Figures of Play

FIGURES OF PLAY
Greek Drama and Metafictional Poetics

Gregory W. Dobrov

OXFORD
UNIVERSITY PRESS

2001

OXFORD
UNIVERSITY PRESS

Oxford   New York

Athens Auckland Bangkok Bogotá Buenos Aires Calcutta
Cape Town Chennai Dar es Salaam Delhi Florence Hong Kong Istanbul
Karachi Kuala Lumpur Madrid Melbourne Mexico City Mumbai
Nairobi Paris São Paulo Shanghai Singapore Taipei Tokyo Toronto Warsaw

and associated companies in
Berlin   Ibadan

Published by Oxford University Press, Inc.
198 Madison Avenue, New York, New York 10016

Library of Congress Cataloging-in-Publication Data
Dobrov, Gregory, W., 1957–
Figures of play : Greek drama and metafictional poetics / by
Gregory W. Dobrov.
p. cm.
Includes bibliographical references and index.
ISBN 0-19-511658-5
1. Greek drama—History and criticism. 2. Performing arts in
literature. 3. Theater in literature. 4. Aesthetics, Ancient.
5. Drama—Technique. 6. Poetics. I. Title.
PA3136.D63   1998
882'.0109—dc21   97-23895

1 3 5 7 9 8 6 4 2

Printed in the United States of America
on acid-free paper

To the memory of my father
Wadim Ivanovitch Dobrov
1926–1997

Вѣ́чнаѧ па́мѧть

Preface

This book is situated at the crossroads of several disciplines—classical philology, dramatic theory, literary criticism—and many separate lines of inquiry. It is therefore written with an eye to a wider audience outside classics. I argue that the emergence of drama in classical Athens marks the invention of sophisticated, self-aware genres in which the "play" was, fundamentally, play with already established fictions (of myth, epic, lyric, drama, etc.). This playful—more precisely, *metafictional*—temperament manifests itself in a variety of phenomenologically distinct "figures of play," whereby drama reveals and exploits an awareness of its own theatricality. Like a figure of speech, each of my "figures of play" is a unique strategy of dramatic syntax that is used to extend and complicate the signifying process; and, like figures of speech, these theatrical strategies mask a high degree of reflexivity and artifice with the pretense of innocence.

Such is the theory. In practice, I take a close look at a series of plays where this more abstract "syntax" is applied to specific and familiar terms. Hence the other meaning of "figures of play," stage-figures, that is, characters in the plays chosen here as test cases for my argument: Aias, Pentheus, Bellerophontes, Tereus, and Herakles. Each of these figures acts as a focal point for the transformational poetics of the script in which he has the leading role. The mythological lineup appears to be uniform, but it conceals a generic divide, as Aias and Pentheus operate in the world of tragedy, while the latter three are comic protagonists who have been "recycled" from tragedy. This study deviates from scholarly tradition by engaging tragedy and comedy simultaneously from a single theoretical perspective. Anxiety about the strict separation of genres is as old as Plato, but it is encouraging to see a new wave of comparative work unintimidated by ancient strictures. In fact, it is fair to say that scholars currently studying the intertextual and metatheatrical aspects of Greek drama have recently established a thriving subfield with strong theoretical links to many fields outside classics. It is my hope to further encourage communication across the generic divide and between the equally formidable divides of discipline and theoretical orientation.

Readers will not find here evidence of strict adherence to a single theoretical school or critical trend, though the influence of Russian formalism may be detected here and there. The uncharacteristically modern look of ancient theater in this study has less to do with theory per se than with a tradition of defining the poetics of contemporary genres *against* the past, with Greek drama the naive child of the European canon. I prefer to let the evidence—our texts and testimonia—speak for itself. However, just as native speakers of a given language will be perfectly competent without necessarily understanding the complex phonology, morphology, and syntax which they control, so the artists of the ancient Greek stage did much for which they may not have had an explicit vocabulary or conceptual framework. We, as students of antiquity, owe our contemporaries an account of our analytical framework for, if one thing should be obvious at this late point, no intellectual enterprise can honestly claim to be "theory-free."

Finally, this study is an expression of love for literature that has been with me since childhood. I have felt, at times, a sort of hubristic joy in daring to formulate my own approach to material freighted with tradition and a long critical reception. For the hubris I take full credit; for the daring and good sense to try, I thank the one who taught me to read in the first place—my father.

Contents

PART I

METATHEATER

Three Phenomenal Modes

Drama and Metafiction

Yes, I have tricks in my pocket, I have things up my sleeve;
But I am the opposite of a stage-magician:
He gives you illusion which has the appearance of truth
And I give you truth in the pleasant disguise of illusion.
To begin, I turn back time.

Tennessee Williams

Dionysos has returned to claim a central position in the study of Greek drama. He is being aggressively rehabilitated as both a god of the polis and god of the theater in ways that subvert the ancient rhetorical question τί ταῦτα πρὸς τὸν Διόνυσον, "What does this have to do with Dionysos?" The inevitable οὐδέν, "Nothing," now has an ironic ring as issues of cult, festival setting, civic ceremony, politics, and social organization are brought to bear on the extant scripts of tragedy and comedy. While Hellenists may appear less than progressive in touting their awareness of the sociopolitical context of drama as something new, "Dionysos" continues to inspire excellent work across disciplines from classics to contemporary cultural theory.[1] The approach taken here, however, departs from the trend of exploiting the symbolism of Dionysos (ancient theater) and Narcissus (modern fiction). It is actually Hermes—master of child's play and a "shrewd and coaxing schemer"—who best exemplifies the reflexive poetics explored in this study.

Hermes is the bearer of communication from author to audience who "ponders word and deed at once." "Born at dawn," according to the Homeric Hymn, "by midday he played his lyre, and at evening he stole the cattle of far-shooting Apollon . . . the very day mighty Maia bore him." In our first encounter with him we, like Apollon of the hymn or Sophokles' satyr trackers, are at once bewildered and amused by how much this child seems to have mastered within moments of his birth. His lyric improvisations and the invention of fire call to mind the quintessentially creative Prometheus. Meanwhile, his associations with deception, rhetoric, communication, travelers, merchants, thieves, the dead, and so on reveal a complex and polymorphous character whose civic and cultic importance rivals that of Dionysos.[2] Most striking about the newborn Hermes is his exploitation of an apparent immaturity that masks precocious competence and self-awareness, a hermeneutics of self. His answer to the angry Apollon involves a detailed description of his infant condition that caters,manipulatively, to an adult perspective. Though immediately inspired by an appetite for meat, he claims only to know his swaddling clothes and mother's breast. "I surely do not resemble a hardy rustler of cattle," protests the trickster. "I was born yesterday!" We know, however, that the day before, he had invented a musical genre through which he mythologized his own conception and birth in a charming performance. Zeus laughs at the child's ruses and Apollon is appeased by the beauty of his invention. Hermes, the self-conscious artificer and singer, is appropriate as the symbolic patron and antecedent of the classical Athenian theater in its reflexive and playful aspects. In a way that develops Odysseus' metafictional role as bard (*Odyssey* 11.368) — a role that is paradoxically a model (as literature) and imitation (as myth) — Hermes is endowed with qualities exemplifying the mode of representation of which he is the subject. Not only does he narrate his brief past in a song mingled of truth and falsehood, he has invented the mode of singing itself.

Not long after we catch the thread of tragedy and certainly well before the beginning of Aristophanes' career, plays of both genres began to reflect the fact that the City Dionysia and Lenaia were increasingly celebrations by the polis of itself, the city involved in self-validation and self-representation. The power of communication, the invention of new modes of expression at the interface of orality and literacy,[3] and an acute self-awareness are qualities that characterize drama as it pretends to know only the traditional language and themes of its birth. Latent in this metaphor, however, is a warning: The critic who turns with some amusement to investigate the metafictional dimension of tragedy, in particular, should be prepared to hear: "But I was only born yesterday!"

Prolegomena

Depicting madness and delusion was a specialty of the Greek tragedians for several generations while utopianism endured as a mainstay of the Old Comic imagination. In their separate ways the two genres were vitally interested in crisis and its consequences. It is hardly surprising, therefore, that tragic representations of irrationality and the utopian schemes of comedy should reveal much about the nature of Greek dramatic art. It is at the points of deepest crisis engaging the core of its being and its relation to the social order, in fact, that the theater is forced to confront itself and to summon its most powerful resources. A leading exemplar of such a crisis in tragedy is the final third of Euripides' *Bakkhai* with the "robing of Pentheus," which highlights mimesis whereby theater self-consciously establishes and maintains its status as a festival *agon*. The followers of Émile Durkheim have even suggested that this play retraces the violent origins of the dramatic festival.[4]

As the genres of tragedy and comedy matured in the latter quarter of the fifth century, their range of expression extended and deepened to become increasingly metafictional. They came to exhibit a heightened awareness of their creative powers and their own theatricality as influential forces in the Athenian polis. Work on Euripides and Aristophanes now commonly employs the term "metatheater" in a way that identifies reflexivity as an inalienable dimension of their stagecraft. "The city established . . . a spectacle open to all citizens, directed, acted, and judged by the qualified representatives of the various tribes," writes Jean-Paul Vernant of tragedy. "*In this way it turned itself into a theater; its subject, in a sense, was itself and it acted itself out before its public*" (italics added).[5] Recent scholarship has explored the explicit reflexivity of comedy.[6] Social and dramatic self-consciousness went especially hand in hand at the City Dionysia as we see from the other festival events such as the Proagon, Eisagoge, Pompe, and, above all, the civic ceremonies that inaugurated the dramatic competitions: public recognition of benefactors of the state, display of the allies' tribute to Athens, front-row seats and gifts for orphaned sons of the war dead, and the selection of judges. It is clear that the polis became a theater of literary and political fictions played by the demos to itself. This process of self-representation, however, was animated by the impulse to call established values, institutions, and practices into question, and it is this self-critical force that reveals ancient metatheatrics as an important accomplice of the Athenian theater in its transgressive dimension.

The chief currency of tragic composition is what we call myth, the traditional legends handed down orally, in art, and in the various genres of pre-dramatic poetry.[7] Tragedy regularly transforms this material from a more-or-less linear narrative into a three-dimensional play whose metafictional qualities are *inevitable* as the culture of the fifth-century theater is injected into the traditional fable.[8] Comedy, for its part, reveals its dialogical relation to tragedy by performing a second-order transformation on this tragic myth. Thus *Tereus* (Sophokles) or *Bellerophontes* (Euripides) is refashioned yet again by Aristophanes into a new scenario with special attention to the moments of tragic invention. The resulting comedies, *Birds* and *Peace*, respectively, exploit, transform, and improvise upon their models to serve the counterpoint between the fantastic comic plot and the sociopolitical satire.

Far from being a fin-de-siècle symptom of decadence of the sort claimed for the metafictional novel by Roland Barthes,[9] self-awareness in Greek drama arises from the dynamics of the festival agon in the context of a democratic polis and is evident in Aiskhylean tragedy before the beginning of Euripides' dramatic career (and before Aristophanes' birth, for that matter).[10] The design of *Eumenides*, for example, depends on the acknowledgment of the Athenian demos as spectators with sustained audience participation in the trial scene. Thus, after the second stasimon Athene gives the following order (line 566): κήρυσσε, κῆρυξ, καὶ στρατὸν κατειργαθοῦ, "make the proclamation, herald, and call the public to order." The most natural and practical realization of this moment is to take στρατόν, "host," "ranks," as referring to the spectator-demos, a reference reaffirmed in lines 572–73 in which the goddess bids the "whole city" to be silent and to learn her "laws" (θεσμοί). At several points the script stretches convention to address the spectators[11] in a way that might be characterized as "direct address by synecdoche," that is, a direct address to "humankind" of which the audience is a subset and concrete representative. The Athenians are summoned from a passive role outside the play to enter the fiction as witnesses to an event of great moment for themselves and their city.[12]

As in the prologue of Sophokles' *Aias*, Athene here plays the part of an internal director who designs and controls the scenario.[13] The style and tone of the second stasimon and final sequence have even been likened to that of an Aristophanic parabasis.[14] This bold comparison captures the important advance in awareness on the part of the dramatic event of its civic and social contexts. There is surely a similarity between *Eumenides* and the first extant Aristophanic comedy (*Akharnians*, produced 425) whereby the body of spectators becomes implicated in the action as a collective "extra" representing jury or assembly.[15] In *Eumenides* the audience and Athenian demos are made to participate in the play, to respond to the stage. The last thing the spectators hear, in fact, is an echo of their own voices.[16] Herein is a phenomenology fundamental to the subsequent development of Greek tragedy and comedy as the stages of communal self-display.

A connection with the audience, a recognition of the spectators in their double role as *politai*, "citizens," and *theatai*, "spectators," is complemented by self-referentiality on the part of the play and players themselves. The theatrical community is bound closely together by an exchange in which the stage acknowledges the duplicity of the spectatorial function, or competence, and responds by admitting and exploiting its own complexity as a construct. Vernant has argued that tragedy "played a decisive role in man's apprehension of *fiction* in the strictest sense,"[17] and so we confront important constitutive ambiguities of the genre that complicate the metatheatrical moment. The epic otherness of the tragic hero paradoxically turns out to be the locus of contemporary problematics; passive spectators watching mimesis of the legendary past find themselves implicated, as citizens of democratic Athens, in a network of modern issues realized on stage. Theatrical self-consciousness is thus vitally dependent on the fundamental mutual awareness of Self and Other on both sides of the dramatic equation.[18]

One may, in fact, speak of a distinctly *Athenian* metatheatrics that is most vividly discernible in the transformation of myth at moments of crisis central to the respective genres: the tragic crises involving madness and the utopianism of comic "salvation" (μηχανὴ σωτηρίας) characteristic of the Aristophanic plot. Study and criticism of the polis as a locus of salvation recurs across genres.[19] Dionysos as choreographer of doom in *Bakkhai* and comic improvisor in *Frogs* is emblematic of the varieties of metatheatrical commentary possible in tragedy and comedy. Although this god is unparalleled as a symbol of spectacular power and ambiguity, it is excessive to equate him in a global manner with "theater" or "metatheater" inasmuch as these phenomena exhibit a breadth and diversity beyond what is Dionysiac, strictly speaking. The explicit mention or onstage presence of Dionysos will often have metatheatrical significance but metatheater is not exclusively Dionysiac. Reversing the priorities of other studies that use Greek drama as documentary evidence for religion and ritual, the transformed theatrical mythoi of madness and utopia are foregrounded here as analytical focal points, as natural means of structuring a discussion of the "figures of play" in the double sense of "tropes" and "protagonists" — at the dawn of dramatic history.

A recent discussion of ancient comedy's "play with its own playness"[20] laments that "the study of the subject has been rather piecemeal." Attention to the reflexive aspects of Greek theater is scattered far and wide in works largely given to something else. Though hardly a recent coinage, "metatheater" is still new enough to be absent from standard works that present Greek drama as something closer to mimetic mythography than to a self-justifying fiction comprehending both text and performance.[21] Stimulated by developments in other fields, however, classical scholarship has for some time shown an interest in the self-referential and metafictional aspects of the ancient festival genres. The potential for a combination of philological and performance analysis makes the study of dramatic metafiction especially interesting and, it is hoped, rewarding. Current work on ancient drama extends to Euripides, Aristophanes, and Plautus critical approaches developed in literary studies outside classics.[22] All aspects of the theatrical event are seen to be implicated in metatheatrical experimentation: language, spectacle, choral parabasis, political satire, representation of gender, and so on.[23]

Tragedy's metatheatrical potential has not been acknowledged as readily as that of comedy owing to lingering assumptions about the limitations of tragic discourse.[24] *Bakkhai* is the exception that proves the rule: widely regarded as a fin-de-siècle masterpiece, it continues to figure as Euripides' markedly self-conscious effort.[25] In light of the work of scholars such as Charles Segal and Anton Bierl, it is no longer possible to ignore this aspect of tragic drama. We are beginning to see, in fact, the publication of studies demonstrating that many supposedly unique features of *Bakkhai* are present in Euripides' other plays and in the work of Sophokles and Aiskhylos, albeit in varying degrees of concentration.[26]

Given the proper level of analysis, tragedy and comedy reveal an undeniable kinship in sophistication and technique. The poetics of satyr-play, on the other hand, has been more controversial. François Lissarague, for example, denies the satyr-play any metatheatrical potential, pointing out the striking absence of parody, burlesque, or topicality from the genre.[27] In light of how poorly this genre is attested, we would do well to respect apparent evidence to the contrary such as the papyrus fragment (P.Oxy 2162; fr. 78a Radt) of Aiskhylos' *Isthmiastai* (or *Theoroi*, dated before 456 BC) in which satyr-choristers at the temple of Poseidon Isthmios carry and discuss likenesses of themselves that may very well be masks.[28] Reticence in this study concerning the satyr-play has more to do with caution and should not be interpreted as a silent affirmation of Lissarague's position. If the genre were attested as well as Aristophanic comedy, we would no doubt find a wealth of surprises on the levels of stagecraft and aesthetics. In the controversial Pratinas fragment (*TrGf* 4 F 3), for example, Richard Seaford has observed satyric "self-presentation, 'literary' invective and reference to the theatre rather than dramatic illusion and plot."[29] Similarly, Euripides' *Kyklops* and the fragments of other satyr-plays have a lively interest in dramatic convention, paratragedy, and topical humor that would justify further investigation.[30] Comedy's dialogue with its fellow genres offers a promising perspective: in chapter 6 below I argue that an important scene in Aristophanes' *Peace* is, in fact, an adaptation of the Sophoklean satyr-play *Sphyrokopoi* ("Hammer-wielders," or *Pandora*).

Consisting of three chapters on the phenomenal modes of dramatic metafiction, this first section outlines an approach that constrains the discussion while allowing for the juxtaposition of genres. Without attempting an encyclopedic overview of all relevant passages, the second chapter suggests a working typology of metafictional strategies. The discussion is then limited primarily to the two that best exemplify the way in which metatheater structures and defines a play, thematically and ideologically: modes termed *mise en abyme* (chapter 2) and "contrafact" (chapter 3). The subject of this study, then, is a group of plays in which the *dramatic representation and the culture of the theater inform and organize sustained sequences in tragedy and comedy*.[31] This macroscopic approach to design and meaning guarantees a preoccupation with actors' scenes and roles (as opposed to choral passages) since it is an actor who invariably directs and enacts the metatheatrical performance. In practice much space is devoted to the play of literary fictions involving madness (in tragedy) and utopianism (in comedy).

The second and third sections of the book, "The Anatomy of Dramatic Fiction," take up five case studies featuring as many (stage) figures at play: Aias, Pentheus, Bellerophontes, Tereus, and Herakles. The first two chapters examine tragic sequences that exploit the dynamics of madness to innovate memorable "shows within": the presentation of Aias in Sophokles' play of that name and the costuming of Pentheus in *Bakkhai*. The tragedy of Aias is framed so as to enact an agon between conflicting ideologies embodied in Odysseus and Aias, a confrontation negotiated explicitly by the theatrical dynamics of playing and seeing. In *Bakkhai*, Euripides extends qualities inherent in the god Dionysos to invent an explicitly theatrical god who destroys Pentheus in a deadly contest of fictions and authority.

The next three chapters explore connections across the generic divide. Chapters 6 and 8 present the metatheatrics of the comic hero's ascent to Olympos and descent to Hades in Aristophanes' *Peace* and *Frogs*, respectively. These two plays are prime, though neglected, examples of the "comic contrafact," that is, transformations of Euripides' *Bellerophontes* into *Peace* and (the same playwright's) *Peirithous* into *Frogs*. These ideologically charged utopian scenarios emerge from the apparently spontaneous improvisation of the protagonist on tragic material. The self-aware Dionysos of *Frogs* is symbolically appropriate as the concluding example, being a splendid and complex figure standing on the threshold of a period in which comedy underwent profound changes. Between these two figures of play, chronologically, falls Aristophanes' *Birds*, interpreted here as a contrafact of Sophokles' *Tereus*. One of the better-attested lost plays of Sophokles involving irrationality and sacrificial violence, *Tereus* shares common features with Euripidean plays such as *Bakkhai* and *Medeia*. In *Birds*, murder and madness mutate into a utopian solution (Nephelokokkygia), which sheds light on the intertextual and interperformative relationship between genres. This chapter concludes by suggesting another important link between tragedy and comedy in an exchange between Aristophanes and Euripides between 414 and 411: *Helene* is argued to involve a metatheatrical response to *Birds*, which is answered, in turn, by *Thesmophoriazousai*.

Fifth-century tragedy and comedy sublimated the agonistic basis of Greek civilization in a way that invited the community to confront itself. In the theater, as in the courts and assemblies, a significant subset of the Athenian public was spectator and judge of contests where important social and ideological issues were played to it by its own members. The metafictional spheres of both genres emerge as sites of multiple negotiations. This reflexive communication between political and dramatic aspects of agon is therefore rich with implications about the dynamics of the first democracy.[32] Aristophanes' intergeneric operators, that is, characters such as Bellerophontes and Tereus, are constructed between a stage-figure proper, a fiction of the author, and a member of the common demos. By disrupting the fabric of tragedy's ethnic and social configurations—for example, recostuming tragic princes as rustic commoners —Dikaiopolis and Trygaios expose fissures in the ideological fabric of the polis, positioning themselves between factions, between "classes," between members of a subcommunity, even between poleis.

The serious work of politics drew heavily on dramatic modes of representation while the plays of the tragic and comic poets were deeply influenced, indeed shaped, by the new art of rhetoric and modes of public debate. By subsuming aspects of "work" (cf. Johan Huizinga's "earnest") and "play," the dialectical agon facilitated a lively reciprocity between the equally self-conscious competitions in the courts, the assembly, and the theater of Dionysos. Drama proper comes into being as a transformation from unreflective protodrama (ritual play, *paidia*) to a highly reflexive, public, and political agon.[33] Crossing the boundary between "earnest" and "play(ful)," this transformation is a natural result of the democratic dynamic. To make sense of Greek political and theatrical agons it is important to recognize their potential as competitive appeals through argumentation to the Athenian body politic in its double capacity as spectator and judge. In different ways, the work of tragedy and comedy was to appropriate material from other fields and genres and to invent new, reflexive discourses with the Athenian state in the roles of both producer and spectator. The similarities and mutual influences of the formally separate discourses in the polis are compelling and suggest a different level of analysis for the metafictional aspects of Athenian drama.

Metatheater

Dramatic theory has been developing in recent decades along two lines that often overlap and intertwine. The first seeks to articulate from a structuralist-semiological perspective how elements of the theater operate as a coherent system of signification; the second—the principal orientation of this study—is focused more on the descriptive phenomenology of the theater and on interpretation within a "complex of signs thrown like a net over our field of perception."[34] The steadily growing special interest in theatrical metafiction has, by now, a vast bibliography ranging from the rather abstract work of semioticians such as Keir Elam to the close readings of the Montpellier conference on "The Show Within."[35] Despite the apparent differences among scholars such as Lionel Abel, Anne Righter, James L. Calderwood, Judd D. Hubert, and Jean-Pierre Maquerlot in the use of the terms "metatheater" and "metadrama," the current literature exhibits considerable flexibility and a healthy, mutual intelligibility with respect to terminology and definitions. The theoretical distinction between the script (drama as "play-text") and its re-created or imagined performance (theater as "performance-text") is not commonly reflected in scholarly usage. Since "metadrama" and "metatheater" are, on the whole, used interchangeably, both terms figure in this study as a theatrical subset of a generalized "metafiction"—that process whereby a representation doubles back on itself, where a narrative or performance recognizes, engages, or exploits its own fictionality.[36] The term "metafiction" characterizes a work "which self-consciously and systematically draws attention to its status as an artefact in order to pose questions about the relationship between fiction and reality." This definition might be augmented to include a "critical return to history and politics *through*—not despite—metafictional self-consciousness and parodic intertextuality."[37] Featuring a "macroscopic" approach to ancient genres played quickly—and often only once—in real time before a restless audience, this study shall be mainly concerned with the *palpable contributions* of metatheatrical sequences and strategies to the performance as a whole.[38] Dr. Johnson's assertion that "[a] play read affects the mind like a play acted" represents an ideal attainable only through familiarity with the specifics of theater production.[39]

At the forefront of the inquiry, scholars of English Renaissance drama have presented metatheater from a variety of perspectives.[40] At the metatheatrical level the elements of dramatic discourse call attention to themselves, to their relative arbitrariness and materiality.[41] Text and performance offer a glimpse through the conventions of their respective "grammars" at the signifying process in which a constructed signifier—word, mask, space, prop—points to, and marks the absence of, a signified that is only indirectly and often arbitrarily related to a "real" referent.[42] Metafiction lays bare the process of poiesis that thus becomes implicated in the pleasure of reading or viewing.[43] As Pentheus superimposes one identity on another in the scene mentioned earlier (*Bakkhai* 912–70), for example, the action draws the spectator's attention to the paradox of costume as comprising "reality" (actor), role (Pentheus), and illusion (the maenad). Pentheus' onstage costuming reminds us that his original apparel is also a disguise and therefore illusory (or, as a sign, arbitrary). At this moment, the stage-play reveals that there is, of course, no absolute reality in which to ground the constructs "Pentheus" and "maenad" but only layers of meaning that we as spectators organize to make sense of our theatrical experience.[44] Euripides here appears as much concerned with the nature of mimesis as he is with innovating a grim moment in Theban legend.[45]

In drama, "the metalinguistic function often has the effect of foregrounding language as object or event by bringing it explicitly to the audience's attention in its pragmatic, structural, stylistic or philosophical aspects."[46] At the reflexive limit, this foregrounding may frame linguistic communication to become part of a broader "metatheatrical superstructure." There is a danger in this abstraction, however, of missing the qualities that distinguish theater from other forms of representation, especially in light of its valorization of real-time performance (as opposed to being a material artifact). We must not, cautions Bert States, "undervalue the elementary fact that theater—unlike fiction, painting, sculpture, and film—is really a language whose words consist to an unusual degree of things that *are* what they seem to be." From a phenomenological perspective,

> image and object, pretense and pretender, sign-vehicle and content, draw unusually close. . . . In the theater light is brightness pretending to be other brightness, a chair is a chair pretending to be another chair, and so on. Put bluntly, in theater there is always a possibility that an act of sexual congress between two so-called signs will produce a real pregnancy.[47]

Even on a pre-theoretical level, the breadth of the reflexive dimension in Greek drama warrants a healthy skepticism about considering it simply as a late and devious "anti-form" imposed on something more primitive and pure, in the sense of Schiller's ancient naiveté. Often ignored entirely, Greek theater appears to be the innocent child of the European canon in discussions of literary self-consciousness.[48]Just as common is treatment of the metatheatrical as a sign of decadent, self-indulgent complexity. It is argued here, however, that the self-conscious aspects of tragedy and comedy, far from being marked or peripheral, *foreground the originary features of the dramatic process*: duplicity, paradox (conveying truth through illusion), and mythopoeic power. We must, of course, allow time for a relatively new genre to react to itself, as it were, and to realize the full potential of its own *physis*.[49] Thus Euripides' later plays are perceptibly richer in self-conscious detail than the earliest surviving work of Aiskhylos. The study of metatheater, nevertheless, reveals a certain commonality between tragedy and comedy with respect to the wider context of the performance situation.

The madness of characters such as Pentheus and Aias, for example, are narrative elements transformed by the dramatists into pivotal moments that expose the stark theatricality of the action by staging one illusion (the delusion of *atê*) in terms of another (the more fundamental "dramatic illusion"). Sophocles and Euripides enhance their respective "fables" by setting up a theatrical situation internal to the fiction where the figures of Dionysos (*Bakkhai*) and Athene (*Aias*) comprise the multiple roles of "god," "actor," and "director." The phenomenology and culture of the contemporary theater are artistically integrated into the scenario of preparation for sacrificial death by means of a creative manipulation of myth, stagecraft, and dramatic illusion. Aristophanes employs similar strategies in a number of comic sequences such as Dikaiopolis' defense in *Akharnians* and the escape routines in *Thesmophoriazousai* that set up a theater of sorts within the play. Both aspects of a dramatic event—the active (performance) and passive (spectatorial competence)—involve a fundamental duplicity. Theater thrives on the inherent tensions between actor and role, theater and *dramatis locus*, costume and disguise.[50] The dialogue, moreover, is split between being a mode of communication between actors and a mode of communication between actors and audience.[51]

The Problem of Dramatic Illusion

The next two chapters continue with a comparative overview of tragic and comic metafictional strategies[52] in order to clarify and constrain the interwoven discussion of comedy (especially the utopian prologue) and tragedy featuring madness and sacrifice. One might begin by saying that, in addition to its habitual and unique usurpation of tragic forms,[53] Old Comedy generates a great deal of surface metatheater by allowing frequent and varied "ruptures of the dramatic illusion." On the other hand, tragedy involves theatricality at a deep level—that of the covert *mise en abyme* (defined later)—to structure situations that, on the surface, appear intertextually innocent. We must be careful, however, in using the term "dramatic illusion" as a synonym for "realism" since the stagecraft of Aristophanes and Euripides did not rely on the latter in the sense that it has for a production of, say, Chekhov or Ibsen. G. M. Sifakis anticipated Kendall L. Walton's work in asserting that a fifth-century play involved an "implicit agreement on the rules of performance (established by long tradition)" between the players and spectators.[54] Greek tragedy and comedy, as forms of "*narration* by means of imitation" (Plato Republic iii. 393c9, 394d2), were played *to* the audience, not just before it. It is important to keep this redefinition of terms in mind when considering the debate over Sifakis's well-known denial of illusion in Greek drama.[55]

For the stage action to be compelling, the spectator must be drawn into the fiction by suspending certain important criteria normally operative in assessing reality, that is, "submitting to illusion" as it is usually put or, in less suggestive terms, accepting the pretense[56] or engaging in the fiction as make-believe. The fictionality of a game or drama does not depend on the verisimilitude of its elements nor is it in any other way a matter of degree.[57] From this perspective, the intensity of "illusionism" in a particular drama has little bearing on its metafictional potential, since the spectators at a performance of A *Doll's House* are not somehow coaxed more easily into the make-believe game than was the ancient Athenian audience of *Persai*. Surely no one is ever fooled by theater into mistaking fiction for reality, a rule proven by the few bizarre anecdotes to the contrary.

A crucial difference between Greek theater and modern realist drama lies in the energy expended to conceal dramatic artifice and to suppress a play's own admission of its theatricality. Exploitation by a play of its "playness"—including disruptions of theatrical pretense—is a powerful means of communication that necessarily relies on specific conventions of play, that is, "illusion" understood as the force permitting one to engage in, and enjoy, a make-believe world, a force that, in J. L. Styan's words, "is the province of all theatre."[58] The argument of the anti-illusionists may be turned on its head: it is precisely the quasi-Brechtian distancing of both players and spectators in Greek drama that invites metatheatrical play with the "dramatic illusion" in a way that simultaneously calls it into question and reaffirms its power.[59] It cannot be sufficiently emphasized that the metafictional aspects of both tragedy and comedy discussed here are constructed at an intellectual distance that alienates the spectator and reveals a dimension in which Greek drama—like Brecht's epic theater—pushes the spectator toward a new level of self-recognition and, perhaps, "activism" understood as the impulse toward change of self or society. At the same time, the recognition of the spectator as a participant in the production of meaning violates spectatorial privacy and involves the spectator directly in the performance. Indeed, a fundamental aspect of metafiction confronted by many students of the subject is the paradox that the spectator is, "at the same time, co-creator of the self-reflexive text and distanced from it because of its very self-reflexiveness."[60]

In order to avoid unproductive controversy and potentially misleading anachronism, however, the phrases "rupture of dramatic illusion" and "play-within-the-play" shall be avoided in this study. Thus in the discussion of Sophokles' *Philoktetes* in chapter 2, I argue that, when Odysseus' charade wanders from its seductive purpose, he, as the "internal director," leaps on stage and assails his "player," Neoptolemos, for abandoning the script. Sophokles stops short, however, of giving his character lines in the spirit of those spoken by Prospero, a famous Shakespearean "internal director," in similar circumstances: "Our revels are now ended. These our actors / as I foretold you, were all spirits, and / are melted into air, thin air," and so on. Prospero's speech shifts explicitly to the circumstances of his play and the theater building ("the great globe itself") and to the "dramatic illusion" ("the baseless fabric of this vision"). The metatheatrics of the Greek poets is distinguished from that of Shakespeare, Pirandello, and Stoppard by assigning specific, and useful, terms to the various phenomena revealed. The next chapter begins with a simple classification in order to place the discussion of individual plays and sequences in the broader context of Greek theatrical self-consciousness.

2

Figures of Play, Part 1

Surface Play and the Mise en Abyme

Surface Play and the *Mise en Abyme*

Studies of contemporary film have produced a taxonomy of reflexive techniques ranging from various uses of the equipment, titles, and dialogue, to the phenomenon of the cinema itself.[1] While there is no comparable survey of ancient metatheater, the genre-specific work of Bain and Bierl, on tragedy, and Rau, on comedy, offers sound points of departure. Taking a somewhat different approach, however, this study will aim at a level of abstraction where tragic and comic reflexivity meaningfully inform each other. The categories are simple, but their realization is complex and varied. Each "figure of play" outlined here, in practice, subsumes dozens of individual techniques and related substrategies. This variety and complexity will be best explored in the context of individual plays and scenes.[2]

The term "surface play" applies to moments in which the performative margin becomes apparent, that is, when an element of the performance briefly admits and exploits its duplicity, moving horizontally, breaking frame from inside the play and theatrical space to the sphere outside the dramatic fiction or between the script of the given performance and text(s) external to it. This mode is the stock-in-trade of comedy that commonly foregrounds a basic duality in this connection: actor/role, theatron/*dramatis locus*, object/prop, face/mask, one's own speech/"borrowed" speech, and so forth. Surface play is usually brought to our attention, moreover, by explicit marking in the script, that is, by verbal or gestural signposting.[3] An effective type of surface play involves polysemous reference to the theater and its equipment—Prospero's mention of "great globe," for example, or Greek play with the term πρόσωπον, "face, mask"—that looks both inward to engage the fiction and outward to the festival and political context.[4] Similarly, the strategic use of ἄτη, "madness," "ruin," in tragedy (cf. *Aias* 123 and 643) may serve as a bridge from the term as used in epic to contemporary usage that connects ἄτη, by folk etymology, to ἀπάτη with its connotations of "deception," "fraud," and even "dramatic illusion." Surface play enriches and problematizes the dramatic fable at a given point by delimiting the boundaries of the fiction as a construct and, simultaneously, linking this construct in a self-conscious way to phenomena external to it.

Play with the "deep structure" of the theatrical event, on the other hand, engages the mechanics of a dramatic situation within the larger, framing fiction and calls to mind the way in which the dramatic festival (in particular the City Dionysia) was a configuration of the polis on a smaller scale. As a species of the *mise en abyme*[5] this second mode, as it manifests itself in Greek drama, differs from surface metatheater and the later forms of explicit dramatic inset (such as the famous "Murder of Gonzago" in *Hamlet*) by being seamlessly incorporated into the dramatic fiction with subtle verbal marking, or none at all. First suggested as a heraldic metaphor in an 1893 diary entry by André Gide, *mise en abyme* has come to enjoy wide currency in contemporary criticism:[6]

> In a work of art I rather like to find transposed, on the scale of the characters the very subject of that work. Nothing throws a clearer light upon it or more surely establishes the proportions of the whole. Thus, in certain paintings of Memling or Quentin Metzys a small convex and dark mirror reflects the interior of the room in which the scene of the painting is taking place. Likewise in Vélazquez's painting of the *Meniñas* (but somewhat differently). Finally, in literature, in the play scene in *Hamlet*, and elsewhere in many other plays. In *Wilhelm Meister* the scenes of the puppets or the celebration at the castle. In "The Fall of the House of Usher" the story that is read to Roderick, etc. None of these examples is altogether exact. What would be much more so, and would explain much better what I strove for in my *Cahiers*, in my *Narcisse*, and in the *Tentative*, is a comparison with the device of heraldry that consists in setting in the escutcheon a smaller one *"en abyme,"* at the heart-point.

Thus Gide defines a formal element that in some essential way mirrors the "subject" (process, format, aesthetics, design) of the whole work on a smaller scale just as the outlines and proportions of a shield, the coat of arms, are reproduced in miniature by the escutcheon mounted at its heart ("abyss," "abysme," and "abyme" are the terms of art). In the context of this study—as it applies to Greek theater—*mise en abyme* will denote a metarepresentational strategy whereby a miniature theatrical *situation* is embedded within a larger, similarly structured dramatic framework. Spectators are invited to contemplate the very process in which they are involved at a given moment from a newly constructed distance where irony interacts with self-recognition. Unlike the Shakespearean example cited by Gide, however, in Greek drama the spectator is never jarred into *formally* acknowledging that an internal sequence is a *play*, a play-within-a-play—and herein is the seductive power and uniqueness of the Athenian mise en abyme: it beckons to the spectator without being presented formally as a play. The ironic potential of this covert strategy is remarkably effective in tragedy (see next section), whereas comedy is more forthright: "Today I must play the beggar's part, / to be myself, yet not to seem myself; / The spectators will know who I am / while the chorus will stand by like idiots" (Dikaiopolis' words to Euripides on the scene from *Telephos* that he will translate onto the comic stage [*Akharnians* 440–44]).

Since the two metafictional modes, surface play and mise en abyme, are not intrinsically comic or tragic, they are illustrated below for both genres with full respect for obvious asymmetries: shifts from the surface of a play beyond the frame of the performance are, of course, far more explicit and frequent in Aristophanes than even in late Euripides. We expect this from comedy that delights in disrupting theatrical convention and pretense as it interacts with the extradramatic world. If the dramatic pretense, or "illusion," is more pervasive and stable in tragedy—indeed a trademark of sorts—then metatheatrical play and disruption of this pretense should be expected whenever comedy engages its sister genre. The increasing frequency of surface play in tragedy (late Euripides in particular) may very well reflect the influence of comedy, a reciprocal connection explored later. The mise en abyme, on the other hand, is well attested in both genres and suggests an important perspective of a shared poetics. In what follows, the questions of quantity and intensity that have concerned Taplin and others are set aside to make way for a qualitative exploration of "figures of play" in action.

The third metafictional figure featured in this study is the "contrafact," a term borrowed from music theory to designate a composition of which part (and sometimes the whole) is based in a significant and systematic way on another composition. Effectively coined for the field of jazz studies in 1975 by musicologist James Patrick in a study of the harmonic sources of modern jazz (as inaugurated by Charlie Parker), "contrafact" or "melodic contrafact" has entered the mainstream theoretical vocabulary as a general term for the "borrowed-harmony technique" whereby "an original piece is selected; the original harmony is retained and the original melody is discarded; a new melody is then fitted to the borrowed chord structure, yielding a new composition."[7] The field (kind, species, genre) of the contrafact and that of its model are necessarily at some remove from each other in time, form, or style. The two (or more) texts are made to interact creatively in a way that dramatizes their difference. The prominence of "old" material outlines a recuperable model behind the composition while the "new" operates at the contrafact's creative focus. The term "contrafact," modified appropriately, suggests the programmatic refashioning of a model into a new composition and offers the dramatic critic a refreshing alternative to the more limited "parody" with its ineluctable connotations of mockery and distortion in the service of humor.[8] A similar strategy is seen in the work of P. Pucci, who reserves the terms "tragicomedy," "paratragedy," and, more recently, "remake" for essentially the same purpose.[9] Besides being potentially misleading, however, these terms lack a certain breadth. Regarded in light of the musical metaphor, for example, the first half of Virgil's *Aeneid* and Joyce's *Ulysses* might be contrasted as vastly different contrafacts of the *Odyssey*, each with its own poetics of transformation and literary agenda. What these works have in common is the systematic reworking of Homer, not any specifically comic or parodic purpose.

There is, moreover, a quantitative dimension to this third figure of play, an issue of scale. The term "comic contrafact" describes a process whereby the comic protagonist appears to improvise on tragedy as he goes along, sustaining a dialogue between genres on many levels: language, character, situation, spectacle, theme, and so on. Like its musical cousin, the comic contrafact puts its poetics of transformation on display so that the spectators are seduced into new, and unexpected, acts of interpretation. Regarding the scripted plays of Aristophanes, of course, we can only speak of the *appearance* of improvisation, a conspicuous "now-what-shall-I-do-next" factor. For all their superficial differences, most Aristophanic contrafacts arise from the creative manipulation of tragic elements (though comedy and dithyramb are also engaged on a smaller scale). More precisely, Aristophanes has his characters, as they go along, appear to be improvising their own scenarios from tragic material that is to hand. In most of the fifth-century utopian comedies the lead role is closely bound up with, indeed *defined* by means of, a tragic model. Here we appear to be dealing not only with an Athenian style of metadrama but with a specifically Aristophanic trademark. Important sections of his plays are successful contrafacts of Sophoklean and Euripidean tragedies in that the latter serve as the underpinnings of a comic construction. The central concern of this study shall be the comedies—*Akharnians, Peace, Birds, Frogs*—in which transformed tragic material furnishes the protagonist early in the play (most fully in the prologue) with the materials for his utopian or quasi-utopian "plan." The contrafact technique is also important—albeit in a reduced and iterated application—in *Thesmophoriazousai*, which presents a synopsis of escape strategies imported from tragedies such as *Helene, Andromeda*, and *Palamedes*.

Although *Thesmophoriazousai* is a departure, on a whole, from the utopian scenarios of plays such as *Akharnians* and *Birds*, it has much in common with these comedies in its technique and offers a commentary on the paratragic solution as a dramatic device. *Ekklesiazousai*, one of Aristophanes' last works, is remarkable for realizing its metatheatrical utopia *without* an underlying tragic framework. Ever the innovator, the playwright revives the familiar idea of a female "revolution" (cf. *Lysistrata, Thesmophoriazousai*, and other comic *gynaikokratiai*) by engaging metafictional strategies developed in earlier utopian contrafacts of tragedy. The result is a delightful hybrid standing on the threshold between Old and Middle Comedy taken up briefly in the discussion of the comic mise en abyme below.[10]

The dramatic contrafact participates to a degree in the features of both surface play and the mise en abyme. It may be intertextual, interperformative, and in most cases explicitly signposted in (marked by) the script and so aligns itself with intertextual and interperformative surface play—for example, a brief verbal or situational allusion—that calls explicit attention to the phenomenon of the theater. As it incorporates and transforms a significant portion of its model (theme, character, situation, script, spectacle, vel sim.), the comic contrafact has more in common with the mise en abyme in that a specific performance and a self-conscious enactment of the theatrical process itself are central to its design. The phenomenon of the contrafact will be seen at many points to overlap with Genette's notion of "hypertextuality" in the sphere of drama where script and performance are coextensive.[11] The specifically Aristophanic contrafact, on the other hand, approaches Gentili's specialized use of "metatheater" as plays made of other plays, in which connection one thinks of Roman comedies largely given to the "translation" and "recycling" of Greek originals.[12] The notion of the contrafact foregrounds something specific to the work of Aristophanes, that is, his sustained and critical involvement with other plays. "Parody" and "travesty" when applied to Aristophanes misleadingly limit the range and importance of his *extended* cross-generic experiments.[13] *Peace*, for example, involves a contrafact of Euripides' *Bellerophontes*, a tragic original transformed into a comedy sporting a variety of specific parodies and travesties. As such, it transcends recent attempts to redefine parody in the very different works of Margaret Rose, Linda Hutcheon, and K. J. Dover.[14]

Preoccupation in this study with the Aristophanic transformation of tragedy should not obscure the conceptual flexibility of the contrafact as a "figure of play." K. Sidwell, for example, has recently studied the intertextual and performative rivalry between the comic poets.[15] There is also a growing awareness of the way later tragedy "read" earlier performances of the same genre and much recent work has shown an interest in tragic intertextuality.[16] While the extended usurpation of tragedy is relatively overt and central to a given comedy, the status of the contrafact technique in tragedy is more elusive. There can be no doubt, for example, that Euripides' plays dealing with the Mycenaean saga are heavily indebted to Aiskhylos' *Oresteia* and, in one notorious case, openly critical of the older poet. Given that one accepts the authenticity of *Elektra* 518–44,[17] this scene plays as a pointed refashioning not simply of the old fable but of the rather unrealistic recognition in *Khoephoroi*. Elektra, representing the new discourse of Euripides, chastises the elder's attempts to engage the old Aiskhylean recognition pattern (lines 520–31: he has found a lock of hair, and shortly some footprints, at the altar and hopes that it may belong to Orestes):[18]

> ELDER. Look at this lock of hair and set it alongside yours
> to see if your color matches that of the clipping;
> For those who share one father's blood are likely
> also to share many physical features.
>
> ELEKTRA. Your words lack sophistication, old man, if you
> think my brave brother would return to this land
> secretly, in fear of Aigisthos. Besides, how could
> these two locks match? One of a noble youth
> trained in athletic competitions, the other delicate,
> caressed by the comb? It's impossible! What's more,
> old man, you'll be sure to find many with similar
> hair who belong to different families.

The practical impossibility of establishing kinship by comparing superficial features is compounded by the almost comical tone of Elektra's comment on the soil conditions (no good for footprints) and her dismissal of the old man's hope that Orestes might have returned wearing a garment of her own making, ἐξύφασμα, as a recognition-token (Orestes was much smaller when he left and she far too young to weave). Elektra speaks for her genre as it has evolved since 458 BC emphasizing that the Aiskhylean recognition is implausible and lacking in verisimilitude. For the modern reader constrained by distance and ignorance (esp. of lost plays) the vigor of Euripides' innovation overshadows his tragic models to the point where an older poet appears to blend with the notion of the preexisting mythical tradition.[19] The operative term for Euripidean sophistication and invention is Elektra's *sophou* (line 524): the old man is lacking in *sophia*, which belonged to an emergent late fifth-century literary-critical jargon and which comprised both δεξιότης, "intelligence," and νουθεσία, "instruction."[20] The large-scale revision of the themes and characters of the *Oresteia* signaled by Elektra's challenge is famous, the sophistic virtuosity of the new Klytaimnestra being perhaps its most vivid moment. But the controversy surrounding the lines quoted above marks them as unusually explicit in their reaction to an earlier text. A scholarly tradition hostile to any suggestion of tragic metatheatrics has, of course, doubted the authenticity of the passage, just as it has resisted suggestion of Euripidean reaction to Aiskhylos elsewhere. Owing to the relative uniformity of tragic language and the meager survival record, larger-scale "hypertextual" connections in tragedy remain elusive. To make a case for late fifth-century tragic contrafacts on a significant scale, in other words, we should need more from both the early trage-dians and the younger contemporaries of Euripides.

Even with a script as suggestive as Euripides' Theban pastiche (*Phoinissai*), moreover, we must confront a problem stated in humorous form by the Middle Comic poet Antiphanes in a famous lament (*Poiesis*, fr. 189 K.-A.): "Isn't tragedy altogether fortunate (as a genre)? To begin with, the spectators know the plots already, before anyone says a word! All the poet has to do is to remind them. I need only say 'Oidipous' and they know the rest—his father Laios, his mother Iokaste, his daughters, sons, what will happen to him, what he's done, etc." While Aristophanes relies on the marked nature of figures such as Telephos and Bellerophontes to indicate an inter-generic involvement with tragedy, the status of the intrageneric contrafact is harder to assess because the "source" and "target" texts are harder to distinguish.[21] Thus the strong allegiance in the surviving tragedies to the epic past makes it difficult to iden-tify much in the way of explicit contrafaction in the extant scripts.

Only in the tragedy's creative twilight and for poets whose work has not survived do we hear of something that approaches the freedom exhibited in this respect by comedy. In formulating his notion of the "tragic moment," Vernant located tragedy between two defining points: the day that Solon (in Plutarch's anecdote) walked out of a performance by Thespis in disgust, and the close of the fifth century. Concern-ing the latter, Vernant reminds us of Aristotle's discussion of Agathon (*Poetics* 1451b), Euripides' younger contemporary whose technique marked a break with the past in that tradition gave way to free invention.[22] Recent work that reads later tragedy against Aiskhylos has broken fertile ground for further research.[23]

It is important to point out here that the modes outlined above are not mutually exclusive. Despite the apparent tension between "surface" and "deep" levels (sur-face play and mise en abyme) with respect to explicitness and self-referentiality, for example, their dynamics are sufficiently different for them to coexist and even co-operate. Thus the surface play of explicitly theatrical language in *Helene*, *Bakkhai* and *Ekklesiazousai* does little to rupture the dynamics of the inner fiction (i.e., the quasi play-within-the-play) of the mise en abyme. Such surface play encourages the audience to bridge the dramatic fiction and its surrounding context through the polysemous use of words such as "spectator" and "mimesis" without detracting from the deeper dynamics of the embedded performance. Comedy, moreover, trades extensively in surface play all throughout scenes that otherwise participate in a larger-scale contrafact. There is no reason for conflict here either. Plays such as *Peace* and *Frogs*, in fact, mingle all three metatheatrical modes with great facility. *Birds* is based to a large extent on the characters and themes of Sophokles' *Tereus* while simultaneously involving a brilliant mise en abyme and a stream of the usual, irrepressible surface play. Similarly, Aristophanes' contrafact of Euripides' *Telephos* sustained in *Akharnians* reaches a climax in a mise en abyme where the protagonist assumes a new identity and delivers his impassioned "great speech." Tragedy's apparent shyness to engage in surface play, on the other hand, is a rather different matter bound up with fundamental issues of generic self-definition. It has little to do with the potential (or failure) of this and other metatheatrical modes to interact.

Surface Play: Examples

Surface play is best illustrated by what has been called "rupture of dramatic illusion," though the picturesque label "the art of interruptions" might be more to the point.[24] In the comedies of Aristophanes such moments are frequent enough to be a trademark of sorts. At *Peace* 149, for example, Trygaios mounts his comic Pegasus (a dung beetle) and, by line 154, is lifted by means of the crane into the air. In the nineteen-line anapaestic system (lines 154–72) that follows, the protagonist mingles paratragic exhortation (cf. Euripides fr. 307 Nauck) to his "steed" with expressions of terror at the prospect of falling to earth. Although the threats to Trygaios' safety are extravagantly comic — he fears the aroma of fresh feces in the Piraeus — they are confined to the comic fiction of the flight from Athens to Olympos. As the meter changes, however, he blurts out in plain colloquial Attic (lines 173–76):[25]

> Help, I'm scared! Hey, engineer,
> jokes aside now, listen to me!
> I've got gas spiraling inside my gut and,
> if you don't watch it, I'll end up feeding the dung beetle.

Here, quite obviously, Trygaios expands the range of his speech to include the circumstances of performance. The shift from anapaests to trimeters marks a transition from inside the comic fiction to the theatrical environment in which an actor, dangling from a rudimentary crane, expresses his misgivings about the stunt. The threat in line 176 (χορτάσω κ.τ.λ.) harmonizes with the preceding scatological humor and there is little reason to dwell on a "rupture" of dramatic illusion here. Nevertheless, the passage places unmistakable emphasis on the theatricality of the comic flight and is clearly marked in language, mood, meter, and action: 1) lines 154–72 colored by tragic turns of phrase such as δρομαίαν πτέρυγ᾽ ἐκτείνων / ὀρθὸς χώρει Διὸς εἰς αὐλάς, "extending your fleet wings advance straight to the halls of Zeus" (lines 160–61), yield to uniformly colloquial speech (lines 173–79); 2) the humor of lines 154–72 is self-consciously suspended as the actor (Apollodoros, so Hypothesis I) lays joking aside in his new show of fear; 3) recitative anapaests are followed by iambic trimeter; 4) Trygaios-Apollodoros no doubt emphasizes his words to the crane operator by means of some upward gesture. There is an effective comic irony here as the lofty diction and position of the hero are briefly interrupted by the down-to-earth details of production. We may infer from the addresses to the crane operator in Aristophanes' *Gerytades* (fr. 160 K.-A., most certainly later than *Peace*) and elsewhere in the fragments[26] that the joke was popular enough to have a certain currency and to be repeated in modified form by the same poet.

The frequent instances of audience address in Aristophanes are a variety of surface play that incorporates the spectators into the dramatic fiction. In the prologues of the early plays, for example, it is common for characters to digress briefly and to engage the spectators as do Bdelykleon's slaves at *Wasps* 74–87. Thus the one designated "Xanthias" begins by saying φέρε νῦν κατείπω τοῖς θεαταῖς τὸν λόγον, "Well now, let me tell the spectators the plot." After a few conspicuously parabasis-like comments (lines 56–66) he gestures upward and informs the audience that Bdelykleon is asleep, literally, "on the roof" and that they, the slaves, have been charged with making sure that his father, Philokleon, does not escape from the house arrest imposed on him by his son. The ensuing dialogue begins with the exchange (lines 71–77):[27]

> XANTHIAS. Our master's father has got a strange sickness
> which no one could ever recognize or diagnose
> without our help. Go ahead, try to guess what it is!
>
> SOSIAS. Amynias there, son of Pronapes, suggests
> "gambling fever."
>
> XANTHIAS. Nope, wrong as can be.
> He's judging from his own behavior, I'll bet!
>
> SOSIAS.   .   .   .   .
>
> XANTHIAS. Well that's not it, though a "fever" is at the root of the problem.

There follow several more jokes at the expense of individual spectators as the slaves pretend to take and reject suggestions from the audience. At line 85 Xanthias finally gives up and resumes his prologue narrative in which he reveals that Philokleon is, in fact, sick with *jury* fever. The script has thus briefly expanded the slaves' private conversation into a confrontational exchange between citizens outside the narrowly circumscribed initial fiction. A common device used to conclude a surface break is to bring on a character who has not been involved in it. Thus at *Wasps* 136, Bdelykleon awakens and calls for his slaves and shortly thereafter Philokleon emerges from the smoke-hole for a comic jack-in-the-box routine.

Aristophanic comedy exhibits great variety of such "play at the surface." At *Peace* 43–48, for example, one of Trygaios' slaves looks out into the audience and relates a conversation that he imagines to be taking place in the audience: an Ionian visitor explains to a young man seated next to him that the dung beetle is a riddling representation (αἰνίσσεται) of Kleon inasmuch as he "eats shit shamelessly." In this case the script hypothesizes its own interpretation, revealing an awareness of an audience response that survives the ephemeral performance. This moment reminds us how easily the Old Comic fiction moved beyond the world of the play to embrace the three-dimensional reality of the theater (and polis) in the process. In a somewhat different spirit, the opening of *Frogs* presents a comic Dionysos who is self-conscious about the quality of his humor and who, like Dikaiopolis of *Akharnians*, speaks overtly as an actor (cf. lines 1–2), spectator (lines 16–18), and reader (lines 52–53).

Perhaps the best-known type of surface play in Aristophanes involves parody of more or less brief bits of tragic language. The vast majority of listings in Rau's catalogue[28] are no longer than a single line and serve a variety of purposes ranging from entertaining with near-nonsense to providing important thematic clues. In the very best examples of this intertextual game the tragic graft enriches its context and suggests deeper connections between its source and the given comedy. Generally, isolated moments of surface play between genres cannot rival the contrafact in extent or thematic significance. Thus a throwaway tragic quotation such as the ξουθὸς ἱππαλεκτρυών, "tawny horsecock," at *Peace* 1177 (from Aiskhylos' *Myrmidonoi*, used also at *Birds* 800) is far less significant, in and of itself, than the network of allusions to Euripides' *Bellerophontes* in the same play.

Finally, the most obvious and powerful shift between the world of the play and the extradramatic world is the parabasis. In the hands of Aristophanes this was a regular component of comedy for many years in which the audience was addressed and, in some form or another, included in the dramatic performance. This institutionalized self-referential digression participates in a long tradition of allusion and self-citation whereby playwrights presented themselves to their community. The parabasis, as Thomas Hubbard has eloquently demonstrated, "is precisely the nexus between poet, chorus, dramatic characters, and polis that gives us critical insight into the drama's articulation of meaning."[29] On a metatheatrical level, however, the surface play of the parabasis is not as unique as it may appear. We shall see that the link between political and dramatic self-consciousness in the other modes of metatheater is no less significant.[30]

It was common for critics in late antiquity to characterize Euripidean drama in what amounts to metatheatrical terms.[31] Modern opinion is tending in the same direction despite the limitations of surface play in tragedy and satyr-play (as compared to comedy).[32] At *Elektra* 698, to cite a well-known example, Orestes and his sidekick exit to kill Aigisthos. The stichomythia that follows the choral interlude (lines 699–750) reveals a distressed heroine who is beginning to doubt the success of what she calls their agon (line 751). As her anxiety mounts, she and the koryphaios exchange heated words that culminate in the question "where are the messengers?" (lines 757–60):[33]

ELEKTRA. You proclaim my death; why do we linger?

CHORUS. Hold it! Wait to learn your fate clearly.

ELEKTRA. Impossible! We are defeated, for where are the messengers?

CHORUS. They will come; the slaying of a king is indeed no small matter!

At this point (line 761) a messenger bursts in with the words ὦ καλλίνικοι παρθένοι Μυκηνίδες, νικῶντ' Ὀρέστην πᾶσιν ἀγγέλλω φίλοις, "Victory! Maidens of Mykenai! I announce Orestes' victory to all friends!" This juncture resembles comic surface play in that Elektra's despair is expressed through a reference to stage convention. She justifies her pessimism within the fiction by stepping forth, as it were, to emphasize a concrete detail of the production: there is no sign of a messenger to narrate the offstage violence. The point of the koryphaios' reply is that, in the dramatic scheme of things, the murder of a king is important enough to warrant the entrance of a messenger with the customary speech. Aigisthos has been slain, in other words, and the messenger will come (as he does).

A more matter-of-fact type of audience address in tragedy is found at lines 128–29 of Euripides' *Orestes*.[34] Helene and Hermione have exited following a brief introductory scene, leaving Elektra alone on stage. The chorus has not yet entered and will not be acknowledged by Elektra until line 136. After a brief address to physis, Elektra says:[35]

Did you [pl.] notice how she trimmed the tips of her hair sparing its beauty? She's still the Helene of old!

It is clear that, for an instant at least, the heroine speaks directly to the spectators involving them in the criticism of a character who has just left the stage. Though not exploited for topical or overt comic effect (though there may be humor here), such a moment of surface play certainly foregrounds the theatricality of the moment. The spectators are expected to have a critical reaction (cf. *Peace* 43–48, mentioned earlier) and are asked to align themselves in this with Elektra-as-spectator. The fictional isolation of a lone figure on stage is thus broken and a new pan-theatrical level of discourse briefly engaged. Such emphasis on, and subversion of, dramatic conventions is not uncommon in mature Euripides; it constitutes the bulk of what qualifies as examples of surface play in tragedy. One could cite quite a few moments of implicit metatheatrical commentary throughout Euripides' plays such the anti-teichoscopic comments by Theseus at *Hiketides*, lines 846–56, or Eteokles at *Phoinissai*, lines 751–52. Though not often underscored as explicitly as is *Elektra* 759, manipulation and criticism of dramatic microstructure is a pointed way in which the dramatist articulates the relationship of his work to society: he acknowledges the presence, expectations, and critical abilities of his audience.[36] From direct allusions to more complex "palimpsests"[37] of reference, tragedy has much to offer the eye trained on intertextuality.

A final example of Euripidean surface play reveals a rare aspect of surface metatheater. In an ode immediately preceding the famous escape scene in *Helene*, the chorus of captive Greek women begins with an address to the nightingale (lines 1107–13) that draws upon a comedy (*Birds* 209–16) produced two years earlier. The most striking of several correspondences between these passages is the tragic phrase ἐλθὲ διὰ ξουθᾶν γενύων ἐλελιζομένα, "come trilling with your vibrant throat" (*Helene* 1111), which imitates Aristophanes' lines ἐλελιζομένη διεροῖς μέλεσιν γένυος ξουθῆς, "quavering with the liquid notes of your vibrant throat." It is *communis opinio* that we have here a reversal of the usual dynamic and that tragedy quotes comedy.[38] This instance of tragic surface play is taken up in chapter 7 in the broader context of the dialogical relationship between genres.

Despite the prominence of surface play in that most reflexive of tragic forms, the Euripidean expository prologue, we must not be too quick to relegate it to the outer fields of the genre's evolution. Our evidence before 450 is limited and, yet, there are traces of intertextuality and audience involvement in the work of Aiskhylos, as we have seen. To the trial scene of the *Eumenides* discussed earlier we could add, by way of another example, the important connection between *Persai* and Phrynikhos' *Phoinissai*.[39]

Mise en Abyme: Examples

Metatheater on the level of the "deep structure" of drama differs from surface play by doing more than simply exposing the duplicity of isolated theatrical elements to bridge the inner and outer worlds of a play. Instead, the playwright amplifies the theatricality of a whole scene by structuring it *internally* like a dramatic performance, that is, with an internal "director," "player(s)," and "audience," all of whom participate in the embedded fiction. Foregrounding the theatrical process itself is more comprehensively a "laying bare" of dramatic poetics. It is a display, *en abyme*, of the theater in its three-dimensional totality. For all its sophistication and power, as noted above, in Greek drama this mode never quite attains to Lionel Abel's Shakespearean "anti-form" of a play-within-the-play. The most obvious explanation for this in the case of Greek tragedy is the absence of the theater from its source-culture (the "heroic" past), whereas Elizabethan plays commonly included references to the culture of drama and its production. Thus, while the theatrical inset ("The Murder of Gonzago") cited by Gide fits comfortably into its fictional context, importing a theater into the court of, say, Agamemnon would strain Athenian tragedy's well-known tolerance for anachronism to the breaking point.[40] There is, moreover, the risk of banality in pushing metatheater to the limit of making a formal theatrical performance a rank-and-file dramatic event within the fiction, that is, literally incorporating the production of a play into the plot, witness modern cinema with its cliche of films-within-films.[41] Similarly, the catalog of nearly three hundred metadramatic insertions in Renaissance English drama compiled by J. Fuzier[42] suggests a vast topos in which we must situate well-known examples such as "The Murder of Gonzago" or "Pyramus and Thisby." Shakespeare's success with this device would appear to owe less to the technique per se than to the genius of a poet who was able to make splendid drama from common materials. In the case of *Thesmophoriazousai* we see Aristophanes, in fact, beginning to move toward the explicit play-within-the-play, that is, to the formal endpoint of the dramatic mise en abyme. Even at the very end of his career—as we surmise from titles such as *Aiolosikon*—Aristophanes appears not to have exhausted the more subtle open-ended approach that he combined with other metatheatrical modes such as surface play and the contrafact.[43]

An exemplary instance of the mise en abyme in comedy is the trial of the dog Labes in Aristophanes' *Wasps* 835–43, 891–1008. Following the agon between Bdelykleon and his waspish adversaries, the spectators are drawn into a domestic mock-up of a law court designed to temper Philokleon's lust for litigation. One dog (literally 'kuon' = Kleon) prosecutes another, Labes (= Lakhes), "snatcher," for the theft of some Sicilian cheese in an allegory of Kleon's pending prosecution of Lakhes, son of Melanopos.[44] Philokleon is tricked into acquitting the offending dog and is quite upset by the spectatorial delusion into which he is made to fall through the machinations of his son. The trial scene is complete with director (Bdelykleon), players (dogs and Bdelykleon), and audience (Philokleon = the jury by synecdoche).[45] The comic picture of the poet as behind-the-scenes manipulator who can orchestrate misunderstanding on the part of his spectators suggests a great deal about the power of drama as a means of persuasion and influence. This hilarious trial scene, in fact, may have made a strong enough impression on the public to dissuade Kleon from following through with his intentions (at any rate, no evidence for the actual trial survives).[46]

Another example of a comic mise en abyme is found in Aristophanes' masterpiece, *Birds*, which features quite a few innovations such as an expository "lesson" in lieu of an agon and a parabasis delivered by the chorus in *propria persona*.[47] For the first time in the extant comedies (414 BC—thirteen years into Aristophanes' career) the poet's voice is heard neither in the anapests nor in the following epirrhematic syzygy. Attempts to interpret the apparent anomaly[48] have failed to take into account the wider context of the parabasis that involves the shaping of a disorganized "natural" community of "birds" into a well-rehearsed chorus of Cloudcuckooland citizens. The transformation of the chorus accompanies an equally significant transformation on the part of the protagonist, Peisetairos, from an elitist who prefers the quiet life (ἀπράγμων) to active sophist and city planner to tyrant-god. The metatheatrics of *Birds* fuses drama and politics in a novel manner: Nephelokokkygia, the Great Idea of the play, is a manifestly dramatic construct involving the enactment "nowhere," that is, suspended in midair of a polis whose name appropriately connotes a booby trap (νεφέλη, "gauze net," κόκκυξ "lightweight," "fool") set for the gullible followers of Peisetairos' teaching. The very invention of this outlandish colony is based on a pun, and its justification and foreign policy rest on a tangle of specious arguments and farcical episodes. What strikes the spectator is that Peisetairos' bizarre (and very funny) scenario within the play is given an explicit political form; that is, it is supposed to be a polis. The "quiet Athenian" becomes a busybody who combines the functions of demagogue and poet-director (χοροδιδάσκαλος) as he hijacks the action for his own political and metatheatrical purposes. Nephelokokkygia unfolds as a performance composed and directed by Peisetairos, who supervises the entrances and exits of characters from his polis-as-comedy. It is the transformation of the chorus, however, that foregrounds most vividly the way in which the mise en abyme may be coupled with innovation in generic form.

The first encounter of the Athenian refugees and the bird-chorus is a disaster in which the two sides array against each other in the epirrhematic agon (lines 327–99). A "military" confrontation is avoided, however, owing to Tereus' diplomatic skills, which facilitate a temporary pact (line 445) between men and birds on the condition that the "birds" (as chorus and as play) win the dramatic competition. Peisetairos, characterized as a sophist in familiar terms (lines 427–30 and 372–73), is invited to teach the birds. The several forms of διδάσκω, "to teach," "to choreograph," used in this context (lines 438, 548, 550; cf. also 375–80, 912) economically express his dual role as sophistic teacher and poet-director: he will convert the hostile array of birds into a chorus by teaching his revisionist theology and new political mythos in the form of an epideictic speech that is simultaneously an act of training and choreography.

Peisetairos is a most literary protagonist whom Aristophanes places amidst many references to books and writing.[49] The double διδασκαλία of the main agon is a great success and may be regarded as illustrating the complementary distribution of military and choral disciplines in a comic corollary of Winkler's "ephebic" hypothesis:[50] the array of bird "hoplites" in military formation (cf. the explicit language at lines 353, 400–402, and 408) is transformed into a stately chorus of Nephelokokkygians, compliant citizens (κόκκυγες = young fools) of Peisetairos' tricky scheme (νεφέλη = gauze trap). Perhaps a further jab at the theatrical process, tragedy in particular, is intended in the fact that the foundation of Nephelokokkygia involves the sacrifice of a billy goat (lines 902, 959, 1056–57). Comedy as trugedy (τρυγῳδία) inaugurates its metatheatrical polis with the one genuine instance of a goat sacrifice accompanied by song (i.e., lines 1058–71 as τραγῳδία) on the fifth-century stage!

In the parabasis of *Birds* Aristophanes replaces the customary direct appeal with a metatheatrical display: the "stepping-forth" is reserved for the first entrance of this new chorus, that is, the chorus of *Nephelokokkygia*, Peisetairos' new city-as-comedy. A point-by-point analysis of the "sophist's" lesson (lines 465–626)[51] reveals that the birds assimilate the choreography well and accurately reproduce their lesson in an amplified poetic form. It is significant also that in the main agon (lines 451–626) Peisetairos' directorial monologue replaces the agonistic contest of earlier comedies.[52] For the dialectic of the agon and polyphony of the parabasis Aristophanes innovatively substitutes monophonic performances in which we hear only the protagonist in one and the "new" chorus in the other. The poet's dramatic purpose in *Birds* is thus expressed through a conspicuous manipulation of older forms. The "rules" of the agon are not inviolable and the parabasis has already undergone a great change, never to return to the style of the 420s. Whether or not the parabasis was the earliest ritual kernel of the Old Comic form and substitute for the parodos (and this is doubtful),[53] the anapestic tetrameter is ideally suited for comic allusion to the conventional presentation of the chorus in tragedy. Again, dramatic convention is important: Aristophanes has sublimated the moment of parabatic direct address and incorporated its force into his metatheatrical design in the famous anapests (lines 685–94):[54]

> Come now, you men whom nature gives but feeble life, like to the race of leaves, weaklings modeled from clay, shadowy strengthless tribes, flightless creatures of a day, suffering mortals, men like the figures of dreams—pay attention to us, the immortal, the everlasting, the celestial, the ageless, whose counsels are imperishable, so that you may hear correctly from us all about the things on high, and with accurate knowledge of the birth of birds and of the origin of gods and rivers and Erebos and Khaos may tell Prodikos from me that in the future he can get lost! In the beginning there was Khaos and Night and black Erebos and broad Tartaros, and there was no earth or air or heaven.

It would be inappropriate for Aristophanes' voice to be heard here, as it would interfere with this presentation. His "representative," Peisetairos, is also significantly silent throughout the parabasis, which is thus played as the entrance of a new chorus: the stately formation reveals a new persona that has assumed the authoritative verbal mask of cosmogonic poetry. The Nephelokokkygians step forward, identify themselves, deliver the impressive ornithogony and invite all spectators to join their play and their polis. As "gods" and "muses" they need not admit to an antecedent discourse. Consequently, their authoritative text conceals its source, that is, the ideas and training of the sophist-poet Peisetairos. The birds' dismissal of Prodikos (line 692), moreover, harmonizes well with their promotion of the new avian order in an effort to secure the first prize for their revisionist composer. Peisetairos' status as director and the birds' awareness that they are the chorus-as-demos of a new performance (Nephelokokkygia) is emphasized in a sequence of fairly standard parabatic surface play (in the syzygy, lines 753–68).

Ekklesiazousai and *Philoktetes*

Manipulation of costume is the ineluctable shadow of dramatic metafiction; it figures in most contemporary discussions of plays such as *Akharnians* and *Bakkhai*. Disguise and transvestitism are the metatheatrical devices par excellence as we continue to learn from the work of Helene Foley, Sandra Gilbert, Frances Muecke, Suzanne Saïd, and others. The metafictional deployment of costume invariably frames the central themes of such plays: the study of gender and mimesis in *Thesmophoriazousai*, fiction and authority in *Bakkhai*, political and social advocacy in *Akharnians*, tragic poetry and civic renewal in *Frogs*, and so on. In its aggressive assault on traditional and socially sanctioned roles and categories, play with costume is a natural and unruly product of the self-representational dynamic of Greek drama; it is by definition metatheatrical.

Aristophanes' *Ekklesiazousai* contains a splendid comic mise en abyme that exploits transvestitism for its metatheatrical purposes, as recent productions have revealed to modern audiences.[55] In this comedy the women of Athens conspire to infiltrate the assembly and to propose measures that would effectively arrogate political power to themselves. We learn later in the play, moreover, of a new communist program that complements the shift in the power structure. Praxagora, the lead player and architect of reform, assumes the role of "internal director" and composes a script for her women to be played in the pnyx. Once again we confront the equation between political and dramatic agons as the usurpation of (male) civic discourse by women is framed in theatrical terms: the political scheme in which women will take over the assembly is realized through careful attention to costume, language, gesture, and performance, all of which receive commentary from the "director" as she rehearses her players. Praxagora emphasizes the notions of μελέτη, "practice" (e.g., line 119), and mimesis (e.g., line 278) as she supervises the "play." Her attention to detail and mimetic accuracy is remarkable: "I won't take another step in this assembly rehearsal," she cries in exasperation at her players' mistakes, "unless you are strict and accurate!" (lines 160–62). The costumes (to be put on in a specific order) are complete with Laconian slippers, chiton, cloak, walking stick, and artificial beard that the cast must enhance with appropriate acting. Of particular importance are the women's "verbal mask" and technical matters of assembly procedure. Here we have a clear presentation of the tension between player and persona, a meditation that the political mise en abyme of *Ekklesiazousai* suggests at every turn. The actors are comically marked within the primary fiction as "women" in a way that exploits the tension between their "real" and first-order fictional genders ("real" men playing "[real]" women). The secondary fiction of Praxagora's script, however, requires the assumption of a third gender category, namely, "pseudomale," which ironically closes the circle as it suggests a return to the point of departure (a cast of men playing to mostly male spectators). Men who must play women struggling with male discourse will not fail to amuse: if they play well, for their skill; if badly, for their sheer absurdity.[56]

As the women practice their parts, they naturally encounter pitfalls that furnish much of the comic stuff of this scene. One woman is misled by the chaplet she must wear (to address the assembly) and expects a drink before anything else, mistaking the assembly for a symposium. Another absentmindedly utters the women's oath μὰ τὼ θεώ, "by the two goddesses (Demeter and Persephone)," thereby eliciting a shriek of indignation from Praxagora, who had taken special care to coach her on masculine bearing and diction, for example, "lean your weight on your walking-stick and speak your words manfully and well" (lines 149–50). A third attempt fails when the speaker addresses the "women in assembly," and so on. A fascinating aspect of this rehearsal is the prominence of apparent improvisation. For all the explicitness of costume, language, timing, and *dramatis locus*, the heart of Praxagora's "play" is played as an improvisation on her idea of the legislative discourse in the ekklesia. Like any improvisation, this script for a women's utopia involves the freedom of invention constrained by rules, in this case, those of male diction and assembly protocol. Again, a curious feature of *Ekklesiazousai* is the way in which one agon (assembly) has replaced another (tragedy) in a dramatic mise en abyme.

In his penultimate play, then,[57] Aristophanes has revived the political metafiction of *Wasps* by shaping his theatrical inset along the lines of institutional procedure in a way that cleverly points up the kinship between political and dramatic agons. Since tragic productions had long furnished the material for comic "improvisation" (most evident in the fifth-century contrafacts), the substitution of a performance "played" in a court of law or in the pnyx for one played in the theater of Dionysos was a natural way to impart a satirical force to a mise en abyme and to underscore a connection between that technique and the contrafact. *Ekklesiazousai* is complete with its internal poet-director, players, and audience and transcends many earlier comedies in its self-reflexive emphasis on theatrical terminology and paraphernalia. Unlike the trial scene in *Wasps*, however, the performance is not fully realized before the spectators; we do not actually witness the assembly for which Praxagora has been preparing her women. The banishment of the main spectacle to a messenger-style report paradoxically sharpens the metafictional point of the sequence. We are present at the rehearsal and later witness the reaction of the "internal" audience (of men at the assembly) in the person of Khremes (lines 372–477). The absence of the performance itself yields to detailed (and hilarious) commentary that is itself metacritical, that is, a report and discussion of the proceedings of the assembly with its own debates. Khremes describes Praxagora's performance from the perspective of a spectator seduced by the fiction: a thin, pale young man "resembling Nikias" spoke at length juxtaposing female virtues and male vices (lines 441–54):[58]

> A woman, he said, is full of common sense
> and business sense. Women don't divulge
> the secrets of the Thesmophoria whenever it's
> held, while you and I blab state secrets at every
> occasion . . . . They always return what they've
> borrowed, withholding nothing while most of us
> do the reverse . . . . Women do not inform or
> prosecute or injure the demos: they do much
> of value and virtue. He said much besides
> in praise of women.

The general acceptance of these criticisms by Khremes and Blepyros underscores the glaring tensions between male and female, insider and outsider, player and persona. It twists the tongue even to describe: men playing men agree with the judgment of their gender on the part of pseudomen who are, in fact, women played by men! It does not stop there, however, since the men playing men turn out not to be "real" men after all (in the figurative sense): they have, after all, let the impostors foist their reforms on them and their compatriots. "Manly" men (in the conventional sense of Aristophanic comedy) would surely not have so utterly lost control of the ekklesia. The seduction of these unworthy but "authentic" males by Praxagora's script (delivered by bogus men) is ultimately reversed as Aristophanes ridicules the women's utopia in the latter half of the play.

There can be little doubt that Aristophanic comedy reinforced communal attitudes on a fundamental level and that a play such as *Ekklesiazousai* subjected the normative notions of gender and virtue to only a minor test that might be likened to a vaccine. Much like the excitement some years ago over a spate of films with transvestite thematics,[59] the minor affront to established sensibilities suggests an "inoculation" against threatening disruption and subversion. Although far removed from suggesting change in the social order, such an inoculation is nevertheless significant. Fissures in the social fabric have opened to allow exploration and exposure, never again to close or be concealed. The very intensity and complexity of the play with social categories in *Ekklesiazousai* suggests a new level of awareness on the part of poet and, perhaps, his public.

In the merchant scene in Sophokles' *Philoktetes* (lines 542–627) we have an example of an extended tragic mise en abyme. This fascinating sequence involves the orchestration of a very human charade by Odysseus, the play's "internal director."[60] Neoptolemos is the main player in this minidrama and has already met and ingratiated himself with the suffering Philoktetes following the general instructions of his "director": he must be conniving (σόφισμα, line 15; σοφισθῆναι, line 77; σοφός, line 119) and thievish (κλοπεύς, line 77) in order to overcome the ailing hero by means of a trick (δόλῳ λαβεῖν, line 101). In this respect Neoptolemos' role has much in common with that of Peisetairos and Praxagora: he is featured in a theatrical maneuver involving trickery, persuasion, and the alteration of forms. Odysseus' general plan is to abduct Philoktetes (αἱρήσειν, line 14; λαβεῖν, line 101) from Lemnos in order to fulfill the prophecy of Helenos concerning the capture of Troy. Sophokles modifies tradition, however, beginning with the oblique and fragmented presentation of the prophecy.[61] Similarly, the Homeric polytropy of Odysseus is amplified and complicated in a specifically (meta)theatrical way.[62] In combining aspects of villain, realist, and buffoon, he furnishes a vivid illustration of the shifty role he expects Neoptolemos to play. Following a forceful exhortation to use craft and persuasion, Odysseus sends the youth on and withdraws, implying, however, that he will continue to monitor his progress (lines 126–31):[63]

> And if you seem to me to be lagging
> behind time at all, I shall disguise
> this same man to look like a ship's captain,
> in order to maintain Philoktetes' ignorance,

and send him out back here again.
His speech, of course, child, will be intricate:
accept and use what is serviceable at the moment in his story.

The articulation here of the play mise en abyme into three separate parties, director, actor, and spectator, has much in common with the madness scenes discussed in chapters 4 and 5. The discourse of tragedy is complicated by the introduction of ignorance (ἀγνοία here, δυσφόρους γνώμας *Aias* 51–52) that enforces the inner dramatic "illusion." The multivalence of the script, moreover, is underlined by language that is delivered ποικίλως (line 130), an adverb ranging in force from "intricately," and "elaborately," to "subtly," "with many meanings." There arises a tension, moreover, between the internal and external audiences of the inset, an ever-present and important feature of the mise en abyme that defines the intellectual distancing of the spectators.

The first "episode" of the charade turns out to be a success as Philoktetes accepts Neoptolemos and asks him to carry him from the island. The length of this exchange exceeds Odysseus' patience, however, and he initiates the second "episode" by sending his men to play merchant and sidekick. Their entrance (line 542) complicates matters somewhat and, ironically, retards Neoptolemos' progress. Euripides, Sophokles' immediate predecessor in staging this story (431 BC), had a disguised Odysseus himself confront Philoktetes in the spirit of the latter part of the *Odyssey*.[64] It is therefore remarkable that Sophokles departs from Euripides' Homeric model (with an active Athene and a "feral" Philoktetes reminiscent of Polyphemos). He redesigns, indeed modernizes, the inset to be a theatrical situation in a way that allows a "behind-the-scenes" Odysseus to direct a group of players in the foreground. That Odysseus has been monitoring the progress of the inset is made clear when he intrudes at line 974. Neoptolemos had abandoned the "script" in an improvisation that was ethically more compelling but that destroyed the fiction and prompted the enraged "director" to leap on stage with a shout: "you wretch! What *are* you doing?!"[65]

It is interesting to consider here certain similarities between internal directors in comedy and tragedy. Both Peisetairos and Odysseus embody poetic authority. The former, like the comic poet himself, mingles a variety of obvious sources in a distinctly sophistic manner that eventually incorporates the author into the "play." Similarly, though with greater realism, Odysseus' plot is remarkable for its involvement with previous models. Like a comic poet, moreover, Odysseus himself figures in "his" internal fiction. Thus Neoptolemos is encouraged to speak ill of Odysseus for greater realism (lines 64–66). As a result, Neoptolemos makes a point of criticizing him several times (lines 441, 457, 568–69) while the sailor playing the part of the merchant does the same (lines 607–9) and conveys alarming "news" involving Odysseus.[66] The Greeks' intentions concerning Philoktetes are revealed by means of clever use of dramatic convention: lines 573–74 are an aside the "boundaries" of which are broken so as to arouse the ailing hero's curiosity (lines 572–78):[67]

NEOPTOLEMUS. Who was this that Odysseus was personally sailing for?

MERCHANT. There was one . . . but tell me first who this is.
Whatever you say do not speak loudly.

NEOPTOLEMUS. This is the famous Philoktetes, stranger.

MERCHANT. Ask me no more now, but get yourself on board
and sail from this country as quickly as possible.

PHILOKTETES. What is he saying, boy? Why is the sailor darkly
bartering in words with you?

The word διεμπολᾷ, "drive a bargain," "sell off," in the mouth of the ignorant Philoktetes appears to be a fine self-conscious touch on the part of the playwright pointing up the deep role of the merchant. There is a further and subtle irony to the fact that, although in *Philoktetes* theatrical technique and "illusion" are associated with Odyssean μῆτις and δόλος, the core of the inner plot is true (the merchant's story, lines 603–19) and sets in motion the events that will lead to Neoptolemos' change of heart, that is, beginning with so distressing Philoktetes that he suffers another paroxysm.[68]

The stasimon that follows the merchant scene involves an apparent lapse on the part of the chorus. In the concluding antistrophe (lines 719–29) they say that Philoktetes has finally "encountered a descendant of good men, and will emerge after those troubles famed and happy." They go on to claim that Neoptolemos is "taking him, after the lapse of many moons, on his sea-traversing ship to his family home." After discouraging the interpretation of these words as some sort of deceit, R. G. Ussher notes that "for whatever reason, [the chorus] seem not to be concerned— even in this rare case of the actors' total absence . . .—to stand outside the dramatic situation."[69] The reason is to be sought in the metatheatrics of stasimon's context. The second "act" of the charade is finished but the internal fiction is not yet complete as Philoktetes is still under its spell. We shall have to wait for the hero to fall asleep for its hold to weaken, a process felt throughout Neoptolemos' inner struggle and confession and completed by the intrusion of the "director" at line 974. In the stasimon the chorus assimilate their presence *formally* to the fiction of the mise en abyme and perform along the lines of the appropriate mythos, that is, as a chorus to the inner drama with its three actors and silent character. On this reading, then, the chorus is seen as neither engaging in outright deceit (Jebb) nor creating violent cognitive dissonance (Ussher and others), but rather being complicit in a striking theatrical experiment.

Philoktetes vividly illustrates the power of metafictional strategy as an instrument whose meaning is uniquely determined with every application. By reflexively foregrounding in Neoptolemos the duality of actor and role, Sophokles deepens his stage figure to embody the play's multiple ambiguities. Neoptolemos is used, among other things, to explore the tensions between rhetorical manipulation and ethics, form and content, speech and thought. There is an important difference, moreover, between such play with theatricality and conscious lying, as we learn from the comic example of *Akharnians*. In the manner of Sophokles' Odysseus, the comic character Euripides participates in *Akharnians* from behind the scenes, as it were, wheeled out on the *ekkyklema* to set before Dikaiopolis an inventory of pathetic disguises. As in the tragedy, the protagonist explicitly distinguishes inner audience (the "foolish" coal burners and dupes of his performance) from the external audience intended to gain insight from the metafictional sequence (*Akharnians* 440–44). *Philoktetes*, like *Thesmophoriazousai* and *Ekklesiazousai*, sustains its interest in the (mis)match between theatrical coordinates: It is doubtless the influence of contemporary Euripidean plays (e.g., *Helene*) that prompted comic and tragic poet alike to frame their work in terms of dramatic representation and its inherent duplicities.

3

Figures of Play, Part 2

The Comic Contrafact

A Poetics of Transformation

Aristophanes' *Akharnians*, the earliest extant Greek comedy, is a natural point of departure chronologically and technically for a presentation of the third metafictional mode briefly outlined in chapter 2. This comedy has recently received considerable scholarly attention, much of which has been directed at the contrafact—the "improvisation" of a new stage play from tragedy that is transposed into a comic key. Euripides and his *Telephos* are integral to the design of *Akharnians* in a sophisticated sequence that serves well as a paradigm for other contrafacts whose technique may appear, superficially at least, quite different. A review of this familiar example will set a hermeneutic pattern for the less familiar transformations presented in chapters 6, 7, and 8 such as that of (Sophokles') *Tereus* in *Birds* and (Euripides') *Peirithous* in *Frogs*. Taking translation as the governing metaphor, however, it is necessary first to consider the discourse that serves as the "target language" for Aristophanes' renderings of tragedy: the "idioms" and "grammar" of a comic poetics developed in the last quarter of the fifth century.

As fate would have it, with the exception of Euripides' *Helene*, all the tragedies upon which Aristophanes "improvises" are lost. To avoid circularity and enhance clarity, each chapter (6, 7, 8) devoted to a contrafact begins with an overview of the lost play in question, that is, Euripides' *Telephos*, *Bellerophontes*, and *Peirithous* and Sophokles' *Tereus*. Juxtaposition of two intertextually related plays allows for the development of a critical dialogue: the tragic reconstruction adumbrates many of the issues raised by the comedy, while the "anatomy" of the contrafact reviews and redefines much of what was said about the tragedy.

Telephos and *Akharnians* are unique, however, in that they have received thorough scholarly coverage in the years between Pucci's groundbreaking *Aristofane ed Euripide* and Collard, Cropp, and Lee's edition of the tragic fragments. The same cannot be said for the other lost plays presented below. The *Akharnians-Telephos* case is presented here as a programmatic example in which demonstration is given priority over originality. The familiarity of this example will help clarify the approach taken in this study. Aristophanes' first surviving play is appropriate, moreover, for a general characterization of the discourse and poetics that make the contrafact possible. Special emphasis is placed on comedy's *systematic* transformation of tragedy, both formally and thematically.

The Nature of Comic Discourse

A striking aspect of an Aristophanic figure such as Dikaiopolis is the way in which he is used to organize an impressive array of verbal and thematic elements in a performance that, strictly speaking, is unrealistic and discontinuous. Such a stage figure is a locus for multiple linguistic registers and multiple voices that may even appear as discontinuities of character. The ventriloqual nature of the comic stage figure, though bewildering, is a defining characteristic of Aristophanic drama that is intimately bound up with its metafictional strategies. The playwright tempts us, as it were, with glimpses "behind the scenes" into the poetic process where the leading figure appears to act as a metafictional operator. A notorious problem in *Akharnians*, for example, is the extent to which Aristophanes' authorial "I" invades the character of Dikaiopolis.[1] Having criticized the litigiousness of old men, the protagonist says (377–82):[2]

> I know well what I've had to take from
> Kleon for last year's comedy—do I ever!
> How he dragged me into the council-chamber,
> and slandered and tongued me with his lies,
> roaring like a torrent and showering me with spit.
> I nearly died, overwhelmed by slime.

The personal response to Kleon is resumed in Dikaiopolis' Great Speech in which comedy is advanced as a suitable medium for telling the truth, however unpleasant (502–5):[3]

> And Kleon can't slander me for
> trashing the polis before outsiders.
> This here's the Lenaia, and we're all alone;
> No visitors have come yet.

Is Dikaiopolis at these points to be seen as identical with the author, a generalized comic hero, a momentary parabasis-like interlude, a more sophisticated fiction of the disguised poet, or simply an opaque and confusing joke?[4] The inextricable connection between dramatic character and discourse is particularly complex in Aristophanes as the "inner landscape" of a figure such as Peisetairos or Trygaios draws on the full linguistic and thematic resources of the entire play. The latter, in turn, is a fiction coextensive with the world of the spectators and, as such, is particularly rich in simultaneous possibilities. Salient features of this comic poetics are polyphony, discourse irony, and apparent improvisation.[5]

Polyphony

The comic script is woven of a mingled yarn, the single strands of which are distinct and particular: colloquial speech, parody, topical allusions, comic formations, and technical language.[6] The presence of the poet as the controlling mind is quite palpable in such writing, not necessarily as an intrusive "I" but rather in the unhomogenized variety of linguistic resources gathered together within a single character. The diversity of these resources and the rapid transitions from one level to another are an undisguised display of the poet's creativity at the expense of realistic character. Being a poetic microcosm of the entire play, the dramatic figure is not a bounded individual easily separable from his (con)text. At the same time, the language of Peisetairos, for example, would appear to differ from that of Dikaiopolis in its composition. Insofar as the former draws on the sophistic vocabulary and mannerisms,[7] he is distinct from Dikaiopolis, who sustains the persona of a farmer critical of the behavior of his compatriots, especially those of the urban center. Dikaiopolis specializes in Euripides while Peisetairos "speaks" Aisopos and Pindaros. The language of both exhibits typical Aristophanic polyphony but differs in the relative concentration of the various strata identified above.

(Apparent) Improvisation

Throughout its transformation in the hands of its most famous fifth-century practitioner, comedy never forgot its improvisational beginnings.[8] The unself-conscious facility with which simple personae such as Trygaios and Philokleon are made to manipulate both language and the very scenario of which they are a part results in a character development of sorts.[9] The plot and fundamental "comic idea" are often directly dependent on the inspirations and decisions of the lead character, who appears to invent as he goes along, propelling the blatantly unrealistic action. The evolving comic scenario, in turn, appears to change the character or at least to reveal new, unexpected potential. The interaction of internal invention (a character's self-expression) and external invention ("improvisation") are vital for the Aristophanic plot. The actions and speeches of Peisetairos, for example, trace a path of conversion from a self-professed *apragmôn* to an ambitious city planner and, finally, tyrant-god. The creative, improvisational aspect of Aristophanes' lead roles are, in an important sense, metaphors of poetic creativity. The identification between poet and protagonist ranges from explicit (Dikaiopolis) to subtle (Bdelykleon). "By projecting his own experience onto his main character," notes Hubbard of this phenomenon, "Aristophanes clarifies both the potential and the limitations of his comic art."[10]

Discourse Irony

More subtle than an intrusion of the authorial "I" are moments when a character behaves like a puppet in the hands of a clever ventriloquist. The author's presence is revealed in a fictional figure's speech as it departs from, or surpasses, its speaker in intelligence, sophistication, tone, or scope. It is tempting, if anachronistic, to regard a tragic figure as the tip of an iceberg concealing a subconscious, a family, and a recuperable past. The Aristophanic character, by contrast, is entirely on display to the point where the spectators are aware of more about him and the meaning of his words than is the character himself. Thus when a figure such as Tereus uses tragic language[11] or when Trygaios enacts a burlesque of Euripides' *Bellerophontes*, the spectator is given a broader perspective on the action than the dramatic figure is really supposed to have. At many points in a play, the protagonist (and sometimes the chorus) communicates to the audience the jokes and ideas of the poet in spite of himself and his role. When a slave includes in his exposition of the dramatic situation an endorsement of Aristophanic comedy and its methods,[12] we do not struggle with a discontinuity between "slave" and "dramatic critic," but rather allow the figure to assume temporarily a new fictional dimension (an aspect of "poet"). The complexity of Dikaiopolis' opening harangue is similarly presented for the reader/spectator to enjoy in its fullness while the dramatic figure is intent on his central problem. His mention of Kleon "disgorging five talents," for example, in all probability looks back to Aristophanes' *Babylonians* and, as a self-citation, conspires with the chorus' promise to "cut Kleon to shreds for the Knights."[13] Here the characters of the comedy are bearers of a sophisticated literary message that is beyond the roles of "farmer" and "rustic." The pleasing irony in which a stage figure's speech exceeds his awareness and abilities is a hallmark of Aristophanic characterization.[14] At times, in fact, the comic script offers ventriloqual moments when the "poet" usurps the voice and role of a stage figure. The most sustained example of such ventriloquation is the parabasis in which the chorus appears to suppress its own identity to speak for the playwright.

The polyphony, apparent improvisation, and discourse irony of linguistic characterization in Aristophanes are representative of a genre that is "in its very essence grounded in an atmosphere of developed agonistic competition and intense literary allusion, wherein the poets sought and created for themselves visible public identities."[15] Old Comedy is, in this respect, part of a long poetic tradition of allusion and self-consciousness.[16]

The full theatricality of the Old Comic fiction encompasses the situation in which a community is spectator to itself in the curved mirror of the poet's genius. The transformational poetics of the contrafact is closely bound up with how Aristophanic figures interact, in varying degrees, with the fictional persona of the "poet." This collaboration makes comedy a patently nonillusory performance played for the poet by the actors to the spectators. In the case of metafictional sequences, the genre clearly transcends binary opposition between "inside" and "outside" the play, "the world of the play," and "the world of the audience." In the latter quarter of the fifth century comedy is still far from dramatic realism, or a theater of "the probable," in the Aristotelian sense.[17] A performance such as *Wasps*, for example, embraces the spectators by fictionalizing them (*demos* by synecdoche), its own context (polis), the poet, and the dramatic process itself.[18] Informed by the aspects of comic discourse outlined above, the contrafact is facilitated by this three-dimensional fiction that at once admits to having author, context, players, and spectators. With a reflexivity operative at every point in the performance, the polis is presented, *re-presented*, to itself by a playwright-citizen whose role as "teacher" and "advisor" of the body politic is an integral part of the comic fiction. Let us turn now to examine in some detail the workings of the comic contrafact under the able "direction" of that metafictional operator, Dikaiopolis.

Telephus Tragicus

Aristophanes' career is framed by conspicuous contrafacts of Euripidean tragedy. Near the beginning (425 BC) stands *Akharnians* with its reworking of *Telephos*, while *Aiolosikon* of the 380s (reworking *Aiolos*, now lost) appears to be the final example indicating a lingering metafictional energy in the evolution to Middle Comedy. Some years ago, Roland Barthes characterized comedy as a parasitic discourse, a "rhetorique noire," which "traces with severity and precision the transgressive places where the taboos of language and sex are lifted."[19] *Akharnians*, the first fully extant specimen of European comedy, devotes these omnivorous and metamorphic energies to *Telephos*, whose ideas, themes, and prestige it appropriates in a systematic and thorough-going manner. In 438 BC, thirteen years before Aristophanes won his first prize with *Akharnians*, Euripides produced this play that was destined to enjoy a paradoxical fame. Though lacking a mediaeval tradition—it is one of the poet's "lost" plays—*Telephos* has remained in the focus of literary-historical inquiry as Aristophanes' most prominent tragic model. It is featured in *Akharnians* and *Thesmophoriazousai* and many scattered allusions. In the decades following the presentation of important papyrus fragments and the scholarly reconstruction by Handley and Rea (complemented by Rau's analysis), the bibliography on the subject has been growing steadily. The ensuing rash of work with *Akharnians* at the focus (or as a ceremonial beginning) by Helene Foley, Niall Slater, Thomas Hubbard, A. M. Bowie and others has established that play's status as its genre's fullest representative, the archetypal Old Comedy. Taplin's *Comic Angels*, which connects iconography with dramatic intertextuality, offers an especially valuable perspective.

This presentation involves an account of how *Telephos* has been transposed into the new (comic) environment outlined above, and so it is appropriate to begin with an overview of the tragic model behind *Akharnians* as it emerges from papyri, book fragments, and other testimonia. A point of departure is offered by Apollodoros' sketch (*Epitome* 3.17–20):[20]

> Ignorant of the course to Troy [the Greeks] put in at Mysia and sacked it, thinking that it was the Trojan city. Telephos, the son of Herakles, was king of the Mysians. Seeing his country plundered, he armed his subjects, chased the Greeks to their ships, and killed many men, including Thersandros, son of Polyneikes, who stood his ground. When Akhilleus charged at Telephos, he turned and ran, but while fleeing he became entangled in a grape vine and was wounded in the thigh by a spear. The Greeks left Mysia and put out to sea. A violent storm arose during which they were separated from each other and landed in their own countries. The war is said to have lasted for twenty years. For they set out on the expedition two years after Helene was carried off, having made their preparations during that time. Eight years after they came back to Greece from Mysia, they returned to Argos and went to Aulis. When they assembled again at Argos after those eight years, they were at a loss as to the way to Troy since they had no commander who knew the course to sail. But Apollon told Telephos, whose wound would not heal, that he would be cured if the man who wounded him were to treat him. So he went from Mysia to Argos disguised in rags and begged Akhilleus to cure him. After Telephos promised to show the way to Troy, Akhilleus healed him by applying to the wound rust

which he had scraped from his Pelian spear. Now made well, Telephos plotted the course for them, and Kalkhas confirmed its accuracy by means of his art of divination.

The Euripidean fragments and testimonia attest to nearly all of the elements in this account. The most important literary and thematic memories of the tragic *Telephos*, however, are of the scene in Argos where the disguised protagonist defends himself and the Trojans. Threatened by Odysseus, who arrives with news of a spy, Telephos seizes the baby Orestes and takes refuge at an altar whereupon he is recognized for who he is: a Greek who, by a series of accidents, has become ruler of Mysia. The crisis of *Telephos* unfolds in three principal "movements" dominated by the Atreidai (debate and quarrel), Odysseus (search and discovery), and Akhilleus (resolution and healing), respectively. In the absence of a precise articulation by choral odes, entrances, exits, and so on, these "movements" shall be used to present the more significant remains of Euripides' script along the lines of a hypothetical reconstruction.[21]

Telephos, Part I: Prologue, Debate, and Argument

Telephos enters, already in his lowly disguise, and speaks a prologue from which we learn that he has returned to Argos from Mysia. The sixteen-line fragment of this speech preserved in the Milan papyrus outlines a brief autobiography culminating in the Greek attack on Mysia:[22]

> Hail, my fatherland, marked out by Pelops   fr. 696 (etc.)
> as his own! And you, Pan, haunting the stormy
> Arkadian crag whence I claim descent!
> Auge, daughter of Aleos, bore me secretly to
> Tirynthian Herakles. My witness is
> Mount Parthenion, where Eileithyia freed [Auge]
> from her labor-pains and I was born. Then many
> were my hardships . . . but I shall abbreviate my story.
> I came and settled in the land of Mysia,
> having found my mother. Mysian Teuthras
> entrusted his rule to me; and the people
> throughout the land have since called me
> by the significant name, *Telephos*, for I
> have settled *far* from home. Though Greek,
> I ruled barbarians with the support of
> many armaments, until the Akhaian force
> arrived to roam the plain of Mysia.

The point here, and in the remaining two-thirds of the prologue (50–60 lines?), is to provide a context for the dramatic intrigue at Agamemnon's court. Telephos, therefore, suppresses his early history to relate more recent events: the successful repulsion of the Greek attack, his injury at the hands of Akhilleus, the oracle (ὁ τρώσας ἰάσεται, "he who wounded [you] shall heal [you]"), and his plan to seek the cure at Argos in disguise. In fr. 705 N[2], which may be part of this narrative—"lord of the oar, disembarking in Mysia, I was wounded by an enemy hand"—Telephos falsely accounts for his injury[23] and in the cryptic fr. 707N[2] may even wish himself well.[24]

The fragments of Accius' *Telephos* applied here by Handley and Webster[25] add color: "the mighty mass of war stirred by the daughter of Tyndareus, the house of Menelaos, and the Trojan shepherd"; "ablaze with bronze and steel, alight with flags"; "waves of Mysian blood rolling"; and "they swiftly sped in flight to the left, where the sea was calm under a mountain."

Telephos' account of the journey to Argos may include a reference to having left home already in disguise.[26] The important fragments 697 and 698 (N[2]) belong to this context:[27]

These humble rags thrown about my body   fr. 697
I wear to ward off misfortune.

Today I must seem to be humble,   fr. 698
to be who I am, but to appear otherwise.

The gnomic fragments 701 N[2] (whoever would prosper must toil) and 714 N[2], (health with poverty is superior to wealth with illness) may be spoken here by Telephos in justification of his plan. The last line of fr. 698 above expresses the metatheatrical tension between actor and role and lies at the heart of Aristophanes' fascination with this particular tragedy. It is important to follow this idea in its transformation from tragedy to comedy. In the former it fuses a reflexive acknowledgment of dramatic duplicity with the mythic situation, while in comedy it is emblematic of the poetics of transformation informing the contrafact.[28] Dikaiopolis emphasizes this with his self-conscious insistence on "assuming the most pathetic disguise possible."[29]

Taking his cue from Hyginus' "*monitu Clytaemnestrae*,"[30] Handley suggests that the protagonist next "secures admission from Clytaemnestra (like Orestes in *Choephoroe*, 653 ff.), and so achieves the position which makes it possible for him to speak in the leaders' debate which we know from Aristophanes."[31] If this is correct, she may be referred to in fr. 699 N[2] as "queen of this deed and stratagem"[32] and may have appeared with the baby Orestes suggesting that Telephos take him hostage in the event of the (nearly inevitable) crisis. The hortatory fr. 702 N[2] may be spoken in this context as well: "Take courage even in the face of god-sent adversity."[33] Webster sees her setting off for the sanctuary of Lykian Apollon, a deity subsequently addressed (by Telephos?) in fr. 700 N[2]: "O Phoebus, Lykian Apollon, whatever will you do to me?" A possible, if somewhat far-fetched, feature of Euripides' plot may be gleaned from Tzetzes' suggestion that Telephos became Agamemnon's gatekeeper.[34]

Despite the tantalizing glimpse offered by the Berlin papyrus (9908) in connection with P.Oxy 2460, there is no conclusive evidence for the identity of the chorus, and scholars remain divided between three possibilities: ordinary Akhaian soldiers, Akhaian leaders, and Argive elders.[35] Although there are good reasons for favoring the latter,[36] there is insufficient data to locate or describe specific choral entrances and songs.

An important issue in reconstruction has been how to combine defense of Troy and defense of Telephos by the "beggar" in a single context. Given the history of awkward solutions to this problem, Malcolm Heath's argument for dividing the rhetorical activity of the protagonist into two speeches is attractive. In this interpretation, Telephos speaks once in defense of the Trojans and a second time in self-defense.[37] The present "movement," then, reaches its climax in a quarrel between Agamemnon and Menelaos that prompts Telephos' first speech.

Menelaos urges a new attempt to rescue Helen with, perhaps, even a raid on Mysia to settle the old score. He says of an enemy (Paris, Telephos?), "May he come to a bad end: it would be a good thing for Greece!"[38] Agamemnon, on the other hand, is inclined to quit. An argument arises about the war against Troy, eliciting the choral comment that "fraternal strife is hard to bear."[39] It is most likely Agamemnon who exclaims, "O city of Argos, do you hear what he is saying?" (fr. 713N²) and continues with the heated anapests clearly directed at Menelaos (fr. 722–723 N²):[40]

> Go wherever you must. I shall not perish   fr. 722
> on account of your Helen.
>
> Sparta is your realm; attend to it.   fr. 723
> Mycenae shall be our concern.

In the context of this argument, Telephos responds to the quarrel by defending Troy in a speech beginning with the following words:[41]

> Do not begrudge it me, leaders of the Greeks,   fr. 703
> if I, a lowly man, dare to speak in the company of my betters.

Telephos addresses Agamemnon and asserts his determination with the famous words that Aristophanes was to enact literally in a scene of hilarious concretization:[42]

> Agamemnon, not even if someone with an axe   fr. 706
> in hand was ready to bring it down upon my neck
> would I be silent: I have a just cause to plead.

The theme of justice is important in both the tragedy and its contrafact, and is emphasized by Aristophanes, who has his protagonist say at *Akharnians* 500: "even comic discourse is familiar with justice." Dikaiopolis goes on to say that his words will be difficult, but just—δεινὰ μὲν δίκαια δέ. Drawing on the logic of the Aristophanic adaptations, Heath suggests the following line of argument:[43]

> I have as much reason as any to hate the Trojans—I, too, have suffered because of them [*Ach.* 509–12, *Th.* 469–70]. But we are among friends here, and may be frank [*Ach.* 513 (cf. 502–8), *Th.* 471–72]: why do we blame them [*Ach.* 514, *Th.* 473–74]? The provocation came from our side, and women have been abducted by both sides [*Ach.* 515–27]; and it is absurd to fight a war for such a cause [*Ach.* 528–29]. You know that we have done such things; so why are we angry with the Trojans?

The speech concludes with the following sentiment expressed:[44]

> Are we then angry [at the Trojans]   fr. 711
> having suffered nothing more than we have done ourselves?

The quarrel betweeen the Atreidai is now diverted into an expression of shared indignation directed at Telephos. A choral outburst in *Akharnians* (line 558) captures the spirit: "how dare you, a nobody, say this of us?" Two fragments, 712 N², "he vilifies our whole city!" and 717 N², "will you be persuaded by this fellow, you wretch?" appear to be spoken at this point by an angry Menelaos to his brother.[45]

Telephos, Part II: Search, Discovery, and Crisis

It would appear that at *Thesmophoriazousai* 76–77 the character Euripides adapts ominous verses from *Telephos* concerning the impending crisis. A simple change restores them as follows:[46]

> On this day it shall be decided [κριθήσεται]
> whether Telephos lives or dies.

This *crisis* is precipitated by Odysseus or his messenger, who enters with news of infiltration by Telephos. We cannot know exactly how he learned of the stranger's arrival or what he reported, but fr. 1 of the Oxyrhynchus papyrus (2460) suggests that a search ensued: "catching sight of him . . . we will search the city . . . a search must be undertaken."[47] The "beggar" resumes his apology, this time focusing on himself in the third person in an effort to diffuse a very dangerous situation. For this second speech Heath suggests the following logic:[48]

> Telephus does not deserve this degree of hatred: you attacked his territory, and it was natural for him to resist. You may say that there was no need [fr. 708, *Ach.* 540]; but if someone made a landing here [fr. 708a, *Ach.* 541], you would not have done nothing [fr. 709, *Ach.* 543]. You know how you would have reacted; do we suppose that Telephus is any different [fr. 710, *Ach.* 555–56]?

The stranger thus attracts attention to himself and is interrogated more closely. *Akharnians* 430 — "I know the man, Mysian Telephos" — echoes the moment at which Odysseus presses the "beggar" to reveal all he knows:[49]

> I know the man, Mysian Telephos . . . be he   fr. 704
> from Mysia or from somewhere else,
> how . . . shall I recognize him?

Heath suggests that the "beggar" claims to be under Klytaimnestra's protection — much to Agamemnon's displeasure — thus bringing her back onstage. Here may belong fr. 721 N[2] in which someone (Odysseus?) warns his interlocutor that "some wicked fellow is using you as his sponsor [proxenos]." Despite the uncertainty of the action, there can be little doubt that it culminated in the famous crisis. The breaking point is suggested by a quotation from *Telephos* at the end of an interrogation at *Knights* 1240 (fr. 700 N[2], cited earlier) where the exasperated Paphlagonian exclaims, "Phoebus, Lykian Apollon, whatever will you do to me?" An alternative to Webster's attribution (Klytaimnestra) is to see in these words the cry with which the tragic Telephos abandons his disguise, seizes the infant Orestes,[50] and seeks refuge at the altar of Apollon (as Webster suggests on the evidence of the relevant vase paintings).[51] The anguished dochmiacs sung by the chorus of women in *Thesmophoriazousai* at the corresponding moment (lines 689–91, etc.) no doubt reflect something from the original production. Telephos' defiance may be exemplified by fr. 727 N[2] in which he repudiates "the most hateful child of a hateful father" and the lurid threat echoed by Euripides' Kinsman at the corresponding moment in *Thesmophoriazousai* (lines 693–95): "Soon his bleeding veins, slit by this knife, shall stain the sacrificial meat upon the altar."

Telephos now explains why he has come. Two difficult fragments of the Oxyrhynchus papyrus (9 and 10) point to a scene in which he is pressured to act as a guide to Troy in response to the "leadership oracle," stipulating that it cannot be taken without his help. In the negotiations that ensue, someone offers healing in return for this favor and asks, "What then prevents you [*i.e., from acting as our guide in an attack on Troy*]?" "Loyalty" (*literally, "not to betray"*), answers Telephos, thinking perhaps of his father-in-law, Priam. From Hyginus' account cited above it is fair to assume that Euripides resolved the impasse by means of a compromise: Telephos led the Greeks to Troy, "pointing out the lay of the land and routes," but did not participate in the actual fighting. This agreement is yet to be threatened by a final obstacle—the wrath of Akhilleus.

Telephos, Part III: Resolution and Healing

At this point in the action we get help from the Berlin Papyrus, which preserves the end of a choral ode and the beginning of the final episode of healing and resolution.[52]

> gust of southerly or westerly breeze   P. Berol. 9908
> will bring . . . to the shores of Troy;
> and you, stationed at the steering-oar,
> will instruct the prow-man to observe a course
> straight for Ilion for the Atreidai.
> For a Tegean mother, Greece not Mysia, bore you
> to be—with a god's influence, surely—a sailor
> and guide of our sea-going ships.

Webster distills the salient points as follows: "1. Telephos has promised to lead the host to Troy (Col. ii, 3). 2. Telephos has been accepted as leader because he is an Arcadian and not a Mysian (Col. ii, 7). 3. Odysseus is on the stage eagerly awaiting Achilles, who comes at the right moment. Telephos has therefore been promised that Achilles shall heal him."[53]

Akhilleus and the Thessalian contingent arrive late and are greeted by Odysseus: "The expedition is agreed . . . you have come at a vital moment, son of Peleus." This entrance makes possible the solution of the second oracle—"he who wounded you shall heal you"—and the healing of Telephos. The minimal configuration for this scene, then, is an animated three-way discussion between Telephos, Akhilleus, and Odysseus in which the latter plays the role of a mediator. Hyginus 101, cited earlier in connection with Apollodoros' account, appears to follow Euripides closely:

> As the Greeks had an oracle that Troy could not be captured without Telephos' guidance, they were easily reconciled with him [after the seizure of Orestes] and asked Akhilleus to heal him. When Akhilleus answered that he did not know the art of medicine, Odysseus said, "in naming the agent of the wound [in the oracle "he who wounded you must heal you"] Apollo does not mean you but the spear. Using shavings taken from this they healed Telephos. Whereupon they asked him to take part with them in the capture of Troy. Telephos refused as he was married to Priam's daughter, Laodike. In return for the favor of healing him, however, he led them to Troy, pointing out the lay of the land and routes. He then returned to Mysia.

The best preserved portion of P.Berol. 9908 (Col. ii, 11–23) contains a rapid exchange between Odysseus and Akhilleus, who are both clearly identified:[54]

> AKHILLEUS. Can it be, Odysseus, that you also have just now   P. Berol. 9908
> arrived from your sea-girt island? Where is the
> gathering of our comrades? Why the delay?
> This is no time to be cooling your heels!

> ODYSSEUS. The expedition has been ratified and is now the concern of those
> in command. You have come at a critical moment, son of Peleus.

> AKHILLEUS. I see no army of rowers on the beach,
> no contingent of soldiers awaiting, being reviewed.

> ODYSSEUS. Soon enough, soon enough. One should hasten when
> the moment is ripe.

> AKHILLEUS. You people are always sluggish and delaying, each
> sitting about making countless speeches
> while there is no progress at all in the work to be done.
> Now I and my Myrmidon host are ready for action,
> as you can see, and we shall sail <without waiting on>
> the delays of the Atreidai.

Akhilleus, true to form, is irate and impatient: "Shall we, Greeks, be barbarians' lackeys?" (fr. 719 N[2]). Odysseus tries to calm him, saying, "It is time to put your judgment before your anger" (fr. 718 N[2]) and is careful to explain: "He is to be cured by the filings of the spear" (fr. 724 N[2]). The last voice preserved in the fragments is that of Telephos entreating the harsh Akhilleus to cooperate and to heal him:[55]

> Yield to Necessity and do not resist the gods.   fr. 716
> Bring yourself to look at me, and calm your
> proud spirit. A god makes even the greatest
> things small and humbles their height.

The healing itself may have been reported in a messenger speech followed by a final celebration and departure.[56] "Telephus, healed and restored," speculates Heath, "enters from the palace, accompanied by Achilles and Odysseus or Agamemnon, and they depart ([to the] side, followed by the Chorus) on the way to launch the fleet against Troy."[57]

Telephus Comicus

For a proper appreciation of Aristophanes' metafictional strategy in *Akharnians*, it is important to consider the contrafact both on the formal level of text and structure, and from the point of view of poetics, to observe how tragic material mutates in a comic environment to produce new meaning. There is discussion of verbal parody and intertextual play in one sector, and thematic, situational, and genre-oriented analysis in another. The philological work of Eric Handley, Peter Rau, and Michael Silk is largely devoted to the former, while the latter remains less charted territory in which the leading efforts are those of Hubbard, Foley, and Bowie. It is important to emphasize the concern in this study with extended transformation of one play into another, a complex process that assumes unique aspects in each Aristophanic experiment. Accordingly, the contrafact of *Telephos* will be traced in a nearly linear fashion as it develops through *Akharnians*, weaving together the various strands of Aristophanes' invention from prologue to exodos.

On a formal level, *Akharnians* exhibits creativity in appropriating specific words (e.g., line 7) and sequences (e.g., Telephos' speech) from tragedy.[58] In each instance there may or may not be distortion of the tragic material or collision between it and the comic context.[59] Furthermore, the order of the tragic elements is retained or disrupted according to the requirements of the comic plot.

In his opening monologue Dikaiopolis identifies himself first and foremost as an opinionated spectator of drama—he emphasizes tragedy (line 9)—and hints at his forthcoming association with *Telephos* by marking his dislike for Kleon with a quotation, "it is a good thing for Hellas" (fr. 720 N²: ἄξιον γὰρ Ἑλλάδι). Conspicuous by omission, the suppressed part of the tragic curse—"may [he] come to a bad end"—lends an elliptical virulence to the comic line. The close association between the theater and the pnyx (assembly), moreover, marks the beginning of an evolving frame within which the protagonist will refashion Euripides. He will manipulate appearance and reality, costume and disguise, truth and fiction. For a start, the comic hero replaces the tragic enemy with his own, thereby adumbrating the thoroughgoing link between Telephos' plea for justice and the comic case for "justice" in the fictionalized conflict—the largely imaginary rivalry—between Kleon and the poet-citizen Aristophanes.[60]

The geographical, spatial, and ideological connections established in the prologue are subtle, but important. As we have seen, Telephos greets the Arkadian landscape, to which he has come seeking relief from his illness, and explains the process whereby he, a Greek, has become a barbarian monarch. Dikaiopolis transforms this situation to fit his position in the polis and his agenda: he is indeed an Athenian, but also a member of a rural deme (Kholleidai) and, thus, an "alien" in the city center that recently had been so quick to sacrifice the countryside to the invading Peloponnesians.[61] His "disease"—and this word is often used of the initial premise or problem in comedy[62]—is the war that has been particularly harsh for residents of inland communities. Dikaiopolis' nostalgia for his deme and his hatred of the city center (ἄστυ) are echoed later by the chorus (lines 990–99) in a way that underscores the division between fellow Greeks in the context of the war. It is surely significant that *Telephos* is, in a sense, a Peloponnesian play!

The paradoxical juxtaposition of exile and return is thus given a new twist. From Mysia, where he had settled in permanent exile, Telephos returns to his native country—the "ancestral land, which Pelops marked out as his own"—as a stranger seeking help, while Dikaiopolis has been forced to leave his rural home to seek refuge downtown as an "exile." The tragic process whereby an initial conflict between the Greeks and a "foreigner" is resolved through recognition and negotiation is reversed in the comedy as Athenians are divided along regional lines. In the end, Dikaiopolis enjoys his separate peace with no prospect of reconciliation between urban and rural factions. The tragic exclamation "O city, my city" (line 27) is appropriate in this context with the repetition of "polis" suggesting a divided mind. The comic prologue postpones the element of disguise, allowing Dikaiopolis to improvise his way toward the

Euripidean climax in a metaphor of Aristophanes' creative process. For now, how-ever, he bides his time waiting to see what will happen (lines 29–33): "And here I take my seat; then all alone, I pass the time whining, yawning, stretching, farting, wondering, doodling, plucking myself, pondering the situation, gazing fondly toward the country, yearning for peace. I hate the urban center here and long for my home in the village!"

As many have noted, an important aspect of Dikaiopolis' role is a dual political-theatrical spectatorship that points up the analogy between dramatic and forensic rhetoric.[63] The central Telephean theme of layered identity begins to unfold with the arrival of various figures starting with Amphitheos. This character's name itself involves a play on the possible meanings of ἀμφι-: Amphitheos is either "thoroughly divine, divine on both sides," or "of dubious divinity."[64] He presents himself by mim-icking Euripidean genealogy in an attempt to underwrite the first interpretation. His comic nature and the ease with which his mission of peace is brushed aside suggest the second, that is, either his "divine" pedigree has long since ceased to matter to anyone, or he is a fake. This mismatch between appearance (costume) and reality (identity) is amplified in the subsequent performances by the ambassadors to the Persian King, the King's Eye ("Pseudartabas"), and the ambassador to Thrace with the Odomantian host in tow.

In this sequence that bears a curious resemblance to the intruder parades char-acteristic of the typical latter half of an Aristophanic comedy, Dikaiopolis reveals that he intends to go beyond the passive spectatorial role outlined in his mono-logue (lines 38–39). He first offers humorous commentary in the form of deroga-tory asides (βωμολοχεύματα) and finally conducts an active examination of the King's Eye, the upshot of which is a revelation of fraud and penetration of disguise. Having questioned "Pseudartabas," Dikaiopolis deduces that he and his attendants are impostors sent as propaganda by the pro-war faction to encourage the Athe-nian demos: "I do believe they come from right here. Why, one of these eunuchs is Kleisthenes, son of Sibyrtios! Do you—O ape sporting the clean-shaven, hot-spirited arse—dare come to us like this, wearing a beard, costumed like a eunuch?" (lines 116–21). This moment serves as a fine example of intertextual surface play in which several texts are superimposed to produce an absurd interaction between their respective contexts.

The first of these lines (wrongly attributed to Euripides' Medeia by the scholiast)[65] appears to be an adaptation of the tragic phrase ὦ θερμόβουλον σπλάγχνον, "O hot-tempered heart!" The participle ἐξυρημένε, "shaved," may similarly conceal a more common form such as ἐξευρημένε, "discovered" (so Rogers). Line 120 substitutes πώγων', "beard," for πυγήν, "rump," in the verse of Arkhilokhos: τοιάνδε γ᾽ ὦ πίθηκε τὴν πυγὴν ἔχων, "having such a (laughably small) rump, you ape." Despite the ob-scene potential of the parodic substitutions, we note a curious economy whereby "arse" replaces a tragic word in the first line while "beard" replaces the "rump" of Arkhilokhos' ape (and the Aisopic tale that appears to be the source of this byword). There does not appear to be deeper significance to this jumble of the tragic and iam-bic beyond the sheer fun of pointing out that just as the ape in popular imagination had no rump to speak of,[66] so Kleisthenes—both as "eunuch" and effeminate—had no beard. However, ἐσκευασμένος, the last word of line 121, reveals the "layered identity" theme with its etymological connection to σκεῦος, the technical term for "prop" (and, by extension, "costume"), a participle repeated several times thereafter.[67]

The lines of the tragic model and its transformation begin to emerge more clearly. We have been introduced to the homology between theater and assembly and have seen a demonstration of how rhetorical manipulation and physical disguise collaborate to deceive the Athenian demos.[68] Having come to a deceptively foreign land (the city center) to engage a hostile ideology (the urban demos, and pro-war faction) in search of a solution to his crisis, Dikaiopolis learns early on that it is not to be found in an adherence to convention and conformity to procedure. Something drastic is needed. Thus when the assembly is dismissed, Amphitheos is commissioned to conclude a separate treaty, and Dikaiopolis faces the chorus whose entrance signals a series of new developments. With the first line of the parodos (204) we recognize a violent disruption of the tragic order as the search inspired by Odysseus in *Telephos* is transposed to the beginning of the action in *Akharnians*: "This way, everyone! After him! Pursue him! Question every passerby about the fellow's whereabouts!" Bristling with words for pursuit, search, flight, and capture,[69] this passage marks itself clearly as the counterpart of Odysseus' tragic search: the vivid diction of πόλιν μαστεύωμεν . . . μαστεύειν χρή, "let us search the city . . . a search must be undertaken," of P. Oxy 2460 becomes the more verbose and prosaic τῇ πόλει γὰρ ἄξιον ξυλλαβεῖν τὸν ἄνδρα τοῦτον . . . δεῖ ζητεῖν τὸν ἄνδρα, "he must be caught for the good of the polis . . . a search for the man must be undertaken" (lines 205–6, 234).

The old Akharnian charcoal burners problematize the protagonist's immediate community so as to highlight the dichotomy between city and country, war and peace, citizen as destroyer,[70] and Dikaiopolis as a potential citizen-savior.[71] Like Dikaiopolis they hate Kleon (lines 300–301) but they are incensed at the conclusion of a private treaty with an enemy at whose hands they have suffered far beyond others (especially in the urban demes). Here we have further, obvious transformation of *Telephos*. The result of Dikaiopolis' appropriation of the tragic persona, rhetoric, and strategy is to split the chorus along ideological lines—into pro- and antiwar factions—in a reflection of the discord incited by the advent and activities of Telephos amidst the Peloponnesian Greeks. Telephos' purpose in coming to the "hostile country" was to engage his compatriots in discourse, persuade them, and win "salvation" for himself and the city. The comic hero's countermimesis certainly achieves the first of these; the second, however, is only a partial success, and the third is a failure. The arrival of the chorus, in hot pursuit of the offender, singing their tragicomic binding-song,[72] amplifies the formal alienation of Dikaiopolis. Having made his private deal with the enemy, he celebrates his separateness in a festival (the Rural Dionysia) marked by its relation to the deme in stark opposition to the polis center. Even in the country-side, ἐν ἀγρῷ, moreover, there is stasis, and the isolation of private land by boundary markers and the establishment of a private market are to follow. In an arresting irony, Aristophanes will reverse Euripides' happy ending by developing Dikaiopolis' progressive alienation and separation from his country—quite the reverse of Telephos' healing and reintegration. The basic dualities inherent in Euripides' *Telephos* are thus refracted throughout Aristophanes' comedy into a number of interacting tensions organized around the visible and aggressive appropriation of tragedy.

The search of the chorus precipitates the next Telephean moment in which Aristophanes boldly continues to rearrange Euripides' sequence by enacting the hostage scene *before* the protagonist's rhetorical appeal. Aristophanes' shuffling of principal elements may be illustrated schematically as follows:

Telephos	*Akharnians*
[a. Telephos assumes disguise]	b. prologue: arrival of undisguised figure
b. prologue: arrival in disguise	whose identity is withheld (until line 406)
c. argument of Atreidai	self-presentation
d. speech #1: *pro Troia*	e. entry (parodos) of chorus and search
(in disguise)	g. discovery
e. entry of Odysseus and search	c. argument between Dikaiopolis and
f. speech #2: *pro Telepho*	chorus
(in disguise)	h. hostage scene
g. discovery	a. Dikaiopolis assumes disguise
h. hostage scene	d. & f. Great Speech fuses speeches #1 & #2
i. healing and reintegration	c. hostile division of chorus
	i. "healing" of Lamakhos and the Dionysiac
	celebration of separate peace

In this sequential transformation, Aristophanes has made of Telephos' rhetorical performances a climax, combining the tragic hero's two speeches into a single great *rhesis*. The violation of logic whereby Dikaiopolis assumes his disguise only after being discovered emphasizes the comic irony in which "illusion" is deconstructed laying bare the poetics of the contrafact. In a sense, element "a" above belongs with the "chopping block" of element "d" as an instance of the concrete enactment and transformation of purely verbal material in the tragedy—in this case, Telephos' explanation of his disguise in the expository prologue. The fusion of tragic elements "d" and "f" in *Akharnians* may be juxtaposed with the "splitting" of element "c" and the reduplication of element "e" in the contrafact of the same play in *Thesmophoriazousai*, lines 598 ff. and 655 ff.[73] In general, the latter is a more linear—though shorter and more limited—transformation of *Telephos* than is *Akharnians*.

Another interesting complication of Aristophanes' contrafact is the way in which the preliminary Dionysiac procession is sandwiched between tragic elements "e"—the search, lines 204–44—and "f"—the discovery, line 281, with its anagram of the tragic Furies's cry.[74] Members of the protagonist's family are terrified and run for cover (offstage) where they shall have to wait until after the parabasis for the festivities to resume in the form of a private market and comic Anthesteria. Meanwhile, Dikaiopolis and the charcoal burners face off in a heated exchange that appears to be informed by the argument (lines 285–324) between Agamemnon and Menelaos (and Telephos) about Troy. This altercation comes to a climax at line 325 as Dikaiopolis grabs the Akharnians' "dear one"—a scuttle of coal—and threatens to slay his hostage(s). Aristophanes has fun with this moment by creating a fleeting misunderstanding while the chorus struggles to process the metonymic substitution of "coal" for "*philos*": "Do you think," they ask, "that this fellow has a child of ours locked away inside? Well, why is he so bold?" The frustrated protagonist points to the coal and shouts, "I mean this, here's whom I'll slay!" The effect is profound and achieves the desired result: the chorus agrees to anything to spare the life of their dear "demesman." This moment in *Akharnians* engages the most famous scene of Euripides' *Telephos* featured in later comedy[75] and a number of vase paintings. There is little doubt that this episode was an innovation on the part of the tragedian[76] and, as such, was especially noteworthy. We have here our first, most vivid, example of the way Aristophanes targets innovation on the part of the composers he is "remaking" to produce equally innovative comedy. This is a very important aspect of the metafictional process exhibited by *Akharnians*, *Peace*, *Birds*, and *Frogs*.

The much-discussed scene with Euripides has programmatic value for all subsequent Aristophanic contrafacts in that it puts on display the "polyphony" and "discourse irony" of the protagonist as he improvises his new scenario from a source tragedy. In order to present his character, Aristophanes utterly transforms the initial premise of Euripides' *Telephos* in which the hero *arrives already disguised*. In *Akharnians* we will have the voyeuristic pleasure of watching the selection and assumption of the new identity in which Dikaiopolis speaks his Great Speech. The costuming and grand comic apologia are introduced by an example of concretization wherein Aristophanes stages Telephos' hypothetical and hyperbolic words to Agamemnon in fr. 706 N². In his argument with the Akharnians, Dikaiopolis had alluded to Telephos' words by saying, "and if, in the eyes of the public, my words fall short of justice, I'll gladly lay my head upon a chopping block to speak" (lines 317–18). He now makes good his promise in a performance punctuated by the choral call for the block and its ceremonial establishment onstage for the Great Speech (lines 355–58, 366–69):[77]

> And I am willing to say whatever I will on behalf of
> the Spartans with my head on a chopping-block,
> Although I do dearly love my life.

[The chorus agrees and calls for the block to be brought out, lines 359–65.]

> Well, look and see, the chopping-block is here
> and I'm to speak, just little old me here.
> And don't worry, I won't shield myself, by god,
> but will say what I think on behalf of the Spartans.

Here, then, the potentially bathetic outburst of the tragic hero is given a ridiculous enactment that will have many parallels in later plays in all manner of literalization and concretization.[78] Aristophanes derives his own brand of humor from pushing the limits of language in performance.[79] We are prepared for the Euripides scene by an equally remarkable moment in which the fictionalized "I" of the poet ventriloquates through the character of Dikaiopolis in a passage cited above (lines 377–82). The wider context of this Aristophanic interlude, with its explicit mention of comedy (line 378) and criticism of Athenian gullibility and vanity, looks forward to the Great Speech as well as to the parabasis. In fact, Aristophanes begins his parabatic self-presentation early in several sporadic "ventriloquations" through his protagonist (*Akharnians* 377–82 and 497–505) that are extended and synthesized in the choral anapests (lines 626–59), a technique employed by the composer throughout the 420s. An important and neglected reason for the first of these ventriloquations is to make vivid the dynamic of the contrafact in which it is *Aristophanes himself* who arrives at Euripides' door intent on improvising something new from his old tragic bag of tricks. In partial imitation of Kratinos in his *Pytine*, the poet lets us see a first-person fiction of himself[80] composing a new literary-political myth animated by an imaginary rivalry with figures such as Kleon and Euripides. Note that in the first exchange, "knock, knock!" . . . "who's there?" the visitor does not identify himself to the servant, reserving that honor for Euripides himself: "Euripides dear, it's me, Dikaiopolis!"

The seventy-line exchange between Dikaiopolis and Euripides (lines 407–79) is a metafictional display that "makes possible a visual as well as verbal means of commenting on the relations among language, art, truth, and reality that characterize the sophistic age."[81] Euripides' being wheeled out on the theatrical trolley simultaneously points up his inability to appear (as a poet-director "behind the scenes") and his function as the source of a composition upon which this comedy will improvise a new script. The mixture of styles and linguistic registers here celebrates the comic character's polyphonic mastery of comedy, tragedy, and all public discourse for that matter. The language of "Euripides" is colored with mock-tragic diction—for example, "what say'st thou?" τί λέλακας—while Dikaiopolis' lines are more fluent and colloquial. They are not without playful admixtures, however.[82] We are entertained first by a visual metaphor reflecting this diglossia[83] as Euripides is revealed composing "aloft" and, like Sokrates of *Clouds*, unwilling to descend to the quotidian level of his visitor's language and concerns. Dikaiopolis has already dropped many hints about who his tragic model is, but lest any spectator misunderstand, he announces himself as "Dikaiopolis of *Kholl*eidai" in line 406, which is a heavy-handed pun on χωλός, "lame." Telephos' distinguishing characteristic is noted again in the request for help (lines 410–17):[84]

> So, you're writing up there,
> when you should be down here? No wonder your characters are lame!
> And, pray, why are you wearing those tragic rags,
> that pitiful getup? No wonder your characters are so sorry!
> But I beg you, at your feet, Euripides
> Give me some ragged outfit from that old play of yours.
> I must deliver a great speech to the chorus,
> a speech which, if poorly spoken, shall bring me death.

The force of the reference to the chorus here is to suggest that one poet-character is speaking to another in a dramatic inset (mise en abyme). The ensuing exchange is as illuminating as it is entertaining. Dikaiopolis has requested a costume from an "old" play, τὸ παλαιὸν δρᾶμα, which he does not name so as to push Euripides to "figure it out." The tragic poet pulls out one example after another, allowing Dikaiopolis-Aristophanes to demonstrate his mastery over his rival. "Oineus?"—"No, someone more miserable"; "Phoinix?"—"No, someone even more miserable still!"; "You don't mean sorry Philoktetes?"—"Nope, even sorrier!"; "Ah, you must mean the pitiful garb of the lame Bellerophontes?"—"No, but the fellow I have in mind certainly was lame, and a beggar, a chatterbox, and a crafty wordsmith." At this point Euripides sees the light and is made to quote his own line (fr. 704 N^2): "I know the man—Mysian Telephos!" Dikiaopolis emits a delighted "Yes!" and Euripides orders his slave to produce the costume that, he says, lies between those of Thyestes and Ino. As Euripides is wheeled back in, Dikiaopolis faces the audience and performs the most important programmatic transformation of *Telephos* in the comedy. Drawing on the prologue containing the key fragments 697 and 698 N^2 (see above), Dikiaopolis says:[85]

> Today I must seem to be humble,
> to be who I am, but to appear otherwise.
> The spectators will know who I am
> but the chorus will stand by like idiots
> so I can give them the rhetorical "finger."

The metatheatrical tension between actor and role ("layered identity") lies at the heart of this particular transformation from tragedy to comedy. The typically Euripidean "philosophizing" about disguise in *Telephos* is transformed here into an operating formula for the poetics of the extended comic contrafact as Dikiaopolis seeks to "assume the most pathetic disguise possible" (line 384).[86]

Conclusion: Trygoidia, Democracy, and Utopia

An important function of the metafictional process in *Akharnians* is comedy's illustration of its manipulative and mediatory powers in the person of Dikiaopolis. This outspoken protagonist is constructed between a stage figure proper, a fiction of the author, and a member of the demos (spectators). Disrupting the fabric of Euripides' barbarian-Greek configuration, he exposes fissures in the ideological fabric of the polis by positioning himself between factions for war and peace, between city and country, between social "classes," even between inland demes. The agonistic modality of his performance is expressed theatrically in the competitive and critical appropriation of the "rival" discourse of tragedy, "swallowing Euripides," as he puts it in the famous conversation with himself (lines 480–89). The chorus marvels at him: "It appears that you intend to speak in opposition to everyone, presenting your neck as hostage to the polis!" This comment elicits the climactic beginning of the Great Speech with its fusion and transformation of Telephos' two *rheseis* (e.g., fr. 703 N^2) and the introduction of "trygedy" (τρυγῳδία)—a neologism expressing Aristophanes' transformational poetics:[87]

> Do not begrudge me, spectators, if I, a beggar,
> dare to compose a *trygedy* and speak
> on behalf of the polis before the Athenian people.
> For *trygedy*, too, is familiar with justice.
> Thus, what I'll say will be shocking but just.

By means of an economical substitution, *tragoidia*, "goat song," becomes *trygoidia*, "vintage song."[88] This, then, is a technical term for a process at work throughout *Akharnians* and one that will figure in a number of other plays during the poet's career down to *Frogs* of 405 and, perhaps, beyond. The morphological trick suggests an "imaginary" rivalry between genres in which comedy is both comparable to tragedy in prestige and function and superior, inasmuch as it appropriates and digests tragic material. Thus the address to the "spectators" has replaced the elitist "leaders of the Greeks" in the Euripidean script, and "Athenians" have replaced "nobles [my betters]." In his coinage-metaphor Dikaiopolis assures the demos that he is not directing his criticism at them—"I am not referring to our polis"—but rather at a few select troublemakers characterized by a string of nasty adjectives. What better illustration is there of comedy's uniquely pan-demotic appeal? Aristophanes' display of his mastery over tragedy thus participates in the "greater democratic" nature of comic discourse. *His metafictional strategies have a distinctly populist pretense*, in the obvious travesty, deformation, and parody as well as in the more subtle transformations of the extended contrafact. "As a fifth-century icon the comic hero was unique," writes Jeffrey Henderson,[89]

> for only at the comic festivals could the mass of ordinary citizens see one of their own in the limelight, speaking their own language and voicing their own complaints and desires. On all other occasions the limelight was reserved for the citizen élite or their tragic counterparts: that small number of men whose wealth, status and expertise entitled them to compete for leadership of the collectivity of ordinary citizens, who only voted.

The speech that follows is a Telephean pastiche fusing and transforming two tragic appeals into a remarkable tour de force on the part of a protagonist who claims to be a good citizen.[90] How is he good? By enacting a fantasy welcome to the common spectator. This fantasy begins with the ability to express what is perhaps a minority opinion (against the war) and extends to the enjoyment of peacetime prosperity "typifying the restoration of the ideal, popular sovereignty."[91] The clever deployment of the reciprocal abductions theme[92] in a lampoon of Aspasia and Perikles is a travesty of an important element of Telephos' original argument.[93] Not only does Aristophanes collapse the two rhetorical performances of the tragic hero but he hijacks his logic and, as usual, performs a thorough substitution in which the traditional elements are replaced by topical items and given an ideological spin. Aristophanes, in other words, explores a metafictional way to represent the current (Arkhidamian) war in terms of that greatest of legendary paradigms, the Trojan War. Dikaiopolis' clever solo is brought to a close by a final, explicit quotation from the *Telephos*. In good Euripidean style, Aristophanes suggests that the Athenians place themselves in the Spartans' shoes and asks what they would have done (in response to the Megarian decree, lines 555–56):[94]

> I know that's what you would have done. And do we think
> Telephos would not do the same? We've got no brains at all!

In theatrical terms the divisive energy "erupts" at the end of the *rhesis* to cause a rift in the chorus that is vividly enacted: the two groups face off, split by contrary responses to the Great Speech, and thus make way for the entry of Lamakhos, a comic character who further complicates the Euripidean thematics by displaying a mixture of "source" elements; for example, he simultaneously speaks as one of the Atreidai (cf. the quotation in line 578) and as Telephos himself (the wounded victim). Angus Bowie argues convincingly that the scenes with Lamakhos and Derketes are informed by the tragic thematics, noting that in much work on *Akharnians* "it is forgotten that reference to Euripides' play does not cease with the parabasis."[95] Thus the victimization of both characters is informed by the tragic moment where Telephos seeks a cure from "the one who inflicted the wound." There is an important hermeneutic clue here as Dikaiopolis gradually forfeits his "Telephean" qualities of victim and suppliant. The one-man utopia is simultaneously impressive and unpleasantly exclusive as we see from the cruel rejection of fellow farmer Derketes. In the Lamakhos-Telephos connection the spectators are invited to trace the themes of the contrafact to make new associations toward the end of the comedy. Thus in a twist of character development, Lamakhos emerges in a sympathetic light that suggests an unexpected contrast between him and Dikaiopolis.

Thus recent work on *Akharnians* has extended the scope of the contrafact beyond the limits of earlier scholarship and has connected various themes of *Telephos* with the parabasis and subsequent intruder-scenes. In an attempt to reconcile the parabatic claims with the activities of the comic hero, for example, Foley makes a case for a thoroughgoing interaction between the "justice" of Aristophanes' comic poiesis (e.g., lines 630–58) and the fictional "justice" of the transformed Telephos.[96] Hubbard, on the other hand, foregrounds the layering of identities — including the relationship between Aristophanes and Kallistratos — through the parabasis into the later scenes.[97] We should not be surprised to see that Aristophanes' first extant contrafact continues to inspire new readings that focus on the interplay of fictions with a particular utopian spin. Early in his career the poet announced a special, ideologically charged involvement with tragedy, a genre with which he put himself in a curious rivalry and which he was to engage time and again in brilliant, complex, and sustained improvisations. Each subsequent contrafact has a unique character and scope, and deserves individual attention. What unifies them is a distinctly utopian thrust that ranges from the narrow (the separate peace in *Akharnians*) to all-embracing (the new city in *Birds*).[98]

Utopia, by definition, is a conundrum expressed vividly in the punning names of those most famous examples, Aristophanes' Cloudcuckooland and Samuel Butler's Erehwon. Popularly used of an idealized place or visionary scheme since its coinage by Thomas More nearly five hundred years ago, "utopia" (οὐ + τόπος) remains a token of hope undercut by futility. The ancient comic polis in the air and More's fantastic island, after all, are "nowhere" and the designation of something as utopia(n) implies a degree of unreality or impossibility. Dikaiopolis' private utopia is obviously a realization of an unattainable wish. In subsequent comedies, Aristophanes imagines new ways to change the state and its people. Indeed, for the purposes of appreciating the Other dimensions of fantastic literature and Greek comedy in particular, we shall learn a great deal by considering exactly how space, time, and society are represented as *different*: better, worse, or in the process of change.

The chapters dealing with comedy (6, 7, and 8) study the scenarios of political invention in *Peace*, *Birds*, and *Frogs*. These three new and different visions of separatism are precipitated by abandonment of the polis in search of a solution of its real and imagined ills. This metatopia, "transformation of place," is articulated to the spectators in the prologue in various fantastic transformations of language, form, and genre. The catalyst for this experiment is the deconstruction of traditional dramatic forms and discourses, a process whereby comedy makes a political comment on the poetics of its sister genre. While tragedy studies political crisis in veiled terms of a limiting mythos, comedy presents a solution—μηχανὴ σωτηρίας—in a contemporary scenario improvised freely from the linguistic, theatrical, and social materials to hand. The comic contrafacts of Aristophanes operate on a principle of creative reciprocity. The innovative tragedies and the innovative moments within those tragedies such as the hostage scene discussed above are specifically targeted for comic "remakes" that are quite original in their own right. At every point Aristophanes flaunts his mastery over tragic language and tragic form in a competitive display of his status as a shaper of public opinion and his genre's preeminence as a mode of entertainment and persuasion.

THE ANATOMY OF DRAMATIC FICTION

Tragic Madness

4

Aias

*Sophokles' Aias, Madness, and
the Show Within*

This section on the anatomy of dramatic fiction begins with studies of two important and well-known theatrical insets involving punitive madness inflicted on a
mortal by a god.[1] Though quite phenomenologically distinct, tragedy mise en abyme
and the comic contrafact have in common their transformation of myth.[2] They both
reveal, in different ways, how drama projected a familiar narrative of the past into
the dialogic space of the theater as an entry in the polis's ongoing analysis of itself. In
becoming a new play, such a narrative is transformed into a three-dimensional and
politicized fable foregrounding the dynamics and culture of the fifth-century theater.[3]
Sophokles' Aias heads a series of five case studies centered on mythical figures who
become dramatis personae. This "becoming" is significantly metafictional and, phenomenologically, metatheatrical. New and complex meanings arise from the old
structures as they are transposed into a contemporary genre and played physically
before the community in the self-reflexive media of the dramatic festival. As Pietro
Pucci has recently shown, the tragic reconfiguration of epic tradition, the creative
"opening up" and problematizing of a familiar tale, inevitably entails a skeptical re-
analysis of the received (epic) ethics, values, and paradigms.[4]

Sophokles is self-consciously explicit about his refashioning of traditional narratives, variously signposting his innovations throughout a script. A vivid example of
such a pointer is Aias' conclusion of the suicide speech: τὰ δ᾽ ἄλλ᾽ ἐν Ἅιδου τοῖς
κάτω μυθήσομαι, "I'll relate the rest to those in Hades below" (line 865). While the
tragic Aias exhibits little inclination to forget his wrath, this promise to resume a
narrative interrupted by death rewrites one of the most memorable encounters between two men in Homer (*Odyssey* 11.543–67). This unilateral conversation between
Odysseus and Aias is striking owing to the latter's eloquent silence, his refusal to speak.[5]
The tragic scenario unfolds as a curious negative of epic: as a stage figure, Aias speaks
a great deal to various characters—indirectly even to Odysseus—and promises to continue in Hades. Ironically, the dynamics of the "show within" render Odysseus silent with respect to Aias, whose main interlocutor is Athene, a deity prominently
featured in the epic and iconographic traditions as the hostile arbiter at the Contest

of Arms. Any transaction that she supervises, in other words, cannot hold much promise for Aias. Visually, however, the tragic encounter is fractured along lines explored below: Aias cannot see Odysseus, Odysseus cannot see Athene, and the spectators are made to contemplate both failures of perception from a twice-removed vantage point. On the levels of narrative and stagecraft, consequently, a reading of Sophokles' *Aias* forces us to confront innovative departures from the familiar for which we must seek motivation in the contemporary plane.

We begin mid century with the prologue to Sophokles' earliest surviving play in which Athene presents her scenario to an internal audience of one. The archaic narrative of madness (*atê*) and its consequences is self-consciously enacted as a powerful metaphor of the theater involving an internal director, players, and spectators, with clever inversion of the dramatic illusion. The opening chase is resolved by the "show within" to set the stage for the hero's self-sacrifice. Odysseus is shocked, indeed forced, into identifying with his enemy and is transformed by fear and pity[6] elicited by a crushing realization of human insignificance. He returns as Aias' advocate in an agon that sophistically displaces his Homeric "cunning intelligence" (*mêtis*).[7] The force that destroyed Aias now defends his honor in a curious rapprochement between very different ideological positions. In Aias, on a persuasive recent reading,[8] Sophokles constructs an embodiment of the heroic Athenian past, an ideal strained to the breaking point as polis mutated into empire. The audience, for its part, is invited into an alliance with the internal spectator, Odysseus, whose character participates in the new discourses of sophistic persuasion and expediency in the service of power. The present and past collide in a terrible moment that gives an entirely new, social meaning to how sacrifice "draws the boundary between god and man and defines the relation between the sacrificer and his community."[9]

The defeat of Aias and all he represents is euphemized as *sôphrosynê*, a virtue with a bitter aftertaste most palpable to his close friends and family.[10] We have here a curious corollary of Thoukydides' diagnosis of ethical deformations from the ominous symptoms of semantic slippage so that "any gesture of moderation, *to sôphrôn*, was taken to be the facade of cowardice."[11] Aias' presentation of *sôphronein* in the Deception Speech and Odysseus' compulsory acquiescence in the term are equally cynical and betray a modern redefinition of power and the relationships it structures. The protagonist's irreversible transgression leads to the oxymoron of suicide (a highly marked death for a hero!) as *sôphrosynê* in line 677,[12] while Athene's display of power in the guise of patronage forces Odysseus into a self-protective reversal that is given the same name. In terms of the historian's paradox, we might say that the despair and humiliation of defeat have been renamed "*sôphrosynê*."[13] This tragic reaction is precipitated in the crucible of an introductory inset whose reflexive sophistication is remarkably modern.[14] On the level of dramatic structure, the disunity between the halves of Sophokles' "diptych" fades to the extent that we appreciate how the play enacts its own interpretation and assumes its own relevance to crises within the democratic polis.

The pivotal function of Sophokles' dramatic inset is, in fact, one of its most original features. As Moshe Ron argues in his theoretical overview of the mise en abyme, "isolability" of the form is critical:[15]

> Closely related to the question of perceptibility . . . [is] the relation of *mise en abyme* to the text continuum in which it is inserted: How the figure is distinguished from its immediate neighbors in the syntagmatic chain. *Mise en abyme* must be located "on the scale of the characters," i.e., intra- or hypodiegetically. If it is a distinct figure, it must have its own distinct identity within the diegetic chain. It is tempting, therefore, to stipulate that it must be inaugurated each time by a diegetic downshift.

That Sophokles has framed his minidrama to be diegetically distinct from the rest of the play is obvious. The complex three-way interaction in which Athene presents Aias to Odysseus as Sophokles presents all three to the spectators is unique to the introductory sequence. Whether we call this a "downshift" or not—and this metaphor is awkward when applied to a dramatic performance in any case—the narrative structure is further reinforced by the phenomenon of Aias' madness. He is not on stage for very long in this condition: we learn of it in the initial exchange between Athene and Odysseus before Aias enters at line 91. He exits at line 117, leaving Odysseus and Athene to discuss his "performance." The response to Athene's "show" continues in the lengthy interchange between Tekmessa and the chorus, toward the end of which Aias is heard groaning within (lines 333 and 336). With these exclamations and the protagonist's entrance at line 348, we behold essentially a new character, a man humiliated by his return to sanity. The minidrama is thus intellectually and aesthetically distinct from the greater body of the play in which it is set, much in the same way as the robing of Pentheus (chapter 5) is placed in relation to *Bakkhai* as a whole.

The very distinctness of this particular mise en abyme draws attention to its unusual initial position, one that would preclude effective framing by its "neighbors in the syntagmatic chain." It is a curious feature of Sophokles' design, however, that the position of the mise en abyme and its dramatic function do not coincide in an obvious way. In order, perhaps, to effect a striking opening, the inset is thrust forward to head the action in lieu of a more unitary narrative, such as Deianeira's introductory speech in *Trakhiniai*. Its deeper role in the design of *Aias*, however, is that of a fulcrum between the "suicide" and "debate" halves of the diptych. As the (internal) spectator of the show within, Odysseus is affected in a profound way that influences his behavior in the final agon. Between halves of the play, behind the entire action, in fact, we sense the powerful influence of Athene's choreography and the brief performance she "produced," which might be called *Aias mainomenos*.

Rapture of the Deep

From the brief discussions of *Birds* and *Philoktetes* above, it appears that (meta)theatrical technique is a sort of *dolos* (ruse, strategem) on the formal level.[16] Its association with tricky characters such as Peisetairos and Odysseus suggests an acute awareness on the part of the classical dramatists of their powers. A special characteristic of the Greek tragic mise en abyme is its ability to negotiate a connection between the tragic delusion of a character on stage and what has been somewhat misleadingly called the "dramatic illusion." Within the fiction, madness splits reality to create an embedded theatrical dynamic. A character such as Aias is in one sense the deluded spectator, in his madness, of a hallucinatory scenario conjured by Athene. His delusion gains force as a metaphor of the main "dramatic illusion." He sees, and is swayed, by what is not real. More immediately, however, he himself is the spectacle presented by Athene to Odysseus. This curious correspondence between madness and theatrical illusion draws attention to how both constitute a cognitive boundary between spheres of perception. In the theater proper it is the spectators who submit to an *apatê*, "deception," or, in the terms outlined in chapter 1, to accept the stage mimesis in a game of make-believe. Within the play, however, it is the player who is deluded and thereby made into a spectacle by the internal director for a third party. This internal spectator may be impressed enough with the interplay between illusion and delusion to react to what he sees, to comment on and perhaps even learn from it. The audience thus gets an opporunity to study spectator response *within* the fiction and to gain reflexive insight into its own part in the transaction between stage and theatron.

In speaking of madness as a scenic correlate of "dramatic illusion," it is important to note that in both degree and manifestation there are significant differences that complicate the metaphor. It is in the nature of metaphor, after all, for one sign or image to replace another in a way that is not fully controllable or predictable. The delusional and aesthetic aspects of *apatê* interact to yield the special meaning of "suspension of disbelief," as Bierl has emphasized in connection with a dictum attributed to Gorgias: "the one who deceives is more just than one who has not, and the one deceived is wiser than the one who has not been deceived."[17] This formulation makes a connection between *dike* as "relationship of equilibrium between action and reaction" and *apatê* as "suspension of disbelief" and is the earliest extant theoretical statement concerning the problem of dramatic illusion. Gorgias here adumbrates in a significant way the recent debate about dramatic illusion outlined above.[18]

Complete immersion in illusion, enchantment to the point of belief, is an asymptote (an approachable, but never attainable, limit) that defines spectatorial experience. The mathematical metaphor is appropriate, indeed, for no matter how vividly our emotions of pity, fear, surprise, joy, and so on, are engaged by a performance, we remain conscious of the boundary between the play and our own reality.[19] The treatment of madness in several Greek tragedies exhibits a bold approach to this asymptotic plane of illusion from both sides, that is, from the world of the play and world of the theatron, from within and without the primary fiction. On the one hand, *atê*, "madness," as it figures in pre-dramatic legend is assimilated ever more closely by the tragedians to natural human experience, that is, to what we would identify as mental illness on the part of the dramatic subject. This tragic *atê* however, is of limited duration and, as such, invites self-conscious reflection as it comes over a character (Pentheus) or once its spell has been broken (Herakles, Aias). From the spectator's perspective, on the other hand, the madness of a tragic character as well as the deceptions of Aristophanic tricksters[20] are metaphors of the *apatê*, dramatic illusion, and provide a touchstone for one's experience of the theater.[21] Madness, in other words, may be used to highlight the cognitive boundary between worlds that collude and collide in an entirely novel way that problematizes what is familiar and expected. The Athenian spectator could not stand apart from the dramatic subject but was implicated in the unfolding crisis.

Aias Mainomenos

In a stimulating study of madness and the tragic self Padel suggests that "tragic emotion is represented essentially . . . as other in self. A destructive other, sent to hurt innards; a god's most effective weapon."[22] She emphasizes that the tragic *personification* of madness is never *Atê* but either *Lyssa* or *Erinys*. *Atê* fades from the Homeric figure (*Iliad* 19.91–94) to a brief sketch in Aiskhylos, to become a more abstract concept of mental blindness and disaster. From the primary mode of psychic disintegration in epic, *atê* yields the center stage of physical representation to Lyssa in the fifth century.

> Lyssa, "Madness," is the fifth-century's personification of madness, especially in tragedy and in vase-paintings of tragedy. She has speaking parts in one surviving Euripidean tragedy and at least one lost play by Aeschylus, possibly more. Illustrations of other lost plays show her attacking men with a goad, like Erinyes, and urging on destruction . . . . Other contexts suggest that *lussa* generally had mad-dog overtones. Lyssa is "madness," but also "rabies." Lyssa, it seems, is "wolfish rage" personified, raging and destructive.

In this respect the function of madness in *Aias* and *Bakkhai* is distinct from the explicit, personified madness in Euripides' *Herakles*—the dialogue between Iris and Lyssa, for example—in that it is less overt and more deeply implicated in the process of dramatic representation itself.

Recent scholarship on *Aias* has shown considerable interest in the play's metatheatrical aspects, with special attention to the vocabulary of perceiving, knowing, even reading in the opening sequence.[23] Continued reference to seeing and spectacle (from *theasthai*) underlines the phenomenological link between the opening mise en abyme and its consequences enacted in the unique suicide spectacle. Odysseus has not fully grasped the situation and looks for guidance to Athene, who addresses him with the sympathetic irony of patron and theatrical director. She first describes what he is doing and then asks for his own assessment (lines 11–13):[24]

> There is no further need for you to peer
> into those doors. Tell me why you are so intent
> in your quest so as to learn from one who has knowledge.

Odysseus' response is telling. He admits that what he sees and understands is far from certain: ἴσμεν γὰρ οὐδὲν τρανές, ἀλλ᾽ ἀλώμεθα, "we know nothing clearly, but are distraught" (line 23). The voice of the goddess is, by contrast, "as clear as a trumpet," and her meaning is easily intelligible though she herself is invisible (lines 14–17):[25]

> Voice of Athene, dearest to me of Immortals,
> How clearly I hear your speech and seize
> the meaning with my mind though you are
> Unseen! As clearly as the sound of a
> Bronze-lipped Etruscan trumpet.

Athene as director supervises his entrance into the theatrical space and gives him instructions. The goddess is never directly visible to either Odysseus or Aias.[26] It is significant, moreover, that she marks the moment with the words καὶ νῦν ἐπὶ σκηναῖς σε ναυτικαῖς ὁρῶ / Αἴαντος, ἔνθα τάξιν ἐσχάτην ἔχει, "And now I see you at the naval *skênai* of Aias, his final/outermost encampment" (lines 2–3). Within the fiction we are, of course, to understand that this is the tent of Aias by the sea at the far eastern end of the Greek camp. On another level, Athene is marking Odysseus' entrance and adumbrating what is to come. The scene—literally *skênê*—is set by the sea where Aias has taken his final stand (*eskhatên* in the sense of "ultimate").[27] The lexical and material link between military tent and stage building is not far to seek. It has been suggested, in fact, that the model for the latter was the tent of Xerxes, a military *skênê* (cf. Hdt. 9.70,82) pressed into theatrical service with the expected semantic extension of the word.[28]

Comic exploitation of the emerging technical term is found several decades later in the verses introducing the parabasis of Aristophanes' *Peace* (the kommation, line 731). In Sophokles' play, Aias' military *skênê* is deployed in a patently theatrical way as the stage building of the embedded fiction from which the hero makes his entrance. The terms "inside" and "outside" (ἔνδον, line 76; ἔξω, line 74) delineate the internal stage and define the theatricality of this entrance in response to Athene, who gives the player his cue. There is also here a strong hint at the hero's mental condition. Odysseus may mean to imply that he is interested to know whether or not Aias is in or out *of his mind*.[29] This use of the *skênê* in *Aias* may be compared to the juxtaposition of choral and military disciplines in Aristophanes' *Birds*. Both are examples of metatheatrical comment on the sociohistorical development of theater practice.[30]

The investment of a divine character with the dual function of theatrical choreographer/director (and second actor as well) is certainly not unique to *Aias*.[31] Apollon ex machina at the end of *Orestes* has been described as a "director" who "reserves the right to alter the mythos or adapt it as he sees fit. The difference between him and the actor is that he has control of the proceedings, while the actor does not."[32] Recent analyses of other leading divine roles in Euripides—Dionysos in *Bakkhai*, Apollon in *Alkestis*—suggest a certain currency in the second half of the fifth century of the mise en abyme choreographed internally by a stage figure.[33] Odysseus' words to Athene in our scene give a similar picture (31–35):[34]

> I rush on his track
> immediately; sometimes I read the prints, but sometimes
> I am bewildered and cannot figure out their source.
> You've come just in time! In all things past and future
> I am guided by your hand.

As both actor and spectator Odysseus is certainly not in control of the proceedings and openly relies on Athene's help, which, at this juncture, is colored by terms of perception (seeing, reading, understanding, etc.). Odysseus' status as spectator is enhanced by his temporal and spatial priority "before the entry of the chorus, whose encircling presence would have the effect of locating [him] in the scene rather than detached from it as an objectifying spectator."[35] His quest is introduced through the metaphor of tracking and hunting,[36] which the verb *sêmainomai* serves to broaden into a general act of reading and interpreting *sêmeia*, "signs." The record of the mysterious nocturnal episode that Odysseus seeks to read constitutes an open-ended text, as it were, an introduction to the script of Athene's scenario. This is surely the sense of the middle voice here, "to infer from signs." Odysseus acknowledges Athene's directorial (poetic) control of the performance, past and future, and takes advantage of her presence to observe and understand her work. Lines 38–65 are a carefully structured "interactive prologue" that opens with a series of seven questions. The repetition of the collocation ἦ καί reinforces the stichomythia to heighten the excitement and rapidity of the sequence. The goddess allows Odysseus to first get his bearings and then begins the prologue proper with the following words (lines 51–53, 59–60):[37]

> I restrained him; I threw over his eyes
> obsessive notions of pernicious joy and
> turned him to the flocks . . .
> As the man wandered in diseased delusions, I
> encouraged him and cast him into nets of doom.

Taking δυσφόρους as the active complement to the passive phrase δύσφορον ἄταν (line 643, end of first stasimon) and taking χαρᾶς with γνώμας, we get a picture of Athene's intervention: she has altered his senses and distracted his wits with illusions of joy. The oxymoron "incurable joy" resonates powerfully with the phrase μανίασιν νόσοις, "diseased delusions," to present the separation between Aias' inner world — the diseased fiction of revenge — and the outer world in which Odysseus waits as spectator for the actor's entrance.[38] This separation is later echoed by Tekmessa (lines 272–73), who observes that "as long as the sickness was upon him he felt pleasure in the midst of his evils, though we, his sane companions, were saddened indeed."

   Comparison of *atê*, "madness," of a stage figure such as Aias with *apatê*, "suspension of disbelief" (theatrical illusion), on the part of the spectators highlights the separation between worlds created by an altered state of either the subject or object of the spectacle. "All is possible when god manipulates [theatrical] *tekhnê*," in Odysseus' words (line 86).[39] This line is spoken by one who, oddly enough, has difficulty trusting the power of this *tekhnê* to guarantee his enemy's blindness. Odysseus repeatedly insists that Athene not call him from his *skênê* (line 74). She has to assure him twice that Aias will not see him: ἐγὼ γὰρ ὀμμάτων ἀποστρόφους / αὐγὰς ἀπείρξω σὴν πρόσοψιν εἰσιδεῖν, "I will turn away the vision of his eyes and keep them from perceiving your face" (69–70) and ἐγὼ σκοτώσω βλέφαρα καὶ δεδορκότα, "I will darken his eyes, though they are open" (85). Her purpose is clearly expressed at line 79 in the rhetorical question "Isn't it the sweetest laughter to mock one's enemies?" Aias will be a spectacle and object of derision insulated from the internal spectator by illusion.[40] An important aspect of this setup is the way in which it reveals an unheroic aspect of Odysseus' character in the given situation: he wishes he were outside it (ἐκτός, line 88). His hesitation and fear of being seen elicits from the goddess a blunt warning to guard against cowardice (line 74).

   The presentation of Aias involves a twist of character articulated in a sort of ring-composition. The deluded hero's emphatic use of the terms σύμμαχος, "ally," and παρεστάναι, "to stand beside, assist," with reference to Athene points up the bitter irony of his situation. An important theme of the play turns out to be Athene's anger at his hybris in rejecting her help. This rather un-Homeric behavior was emphasized by Winnington-Ingram, among others, contra Knox's view of Sophokles' Aias as thoroughly Homeric, with the hero's death being the "death of the old individual Homeric (and especially Achillean) ethos."[41] Sophokles' character has rejected the dependence on the gods (and family for that matter) that normally limits a warrior's behavior. The balance of crime and punishment is well presented in a later messenger speech that reports the prophecy of Kalkhas: Aias has angered the goddess but may yet be saved if he survives the day (lines 776–79).

The new Aias, the deluded subject of the internal fiction, by contrast, responds to Athene's question "do you care so little for your ally (σύμμαχος)?" with the confident words "how well you've stood by me (παρέστης)" (92). This exchange is ominous in light of the language Aias is said to have used to reject Athene: "Go stand beside the other Argives, goddess; where I fight, battle will never break the line" (lines 774–75). In Athene's presentation of Aias to Odysseus, a certain "Homeric" quality has been restored to the hero with the ironic effect of intensifying his shame and humiliation. The interview between the goddess and her "actor" proceeds from this point to illustrate the breadth of Athene's fictive scenario. The Atreidai are dead and the current focus of Aias' rage is Odysseus himself. The latter has been scourged and bound in preparation for further torture and death. Athene, as a voice in the internal fiction, intercedes on Odysseus' behalf only to be told that Odysseus must be punished. In all else she may have her way. This hint of the true autonomy of Sophokles' Aias resonates, even inside the embedded fiction, with the gallery of hubristic characters who earned Athene's wrath.

The climax of this tragedy mise en abyme, "Aias Mainomenos," involves the discussion of Odysseus' fate in the internal fiction. In this remarkable situation, an internal spectator is simultaneously represented in the "performance" he is watching. Such topical intensity is put to good use in comedy, of course, as we have seen in the prologue of *Wasps*. The effect on Odysseus of this tragic topicality, however, is far from comical. Aias' words concluding the brief epeisodion are laden with particularly heavy irony: τοῦτο σοὶ δ' ἐφίεμαι / τοιάνδ' ἀεί μοι σύμμαχον παερστάναι, "I bid you," he says to Athene, "to always *stand as an ally by my side* as you have today" (lines 116–117). The ring is complete and the hero's doom sealed. Odysseus is, understandably, shaken by the spectacle. It is here, in this act of watching and learning, that we must situate the emergence of the new ethos of forced humility, as *sôphronein* is redefined with respect to Odysseus and Aias. As spectator, Odysseus passes from fear (just before the mini-epeisodion) to a peculiar, disoriented pity in anticipation of Aristotle's famous formulation. These are certainly among the best-known lines (121–26) of the play, a tragic "parabasis" of the sort discerned in another play by Dodds.[42] The internal player steps forward to comment on his situation:[43]

> Yet I pity him
> in his misery though he is my enemy
> for the terrible yoke of *atê* that binds him.
> I think of him, yet also of myself;
> For I see the true state of all us that live—
> We are dim shapes, no more, and weightless shadow.

Athena endorses this new perspective and gives it a name: "the gods love *sôphrôn* men and hate those who are base" (lines 132–33). In this pronouncement *sôphrôn* is ominously redefined against a periphrasis for *sôphrosynê* applied to Aias a few lines above (119). "Do you see Odysseus," Athene had just asked, "how great is the might of the gods? Who was more prudent [*pronousteros*] or better able to act with judgment than this man?"

The new imperative of *sôphronein*, then, is presented and enforced by means of a spectacle, a performance that has powerful emotional and ethical impact on its spectator(s). Odysseus responds to Athene's "play" immediately and deeply. His general and specific hostilities mutate to sympathy: "I think of him, yet also of myself." The configuration of the internal fiction sets up a stark contrast between appearance and reality for Odysseus to contemplate. In this inversion, a restraining *atê* imposed on the player, Aias, is supported by the ironic participation of Athene.

The theme of *sôphronein* is problematized in terms that reveal the power of dramatic spectacle with its implications for other, more dangerous, ways of seeing. A salient feature of such metatheatrical design across genres is that a leading dramatis persona is given the creative powers and control of a playwright (cf. Dikaiopolis or Peisetairos).[44] Athene in this play has been the composer orchestrating a tragic spectacle with the explicit purpose of making an impression on her audiences both inside and outside the primary fiction. As Odysseus comments on what he has seen, he involves the outside audience in his response, guiding it in a way that links the deeper function of Athene's design with the design of the poet himself. The audience is urged to feel fear and pity, and to learn with Odysseus. "As Odysseus makes connections between himself and Ajax," notes Thomas Falkner,[45]

> he may also question how, or if, his situation really differs from that of Ajax at all. As he watches Athena manipulate and humiliate "her ally," how can he be certain that Athena is not doing the same with him? Is his own knowledge any less illusory, his own security any less precarious? May not he in his turn be a spectacle for another audience whose knowledge is larger that his own? And this in turn affects the audience, as it produces that effect which Borges calls *dédoublement*—that sudden self-consciousness we may have in the process of watching a dramatic representation: our awareness that other spectators are doing what we are doing, and with it the fear that we may ourselves be characters in another story and objects of their beholding, and so on in a kind of infinite regress.

The *Sôphrosynê* of Defeat

The consequences of Athene's choreography for the second half of the *Aias* are profound: the very cunning and verbal skill with which Odysseus humiliated Aias are now employed in the fallen hero's defense. Aias, for his part, has articulated the necessity of death as *sôphrosynê*.[46] What Odysseus accepts as *sôphrosynê* (imposed on him by Athene) is surely, from a mortal point of view, a sensible and self-serving strategy. Beholding the goddess's display of the severe imbalance of power between gods and men, Odysseus is shocked by the relative pettiness of his perspective and realizes the extent to which he has been manipulated by a higher power. Within the tragic fiction he resembles a game-theorist who is forced to calculate how and when a given virtue is consonant with self-preservation or personal gain. After all, Aias' prudence and ability "to act with judgment" had not saved him from destruction by the gods. The resultant self-destruction draws a sharp line indeed between the mortal and divine realms, a barrier felt most acutely by the one whom the goddess favors.

Odysseus' entrance at line 1318 marks the second and final debate around the corpse of Aias, a debate in which he defends the *themis* of burial (it is "the right thing to do") in terms of Aias' valor (*aretê*). Athene's spectacle was an important element of the great plan that culminated in the hero's suicide. After his dramatic lesson was reinforced by the news of Aias' death, Odysseus calculatedly exchanges the rhetoric of hatred for that of reverence (εὐσέβεια).[47] We have already seen that the immediate effect of the spectacle staged by Athene was to move Odysseus to express pity for Aias (lines 121–24) with an alliterative pair of adjectives, δύστηνον, "in misery," and δυσμενῆ, "(my) enemy." Between this moment and the exodos, the concept of *sôphronein* is used many times to define the position of various participants in the tragedy. Thus Menelaos (line 1075), Agamemnon (line 1259), and the chorus (line 1264) invoke *sôphronein* against Aias and the arguments of Odysseus. Aias himself, in his third monologue (esp. lines 677–83), provides a bridge between Odysseus' forced theatrical lesson on sôphronein in the prologue and the enactment of the new ethic at the end of the play in which Odysseus affirms the good reputation of Aias, his former enemy, and secures his right to burial:[48]

> Shall we not learn discretion [*sôphronein*]? I, for one, will!
> For I have recently understood only so much to hate
> my enemy as one who might hereafter become my friend,
> and towards a friend I would wish to show aid and service
> only as much as to one who may not always remain so.
> Most men have found friendship a treacherous harbor.

In light of Athene's cruel lesson, the essential ethos of the hero is qualified by a cynical meditation on the mutability of all things, an idea applied to friendship in the maxim attributed to Bias of Priene, "love a friend as one who will/may come to hate you; hate your enemy as one who will/may come to be your friend."[49] Aias expresses his decision to commit suicide in a deliberately ambiguous and deceptive manner that allows Tekmessa and the chorus to hope for a change of heart. The ambiguity of the Deception Speech affords the poet the means to make an ironic connection between the experiences of Odysseus and Aias, inasmuch as the latter is given words that unwittingly foreshadow the sophistically framed *sôphrosynê* of the final debate. Odysseus, in turn, is made to echo these words to the astonished Agamemnon, who cannot believe that the erstwhile archenemy of Aias is now arguing on behalf of the fallen warrior (lines 1356–59):[50]

AGAMEMNON. What will you do? Will you honor the corpse of your enemy?

ODYSSEUS. His virtue weighs more than hate with me.

AGAMEMNON. Indeed, those who act like this are the unstable among men.

ODYSSEUS. Yes, and many who are now friends soon turn out to be enemies.

The strategically higher ground from which Odysseus defends Aias' right to burial is thus linked rhetorically and thematically through the Deception Speech back to the spectacle of the prologue and, beyond that, to the epic Contest of Arms.[51] Odysseus' new *sôphrôn* behavior contrasts tellingly with Agamemnon's definition of *sôphronein* (lines 1252–63).

Throughout Odysseus' defense of justice (δίκη) and reverence for the gods (εὐσέβεια), the audience is reminded of his combined experience as sophistic persuader and recent cospectator. We think of the Odysseus who is present and also the other epic, lyric, and dramatic Odysseuses who are absent.[52] From this perspective Odysseus' motivation in the final debate cannot simply be the piety suggested by lines 1344–45: ἄνδρα δ᾽ οὐ δίκαιον, εἰ θάνοι, βλάπτειν τὸν ἐσθλόν, οὐδ᾽ ἐὰν μισῶν κυρῇς, "When a brave man is dead, it is not right to harm him even if you hate him." This admonition to Agamemnon reveals an Odysseus who has been fundamentally reoriented (or disoriented) by his experience as spectator, which the "author" (Athene) links with her lesson in forced *sôphrosynê*: τοιαῦτα τοίνυν εἰσορῶν, "being spectator of such things."

Agamemnon responds to his colleague's peculiar behavior with an impressive perspicacity, interpreting it correctly as an expression of self-interest. Having clarified that Odysseus is urging him to bury Aias, he observes: "I see, it is the same in everything. Each man labors for himself." Odysseus agrees: "yes, and for whom is it more fitting that I labor than for myself?" (lines 1366–67). Odysseus' reversal is rendered intelligible through its metatheatrical presentation. Instead of being baffled by Odysseus' behavior, we follow him as he is shocked into identifying with Aias and bullied into what Athene would call *sôphrosynê*. Drawn into Odysseus' predicament, we must confront this ethical transvaluation (with all its implications) and observe its consequences as he deals with the various passions and limitations of those involved in the tragedy.

In his study of the play, Bradshaw has made the case for seeing Aias as the site of archaic polis-values. "Glorious Athens" is the last memory the hero bids farewell before he dies. The interpretation of Sophokles' Aias as a traditional Athenian (as opposed to Aiginetan) hero by assimilation has a long history and is persuasively outlined in Bradshaw's study. Commenting on the complex political enactment of myth in *Oresteia*, he argues that *Aias* "has a similar relation to the polis, for Ajax can be seen as the Athenian agonist, not only in that he embodies traditional values but also in that he confronts the problems of redefinition which the contemporary polis was addressing."[53] While it is difficult to follow Bradshaw's reading fully into its rather narrow allegory of international politics, it is persuasive in identifying Aias and Odysseus as sites of conflicting values, indeed a collision of cultures in the arena of the theater.[54]

Much like Aristophanes several decades later in plays like *Clouds* and *Wasps*, Sophokles in *Aias* dramatizes the death of Athens' legendary past. The agent of change is the amorphous force personified by the goddess of the polis, but it is Aias' peer, his compatriot, who must witness his destruction and struggle to make sense of it. It is no accident that Sophokles chose Odysseus as the figure with whom the spectating demos should identify. In spirit, the literary Odysseus was a prototype of Athenian ambition and jaded, sophistic resourcefulness. His involvement with Aias, *daimôn* of the traditional Athens representing its nobler, mythical past, is therefore fraught with ambivalence and humiliation. The experience of destroying his adversary is bleached of all satisfaction in light of the consequences. Destiny and time cannot be opposed and Homer's "hero of much mêtis [*polumêtis Odysseus*]" must be now clever enough to accept this defeat along with its cynical name. Like a prisoner with a very long sentence, he acquiesces in "good behavior." One thinks of Perikles' final assessment of Athens-become-empire. "While some may look back with nostalgia to a simpler past," he appears to say, "it is lost forever." Unlike Athene, however, Perikles avoids oppressive euphemism (Thouk. 2.63): "It is right and proper for you to support the imperial dignity of Athens . . . . Nor is it any longer possible for you to give up the empire . . . [which] is now like a tyranny: though it may have been wrong to take it, it is certainly dangerous to let it go. And the kind of people who talk of doing so and persuade others to adopt their point of view would very soon bring the state to ruin."

The metatheatrical reading outlined above suggests a somewhat different allegory of the encounter between past and present on the Sophoklean stage. The emphasis has been more on the "how" rather than the "what" of the playwright's design, that is, *how* the metafictional inset (prologue) leads the demos as both primary and vicarious spectators (via Odysseus) of Aias' madness to a reflexive epiphany of a moral crisis. In a transformation that reveals the genre as temperamentally metafictional, tragedy translates a familiar epic narrative and mythologem (punitive madness) into the language of modern theater. Not surprisingly, at a critical moment of transformation the action is constructed explicitly along the lines of a theatrical performance en abyme, at the heart of the framing play. And so, at the outset, we are put on the track of a more complex and disturbing metafictional poetics.

The transgressive discourse of tragedy—this tragedy in particular—does not offer solutions but rather questions social institutions and confronts things that lie beyond human control. Anticipating the dilemma of many postclassical colonial empires, Athens was increasingly torn between an archaic self-image and a rather bleak emerging reality. The aristocratic ethos and the pride of an insular polis, *prima inter pares*, was ever harder to reconcile with the realities of empire and the sociopolitical changes characteristic of the mid fifth century. The double burden of power and change is distributed by Sophokles among his characters in terms of the active (perpetrator) and passive (victim) "voices," respectively. Athene is strongest and Aias, the weakest, while Odysseus is caught in between. As Thoukydides vividly illustrates, naked aggression and clever argumentation were to conspire many times throughout the Peloponnesian War to force a weaker party into an action or position euphemistically termed "just." "The standard of justice," in the words of the Athenian delegation to Melos, "depends on the equality of power to compel and . . . in fact the strong do what they have the power to do and the weak accept what they have to accept."[55] The realization by Athene of the unseen force of destiny moving men about like pieces in a board game is enhanced by the clever introduction within the play of the mise en abyme as a theatrical mirror that reveals a curiously feminized hero. In terms argued by Zeitlin, Aias is driven to "feminine" irrationality, penetration, and death that set him apart formally and thematically from the codes of epic heroism.[56] The spectator, as the role of Odysseus demonstrates, cannot remain uninvolved: simultaneously participating in a spectacle and watching it, he is forced to comprehend his double status as both player and audience. In other words, he is de facto complicit in the events he has come to see represented. Owing to Sophokles' aggressive presentation of Odysseus as spectator, the realization and experience of the player are communicated to the spectators, who are challenged, as a community, to inscribe their own experience into that of the stage figure. It thrills the imagination to picture a large subset of the polis at the City Dionysia, many thousand strong, simultaneously contemplating a dramatic fable and watching each other watch as the implications of the play emerge ever more clearly. As both spectators and participants, they were caught between responsibility and passive observation in a particular type of *dédoublement* that was surely one of the most original and sophisticated achievements of the Athenian theater.

5

Pentheus

Euripides' Bakkhai *as a*
Contest of Fictions

Scholarship on Dionysos and tragedy tends to follow rather different routes as it emphasizes either cultic manifestation, on the one hand, or Dionysiac myth and symbolism as featured in art and poetry, on the other. It is important to distinguish between
the two, and equally important to specify one's focus in the interpretation of a given
text. This chapter aims to contribute to our understanding of how myth was translated
into dramatic fiction, with emphasis on a specific Euripidean expression of the poetics
involved. In the case of *Bakkhai*, the myth reflects the ancient violence and savagery
that was mitigated and suppressed in contemporary cult. Euripides, however, exploited
this "savage" myth as a canvas for aggressive poetic invention to produce an original
work of art in which Dionysos himself was redefined. In other words, the distinctive
features of *Bakkhai*—Euripides' reflexive experiment par excellence—are neither an
inevitable projection of extradramatic cult nor simply a document of Dionysos as general, metaphysical symbol of the late fifth century.

The ancient taunt of "nothing to do with Dionysos" and the excesses of early
ritualist scholarship have inspired a modern reevaluation of tragedy as Dionysiac.
From a postwar renaissance[1] this reevaluation has inspired a number of approaches
to the relationship between drama and various aspects of Athenian culture (ritual,
cult, literacy etc.).[2] Although *Bakkhai* has been a centerpiece in this enterprise, its
innovative and transgressive aspects are strictly subordinated to ritual, not to say suppressed by it. In a strange academic transformation, a highly original work of art
becomes a passive document. It is telling that the agency of the poet-composer has
little place in a hermeneutic strategy that priviliges ritual and cult above all else. "The
myth of Pentheus dramatized in the *Bacchae*," asserts Richard Seaford, "does not
derive from the imagination of a single individual."[3] On his reading, *Bakkhai* makes
sense only as a reflection of initiation ritual dramatized as a "Dionysiac sacrifice"
(for which the play itself, paradoxically, is the main evidence).[4] Against this position
is the view articulated by Gerald Else some time ago that cult-myth and ritual are
secondary to the imagination and creative control of the composer.[5] "To understand
[tragedy]," wrote J.-P. Vernant along similar lines,

we should evoke its origins—with all due prudence—only in order the better *to gauge its innovatory aspects, the discontinuities and breaks with both religious practices and more ancient poetic forms.* The "truth" of tragedy is not to be found in an obscure, more or less "primitive" or "mystical" past secretly haunting the theater stage (emphasis added).[6]

On the other hand, Vernant and many others working in the post-Nietzschean tradition have fashioned a general, metaphysical Dionysos who is made to embody principles such as ambiguity, contradiction, paradox, order-in-chaos, and so forth. Dionysiac genealogy is confusingly equated with Dionysiac essence. From this direction, the god has returned with a vengeance to stake his postmodern claim as the master of illusion and "the god of tragic fiction."[7] Segal argues, for example, that "as patron god of the theater, Dionysus is the culture's symbol for the power of fictional representation and illusionistic drama."[8] Epitomizing fin-de-siècle experiment and self-conscious manipulation of dramatic convention, Euripides' *Bakkhai* has been the focal point of much stimulating and productive scholarship centered on the archaic, "poetic" myth of Dionysos with its violence and transgression. However, just as the ritualist approach can be blinkered by its reductionism, so enlisting "Dionysos" as a fifth-century "god of theater and fiction"[9] fails to recognize that this theatrical Dionysos makes his first entrance specifically in Euripides' last play. Metaphysical generalizations about Dionysos must therefore be modified to acknowledge Euripidean innovation. The playwright's contribution to subsequent Dionysiac symbolism was to invent an explicitly theatrical god and to demonstrate on the tragic stage exactly what this meant.

Bakkhai is considered in this chapter on a pragmatic level as another metafictional transformation similar in spirit and technique to the Sophoklean examples (*Philoktetes, Aias*) discussed above. Again, the composition of tragedy will be seen to problematize traditional narrative by projecting it into a self-conscious performance reflecting the dynamics and culture of the fifth-century theater. At the heart of the play is the transgressive mise en abyme in which Pentheus hastens to dress as a spectator only to die as a spectacle. The injection of theatrical culture into myth is, by definition, metafictional.[10] It is clear that the metatheatrics of *Bakkhai*—the complex interaction of generic elements, the enactment of madness, the play with mask and costume, the blurring of lines between illusion and reality—is produced by specific innovations into the traditions that "transform the structures of myth and ritual from an affirmation of order to a questioning of order."[11] The Dionysos of later literature and iconography[12] who has lately been promoted to be the official "god of drama" is largely the fabrication at a specific historical moment by Euripides within the framework of an increasingly reflexive and dialogical genre.

It may be somewhat iconoclastic to claim that the unique and metafictional aspects of *Bakkhai* do not automatically proceed from the Dionysiac content. The implications of such a claim explored in this chapter are that Euripides single-handedly reinvented Dionysos for posterity as a metatheatrical operator—and, in a limited sense, "god of theatrical illusion"—by innovating several key features into the story of Pentheus. Jennifer March's work on the iconography of Dionysos[13] contributes substantially to this argument. The extensive work on the metatheatrics of this play, complemented by capable surveys thereof,[14] renders a recital of the vari-

ous self-conscious experiments with theatricality unnecessary. Instead we can con-
centrate on the close connection between innovations in myth and metafictional design. In the process of enacting this first-order transformation, that is, Euripides' rewriting of myth, Dionysos becomes explicitly and permanently associated with dramatic illusion and theatricality in a way not evident in the other rare references to
the god in tragedy.[15] This collusion of innovations on the levels of myth and
metadrama participates in a more general theatrical exploration of truth and falsehood, a contest of fictions, as it were. The main plot of *Bakkhai* emerges as a destructive fiction self-consciously orchestrated by Dionysos to punish the authors of
an intolerable fiction concerning himself (lines 26–31). We are invited to contemplate the construction of truth on a number of levels of which the highest is, ultimately, that of a remarkably ambiguous and complex tragic text authorized by the
composer.

Spectatorship and the Travesty of Tradition

Bakkhai has maintained an extraordinary ability to attract interest and engender
controversy.[16] Euripides' last script is notoriously complex and, in light of recent
work, it is hardly necessary to emphasize its status as the preeminent Greek metadrama on the tragic side. It is arguably the most aggressive of tragedies, for example,
in its use of comic elements to problematize Pentheus' seduction in a manner
suggestive of intergeneric influence. There can be little doubt that, in his last play
at least, Euripides was responding to comedy in its own idiom.[17] Inasmuch as the
myth of Dionysos features the collective ecstasy of his attendants, it lends itself to
dramatization as a play en abyme involving interaction between the central divine
figure and his attendants. "The importance of the entourage in myth," notes
P. Slater, "is a direct expression of the importance of the *process* of Bacchic worship as compared with other forms: the profound emphasis on the production of
religious enthusiasm through group activity."[18] A compelling innovation on the
part of Euripides was to translate this cultic dynamic into a theatrical process where
the enthusiasm of the foreign chorus provides a backdrop for the punitive madness of the young Greek king.

Euripides did not limit his involvement with tradition to mere emphasis and
extension, however. In her study March has shown that any interpretation of *Bakkhai*
must take into account the full extent of Euripidean invention that, in the terms
applied to *Aias* above,[19] amounts to the feminization of Pentheus in overtly theatrical terms. Slipping into a passive role, he is prepared for sacrifice by being put on
display as a female stage-figure. "When Pentheus goes to the mountain," observes
Haslam, "it will be without anger, without weapons, without men; in command of
no one at all, not even himself; not leading, but led; and a god-fighter no longer, but
in thrall, and unmanned."[20]

At a pivotal moment in the play, the Stranger sets in motion his new plan that is
to culminate in the destruction of his adversary: Pentheus' double transformation
from man into maenad and spectator into spectacle begins with an invitation to watch
(line 811). The young king had just called for his weapons and abruptly orders the
Stranger to be silent. The sly temptation of the words that follow marks a dramatic

shift in the relationship between the god and his victim (811–16):[21]

DIONYSOS. Would you like to see those women huddling together in the hills?

PENTHEUS. Very much indeed, why I'd pay a great weight of gold for that!

DIONYSOS. What has made you fall into a great lust for this?

PENTHEUS. It would cause me distress to see them drunk with wine.

DIONYSOS. Yet you would enjoy looking upon such a "distressing" sight?

PENTHEUS. Of course, if I could sit quietly beneath the pines.

The equivocal appeal to the lust of the eyes, the eros of seeing, hints at the terror to come. Pentheus' desire comprehends both pleasure and pain in a voyeuristic manner underscoring the paradoxical yearning to see something he loathes and fears. The theatrical connection is clear: like Odysseus in Sophokles' *Aias* he is drawn to a painful spectacle as long as he is afforded the comfort of distance from it, a buffer that is the necessary condition for the "proper [tragic] pleasure," in Aristotle's phrase.[22] Unlike Odysseus, however, Pentheus is to become the deluded subject of a spectacle that he cannot comprehend. Stripped of his spectatorial safety, Pentheus will witness his own transgression trigger another, far more horrible crime.

An important step in preparing for the final seduction is the so-called miracle, where Dionysos appears to supervise the destruction of the Theban palace following his incarceration. Pointing out the discrepancy between the words of the script and what may have been staged, Segal notes "the power of Dionysus to create a fictive and yet convincing world." This moment is a divine epiphany that reveals "the capacity of a fiction to embody truth through symbolic meaning, and the actor's (and spectator's) ability to lose himself in fusion with an alien personality."[23] An interest in the process of dramatic signification is evident in the abundance of terms for seeing and perceiving, which suggests a link between theatrical illusion and Dionysiac *ekstasis*, the spell cast by the god.[24] What adds force to this moment is the process whereby Euripides explicitly associates Dionysos with the power of "dramatic illusion." *Bakkhai*, in other words, is not simply drawing on a theatrical topos but adapting the god and his cult to the aesthetics and semiotics of the late fifth-century stage.

While Dionysiac ecstasy is expressed in terms of unalloyed joy on the part of the chorus, the seduction of Pentheus in the dressing scene involves an additional and subversive layer of illusion that undermines everything the young king has heretofore asserted and that delivers him to his sacrificial death. *Bakkhai* develops vividly as a metadrama featuring a brilliant theatrical inset supported by play with disguise and illusion. It is commonly assumed that these unique features of *Bakkhai* are a direct reflection of ritual dynamics and structures. However, both the argument for *Bakkhai* as an initiatory fable reflecting a weakly attested "Dionysiac sacrifice"[25] and as the global equation of Dionysos with dramatic illusion and metatheater rely critically on a nexus of three elements: the maddening of Pentheus, his recostuming as a woman, and his death at the hands of Agave, who must belatedly recognize her son and reassemble his body to mourn it. Adherents of the ritualist and "metaphysical" (essentialist) approaches have strategically overlooked or undervalued the fact that *these are precisely the elements invented by the playwright*. In the excitement over drama having everything to do with Dionysos, it is certainly unfashionable to claim that this metatheatrical deity sprang fully formed from the head of Euripides!

March's persuasive reading of *Bakkhai* restores to Pentheus a measure of humanity denied him by critics in search of a hubristic tyrant ready for a fall.[26] Pentheus fails in his attempts to navigate using reason alone and, like Oidipous, ends up wrong for all the right reasons.[27] The division of the larger (imaginary) "theatrical space without," to borrow Hanna Scolnicov's phrase,[28] into city and country, the polis and Kithairon, reflects the competing mortal and divine spheres. No match for the god even on his own turf, Pentheus is drawn to the mountain, "the kingdom of Dionysos,"[29] for the final sacrifice. The terrible climax of the play, March argues, dramatizes the "defeat of νόμος by φύσις . . . embodied in the killing of a son by [his] mother."[30] This destructive scenario is realized by means of three primary innovations aimed at sustained travesty of tradition. Each of these innovations is such a radical departure from the pre-Euripidean narrative that the transformational program of *Bakkhai*—the rewriting of the conflict between Dionysos and Pentheus—is certainly relevant to any interpretation of the play:

1. Pentheus is made to lose his mind in order to facilitate his execution;
2. His leadership in open combat is replaced by solitary infiltration "in drag"; and
3. Agave becomes the killing mother, a feature designed for the recognition-scene.

Bakkhai is reviewed below from the point of view of these three elements in order to foreground the extent to which this metafictional tour de force is a product of a single playwright reflecting on the power of his craft. Euripides, far from being the passive transmitter of religious or poetic tradition, was self-consciously able to disrupt these traditions in order to engage his fellow citizens in a contemporary dialogue. *Bakkhai*, in fact, emerges as a great contest of competing fictions. From the very outset, Dionysos identifies the malicious revisionism of the Theban women as an intolerable fabrication that he has come to correct. The means to this "correction" turns out to be a large-scale rewriting of Pentheus' story, a counterfiction designed to punish the city and destroy its king. Throughout the play, moreover, various points of view are expressed in terms of the dichotomy between fiction and truth. Take, for example, Pentheus' view of the activity on Kithairon: "The women have abandoned our homes," he snarls (lines 217–18), "to pursue their pretense of bacchic revelry (πλασταῖσι βακχείαισιν) in the wooded hills." In the person of Dionysos, then, Euripides presents his radical revision of Pentheus' story in which the recostuming of the stage-figure signals the travesty of tradition on the authority of the poet and his leading (divine) figure. "A *consciousness of the fiction is essential to the dramatic spectacle; it seems to be both its condition and its product*" (emphasis added).[31]

From Leader of Men to Solitary Madman

The iconographic tradition preceding and surrounding Euripides' play unequivocally represents the encounter of Pentheus with the maenads as a pitched battle. The young king is the leader of an armed band involved in fighting, hunting, or ambush. The enemy commander is, of course, Dionysos himself: "The god led out his army of Bakkhai," in the words of Aischylos.[32] Never is Pentheus shown in the dress of a

maenad as in the *Bakkhai,* nor is there any trace of his madness.[33] From the prologue to the turning point noted above, the action suggests a commitment to the traditional story in which Pentheus is killed in an open confrontation. The plot development turns critically on the reversal of audience expectations that, for more than
half the play, are set up by reference to the familiar version.[34] Viewed in this light,
the second half of *Bakkhai* is a shock, with one surprise following another. The war
on Thebes outlined in the expository prologue—punishment of the Theban women
and the potential war with the men—mutates into Dionysos' personal campaign
against Pentheus. The key element in this shift is the transposition of the maenadic
frenzy described in lines 32–34 onto the king himself.

While there is nothing unusual in the notion of a woman under the spell of
Dionysiac mania, the attraction of a male to this sphere is disturbingly innovative.[35]
The imminent, overt feminization of Pentheus through recostuming, presentation,
and dismemberment[36] is thus deeply bound up with his madness on a thematic level.
In outlining the extent to which the playwright altered the old story, one could point
out that Euripides complicates the notion of Dionysiac ecstasy from the beginning
by juxtaposing the authentic celebration of the parodos with a wicked travesty thereof.
The joy of the god has been inflicted treacherously on all Theban women as a *punishment* for their revisionist gossip. The first mention of Dionysiac mania implies
the oxymoron "punitive ecstasy," a paradox with an implicit warning: what might we
expect from an angry god in disguise who manipulates his presence and the very forms
of his worship as tools of destruction? Most important, in allowing Dionysos to openly
rewrite the Pentheus myth, Euripides presents a vivid metaphor of his own authority. The agency of Dionysos, moreover, is especially appropriate in that it underscores
the inevitable ambiguity of a text that even a god cannot fully control.

Being the mechanism of Pentheus' feminization, madness provides a broad foundation for Euripides' metadramatic construction. Unlike Aias, who is deep in his
delirium at the very outset, Pentheus is gradually cut off from the real world by a
screen of delusion that rises slowly and perceptibly as we approach the turning point.
Like Sophokles' *Aias,* however, madness strictly defines the formal boundaries of
the theatrical inset in *Bakkhai.* Its full effect is marked by the presentation of the
recostumed Pentheus as a new character and it concludes abruptly with the return
of Pentheus' sanity in his (reported) presentation and sacrifice. While the absolute
change in attitude and awareness from Pentheus' entrance to the dressing scene is
astonishing, Euripides carefully places his seriocomic mise en abyme in a fully accessible matrix of antecedents, parallels, and clues. To begin with, Pentheus' madness, though a literary invention, is quite intelligible as an extension of the punishment already inflicted on the Theban women. Teiresias recalls for us the god's
indictment in the prologue—θεομαχεῖ τὰ κατ' ἐμέ, "[Pentheus] opens war on deity
in my person"—and proleptically links this *theomakhia* with madness. "I will not be
persuaded by you to fight the god," he says to the (still quite sane) king; "you are
mad, cruelly mad. No drug can cure your sickness, but some 'drug' has caused it."[37]
Just before the palace miracle, Dionysos hints at the creeping delusion in a phrase
reminiscent of Tiresias' famous words to Oidipous[38] (line 506): οὐκ οἶσθ' ὅ τι ζῇς,
οὐδ' ὃ δρᾷς, οὐδ' ὅστις εἶ, "you don't understand what your life means, nor what
you're doing, nor who you are." When Pentheus naively responds with "name, rank,

and serial number," Dionysos plays ominously with the etymology of the king's name (*penthein* = to mourn): "you are appropriately named for disaster."

The theme of dangerous disguise provides a concrete backdrop for the evolving split between appearances and reality, a rift maintained by a powerful and permanent dramatic irony. The scenes involving the Stranger and Pentheus exhibit an increasing tension between the ignorant discourse of the former and the understated power of the latter, strangely similar to Jesus' interview with Pilate in the orthodox interpretation. Unlike the New Testament account,[39] however, the misunderstanding here is a cruel joke and is resolved in an epiphany that is virtually simultaneous with the mortal's death. In the prologue, the Stranger twice announces that he is a god in disguise (lines 4, 54) who has come on a punitive mission in the shape of a man.[40] Pentheus, then, is in deep trouble from the very start and we are not much surprised when he begins to slip. Doom structured by various disguises is foreshadowed several times by significant references to Aktaion. Kadmos utters the most explicit of these in his warning (lines 337–41): "You saw that dreadful death your cousin Aktaion died when those man-eating hounds he had raised himself savaged him and tore his body limb from limb because he boasted that his prowess in the hunt surpassed the skill of Artemis. Do not let this fate be yours!" From the spectator's vantage point, Aktaion's crime has only tangential relevance since Pentheus is intent only on doing his duty as king with no thought whatever of rivaling or slighting the gods. Rather, Kadmos' warning points up the manner of death in which the victim was killed and dismembered by his own (in this case, hounds), who fail to recognize him. It is especially alarming that Aktaion's "disguise" in the exemplum is imposed by Artemis as a mechanism of execution. Euripides has projected this idea in a vividly theatrical way by innovating Pentheus' experiment in transvestite voyeurism, that is, by grafting the form of Aktaion's punishment onto the narrative of Pentheus' death.

As in *Aias*, madness structures Pentheus' tragedy en abyme, as a play, by establishing a cognitive boundary between the unfortunate "actor" (Pentheus) and the internal audience (Dionysos and the maenads). In its metafictional transformation madness serves as a force field of sorts that formally demarcates the "shows within," *Aias Mainomenos* and the *Robing of Pentheus*. Pentheus' senses had already begun to betray him during the palace miracle, as we learn from the internal poet-director who sits aloof from the new scene he has composed (lines 616–22):[41]

> Thus I, in turn, humiliated him, in that
> He seemed to think that he was binding me but never once
> so much as touched my hands. He fed on his hopes.
> Inside the manger where he led and imprisoned me, instead of me,
> he found a bull and tried to rope its knees and hoofed feet.
> He was panting forth his anger, biting his lips with his teeth,
> his whole body drenched with sweat, while I sat nearby,
> calmly watching.

"But at that moment Bakkhos came," says the Stranger, formally separating himself as composer from the character of Dionysos. The striking interplay of disguise, presence, and absence[42] begun in the prologue culminates in the dressing scene to emphasize the third dimension of the mise en abyme. Here, as often, we are reminded

that the disguised god comprises several personalities, as it were, with the bull a significant Dionysiac prop looking forward to Pentheus' death.[43] The blurring of boundaries between illusion and reality in Euripides' hall of mirrors is heightened by the
interaction of multiple frames of reference: those of Dionysos, Pentheus sane,
Pentheus mad, Theban women in maenadic frenzy, Theban women "sober," and
so forth.

The split between discourses—the ironic speech of the Stranger and the ignorant passion of Pentheus—along the fault line of the latter's creeping delusion reaches
a climax after the first messenger speech. The Stranger coyly warns Pentheus not to
take up arms against the god and to offer him due sacrifice (lines 787–95). To this
Pentheus replies scornfully (lines 796–97):[44]

> I shall indeed sacrifice: with much female slaughter,
> well deserved, disturbing the glens of Kithairon.

This notoriously ambiguous phrase, φόνον θῆλυν,[45] inscribes the duality noted
above into Pentheus' own speech. He means, of course, that maenads will be slaughtered, but we are invited to imagine Pentheus as a victim of the *sparagmos* just narrated by the messenger (lines 734–68). For a few lines more the Stranger humors
Pentheus as he blusters about leading his men to fight the maenads. Finally the
young king loses patience and, ordering his interlocutor to be silent, calls for his
armor. This is the Stranger's cue to begin his seduction, which he marks with an
extrametrical exclamation.[46] This "'ah' means death," notes Oliver Taplin, "and
yet it epitomizes Dionysus in this play that this terrible moment should be conveyed cooly, enigmatically, monosyllabically."[47] The dressing scene is now inevitable and the impending battle on Kithairon is canceled. The temptation of a
maenadic spectacle enjoyed in safety proves overwhelming. Unlike Odysseus in
Sophokles' *Aias*, however, Pentheus is seduced by his "director" into trusting his
security as a spectator. We know, of course, that it is *he* who is the spectacle and
that this performance shall be his last. To prepare for it, he must be dressed and
we must watch.

Clothes Make the Woman

Euripides' dressing scene has perhaps received more attention than any other for its
reflexive brilliance.[48] The thematic lines underlying the earlier scenes now converge,
and the full extent of Pentheus' madness is put on display. His unexpected and utterly improbable recostuming into a maenad violently derails the action to initiate
an unfamiliar future, the authentic realm of fiction in the modern sense. The king
loses his determination and becomes oddly passive to the point of asking the Stranger's
advice—τοῖσι σοῖσι πείσομαι βουλεύμασιν, "I'll do whatever you suggest." This
request elicits a chilling set of stage directions from the internal *khorodidaskalos*, who
again addresses Dionysos in the second person. It is fascinating to recall a similar
moment in the parabasis of Aristophanes' *Birds*[49] where an entirely new "play" begins: the reinvented society of birds steps forward to demonstrate a new, collective
persona and to advertise the brave new world of their polis. Similarly, Dionysos
launches the scenario he has just composed by introducing a "new character" sym-

bolizing the multiple reversals to come. This is nothing short of a second prologue that outlines Euripides' midstream revision. (lines 847–861):[50]

> Women, the man is now entering
> the trap. He shall come to the bacchants
> and pay the price of death.
> O Dionysos, now action is yours. And you are near.
> Let us punish this man. But put him outside his mind;
> bewilder him with light frenzy. For sane of mind
> this man would never wear female dress;
> but, wandering out of his mind, he will do it.
> After those threats with which he was so terrible,
> I want him made the laughingstock of Thebes,
> paraded through the streets in the form of a woman.
> Now I shall go and costume Pentheus in the clothes
> which he must wear to Hades, butchered
> by his mother's hands. He shall recognize
> Dionysos, son of Zeus, a god with a god's authority,
> most terrible, and yet most gentle, to mankind.

A striking word in this passage is γέλωτα, "laughter," which marks the robing of Pentheus as a curious experiment with comic elements.[51] This is certainly not the first time Euripides has engaged the comic, but it is his boldest crossing of generic lines. In the earlier, extended interaction between Euripides and Aristophanes discussed in chapter 7, the dialogue is softer and its range more constrained. Here innovation in style—the striving after a tragicomic dissonance—goes hand in hand with the travesty of traditional myth. By inventing and enacting a scene of onstage costuming, Euripides could expect a comparison with the established comic topos, be it the Telephos scene of *Acharnians* or the infiltration of the Thesmophoria by his own fictional kinsman. Although impossible to prove, it seems likely that in his later work Euripides consciously imitated and responded to Aristophanes. It is remarkable, after all, how much of the comic poet's stage-play with dress has to do with tragic costume, that of Euripides in particular. A quick glance through the present study reveals sustained instances in *Acharnians, Peace, Birds, Thesmophoriazousai*, and, of course the post-Euripidean *Frogs* and *Ekklesiazousai*. It is as if the tragedian had dared, in his last script, to unite two Aristophanic innovations—the enactment of disguise and the transvestite infiltration—to achieve the sublime mixture of horror with the ridiculous so eloquently explicated by Bernd Seidensticker and Helene Foley.[52] When it comes to the issue of disguising Dionysos in particular, Aristophanes may not have offered much in the way of comic inspiration to Euripides, who died a year before the production of *Frogs*. Kratinos' *Dionysalexandros*, however, a play that probably coincides with the end of Pericles' career (430 BC?), made great capital of disrupting myth by inserting the disguised god into the old story of the Judgment of Paris. Enough of Kratinos' comedy and other fragmentary evidence survives for us to identify Dionysos incognito as a comic topos with at least several potent representatives.[53] Without insisting on this connection, it is worth noting that *Bakkhai*—surely the *tragic* debut of Dionysos in disguise—is marked by unusually aggressive experimentation with formal and thematic elements of comedy. This can hardly be coincidental.

The core of the tragicomic robing is the moment (lines 925–44) when the internal director steps in to manage the new costume that threatens to get out of control. He speaks also with the clear voice of a spectator eager to see something stimulating. His bold and descriptive cue (lines 912–17) begins with an improbable tragic pun[54] and includes physically explicit stage directions: "You who eagerly hasten to mischief, to see what you should not; Pentheus, I say, *come forth from the building and show yourself to me in your woman's outfit*, the maenad costume in which you would spy on your mother and her band." As he emerges, Pentheus describes his hallucinations: his vision is split, he sees two suns, two gates, and so forth, and the Stranger appears to be the "guide bull" associated throughout the play with Pentheus' final journey.[55] In this way, Euripides vividly symbolizes the multiple duplicities and ambiguities of his fable that have so engaged spectators and readers. It is unsettling that this most extreme distortion marked by incoherent language is, in fact, the truest point in Pentheus' field of vision: the Stranger is indeed the Dionysiac beast leading him to his death! While we may find Pentheus' question ridiculous, his words point to truth: "Have you always been a beast?" Dionysos amplifies the irony by again speaking of himself in the third person and assuring Pentheus that he now sees exactly what he should be seeing. Thus Pentheus' madness is articulated metatheatrically as the delusion of a player who thinks himself a spectator, the disorientation of one who knows neither "what he is doing," in the Stranger's words (line 506), nor on which side of the great divide he stands. From our ironic perspective, we can only pity the depth to which this tragic *alazon*, "self-ignorant man," has fallen.[56] In light of Teiresias' drug metaphor cited above (lines 326–27) we could say that the physician who administered the hallucinogenic is now satisfied that it has taken effect. This is peripety of the starkest kind, one that foregrounds the full seriousness of Euripides' tampering with tradition.[57]

Pentheus now begins to play, quickening the dialogue to a sustained and regular distichomythia. Dionysos' victim relishes the transgressive moment by asking if he resembles his mother (or aunt), referring specifically to their *stasis*, their physical *bearing*, "pluming himself on his clever acting."[58] The Stranger's encouraging reply pointedly separates the truth from what appears in a spectacle by repeating the verb ὁρᾶν, "to see": αὐτὰς ἐκείνας εἰσορᾶν δοκῶ σ᾽ ὁρῶν, "as I watch you, why, I think I might even be looking at one of them" (line 927). The fit between appearance and reality is not perfect, in fact, and the choreographer must step in to adjust the costume. He describes a lock that has fallen out of place using a verb (ἐξίστημι) used in expressions for madness.[59] Pentheus' dependence on Dionysos has now become absolute, a fact that is expressed theatrically as the god orders his "actor" to raise his head and wait patiently while he adjusts the costume. "Please, do!" responds Pentheus, "You must play the dresser [σὺ κόσμει], I am in your hands completely." The first verb resonates with theatrical significance while the latter, ἀνακείμεθα, is suggestive of sacrificial dedication[60] and enforces the ominous implications of the "second prologue." This line breaks the regularity of the stichomythia and it is tempting, with E. R. Dodds, to imagine a significant pause accompanied by a gesture.[61]

Although the superficial discussion of costuming continues with technicalities of the *peplos*, the dialogue suddenly fractures along the lines of truth (Dionysos) and illusion (Pentheus) in a way that is a hallmark of this play. In response to Pentheus' discussion of the irregular hemline, Dionysos utters an alarming non sequitur (lines

939–40):[62]

> You shall regard me as your best friend, perhaps, when you see
> how unexpectedly self-controlled the maenads are.

Pentheus misses the point and does not stop to ponder this unexpected assertion of *sôphrosynê* on the maenads' behalf, nor is he interested in comparing rumor and reality. His blind spot, the fear of sexual misconduct, is emphasized against the rift between rumor and truth, a mismatch that traces the clash of divine truth and human ignorance in the dialogue. Similarly, while Pentheus blithely fusses over the details of his performance as an actor, Dionysos continues to speak on a separate plane in carefully ambiguous terms maintaining the separation of realities noted above. His explicit stage directions on holding the *thyrsos* and dance (lines 943–44) are followed by the phrase αἰνῶ δ᾽ ὅτι μεθέστηκας φρενῶν. If he were listening, Pentheus might take these words to mean that the Stranger approves his change of *heart*. To the spectators another meaning comes clear: "I'm pleased to see that you are out of your mind."

As if to illustrate this last point, the conversation now takes a fantastic turn to the "theatrical space without," leaving the polis to imagine the realm of Dionysos on Kithairon. The charged irony of conversation continues as Pentheus gets carried away, losing all sense of what is possible in his "performance" (lines 945–48):[63]

> PENTHEUS. Could I hoist the folds of Kithairon and carry
> them on my shoulders, maenads and all?
>
> DIONYSOS. You could if you wanted to. Before, your mind was
> unsound, but now you have the kind of mind you should have.

Dionysos condescendingly urges his player to stick to the script in which the recently planned military campaign is under erasure. The god reinforces Pentheus' confusion between the spheres of "player" and "spectator" and steers his attention back to the temptation of voyeurism. The pervasive military language that *Bakkhai* has imported from the pre-dramatic tradition[64] flickers and fades from Pentheus' lips at this point: "Indeed, women are not to be mastered by violence. I shall hide my body among the fir trees" (lines 953–54). Watching the play, in other words, not fighting, is the thing. Dionysos' conspicuous and repetitive echoes of his victim's words[65] further underscore the extent to which his meaning differs from that of Pentheus. It is hard to overemphasize how profoundly Euripides has subverted the nature of Pentheus' resistance to Dionysos. Constructing the young king's (false) gender to be the passive antithesis of open and violent confrontation, he problematizes the encounter between man and god in a profound way possible only in the theater. In the disguised Pentheus the fundamental tensions and ambiguities inherent in the Theban crisis are given a vicious spin and put in full view of the polis.

The scene concludes with an ironic crescendo celebrating the consequences of the grand illusion, that is, Dionysos' success in putting Pentheus on display with the promise of safe spectatorship. This is a terrible theater indeed, an agon of death. The entrance of the new Pentheus inaugurates a fundamentally reconfigured spectacle that retraces in reverse the familiar tragic pattern in which the polis is a site of salvation.[66] The transvestite "maenad" is dressed to leave the safety of the city for a dangerous beyond where he shall die. Even his experience in this imaginary space is suggestive of the dynamics of theatrical agon and spectacle. Upon his final exit Pentheus will "labor (suffer) for his city" in "ordeals" (*agones*) to which he will be led by his "saviour" (Dionysos) and from which he will return "carried in his mother's arms . . . a spectacle for all to see." The distichomythia disintegrates into the pathetic final exchange of this tragedy mise en abyme in which Pentheus babbles, dizzy with anticipation and delight. He has no idea what he is saying and his last words are no longer his own. They stand apart from him as a grim inscription over his place of execution: "I am getting what I deserve." This is the last exchange between Pentheus and the Stranger (lines 963–70):[67]

> DIONYSOS. You and you alone will toil for your city.
> Ordeals await you, ones that you
> deserve. I shall be your escort and protector,
> but another shall bring you back.
>
> PENTHEUS.   Yes, my mother.
>
> DIONYSOS. Conspicuous to all.
>
> PENTHEUS.   That is why I am going.
>
> DIONYSOS. You will be carried home. . .
>
> PENTHEUS.   O luxury!
>
> DIONYSOS. In your mother's arms.
>
> PENTHEUS.   You are forcing me to be pampered.
>
> DIONYSOS. Pampering, yes, in my own way.
>
> PENTHEUS.   I am getting what I deserve!
>
> DIONYSOS. You are an amazing young man, amazing, and you are
> going to amazing sufferings. You will attain a glory towering to
> heaven.

"The δέσις of the plot is now complete," notes Dodds (*ad* lines 973–76), "the λύσις about to begin." Dionysos turns away from the retreating Pentheus to formally conclude choreography of his show within by addressing the Theban women. Once again he uses the word *agon* to bridge the theatrical and experiential aspects of the mise en abyme: "I bring you this man for his great *agon*." We do not hear from Agave and her kin, however; rather it is the chorus of Asian maenads who reply in a violent appeal to *dikê*, *sôphrosynê*, and *eusebeia*. Their opening invocation calls on the hounds of lyssa, "madness," to incite Kadmos' daughters against one they call τὸν ἐν γυναικομίμῳ στολᾷ λυσσώδη κατάσκοπον μαινάδων, "costumed in imitation of a woman, the madman who spies on the maenads" (lines 980–81). They help us see coming events as they read from Dionysos' script the lines of Agave: "Who is this spy who has come to the mountains to peer at the mountain revels of the women of Thebes?" and so on. Agave's own delusion is anticipated by the chorus who attribute the following words of the text to her: "this

man was born of no woman. Some lioness gave him birth, some Libyan gorgon!"
(lines 986–88). Though we cannot appreciate them now, we shall remember these
lines when the unfortunate woman returns from Kithairon with the bloody head
of a "lion" on her *thyrsos*.

The Killing Mother

The maddening of Pentheus and his robing in the tragicomic mise en abyme lay the
foundation for what is perhaps Euripides' most daring innovation, that of having *Agave*
kill her son in a bacchic frenzy. Beginning with the second prologue (lines 847–61),
the ominous "soundtrack" of the play has been rising to the crescendo of Pentheus'
approaching doom. This is to be a moment of unspeakable violence where mother
and son meet (indeed, touch!) though still separated by the barrier of madness. There
must be no anesthesia in this operation, however, so Dionysos suddenly breaks the
illusion by restoring to Pentheus his wits at the very last moment in order to heighten
his pain. Thus, although Agave appears to "cure" Pentheus of his madness—as
Kadmos does Agave—the parental role is subverted as the "cure" turns out to be worse
than the "disease."[68] The climactic innovation of the killing mother theme moves
the mise en abyme outward to Kithairon for an abrupt conclusion as Pentheus regains his sanity during his presentation and *sparagmos*. Agave will then emerge as
the focal point of the tragedy when the effect of the Dionysiac "hallucinogen" wears
off leaving her alone to face the truth. She is not the first killing mother in tragedy
but certainly the most pitiable.

   To anticipate chapter 7, in his *Tereus* of the 430s, Sophokles shocked his audience by presenting the tragedy of Prokne, unquestionably the original killing mother
of the tragic stage. In that play, the Athenian princess butchered her only son and
fed his remains to her husband in mad revenge for his rape and mutilation of her
sister. *Tereus* was enormously influential and the available evidence identifies
Sophokles' Prokne as the model for Euripides' Medeia, whom in 431 the playwright
quite unexpectedly made to slay her children.[69] While the dramatic significance
of Euripides' second killing mother is well analyzed by Jennifer March,[70] it is worth
extending our study of Dionysos' counterfiction above to trace how the messenger
speech incorporates the new fable of Pentheus *transvestitus* into the larger design
of *Bakkhai*.

   The presentation of Pentheus as a sacrificial spectacle continues to bear the marks
of self-conscious theatricality in the afterglow of the dressing scene. The absurdity of
his situation is revealed in living color as he comes upon the maenads going about
their pleasant business, trimming their *thyrsoi* and singing antiphonally (βακχεῖον
ἀντέκλαζον ἀλλήλαις μέλος), a detail that underscores the formal connection of these
characters in the narrative with the actual choristers on stage. For the last time, Pentheus
disparages maenadism as a loathsome fiction. The phrase he uses (μαινάδων νόθων,
line 1060) is a strong condemnation of the activites he sees as counterfeit, illegitimate,
a "bastardization" of proper behavior. We now realize that, by grafting a theatrical fiction of his own into the plot, Dionysos stages a showdown between members of the
Theban community (with the royal family at the focus) who had dismissed his pedigree and cult as an evil fiction. They are face-to-face, but on the unequal terms of

players and spectators separated by a veil of madness and held in place by a powerful director. It is fascinating to compare this moment as it is reported with a similarly tense point in Sophokles' *Aias* when the enemies Odysseus and Aias actually come face-to-face. Despite Odysseus' fears, as we have seen, the boundary of illusion symbolized by the *atê* of Aias is strictly enforced though violence retains its terrible potential. It is this internal dramatic illusion, in fact, that serves to utterly reverse the promise of pursuit and punishment with which *Aias* opens. In *Bakkhai*, on the other hand, the internal director destroys the cognitive membrane between the world of the stage (the disguised Pentheus in his tree) and the world of the audience (maenads). Fiction and reality collide with catastrophic results (lines 1075–81):[71]

> He was presented to the Maenads' view rather than
> seeing them himself. He was just becoming visible
> in his perch on the tree when the stranger vanished
> and there came a great voice from the air of heaven
> —Dionysos one may guess—crying: "Women, I bring you the
> man who made you, me, and my rites the object of
> laughter. Punish him now.

Euripides' flirtation with comedy is now placed in a grim context indeed and we note that the theatrical inset is framed by two conspicuous references to laughter (lines 854 and 1081). For Pentheus, the real Dionysos has always been marked by an absence, for us, by being under erasure in the figure of the Stranger. Paradoxically, we are prepared for the epiphany of the god by a report of the abrupt and final disappearance of the main stage-figure ("Stranger"). The last internal "stage directions" announce that the play of fictions has come full circle: Pentheus was made ridiculous as the "star" of a quasi comedy, the mise en abyme contrived for him in direct retaliation for making Dionysos and his cult "the object of laughter." The inherent qualities of tragedy's sister genre were imported into Euripides' metatheatrical contest of fictions in order to render the final revenge all the more devastating. There is nothing funny about the conclusion of *Bakkhai* and we realize that, as spectators, we too were deluded along with Pentheus into being amused.[72]

The focal point of the second messenger speech is the moment when Pentheus reveals his face and cries, "No, no Mother! I am Pentheus, your own son, the child you bore to Echion! Pity me, spare me, Mother!" (lines 1118–20). The victim has regained his senses and demonstratively rejects his maenadic identity, a point in the narrative that formally concludes the mise en abyme of disguise and infiltration begun at line 810. We imagine a frantic attempt to disentangle himself from everything he had so enthusiastically cultivated just minutes before (in real time). As his spectatorial security evaporates, he understands, for a brief instant, that the very forms he had dismissed as fictions unworthy of respect have been used to trap and destroy him. All that remains now is the last wave of punishment, the tragedy of Agave in which she must bear the full brunt of Dionysos' lethal minidrama.

Dionysos' tragedy mise en abyme is traced up to the final recognition (line 1282) by the signifiers of Pentheus' costume and disguise. In a desperate effort to save his life, he terminates the internal charade by tearing off a marker of his maenadism, the *mitra*, a headband holding a wig.[73] There is great pathos in this last moment when the doomed youth touches his mother's face for the last time. After the dismemberment during which pieces of Pentheus are tossed about in gruesome sport, Euripides innovates another metatheatrical detail that keeps Dionysos' fiction in the foreground: he has Agave impale Pentheus' "head" on her *thyrsos* to be her main hunting trophy.[74] The stage figure is thus physically dismembered as he surrenders his mask to be a lonely signifier bearing the full meaning of the past, a message to be read by Agave and that shall destroy her. From a character with an overdetermined costume (maenad superimposed on king) Pentheus is reduced to a tragic mask maintaining his presence on stage by silent synecdoche. As Agave feels the Dionysiac ecstasy subside, she interprets the sign she carries, performing the last spectatorial act of the inner play: "No! I now see . . . this the greatest possible grief!"

Conclusion

Drama furnished a pervasive and powerful metaphor for life in a society that did not yet know "all the world's a stage" as a cliché.[75] In firmly embedding Dionysos and his cult into a theatrical matrix, Euripides made a highly original and lasting contribution to the sphere of the Greek "imaginary"—that complex of representations through which a civilization articulates itself and its world. It is hardly surprising that Dionysos "at large" is often confused with Euripides' metatheatrical stage-god:[76]

> Tragedy thus opened up a new space in Greek culture, the space of the imaginary, experienced and understood as such, that is to say as a human production stemming from pure artifice . . . If we are right in believing that one of Dionysus' major characteristics is constantly to confuse the boundaries between illusion and reality, to conjure up the beyond in the here and now, to make us lose our sense of self-assurance and identity, then the enigmatic and ambiguous face of the god certainly does smile out at us in the interplay of the theatrical illusion that tragedy introduced for the first time onto the Greek stage.

Euripides' complex story of Dionysos at Thebes has been argued here to revise tradition so as to associate the god in a specific and detailed way with the culture of the fifth-century theater. Dionysos was thereby reinvented as an explicitly theatrical symbol. The dramatic revision of myth illustrates, in a special sense, how *Bakkhai* asks "what it means to absorb myth and ritual, this time Dionysiac myth and ritual, into the life of the *polis*."[77] By means of pointed innovations into the tradition used to set up an interplay of competing narratives—traditional myth, Theban gossip, and the actual stage-play—the punishment of Pentheus and the Theban women is realized as a large-scale contest of fictions that emphasizes the authority of one (playwright, god) who controls the "text" against the background of multiple social and "cosmic" rifts such as those between oikos and polis, male and female, man and god. A first impression is that man may play with fiction as long as he remembers that all reality lies within the gods' power to create and manipulate. Just as we are ready to acquiesce in a losing game where "illusion and symbol are the only modes of access to a god who can take whatever form he wishes" (line 478)[78] we are reminded that all truth here, including that of the god, is embodied in the tragic text and performance—

a fiction remarkable for its ambiguity and innovation. The composer and his work emerge as the final arbiters of truth whose construction is a negotiation between an individual and his society.

Dionysos is presented in *Bakkhai*, above all, as a conspicuous "master of truth," to use a phrase well known for its application to poets in ancient Greek society, where "truth" is shown to be coextensive and inextricable from its text. This mastery is established explicitly in the prologue as the god announces that he has come to rewrite history as it is being told in Thebes. More importantly, we watch Dionysos "choreograph" Euripides' own revisionist narrative to produce a new fable that is as strikingly new as anything the Theban women were guilty of. There is here an arresting paradox wherein a narrative condemned for its "innovations" is punished through the enactment of a new narrative that arguably does far more violence to tradition! A warrior is made a woman, the conscience of the polis is left deranged, and a mother is made to perform the gruesome work of executing her own son. There can be no more vivid demonstration of how the metafictional potential of the tragic text may be engaged to study the text's own construction and truth in explicitly transgressive terms. In this connection it is important to remember that *Bakkhai* was performed posthumously at Athens from a "text" in the most literal sense. Transgression in the social sphere was here mirrored powerfully on the level of poetics. For this process Euripides invented a new name and representative, and that was Dionysos.

PART III

THE ANATOMY
OF DRAMATIC FICTION

Comic Utopia

6

Bellerophontes

Euripides' Bellerophontes
and Aristophanes' Peace

Moving from the tragic figures of the last two chapters to the hybrid comic figures of chapters 6, 7, and 8, we encounter an important shift in metafictional
strategy that involves the mediation of a fully articulated tragic text between comedy and tradition. While tragedy alludes, comedy is free to quote. The respective
maddenings of Aias and Pentheus, as we have seen, were reinvented as spectacles
informed by the new reflexive poetics of Athenian tragedy. There, familiar configurations and narrative patterns were transformed into phenomenologically distinct moments of theatrical and political self-study, as myth became theater. In the
contrafacts studied here, on the other hand, the Aristophanic refashionings of tragedy perform a second-order transformation in which a given myth is transposed
into a comic key not from epic (or an indeterminate popular source), but directly
from a relatively recent tragic performance. As we saw in *Akharnians,* and as we shall
see again in *Peace, Birds,* and *Frogs,* Aristophanes organizes his contrafacts around a
tragic problematic to which he advertises a novel, and more powerful, utopian solution (*sôtêria*). In this triumph of comic solution over tragic problem Aristophanes
implies an ideological difference between genres, a fundamentally different point
of view held in a fundamentally different world. In the ongoing rivalry between
Aristophanes and tragedy, the latter figures as a metaphor of failure and social disintegration that comedy has the superior abilities to rectify as it pleases.

At work here is a curious and covert intergeneric, *imaginary* rivalry — in the sense
of "the Greek imaginary" — that is an extension of the intrageneric rivalry institutionalized at the dramatic festivals. Alongside the open and vigorous competition between
comic poets studied by Sidwell and others is, in the case of Aristophanes, a career-
long competitive interest in tragedy, especially in the person of Euripides. Reaching
beyond the frame of the formal dramatic competitions — tragic poet versus tragic poets,
comic versus comic — this rivalry across generic lines exemplifies a new stage in the
self-definition within a genre and on the part of a playwright who becomes concerned
not only with rivals at eye level, as it were, but in a larger city wide agon from which
he emerges the victorious *didaskalos*: teacher, culture maker, and shaper of public

opinion. From the spectacles of madness mises en abyme in *Aias* and *Bakkhai* we turn now to Aristophanes' extended utopian experiments with tragedy. These experiments are complex and unpredictable, each one being a poetic microcosm with rules of its own. The one general theme of the utopian contrafacts, including *Akharnians*, is that transposition of tragic fiction into a new and brighter key always makes better music for a better world.

Tragoedia Transvestita

One of the most visible contrafacts of tragedy in Aristophanes is the flight of Trygaios on his dung beetle that inaugurates the utopian vision of *Peace*, produced in 421. This protagonist is positioned Janus-like between the roles of Dikaiopolis of *Akharnians*, four years earlier, and Peisetairos of *Birds*, seven years later.[1] Like the former, Trygaios is a simple rustic—a vine grower from the inland deme of Athmonon—who undertakes to change his world through immediate and direct action. Like Peisetairos, whose challenge to the gods is celebrated in the apotheosis of the comic hero as tyrant and god (*Birds* 1707 and 1765), Trygaios demonstratively leaves Athens, masters Olympos, and is hailed by the chorus of Pan-Hellenes as αὐτοκράτωρ, "supreme ruler." The opening heroic quest of *Peace* transforms the tragic failure of the protagonist in Euripides' *Bellerophontes* into a spectacular comic success. This chapter analyzes the flight of the new Bellerophontes as a metafictional hybrid—the exalted discourse of tragedy spiked, as it were, with subliterary *ainos* (Aisopos' tale of the eagle and the dung beetle).[2] Trygaios' flight and the business surrounding it emerge as a sustained contrafact of action, character, and theme in which Aristophanes synthesizes his political utopia from an unlikely mixture of "low" and "high" narrative elements within the general framework of an *anodos* myth celebrating the return of fertility.

Throughout his career, Aristophanes maintained an interest in *Bellerophontes*, produced most likely in the 430s.[3] The Euripides scene in *Akharnians* discussed above begins with a pointed allusion at line 411 in which the protagonist finds Euripides perched aloft and says: "Are you composing way up there when you should be down here? No wonder you create crippled characters!" Dikaiopolis shortly reviews the tragedian's inventory of roles and costumes in search of one that would impart to him the greatest persuasive power in an agon that is to be a matter of life and death (*Akh.* 417). Euripides first suggests the costumes of Oineus, Phoinix, and Philoktetes, all of whom Dikaiopolis rejects as insufficiently pathetic. The discussion then turns to Bellerophontes in language with a strong tragic tint (e.g., δυσπινῆ πεπλώματα):[4]

> EURIPIDES. Then perhaps this is what you want, the filthy rags worn by that old lame Bellerophontes here?
>
> DIKAIOPOLIS. No, not him. But the character I have in mind sure was lame, all right; an impertinent beggar, a windbag—the perfect orator!

Verbal echoes in *Knights* (line 1249) and *Wasps* (line 757) place *Bellerophontes* in a rather circumscribed group of Aristophanic favorites, a status secured by the sustained treatment in *Peace*.[5] Trygaios' career reflects the widespread, optimistic anticipation of the treaty with Sparta (concluded shortly after the City Dionysia in 421). He personifies *trygoidia*, comedy's *terminus technicus* for its transformational poetics.

We can only marvel at Aristophanes' choice of a model. Reconstructions of Euripides' *Bellerophontes*[6] reveal a tragic dystopia from which the only escape available to the hero is to die—literally to "crash and burn"—estranged from men and gods. This theatrical flight appears to have been, paradoxically, an act of desperate piety, as passionate as it was futile. The original sequence is clear: intrafamilial strife, ordeals in Lykia, betrayal, loss of his children, melancholy solitude, final crisis, flight, and death. Reversing the dynamics of his Akharnian metafiction (where Telephos' social reintegration is transformed into the disruptive individualism of Dikaiopolis), Aristophanes refashions Euripides' catastrophic finale into a prologue that initiates a fantasy of salvation on an international plane by Bellerophontes reclad as an Athenian rustic! The tragic end becomes a comic beginning: Trygaios fearlessly confronts the gods, successfully negotiates their absence, deals with Polemos and Hermes, and returns with a blessing in which empire mutates into fantastic Panhellenic concord presided over by Athens (of course). The isolated and bitter victim of human treachery is allowed to reenact his exploit in comedy and to join the widest possible community in peaceful utopia. As with *Telephos* in *Akharnians* and Sophokles' *Tereus* in *Birds*, an appreciation of the tragic contrafact in *Peace* requires a review of the tragic model. The importance of Lamberto di Gregorio's work will be evident throughout the following discussion. As a capable synthesis of reconstructions from Welcker to Webster, his study leaves little to add in the way of evidence and detail. Di Gregorio's contribution has been to incorporate all the relevant evidence and scholarship into a new and compelling narrative solution to the fragmentary puzzle.[7]

Bellerophon Tragicus

The action of this play follows on the events of Sophokles' *Iobates* and is closely linked in theme to Euripides' own *Stheneboia*. Homer (*Iliad* 6.200–202) approaches Bellerophontes' tragic end, but does not tell the story:[8]

> But after Bellerophontes was hated by all the immortals,
> he wandered alone about the Aleian plain, eating
> his heart out, skulking aside from the trodden track of humanity.

Though Hesiod supplies important details of the legend[9] we must wait until the fifth century for explicit narratives of the fall. Pindar was interested in Bellerophontes (e.g., *Olympian* 13), and is the first extant author to deal explicitly with the hybris and death of the hero. The sententious conclusion of *Isthmian* 7 (lines 42–48) makes the following point:[10]

> For we all perish, winged Pegasos shook from his back
> though our luck varies. Bellerophontes his rider, striving
> If a man gazes in the distance, to enter the dwellings of the sky
> he is too short and join Zeus' company.
> to reach the bronze-paved Most bitter is the end
> home of the gods: of a sweetness not our right.

From a variety of sources, however, we get at least a general picture of how this moment was dramatized by Euripides in his *Bellerophontes*; recent efforts at reconstruction shed light on the main lines of Aristophanes' contrafact in *Peace*.

Given the scant nature of the evidence, Friedrich Welcker, N. Wecklein, Peter Rau, T. B. L. Webster, and others have had to interpret the scattered testimonia and fragments in light of the two authors who most certainly were familiar with the play, Aristophanes and Aelianus. Di Gregorio has proposed a compelling arrangement of the well-known dramatic elements in a relation to one another—Stheneboia's vendetta, Bellerophontes' sojourn in the Aleian plain, his "melancholy," "atheism," hybris, flight on Pegasos, and death. Crucial in this effort has been the deployment of a neglected testimonium in the reconstruction of the plot: a difficult epigram in the Greek Anthology (3.15: the fifteenth Cyzicene)[11] whose didascalion relates the consequences of Bellerophontes' flight in the following scenario: "Bellerophontes, having fallen from Pegasos into the Aleian plain, is saved by his son Glaukos when he was about to be killed by Megapenthes, son of Proitos."[12]

The initial crises in Argos and Lykia induced Bellerophontes to first avenge himself by killing Stheneboia and then to withdraw to a solitary life in the Aleian plain. This first sequence of tribulations is followed by the climactic confrontation and death dramatized in *Bellerophontes*: Stheneboia's male kin seek him out in his isolation on a mission of counterrevenge. Bellerophontes' resolute misanthropy yields to deep despair and, in a fit of outrage against heaven, he undertakes his fatal flight. *Bellerophontes* thus emerges as a very personal epilogue to the Potiphar's wife intrigue told by other poets and by Euripides himself in *Stheneboia*. Given the inadequacy of the ancient summaries poorly represented by P.Oxy 4017 fr. 4 and P.Oxy 3651,[13] it will be helpful to introduce the reconstruction with a brief narrative summary in lieu of a dramatic hypothesis.

Background to Euripides' Bellerophontes

Having killed Belleros, ruler of Corinth, Bellerophontes seeks refuge at Argos (or Tiryns) where he is purified by King Proitos. The latter's wife, Stheneboia, makes advances to Bellerophontes and, rejected, accuses him of attempted rape. Unwilling to kill his guest, Proitos sends Bellerophontes to his father-in-law, the Lykian king Iobates, with written instructions to do the job for him. Iobates complies by sending the hero on a series of trials that the latter negotiates successfully. Impressed, Iobates relents and gives his daughter in marriage to Bellerophontes, who is invited to share the throne. He eventually learns of Stheneboia's and Proitos' intrigue and returns to Argos to deal with them. While Stheneboia contrives new treachery against him, Bellerophontes induces her to mount Pegasos. Near Melos, he throws Stheneboia to her death. Angry with him for this and jealous of his glory, Megapenthes and Iobates drive Bellerophontes from his kingdom. Further grief comes to the hero with the loss of his children, Isandros, who dies fighting the Solymoi, and Laodameia, slain by Artemis (Schol. Iliad 6.202a). Bellerophontes withdraws to a solitary and rustic life in the Aleian plain in Asia Minor.

Action of the Play

Having lived for some time now in the "field of wandering" (cf. ἀλᾶσθαι), Bellerophontes suffers from severe melancholia brought on by his misfortunes and his experience of human depravity: there is no justice on earth and no gods to speak of. He finds little comfort in his son, Glaukos (cf. the epigram Anth. Pal. 3.15 above), and in members of the local community. Iobates and Megapenthes arrive to avenge Stheneboia's death, and bring Bellerophontes news of his condemnation in absentia by a judicial assembly at Argos. This perpetuation of Stheneboia's crimes throws Bellerophontes into a rage and he mounts Pegasos to confront the gods. Iobates and Megapenthes plot to ambush him when he touches down after the inevitable failure. Punished by the gods for his hybris, the hero falls from Pegasos and lies dying in the Aleian plain when he is ambushed. Glaukos confronts his father's enemies and kills Megapenthes. This belated rescue inspires in Bellerophontes a change of heart and he dies affirming a renewed belief in divine justice.

Bellerophontes is set in the Aleian plain before the hero's dwelling. The play appears to open, like *Medeia*,[14] with Bellerophontes lamenting within his hovel while the expository prologue is spoken by another figure (perhaps Glaukos) who relates the miserable condition of the hero's spirit. The first episode begins with a dramatic transition from pathos to reason (again, like Medeia's) as the protagonist makes his entrance and engages Glaukos and the chorus who exhort him to be of good cheer. Bellerophontes' state of mind is rather grim as we see in the long fr. 285 N^2 (of which I cite the beginning and end) where he strongly asserts the belief that the more one has, the more one stands to lose: it is best not to be born, or if born, to know as little as possible of life's joys:[15]

> I claim that the saying common everywhere is valid indeed—   fr. 285
> that it is best for a man not to be born in the first place.
> Of three possible destinies, wealth, high birth, and poverty,
> —and this is the number I propose—I deem one to be
> superior [i.e., ignorant poverty, as he goes on to argue]
>
> . . . .
>
> It is thus best not have experienced good things.
> For I remember how esteemed I was among men
> while my life was fortunate!

To this context, no doubt, also belongs fr. 287 N^2, in which the hero expresses resolute independence, and two important theological passages, fr. 286 and 292 N^2.[16] In the latter (lines 1–6), Bellerophon answers his interlocutors with a metaphorical reproach, implying that they are like inferior physicians who treat a disease haphazardly in the absence of a correct diagnosis: "The doctor too should apply a remedy when he has studied the disease and not give medicines summarily, in case they do not suit it. Men's diseases are some of them self-chosen, some of them sent by the gods, but we treat them according to our custom." Here we note that the notion of disease (*nosos*) is generalized to include human misfortune in general (and that of Bellerophontes in particular). The doctor is obliged to diagnose and treat any illness, irrespective of the cause. "But I would tell you," he continues, shifting to the ethical problem of god-sent illness (disaster), "that, if the gods commit (such) shameful deeds, they are not gods."

The famous "atheistic" fragment 286 N^2 elaborates this idea (to the chorus? cf. line 13) in a typically Euripidean anticipation of the play's climax. This, arguably the strongest denial of the existence of the gods in Greek drama,[17] has critical implications for our appreciation of both the play's conclusion and its contrafact in *Peace*. Bellerophontes is presented as expressing utter pessimism about divine justice, a state of mind that will be put to the test in a climactic *agon* (in the sense of "ordeal"). Faced with a further, and intolerable, series of injustices, the hero will test his own atheistic hypothesis by flying to see if the gods exist and, if so, to confront them on the charges that he presents in this fragment. His speech shows signs of formal rhetorical technique whereby an orator persuades his audience that he is only expressing beliefs that they already hold (at least implicitly):[18]

> Does someone say that there are gods in heaven?   fr. 286
> No, there are none, unless someone in his
> folly is willing to rely on antiquated reasoning.
> Don't trust my words alone, judge for yourselves:
> A tyranny that kills countless people, confiscates
> their properties, transgresses oaths, and plunders cities,
> is thereby far more prosperous than communities
> that are consistently pious and peaceful.
> I know, similarly, of small cities which honor the gods
> and yet are controlled by larger, ungodly states
> by sheer numerical superiority of weapons.
> I am certain that you would agree: if a sluggard prays
> to the gods and does not labor for his livelihood . . .
>
> . . . .
> [   ] and misfortunes build up religion like a tower.

As Riedweg and others have pointed out, Bellerophontes' somewhat condescending change in tone at line 13 from Realpolitik to a quainter example suggests that his interlocutors (ὑμᾶς) were, in fact, the local peasants of the Aleian plain.[19] The chorus and Glaukos serve as foils in this scene to reveal the full extent of his melancholia and psychic turmoil. Fragments 294, 295, and 297 N[2], with their negative *sententiae* concerning human nature (envy, wickedness, and greed) and technical legal language could well belong to this ongoing discussion between the hero, his son, and the chorus.[20] Bellerophontes and Glaukos exit.[21]

So far, Euripides has limited himself to revealing Bellerophontes' state of mind as a consequence of his well-known misfortunes. Di Gregorio argues that the action of the play only gets underway in the second episode with the arrival of Iobates and Megapenthes, whose respective attitudes to Bellerophontes, however, will turn out to be rather different. Megapenthes, it would appear, accuses Bellerophontes (to the chorus) of his mother's murder and reports the details of an Argive plebiscite that condemned him for this crime.[22] Bellerophontes enters and faces his accuser. "It is a short story," says Stheneboia's son in fr. 68 N[2]; "he killed my mother."[23] Bellerophontes bursts into a rage, at one point apostrophizing the source of all his trouble in fr. 666 N[2]: "O most vile of women! What word of greater reproach for you could one utter than this?" This context seems appropriate also for the death wish of fr. 293 N[2], followed shortly by fr. 296 N[2]:[24]

> Thoughts of prestige exalt you to look with disdain   fr. 293
> on us here before you. I'd rather die then! Life is not worth
> living for one who must see the wicked unjustly honored.

A good man will never hate another good man   fr. 296
while wicked men stick together with pleasure.
Affinity of character is wont to be a person's guide.

Megapenthes is particularly hateful to Bellerophontes, since he has teamed up with Iobates, whose betrayal and abuses are second only to those of Stheneboia. What is more, they believe they are in the process of vindicating their relative by bringing her "murderer" to justice with the support of the Argive council. This distressing perpetuation of Stheneboia's crimes is the event that finally upsets Bellerophontes' precarious melancholic equilibrium and pushes him over the edge. "Thus the plot development," notes Wecklein in this connection, "must have consisted in the intensification of melancholy."[25] Seeing that his efforts to isolate himself from human wickedness have failed, and appalled at the vigor of Stheneboia's vendetta, Bellerophontes begins to ponder his final exploit. As they do not dare lay hands on the hero in the presence of his son and friends, Megapenthes and Iobates exit with a promise to return.

Bellerophontes continues to discuss his situation with the chorus and, perhaps, Glaukos. We detect his slowly maturing decision in the face of a difficult and depressing predicament. The rhetorically parallel frr. 299 and 302 N[2] (juxtaposed by Di Gregorio) appear to come from a context in which someone is attempting to console Bellerophontes: "Everything is weak in the face of necessity (ἀνάγκη)" but "courage has great power in the face of misfortune." Fr. 301 N[2] continues in this vein: "You observe unexpected reversals in the lives of countless men, do you not? Many have escaped the swell of the sea and many excellent men defeated by hostile arms in battle arrive at a better fortune." The episode may have concluded with a choral song in which the lyric meditations on mortality, time, and fate of frr. 303 and 304 N[2] would fit well thematically: the success of the wicked does not last; time has great power to reverse injustice. Bellerophontes is not persuaded, however, and has firmly decided to make his desperate attempt to challenge the gods (if they exist at all!). He exits to be seen again only in flight and, then, in the final tableau in which his broken body is wheeled out on the *ekkuklêma*.

The third episode is devoted to the conspiracy of Iobates and Megapenthes, capped by the physical enactment of Bellerophontes' spectacular flight. In the fragments relating to this episode, Di Gregorio sees the traces of an agon in which Megapenthes disagrees with his grandfather on the issue of how to bring Bellerophontes to justice. Realizing what the hero plans to do, Iobates and Megapenthes debate the execution of Stheneboia's vendetta. Megapenthes, presumably, urges his grandfather to help him kill Bellerophontes as soon as possible, while Iobates counsels restraint. Fr. 291 N[2] is informed by the wisdom of old age: "My son, young men's muscles are indeed flexed for action. The advice of the elderly is better, for time gives the most subtle education of all." The answer to this comes in fr. 289 N[2] where deceit (lit. "theft") is advanced as the only way to get one's way and resolve conflict. This fragment concludes with the sentiment that "the road of truth is ineffectual. War and deception are close friends." In this context Iobates may have spoken the words of fr. 288 N[2]: "deceit and dark machinations have been invented as cowardly remedies [φάρμακα] against need." Frustrated perhaps by losing ground in this rhetorical match, Megapenthes comments that he is far less afraid of a stupid strong man than a "wise" (σοφός) weakling (fr. 290 N[2]).

It seems fairly clear that Iobates prevailed and that Bellerophontes was not attacked immediately, but allowed to act on his decision. The epigram (AP 3.15) mentioned earlier suggests that Iobates' plan involved calculated restraint to see how Bellerophontes' flight to Olympos would turn out. If he were not destroyed by the gods, he would have to return to the Aleian plain where he might be easily ambushed alone. The chorus should probably not know about the intrigue though Glaukos somehow finds out—a feature of the plot necessary for the final "rescue." The agon between Stheneboia's kinsmen is concluded and they exit.

Bellerophontes' penultimate appearance in the play involves his celebrated flight on Pegasos enacted by means of the crane. This must have been a spectacular exit, to judge from the emphasis placed on the moment by Aristophanes in his reenactment. While it is not impossible that Bellerophontes mounted "Pegasos" directly onstage (thus, perhaps in *Peace*), it is more probable, with Webster, to imagine that he does not reappear on stage in the third episode.[26] Rather, having entered the skene (his house) at the end of the preceding episode, he takes off from within his "house," that is, is lifted from the roof to fly across the theatrical space. To this context belong frr. 306, 307, and 308 N^2:[27]

> Come, my dear fleet-winged Pegasus   fr. 306
> Go! Raise your golden-bitted wings!   fr. 307
> Hasten, my soul   fr. 308
>
> . . . .
>
> Let me pass, o shady foliage,
> fly over spring-fed glens;
> I hasten to see the heaven above my head,
> what conditions it offers for a good journey.

It was most certainly a messenger's task to report the punishment of the hero by Zeus, his fall, and how he was ambushed by his enemies and defended by his son. From this speech we may have two fragments, 309 N^2 and 309a Kannicht. The first gives: "[Pegasos] stooping, submitting more, if ever he was more willing"; while the second, from a recently discovered palimpsest, reads: "And to him, from above, the rain-drenched cries . . . ."[28]

The messenger speech was most likely followed by a scene similar to the finale of *Hippolytos* and *Trakhiniai*, with the protagonist revealed in his dying moments, either brought on stage by Glaukos or shown by means of the *ekkyklêma*. His body is broken, but the spectacle of Glaukos' victory has inspired a change of heart: moral order may still be possible on earth and, though they punished him for his hybris, the gods in heaven do have an interest in justice. This sentiment is expressed in fr. 311 N^2, in which Bellerophontes reflects on his life in an address *ad animam suam*:[29]

> You were pious with respect to the gods while you lived.   fr. 311
> You always stood by allies and did not tire helping friends.

Facing his death "heroically and magnanimously" according to Aelianus (NA 5.34),[30] his words suggest resolution: "My misery! But why 'my misery'? We have suffered what mortals must suffer" (fr. 300 N^2). A few fragments look back to recent events, such as fr. 309 N^2 referring to Pegasos' conscientious obedience with regret,[31] and fr. 298 N^2 concerning Megapenthes: "Just as there would be no wounds if weapons were fashioned from marsh reeds, so a base and cowardly mother cannot produce brave and excellent warriors."[32]

The exodos was most likely supervised by a deus ex machina. "The epilogue is narrated by a god," suggests Welcker, "presumably Hermes, who relates the consequences of the crash and the fate of Pegasos."[33] This is probably the story found already in the *Theogony* (285–86) according to which the winged horse was taken up into Olympos to bear for Zeus the instruments of his master's destruction: "alongside the chariot of Zeus he carries the bolts of lightning" (fr. 310 N^2). One of the last lines of the play must have been Hermes' order to Glaukos and his assistants to "Carry the unfortunate man inside!" (fr. 310).[34]

Bellerophon Comicus

As with *Telephos* in *Akharnians* four years earlier, Aristophanes composed his contrafact of a specific tragedy in *Peace* using broad strokes and bold colors. Although Euripides is not a character in this play, he is mentioned repeatedly in connection with the activities of the comic flight in the prologue, and later in the retrieval of the goddess Eirene. Trygaios' daughter, for example, plays the part of the tragic Glaukos in expressing reservations about her father's flight. Aristophanes gives her lines that foreground the metafictional nature of the exploit with emphasis on the "lameness" topos (lines 146–48):[35]

> Watch out for one thing, that you don't slip off and drop
> from up there, and then be lamed and provide
> Euripides with a plot and get turned into a tragedy.

Similarly, Theoria, the silent but "live" personification of Trygaios' achievement, is said to be fragrant with the sweet smell of the Dionysia and the ἐπύλλια of Euripides. This term is usually taken to mean "metrically lighter feet, with frequent resolved feet," but, as J. D. Denniston notes, it can also mean "miniature epic."[36] In other words, Peace, as she is comically represented in the play, smells like a contrafact, a new miniepic *Bellerophontes*! As Rau has illustrated with his customary attention to detail, Euripides is made present to the spectators through conspicuous quotation from his works and more general surface play with tragic diction. The approach to *Bellerophontes* by Pohlenz, Aélion, and others as an autobiographical allegory depicting Euripides "searching fruitlessly for life's meaning" has interesting implications for Aristophanes' contrafact in *Peace*.[37] Mr. Comedy (Trygaios) replaces the tragic protagonist (Bellerophontes-Euripides) to demonstrate the superior power of his genre. In *Peace* as in the other utopian plays considered here, comedy deviously masks its own fictionality in disavowing the tragic imaginary as ineffectual and needing replacement by a "real" and contemporary solution.

The mechanism whereby the last episode of *Bellerophontes* is transformed into the opening sequence of *Peace* involves the catalysis, as it were, of Aisopic *ainos*. As the social, thematic, and narrative antithesis of "high" tragedy, the fable of the eagle and the beetle is precisely the ingredient Aristophanes needs for his ideological transformation of tragic failure into comic salvation:

An eagle once wronged a beetle, either by stealing its young, or by killing a hare which had supplicated the beetle for protection. In revenge, the beetle pursued the eagle wherever it nested, rolling its eggs out and breaking them, until the eagle fled for safety to its divine protector Zeus and was allowed to place its eggs in his lap. Thereupon the beetle flew up to Zeus, and either by buzzing round his head or by laying a ball of dung in his lap made him forget about the eggs and jump up so that they broke.[38]

The discourse of servile trickery and protest, that is, the *ainos*, "fable," as employed by characters of lower social standing,[39] contrasts starkly with the heroic mythos to create a hybrid narrative in which high and low elements coexist in suspension. Thus Hubbard notes that the beetle imagined to feed on Ganymede's "ambrosia" (i.e., excrement; line 724) "illustrates the beauty and the beast theme, the mutual dependence of corporal messiness and aesthetic sublimity within the world of comic drama."[40] As was the case with Dikaiopolis, Trygaios is the active representative of the poet in that he controls the narrative and improvises a new scenario from the old. This function is made clear in many ways. There is the hero's name, which expresses the transformational poetics of comedy, as noted above in connection with the coinage of "trygedy" (τρυγῳδία). Whereas Bellerophontes' name memorializes the beginning of his troubles (the slaying of Belleros) and the resulting tribulations and ultimate disaster, Trygaios is quite literally "Mr. Comedy" with all the transgressive and manipulative power implicit in such a designation. Accordingly, he characterizes his undertaking as "a novel [unprecedented] act of daring" (τόλμημα νέον, line 94) and cites Aisopos as his inspiration, quoting the "text" at lines 133–34 to underscore the connection between this narrative and himself as the new Bellerophontes. He is explicit: "In the fables of Aisopos [the beetle] was the only winged creature found to have reached the gods' realm" (lines 120–30).

From the start of his play, then, Aristophanes provides us with multiple clues for understanding his contrafact. The presentation of Bellerophontes reclad as a rustic commoner is in itself an icon of the transformational poetics at work. On an ideological level, Trygaios represents a member of the common demos who usurps the role of a tragic prince and derails the Euripidean scenario in a demonstration of the carnivalesque energies of comedy. The "underdog" pretense of this protagonist is defined simultaneously with respect to three oppressive and antagonistic parties against whom he directs his poetic and political activities: the archaic upper class that inhabits the bleak and hopeless world of tragedy (as seen from a comic perspective, at any rate), the pro-war faction that had been in control of the Pnyx, and the gods—especially Zeus as the symbolic source of power—whom Trygaios blames for sequestering Peace. Against all these adversaries, Trygaios will prevail, thanks to the egregious success of his vehicle, that is, the beetle who is simultaneously his "little Pegasos" as well as the hero of his secondary narrative who worsts his oppressor (the eagle) and the authority behind the oppression (Zeus). This metaphorical reversal of Bellerophontes' destruction at the hands of the same god informs the contemporary scenario in which Trygaios leads all Greeks oppressed by war to an allegorical victory over War and his accomplices (i.e., perpetrators). Polemos, Kydoimos, Eirene, Opora, and so forth, thus figure in a new utopian myth where novelty, defiance, daring, and salvation by an underdog are key themes.

While Bellerophontes' flight is a desperate metaphysical test of *dikê*, that is, an experiment designed to see if the gods and divine justice exist at all, Trygaios' reenactment is a pragmatic assault on Olympos designed to retrieve a very different and concrete blessing of whose existence and location he is certain. The melancholia of the tragic hero is transformed into a comic madness, a condition on a par with the *nosoi*, "sicknesses," of Peisetairos and Euelpides (*Birds* 31), Philokleon (*Wasps* 71), and other comic protagonists. The emphasis on Trygaios' state of mind and his war with Zeus[41] are prominent aspects of this contrafact as we hear from a slave who, not surprisingly, complains about his master (lines 54–59):[42]

> My master is mad in a new kind of way,
> not the way *you* are, but another way, altogether new.
> All day long he looks up at the heavens
> like this, with his mouth open, and rails against Zeus
> and says, "Zeus, what on earth are you aiming to do?
> Put down your broom; don't sweep Greece away!"

Now this presentation of the comically "melancholic" figure is a clever appropriation of the dynamics of the tragic performance: the protagonist is first described, then heard from within, and finally seen in a climactic entrance. The narrative sequences here, lines 50–61 and 64–81, are a vivid and comic transformation of material that we may assume was featured in the Euripidean opening. Trygaios interrupts the prologue — as Bellerophontes appears to have done — whereupon the slave gives a *paradeigma*, "example," of his madness, which is tellingly characterized as *cholê* (lines 65–66; cf. melancholy). There follows a description of an unsuccessful attempt to climb up to heaven, after which Trygaios is used to reveal the critical project underway. Having harnessed an enormous dung beetle, he identifies his role in the comic contrafact with a conspicuous quotation of *Bellerophontes* fr. 306N[2].

By way of introduction to this exposition, therefore, Aristophanes includes the strikingly reflexive discussion noted above in which the players are made to contemplate the allegorical interpretation of their own performance. There appears to be here the further implication that the literary war on Kleon was widely known and had become a cliché of Aristophanic criticism (lines 43–48):[43]

> SLAVE 2. Well, by now some young man in the audience,
> [who] fancies himself clever, may be saying "What's all this about?
> What has the beetle got to do with?" —
>
> SLAVE 1. Yes, and then an Ionian fellow
> sitting beside him says to him: "My opinion is he's using it to allude
> to Kleon — saying that he's eating muck in Hades."

Aristophanes here appears to be singling out his foreign audience at the City Dionysia, linguistically and intellectually, for a jab on account of their being somewhat slow to appreciate the implications of Kleon's death (both physically and in respect to his importance to the given comedy).[44] It is perhaps with this critical point in mind that Aristophanes included the reprise of *Wasps* 1030–37 later in the parabasis (lines 752–60). With *Peace* it is possible to argue that Aristophanes' work is beginning to depart in many ways from the pattern established in the first five years of his career.[45] Thus the departure from the "Kleon theme," a more subtle metafictional design, and the absence of a dialectical agon are features that *Peace* has in common with *Birds*, the next play in the extant series and the poet's most ambitious utopia on record.

"Quiet, now," says one slave, "I think I hear a voice," as his narrative of Trygaios' melancholia is interrupted by the hero's offstage cry (lines 62–63): "Zeus, what on earth are you trying to do to our people? You'll uproot all the cities before you know what you've done!" This tragic outburst is a pointed appropriation of Bellerophontes' attitude. An interesting way in which Trygaios' madness actually replicates that of his tragic model is in its wrongheadedness: just as Bellerophontes was shown to be excessive in his bitter rejection of divine justice, so Trygaios will learn from Hermes (lines 207–8) that the gods have abandoned Olympos, disgusted with the behavior of the Greeks themselves: "they moved out yesterday . . . angry with the Greeks" (lines 196, 204). This tension between the tragic and comic melancholia culminates in a humorous *aprosdokêton*: Trygaios' passionate rhetoric here and in his confrontation with Hermes leads only to the realization that the gods are not to blame and that the real culprits are back home. What more striking substitution could there be for Bellerophontes' tragic punishment at the hands of Zeus than the glaring absence of the gods, an abandoned Olympos?

In keeping with the spirit of the Aisopic fable, Trygaios shifts gears, as it were, and suddenly redefines his role in a way that resembles the conversion of Peisetairos: the heuristic tone of the prologue, that is, the inquiries involving Tereus and Zeus, evolves into an active campaign in which the hero aggressively avails himself of what he needs (peace, a new city). Although the absent father of gods and men is not available for confrontation, he has left behind an important trace of his authority by installing War on Olympos and sequestering Peace in a deep cavern. This foregrounding of peace as a concrete sign and telos of the hero's quest is also a jarring deconstruction of Euripides' Bellerophontes governed by aporia and epistemological suspension.

The Polemos scene (lines 236–88) is a rare example of comic allegory in which Polemos makes the familiar *myttôtos*-mash in his mortar, with each of the ingredients representing a prominent polis (garlic = Megara, cheese = Sicily, etc.). This sketch is an effective, if minor, instance of the mise en abyme, that is, a farce played by master and slave to an audience of one. Trygaios' lines in this sequence are asides to the theatron with which he identifies as a spectator removed from the action: "What shall we do, unhappy people?" he exclaims at line 263; "You see what great danger we're in!" This dialogue with the audience reaches a climax upon the exit of Polemos and Kudoimos (line 288). The mood of international cooperation is now in the foreground as Trygaios emphasizes the Panhellenic nature of the audience at the City Dionysia (lines 292–95):[46]

> Now, men of Greece, now's a fine chance
> for us to be rid of broils and battles
> and to haul out Peace, so dear to us all,
> before some other pestle can interfere!

The address to the audience is quickly transformed into a summons to the chorus, who make their entrance forthwith: "Come this way, everyone eagerly, straight to our salvation! To the rescue, Panhellenes!" They then address Trygaios as their leader saying, "So you tell us whatever has to be done, and be our *director*."

Anodos and Consequences

The language used here[47] suggests an image of an Eirene literally buried deep in the ground who must be extracted from the earth: μόχλοις καὶ μηχαναῖσιν εἰς τὸ φῶς ἀνελκύσαι τὴν θεῶν πασῶν μεγίστην καὶ φιλαμπελωτάτην, "with levers and contrivance to haul up to the light the greatest and most vine-loving of all goddesses" (lines 307–8). The significance of this situation is revealed in the hauling scene, which has been analyzed as a reworking of the *anodos* of Pandora staged in a Sophoklean satyr-play for which Hesychius gives the alternate titles *Pandora* or *Sphyrokopoi*, "Hammer (*sphyra*)-wielders."[48] There may even be an overt verbal allusion to the source text at line 566 where Trygaios begins his catalog of agricultural implements and fruits with the *sphyra*, a special hammer used to break up the earth: "Certainly, by Zeus, I see that the *sphyra* is a splendid thing when it's ready for action!" Mediating between comedy and the general mythologem of a fertility deity's return from the underworld, this satyr-play may have furnished Aristophanes with an unusual dramatic model from which to improvise his solution. Building on the work of Wictor Steffen,[49] Dana Sutton makes the following compelling suggestion concerning Sophokles' play:[50]

> Several vases show Pandora emerging from the earth in an *anodos*. While no vase in which the emerging female figure can be identified as Pandora features satyrs, these are similar to other vases showing the emergence of a figure better identified as Persephone . . . on which satyrs are shown assisting the *anodos* by breaking up the earth with hammers, picks, and similar implements. If we assume *Pandora* contained an *anodos* of Pandora, this would explain why the satyrs are described as hammer-wielders in the title.

The remains of Sophokles' script are too meager to prove this connection by means of explicit quotation or parody, but as a contrafact of satyr-play, the function of the hauling scene in *Peace* would be greatly enhanced and clarified by such pointed situational connection to the *anodos* motif. Just as Aristophanes had leavened the tragic flight with Aisopos, so now he derails Euripides' tragic conclusion by means of satyr-play, written by a rival tragedian, Sophokles. Bellerophontes' failure and death are thus transformed into a narrative involving a symbolic return from death. The *anodos* of Eirene also has allegorical value, since the work of the Panhellenes (and, eventually, farmers) restores prosperity and fertility to Attica. "The burgeoning prosperity of the countryside," notes Sutton in this connection,[51] "is described in such fantastically exaggerated terms that it is really presented in terms of a miracle attendant on a divine epiphany."

The celebration of fertility and peace in the latter half of the play amplifies the Aisopic motif of success into a pageant of renewal and salvation, *sôtêria*, which now emerges as a leitmotif of the play and of Aristophanic utopia in general. There is always, however, a practical, down-to-earth aspect to these impossible worlds and scenarios of invention and renewal that embrace both theater and political life. Thus,

on the political level, he is careful not to attack the common demos but only prominent demagogues in a gesture that links advice to the polis with efforts to curry favor
with the spectators. In the latter connection (the level of the dramatic competition)
Aristophanes advertises his work in the parabasis as an innovative departure from tired
patterns. Thus he claims to be instrumental in improving his genre by stopping his
rivals from using worn-out gags and stock scenes. He characterizes his renewal of
comedy with language that includes, perhaps, a hint of *Bellerophontes* fr. 286 N^2. In
the latter context it was misfortune that Bellerophontes scornfully identified as the
architect of piety, whereas the parabatic voice here identifies Aristophanes as the
mastermind of comic renovation (lines 748–50):[52]

> Such poor stuff, such rubbish, such ignoble buffoonery, he has removed;
> he has created a great art for us, and built it up to towering dimensions
> with mighty words and ideas and with jokes that are not vulgar.

Within the dramatic fable, of course, it is Trygaios who acts as the architect of renewal (line 305), "Mr. Comedy" who physically brings Peace down to earth and
"unites the Greek poleis in pleasant laughter" (lines 539–40). Trygaios is hailed as
the "savior of the farmer demos" (lines 914 and 919–21) who "saved all Greeks" (line
866). The conjunction of political and theatrical salvation is further emphasized in
the figure of Theoria ("Showtime" in Sommerstein's translation), who is the object
of sustained and aggressive humor in lines 868–908. The erotic thematics of the tragic
model have been reversed: whereas Bellerophontes' troubles were precipitated by
malevolent female eros of which he was the perpetual victim, Trygaios asserts full
"sexual" control over Opora and Theoria, the female personifications of agricultural
and theatrical blessings, going so far as to present the latter to the Prytaneis as a sexual
plaything. The members of the chorus are beside themselves with joy: "Truly any
man who is like this one is good for all citizens . . . You have become a savior of
mankind!" (lines 909–15). While superficially irrelevant to Trygaios' adventure, the
parabasis is central to the play's meaning as it underscores the related activities of
Aristophanes and Trygaios as "saviors" and agents of renewal.

The parabasis is remarkable for its illustration of the complementary distribution of real and imaginary rivalries in Aristophanic comedy. What has been termed
"imaginary rivalry" here is largely the ongoing contest between Aristophanes and
Euripides. It is "imaginary" in two important ways. First, a comic poet could not
formally compete for a prize against a tragic poet, so the agon between Aristophanes
and Euripides can only exist as a dramatic fiction on the order of the "political" rivalry between the comic poet and Kleon. Second, and in keeping with this first point,
Aristophanic comedy exhibits two distinct modes with respect to real and imaginary
rivalries. The latter is conducted in strictly mimetic terms where tragic material and
the tragic poet himself are incorporated into the dramatic fable as part of the fictional scenario. The contrafact, as we have seen, is an important comic mechanism for engaging Euripides and his work. Through this and other mimetic strategies Aristophanes can effectively imitate and criticize tragedy simultaneously (Plays
such as *Peace* and *Frogs* are arguably far more admiring of Euripides than they are
critical). Actual rivalry, on the other hand, is something about which Aristophanes
was deadly serious and, for this reason, it is relegated to the nonmimetic discourse of

the parabasis and parabasislike interludes of the sort discussed in *Akharnians* above. At no point does Aristophanes appear ready to pay a rival comic poet such as Eupolis (*pace* Sidwell) or Phrynikhos explicit mimetic tribute of the sort lavished on Euripides. Accordingly, *Peace* articulates its theme of renewal and *sôtêria* in distinctly different ways with regard to the two genres. In the mimetic sphere, we see Trygaios reenact Euripides to become the *sôtêr* of Athens. In the nonmimetic sphere of the parabasis, it is Aristophanes himself who rescues comedy from the "damage" of his inferior rivals.

Aristophanes' conjunction of dramatic models also sheds light on the problem of the chorus, which in *Peace* shifts its identity from Panhellenes (articulated socially), to Athenians, to Panhellenes again (articulated politically), to peasants, and finally, to specifically Attic peasants.[53] In this mutable identity—which is not unusual for Aristophanes—we discern the traces of the composition process. The "supportive farmer" element is a direct reflection of Euripides' *Bellerophontes* and does much to explain the unusual concord between the chorus and protagonist in this play. The unique absence from *Peace* of an agon, either formal or thematic, is no doubt explained in part by this alliance.[54] With regards to the *anodos* theme, moreover, specifically *Athenian* farmers—as allies of the protagonist—are a necessary and appropriate substitution for Sophokles' satyr chorus:[55] Trygaios is one of their class and together they stand to benefit most from the retrieval of the "fertility goddess." The Panhellenic element is Aristophanes' innovation, a grand utopian feature superimposed, albeit imperfectly, on the underlying stratum of borrowed tragic and satyric themes. The presumed unity of the satyr chorus striving to haul up Pandora is redefined in light of their new comic task. Inasmuch as the chorus of *Peace* is made to cooperate in retrieving Peace, their very identity "expands" to embrace the consequences of this activity, that is, they represent all Greeks united in cooperative pursuit of peace.

It should be no surprise, then, that in the scenes featuring unity and cooperation (parodos, hauling scene) the Panhellenic aspect is thrust to the fore while after the hauling scene the "peasant" substratum resurfaces. Bellerophontes, we remember, fell back to earth to die among his comrades, a tragic conclusion that is reversed as the facilitators of the anodos (Panhellenes) are reduced to the group that most deserves to enjoy its consequences (Greek farmers). Upon Trygaios' return to Athens, their identity naturally narrows to specifically *Athenian* farmers. Aristophanes is not yet ready to depart from his tradition of exploring the consequences of his protagonist's success in a narrowly Athenian context. Thus *Peace*, like the plays before it, focuses on Trygaios as an Athenian by means of the expected local intruders and topical humor. Here the Panhellenic aspect of the play is overshadowed by the specifically Athenian success of Trygaios, which emerges as a curious negative of empire and military superiority: Athens is, in fact, "victorious" over Sparta as "leader" of the Greek states—in promoting peace!

The Athenocentric consequences of the comic *anodos* have been capably discussed by Bowie in connection with various festivals of the polis, particularly the Anthesteria.[56] By means of the *anodos* theme and festival allusions, Athens is simultaneously criticized for its conduct in the war and represented as the locus of peace.[57] There is, furthermore, an important connection between the antiquity of the Anthesteria—a festival that enjoyed Panhellenic status—and the Panhellenic theme of this comedy in which the Greek states cooperate in the ritual return of Peace. In this light, Athens' status as chief city of the Ionians cooperates with the Panhellenic theme to lend plausibility to Aristophanes' utopian conception.

The contrafacts of Euripides' *Telephos* (chapter 3), *Peirithous* (chapter 8), and Sophokles' *Tereus* (chapter 7) reveal the extent to which Aristophanes studied tragic transformations and interpretations of myth, especially in the ideological sphere, broadly construed. Just as he deconstructs the barbarian thematics of *Tereus* to build the utopian polis of *Birds*, so in *Peace* Euripides' intense preoccupation with solitude and melancholic "atheism" in *Bellerophontes* is chosen to support the comic myth of Panhellenic cooperation in the establishment of what is effectively an innovative cult of Eirêne.[58] Tragedy, as comedy's source text, is used repeatedly as a powerful metaphor for comedy's great problem, that is, initial conditions that comic poiesis has the power to change. Thus the tragic Bellerophontes suffers in his self-imposed isolation and exile while Trygaios excels as the motivator and leader of a community. The tragic hero's alienation from his homeland culminates in his denial of the gods and his punishment for this mistake. Trygaios' experiment, his reenactment of Bellerophontes' quest, proves, quite to the contrary, that the gods *are* in fact gone and that responsibility for *sôtêria* is his alone. As we have come to expect, Aristophanes makes his point by establishing a network of agonistic relations between dramatic genres, between the demos and its hawkish leaders, between gods and men, between war and peace. The clever play with these reversals and the Panhellenic implications of *anodos* myth and ritual suggest a comic redefinition of power whereby the ability to transform myth and history in the pursuit of peace emerges as a demonstration of power far superior to the episodic and ephemeral success in war. The most impressive empire of all, in other words, is a Panhellenic empire of peace, "ruled" by Athens who alone, through the agency of her leading comic poet (and his rustic "representative"), has the resources to secure it.

The sustained metafictional experiment formally concludes with Trygaios' return (line 819) at which he comically notes that he is a "bit sore in the legs." Beyond this final reversal of Bellerophontes' fall it is interesting to speculate that Aristophanes may have exploited the parallelism between the violent intrusion of Megapenthes and Iobates in the final episode of *Bellerophontes* and the colorful, if typical, interlopers such as Hierocles and the Arms-dealer. In any event, the celebration of fertility and a productive life in the scenes after the parabasis is the most striking transformation of Euripides' tragic conclusion, made especially absurd as Trygaios' "steed" wanders off to "graze" on Olympos, leaving his master to *walk* home! Lest we forget his source, however, Aristophanes marks this turning point in his comedy with a final and explicit allusion to *Bellerophontes* (lines 720–22, incorporating fr. 312 N[2]):[59]

TRYGAIOS. O beetle, homeward, homeward let us fly!   fr. 312
HERMES. It's not here, my dear fellow.
TRYGAIOS. Why, where's it gone?
HERMES. "Yoked to the car of Zeus, it bears the lightning."

7

Tereus

Sophokles' Tereus *and*
Aristophanes' Birds

This chapter follows a sustained conversation between genres that begins in the 430s with Sophokles' *Tereus*, a performance anticipating *Bakkhai* in its use of disguise and the forms of Dionysiac cult. Following a review of the evidence for *Tereus* and possible reconstructions of the fragmentary script, the connection between it and Aristophanes' *Birds* is explored. The latter is presented as an extended contrafact of Sophokles' play, a comic extravaganza that marks its relation to *Tereus* in a series of specific transformations of character and situation. As was the case with the contrafact of *Telephos* outlined above in chapter 3, Aristophanes plays fast and loose with a number of specific tragic innovations to rival the genre on an ideological level, to offer an alternative to the tragic vision. Whereas Sophokles had mapped the crisis of Prokne and Philomela onto a newly constructed grid of oppositions between Greek (specifically *Athenian*) and barbarian, *Birds* offers escape from Athens into a utopian polis negotiated by Tereus, an ambassador from the tragic stage whose role is to catalyze a new comic fiction. By offering a contemporary solution—μηχανὴ σωτηρίας—in a scenario improvised freely from the linguistic, theatrical and social materials to hand, Aristophanes flaunts his mastery over language and tragedy in a competitive display of his genre's prominence as a mode of entertainment and persuasion.

In 412, two years after the production of *Birds*, Euripides, no doubt impressed by the bold metatheatrics of Aristophanes' play, responded with his flamboyant and innovative *Helene*, which celebrates its revisionist program in the heroine's minidrama of escape, that is, the fictive funeral staged by Helene and Menelaos in Egypt. Rare but incontrovertible evidence that tragedy could indeed "talk back" emerges from the way that this mise en abyme is initiated by a pointed quotation from *Birds*. This intertextual moment underscores comedy's involvement with tragedy as well the self-conscious eclecticism of Euripidean theater. The final word in this dialogue is heard a year later in *Thesmophoriazousai*, a metafictional tour de force in which Aristophanes engages Euripides at every turn, even bringing the tragedian on stage once again as a character. The relevant portion of *Helene*—a hilarious reenactment of the Euripidean inset—is featured prominently in Aristophanes' montage of escape scenes in a demonstration of how comedy can read and (re)write tragic metafiction.

Tereus: A Tragic Ambassador to Comedy

Aristophanes' hybrid bird-man is a remarkable character whose dramatic function as a self-professed refugee from the tragic stage and a mediator continues to engage students of the play.[1] Much work on *Birds* implicitly addresses the questions "Why has Aristophanes chosen Tereus as his intermediary between men and birds?" and "What connection might exist between the legends of Tereus, their literary treatments, and the design of *Birds*?"[2] Though a Thracian,[3] Tereus in the comedy speaks a colloquial Attic as well as an exalted, mock-tragic Greek. He is at times pathetic, at times genial, and always funny. Furthermore, he lives in perfect harmony with Prokne (who in *Birds* has no speaking part) and behaves in a manner that would have been comically familiar to spectators at the City Dionysia. Virtually all distinctive features of the violent legend—the rape and imprisonment of Philomela, the glossectomy, the sacrifice of Itys, and the Dionysian cult-context of the Athenian sisters' revenge—are banished from the comic stage. Finally, and what seems most significant, Aristophanes has made Tereus a benevolent bridge between the Athenians and the comic beyond, between the "here" of the polis and theater and an avian "nowhere" in which Peisetairos invents Nephelokokkygia. Tereus' primary function, in fact, is to have taught and disseminated language among "barbarians" in order to prepare a theatrical and linguistic context for Peisetairos' creative activities. Thus, beyond his transformation from man into bird, Tereus undergoes further and extensive metamorphosis from a tragic character into a comic character at the hands of Aristophanes. This contrafact is not a routine burlesque of traditional material. Through his comic Tereus Aristophanes presents a commentary on Sophoklean innovation (in *Tereus*, ca. 440), in a way that furnishes the complex thematic foundation of *Birds*.

At once innovative and familiar, the contrafact of *Tereus* in *Birds* is a striking example of how Aristophanes uses tragic forms to express comic ideas: by transplanting Tereus from the context that Sophokles had charged with a strong Atheno-barbarian tension, and by subjecting him to a comic transformation, Aristophanes engages the "boundless optimism" that we must suppose was the governing mood in the demos during the spring of 414.[4] At the same time, the character's tragic provenance and the surprising results of his catalytic role in *Birds* have ominous overtones, a dark lining, as it were, that continues to attract attention.[5] Nephelokokkygia is thus located between a present world in which the tragic past may be forgotten and a future world in which past terrors must be reinscribed. This contrafact of tragedy—that is, the programmatic usurpation, assimilation, and transformation of genre, history, myth, and texts—is a particularly sophisticated and aggressive example of the Aristophanic poetics of transformation at work.

Since the early nineteenth century[6] scholars have puzzled over Peisetairos' statement of purpose (especially lines 39–48), which, unlike similar passages in earlier plays (*Knights* 36–72, *Wasps* 54–73), seems to have little explicit relevance to the subsequent action:[7]

That's the thing: the cicadas chirp on the branches
for a month or two, the Athenians chirp away
at lawsuits continually all their lives long.
That's why we're trekking this trek;
with a basket, a pot and some myrtle-wreaths,
we're wandering in search of a trouble-free place,
where we can settle and pass our lives.
Our journey now is to see Tereus the hoopoe,
wanting to find out from him if he's seen
a city of that kind anywhere he's flown over.

The apparent irrelevance of these opening claims along with the general in-determinacy of the Athenians' quest suggests that the design of *Birds* departs from the linear sequence (problem/conflict—*sotêria*—consequences) characteristic of the *engagé* comedies produced in the 420s, that is, before the seven-year hiatus in the extant corpus. Furthermore, as one critic puts it, "*Birds* differs from all the other fifth-century plays of Aristophanes that survive in having no strong and obvious connec-tion with a topical question of public interest, whether political . . . , literary-theatrical . . . , or intellectual-educational . . . ."[8] The prologue, however, in its references to *Tereus* (lines 15 and 46) along with the ensuing dialogue (lines 92–208), far from being irrelevant, points to a neglected and central motive developed through the parabasis and fully realized in Nephelokokkygia (the epeisodia). The themes and situations of a poignant political tragedy are refashioned into a comic polity by means of the contrafact process. Peisetairos combines the rhetorical prowess of a sophist with the comic playwright's creativity as he supervises the many entrances and exits of characters from his polis-as-comedy named Trap (νεφέλη) for Chattering Fools (κόκκυγες). Nephelokokkygia thus unfolds as a play written and directed by the protagonist![9] The process by which a drama derives much of its meaning from its context within the culture of the polis appears reversed: Aristophanes builds an in-substantial city "made of drama" subject to the rules of performance for which the transformed tragic model serves as a living blueprint. *Birds* is indeed "the artistic culmination of Aristophanes' earlier technique"[10] in its unusually balanced synthe-sis of political, literary-theatrical, and intellectual themes.

Flight from Tragic Abuse to Comic Mockery

Entering the theatrical space holding a jackdaw and a crow, respectively, Peisetairos and Euelpides announce that they have been sent on their journey by a certain (other-wise unknown) trader (lines 13–16):[11]

that man from the bird market,
that loony tray-vendor Philokrates, who told us
that these two birds would show us where to find Tereus,
the hoopoe, who was turned <   > into a bird.[12]

After wandering aimlessly about the orchestra for some time, the men finally stumble upon Tereus' dwelling where they confront a slave who has followed his master through metamorphosis. The slave-bird's costume and apologetic description of Tereus' behavior (especially the curious mixture of avian and Athenian diets) prepare the spectators for the hoopoe's bombastic entrance at line 92: ἄνοιγε τὴν ὕλην ἵν' ἐξέλθω ποτέ, "throw wide the wood, that I might enter at last." This mock-tragic stage direction (cf. the "open sesame" pun ὕλην~πύλην), along with other exotic elements deriving from the near-eastern lore of the hoopoe,[13] is emblematic of the uniqueness and comic strangeness of Aristophanes' Tereus. The unexpected appearance, speech, and behavior of the bird-man elicit laughter from his visitors: "You look as though the Twelve Gods had blasted you!" jeers Euelpides. Tereus responds defensively (lines 96–102):[14]

TEREUS. You're not making fun of me, are you,
just because you see this plumage? I was once a man, you know,
gentlemen.

PEISETAIROS. It's not you we're laughing at.

TEREUS. What is it, then?

PEISETAIROS.   It's your beak we think looks funny.

TEREUS. This is the injury Sophocles inflicts on me,
Tereus, in his tragedy.

PEISETAIROS. You're Tereus, are you? Are you a bird or a peacock?

From this exchange it emerges that Aristophanes' Tereus claims the Sophoklean stage as his place of origin. "The Hoopoe of Aristophanes' play is a literary bird," notes Drew Griffith. "He makes it explicit that he is not merely the Tereus familiar from the broad field of myth but, much more precisely, he is *the very same character* that Sophocles staged."[15] This connection is clarified by the entrance of a character whom Theodore Kock calls "der zweite Tereus-Wiedehopf"—the third of the much-discussed "four dancers of the parodos (lines 268–93)."[16] His appearance at line 279 surprises Euelpides, who thought Tereus to be the only representative of the species (lines 280–86):[17]

EUELPIDES. What extraordinary sight is this? So you're not the only hoopoe—there's also this other one?

TEREUS.   He's the son of Philokles' hoopoe [or: "Philokles the hoopoe"] and I'm his grandfather—just as you might say "Hipponikos was the son of Kallias and Kallias [Jr.] the son of Hipponikos."

EUELPIDES. So this bird is Kallias. What a lot of feathers he's lost!

TEREUS. Yes; being a pedigree bird, he gets plucked by prosecutors, and in addition to that the females pull out his feathers.

This oblique joke seeks to express the relationship between the two hoopoes in terms of the Athenian custom of alternating male names for successive generations. A grandfather-father-son sequence in one branch of the Kêrykes family is correlated with a comically contrived hoopoe-succession:[18]

Kallias (PA 7825)	Tereus: deuteragonist of Sophokles' *Tereus*
Hipponikos (PA 7658)	Philokles, i.e., the hoopoe in his tetralogy *Pandionis* or Philokles himself (satirized as *aiskhros*, "ugly")

Kallias Jr. (*PA* 7826)   Tereus: the second hoopoe, i.e., the third of
four dancers in *Birds* 279–84.

Thus the first hoopoe of *Birds* is Sophokles' Tereus, and he is the "grandfather" of the dancer (i.e., hoopoe no. 2 of *Birds*). The intervening "generation" is represented by a hoopoe associated with Philokles, the minor tragedian lampooned elsewhere by the comic poets.[19] This sets up a multilevel joke in which Aristophanes simultaneously mocks (1) Philokles' work (the tetralogy *Pandionis*) as derivative of Sophokles; (2) Philokles' appearance: his pointed head suggests the crest of a hoopoe or lark (cf. line 1295); (3) the profligate lifestyle of Kallias Jr.; and, finally, (4) his own work in that the dancer, who is properly Aristophanes' hoopoe, corresponds to the degenerate younger Kallias, a popular target of comic ridicule (cf. Eupolis' *Kolakes*, ca. 421). Ludwig Koenen improves the text by placing line 287 before 280 to make the phrase βαπτὸς ὄρνις, "dipped/gaudy bird," apply to the second hoopoe, thus restoring another aspect of the joke: the connection between the profligate Kallias-bird and his brother-in-law Alkibiades, who was himself lampooned a year earlier by Eupolis in *Baptai*, a comedy featuring a chorus of female votaries of the Thracian Kottyto.[20]

Although the hoopoe whom Peisetairos and Euelpides first encounter is, therefore, Sophokles' Tereus, he speaks as a refugee from the tragic stage and complains of ill-treatment by the tragedian: λυμαίνεται ἐν ταῖς τραγῳδίαισιν ἐμὲ τὸν Τηρέα, "This is the injury Sophokles inflicts on me, Tereus, in his tragedy." It is most natural to conclude from this response that Aristophanes is here satirizing the Sophoklean *costume* of the transformed Tereus. "In his *Tereus*," notes the scholiast, "Sophokles enacted the metamorphosis of Tereus and Prokne into birds, which inspired the extensive play with *Tereus* [in *Birds*]."[21] While one may wonder about the extent of this "enactment," it is clear that the results of the transformation were somehow emphasized on the tragic stage. First of all, these words, along with the attribution of his sparse plumage to the "winter moulting of all birds," (lines 105–6) are meant as an apology for Tereus' appearance. Secondly, the imperfective aspect of λυμαίνεσθαι, primarily a verb of physical outrage[22] used to account for the funny beak, suggests that the innovation involved visible and permanent changes. Thus it is interesting that Tereus' entrance in *Birds* is immediately marked by an association with Sophokles' tragedy and, more specifically, Sophoklean invention in the form of an unusually pathetic spectacle. From a comic perspective, the tragic pathos is characterized as λυμαίνεσθαι and elicits laughter at Tereus' beak and plumage in anticipation of later jokes about the second hoopoe plucked bare by sycophants and rapacious women. This particular translation from tragic pathos (viewed as λύμαι, "maltreatment") into comic σκώμματα, "jesting," may be regarded as programmatic of Aristophanes' technique in *Birds* with respect to *Tereus* (as well as other literary targets such as the *Prometheia*) and leads us to examine in greater detail the model on which the contrafact is based. A review of *Tereus* is also necessary at this point since neither the fragments of Sophokles' play nor the various attempts at reconstruction have figured prominently in the literature on *Birds*. If Aristophanes' Tereus is indeed a literary bird, his dramatic origins deserve careful consideration.

Tereus Tragicus: The Neglected Source

Tereus, of which fifty-seven or so lines survive, is one of the better-attested lost tragedies of Sophokles. In the century and a half since Welcker's fundamental work,[23] as
much as may be reasonably expected in the way of reconstruction and thematic
analysis has been done.[24] The only new light to be shed on the subject in recent years
has been the publication of P.Oxy. 42.3013, which may derive from the controversial
Tales (hypotheses) of Dikaiarkhos. The point of surveying the evidence for the lost
play is to assess the element of Sophoklean innovation, that is, both the extensive
primary reshaping of the traditional material ("the myth") as well as certain unusual
and striking features of the performance. In re-presenting Tereus Aristophanes is
responding precisely to these aspects of the tragic model.

The papyrus hypothesis is remarkably similar to the several other summaries of
the Sophoklean Tereus story.[25] The lost play can be said to have involved (in narrative or action) at least the following events and situations:[26]

1. arrival of Tereus and Philomela from Athens
2. revelation of Tereus' crime by the "voice of the shuttle"
3. Prokne's reaction
4. the slaughter of Itys
5. Tereus' meal
6. flights of Prokne and Philomela
7. metamorphosis of Tereus, Prokne, and Philomela into birds

Pre-Sophoklean and contemporary primary testimonia are few.[27] Of the many
later passages attesting various versions of the legend ("Theban," "Megaro-Athenian,"
"Asiatic," etc.), the most useful and most likely to reflect knowledge of Sophokles'
play are the nine fragments of Accius' *Tereus* and the well-known passage in the sixth
book of Ovid's *Metamorphoses.*[28] There can be little doubt that here, as in many other
instances, a famous tragedy was an influential model for the Roman poet.[29] Besides
ordering and assigning the fragments, the main points of contention in reconstruct-
ing the play have been (1) the identity and role of the chorus; (2) the distribution of
the elements 1–7 above among actors' scenes (epeisodia); (3) the extent of the
Dionysian theme (e.g., in the choral odes); (4) the nature of the final divine epiphany;
and (5) the character and role of Tereus, especially in connection with the question
of the Dryas episode.

A conservative review of the dramatis personae and their distribution would include: Prokne (played by protagonist), Tereus and Hermes (deuteragonist), Nurse,
Servant, Messenger (tritagonist), Philomela, Itys (silent characters), and a chorus of
Thracian men, most likely Tereus' attendants.[30] Controversial in this list are the identities of the god and the chorus. In light of the reassignment of the "Aiskhylean" fragment, preserved by Aristotle, to Sophokles (fr. 581 Radt, see later discussion), it seems
reasonable to assume that the *rhêsis* relating the metamorphosis of Tereus, Prokne,
and Philomela is spoken by a messenger-god, not the pro-Thracian Ares.[31] The action takes place before the palace of Tereus in Thrace; a major feature of Sophokles'
design was to associate Tereus with historical Thrace (e.g., Haimos, Rhodope) rather

than the "prehistoric" Thracian-occupied Phokis (Daulis), and to place him and Prokne at a considerable remove from Athens. The play is set on a day of the triennial Thracian feast in honor of Dionysos, when local custom may have specified a sacrifice followed by a private royal meal (Ovid, *Met.* 6.647–49 has Prokne invent this feature). Sophokles innovatively exploited the festival context to mitigate the horror of the events and to provide the women an opportunity for revenge.[32] In the absence of explicit structural data, the design of the play is best regarded as involving four sequences of actors' scenes typically articulated by choral songs (parodos, stasima, and exodos-lyrics).[33] The similarity in language and technique between *Trakhiniai* and *Tereus* suggests that the latter "had the diptych form. The first part dealt with the loneliness of Prokne . . . and the return of Tereus. . . . The second part dealt with the vengeance taken by Prokne and the transformations."[34]

The most important issues relating the plot with actors' scenes are (1) whether Tereus' return from Athens is narrated as a past event or incorporated into the action of the play and (2) whether the Dryas episode related by Hyginus (*Fab.* 45) constituted part of Sophokles' design. The time that elapses between Tereus' return and the final crisis (a year in Ovid, *Met.* 6.571) would seem to preclude both events' being incorporated directly into the action.[35] In the absence of evidence to the contrary, the most we should assume is that the first part of the play developed the theme of how Prokne's long-standing despair and isolation in Thrace had been renewed and deepened by Philomela's relatively recent "death." An account of the expedition to Athens and its tragic conclusion fits quite naturally in the context of Prokne's famous lament (fr. 583 Radt), which most likely belongs to an expository prologue.

Hyginus relates a version of the myth in which Tereus, warned by portents of Itys' imminent murder *a propinqua manu*, kills his brother, Dryas, in a misguided attempt to save the boy.[36] Including this episode in a reconstruction, it has been argued, would both "humanize" Tereus and justify the traditional title.[37] The absence of Dryas from all major sources, however, is a strong indication that he did not figure in Sophokles' play. Consequently, of the plot features listed above, items 4 and 5 are reported by a messenger (or a similar character) while the metamorphosis receives somewhat special treatment in a divine epiphany and *rhêsis*. It is also possible that Sophokles marked the symbolic death of Tereus, Prokne, and Philomela visually on the *ekkyklêma* in a tableau involving subtle tokens of the metamorphosis. The arrival of Tereus from Athens and the report of Philomela's "death," on the other hand, must be recounted in the prologue by Prokne as an event of the recent past.

The best-known fragment of *Tereus* (583 Radt), which in all likelihood inspired Medeia's lament (*Medeia* 230–51), suggests that the play opens with an expository monologue in which Prokne bewails her misfortunes, perhaps in the presence of a trustworthy character (nurse?):[38]

But now, separated from home, I am undone. Often indeed,   fr. 583
have I observed how miserable my sex is in this respect.
When we are girls, our life in our father's house
is the sweetest, I think, that can fall to mortals;
for the days of thoughtless childhood are ever glad.
But when we come to years of discretion,

we are thrust out and sold in marriage
far away from our ancestral gods and from our parents:
some of us to other parts of Hellas, some to barbarians,
some to joyless households, some into places of reproach.
And in this, when once the nuptial night is past,
we must acquiesce, and deem that it is well   (tr. Jebb, adapted)

Noteworthy here is the correlation of the general helplessness and isolation of women "sold in marriage" (cf. *ekdôsis*) with the misery of an Athenian princess among barbarians. Her recollection of life at home in Pandion's palace is sharply offset by the phrase νῦν δ', which introduces the present lament: "*now, however,* among Thracians and far from Athens [χωρίς], I am nothing!" The *anoia* of a carefree childhood anticipates the phrase spoken by the god after the final crisis (fr. 589 Radt): ἄνους ἐκεῖνος· αἱ δ' ἀνουστέρως ἔτι ἐκεῖνον ἠμύναντο, "[Tereus] is a fool, but [Prokne and Philomela] exhibited even greater folly in punishing him." Accius echoes these words (fr. 639–42 Warmington) in characterizing Tereus as a savage *amore vecors flammeo*, "mad with burning desire," who committed a heinous crime *ex dementia* (cf. Ovid, *Met.* 6.456–60). Sophokles thus makes a full circle of the Homeric phrase in which the "Daughter of Pandareos, the greenwood nightingale," is said to have killed her son Itylos δι' ἀφραδίας (*Od.* 19.518–23): the Athenian women are forced to pass from the blissful folly of childhood to the madness of revenge in which they assimilate to Tereus' senseless barbarism. To this context also belongs fr. 584 Radt, in which Prokne says she envies the woman "who has not experienced a foreign land."[39]

The entrance of the chorus, consisting of Thracian men, would do little to comfort the grieving queen. "Their constant presence on the stage," suggests Akiko Kiso, "helps to emphasize the loneliness of Prokne."[40] There follows a scene involving dialogue between Prokne and Tereus in which the latter offers words of consolation (fr. 585 Radt):[41]

Clearly, [your loss / this situation] is painful. Yet,   fr. 585
as mortals, we must graciously accept what the gods send.

By encouraging Prokne to accept her sister's "death" Tereus clearly hopes to discourage any further inquiries into his recent journey and crimes. His efforts are thwarted, however, in a subsequent episode when an embroidered *peplos* is brought to Prokne — a gift that at least one source identifies as traditionally offered to the queen on the occasion of the Dionysian festival.[42]

It is clear that a closely following scene involved the delivery of Philomela's *textum* and the subsequent recognition. Placing the journey to Athens and Philomela's "death" in the recent past avoids an awkward lapse of dramatic time in order to bring the action to its dénouement. Prokne, moreover, is not required to pass abruptly from the initial shock of grief to controlled deception as she receives the gift and reads her sister's message. The courier—most likely one of Philomela's attendants (a man: fr. 588 Radt)—is ignorant of the real purpose of his assignment, as are the other Thracian slaves and retainers of Tereus. The passage in the sixteenth chapter of *Poetics* referring to this moment in Sophokles' *Tereus* is reinforced by other evidence in making clear that Philomela's weaving involved a *written* message, a feature invented by Sophokles for his dramatic purposes—in Aristotle's words, a recognition strategy πεποιημένον ὑπὸ τοῦ ποιητοῦ, "invented by the poet."[43] It seems quite clear that the glossectomy was an auxiliary feature introduced to set up the recognition by means of a written message. The language of Tzetzes' "hypothesis" (Radt, *TGF* 435)— τὴν αὐτῆς γλῶτταν θερίζει, "he shears her tongue"—is a distinctly tragic and is most likely a quotation from the play relating to this moment.

Shaken by what she has read, Prokne carefully solicits details of Philomela's whereabouts from the servant who brought the *peplos*, encouraging him to tell the truth (fr. 588 Radt). Ovid's account (*Met.* 6.583–86), as well as several fragments of Accius' play, points to this moment of outrage checked by great self-control: "you practice, woman, the way of many wives," say the chorus disapprovingly, "in that you strain your might against your husband's dignity" (fr. 643–44 Warmington). A painting by the Dolon Painter on a Lucanian bell-krater (see note 55) suggests that Tereus was present at least during the delivery of the *peplos*. Prokne is forced to conceal her grief and must plot silently (fr. 645–55 Warmington) to take advantage of the festival occasion. Once she leaves the palace, she gives free rein to her rage (Ovid, *Met.* 6.594–96):[44]

> Surrounded by her (female) attendants
> Prokne rushes through the forest
> frightful in her frenzied rage of pain,
> *feigning* your fury, Bakkhos.

Our evidence strongly suggests that this Dionysiac element, like "the voice of the shuttle," is yet another feature "invented by the poet" to serve a specific and complex dramatic purpose. Sophokles has Prokne and Philomela use the revelry, maenad dress, and ritual as a versatile disguise for the several stages of their reunion and vengeance— a point in *Tereus* that seems to anticipate (perhaps even serving as the model for) the metatheatrical strategies of Euripides' *Bakkhai* discussed in chapter 5.[45] Being a deity associated with delusion and disguise, Dionysos is a natural choice to preside over the Athenian sisters' grim theater of revenge. Prokne is made strange by the Bacchic transformation, which thus serves to prepare the spectators for the final, violent episode. It is tempting to view Pentheus' paranoia from the Athenian spectators' perspective: the travesty of ritual in *Tereus* would certainly have made it possible to sympathize with his fear of a wicked masquerade on Kithairon involving "bogus bacchanals" (πλασταῖσι βακχείαισιν, line 218) and "bastard maenads" (μαινάδων νόθων, line 1060). Long before *Bakkhai*, however, this combination of sacrificial irony and play with disguise inspired Euripides to draw upon Sophokles' Prokne for his Medeia.[46]

Although the Thracian and Dionysiac elements are complementary innovations on the part of the poet, "it is precisely in this play where the action swirls along the edge of sobriety that Bacchism is to be brought in, and not merely as a dramatic expedient."[47] Prokne leaves the palace to fetch her sister "in great haste, dressed in a maenad's attire" (fr. 586 Radt). The exhortation to address a prayer to Dionysos belongs here as well: *deum Cadmogena natum Semela adfare et famulanter pete*, "entreat in servile fashion the god, son of Kadmos' daughter Semele" (fr. 647 Warmington). There follows another choral song for which Calder suggests "a Dionysiac theme."[48]

That such a theme was present in one or more of the odes is clear from a choral fragment (591 Radt) which Friedrich Welcker, Richard Jebb, and others have recognized as reflecting a basic principle of Dionysiac cult:[49]

> The human race is one; a single day brought forth all   fr. 591
> of us from our father [Ouranos] and mother [Gaia].
> No one is born more exalted than another.
> Yet some of us are fed the doom of evil days,
> others are nourished by prosperity, while others still
> are caught in the ineluctable yoke of slavery.

The glancing cosmogonic reference here may also point to an Orphic theme naturally suggested by the Thracian setting. This may be the sole trace of the dramatic source of Aristophanes' famous parody of Orphic cosmogony in the parabasis of *Birds*. The themes of titanomachy and, by assimilation, gigantomachy are also suggested and may be relevant to the revolt against the gods in the latter half of the comedy.[50] This song of a Thracian chorus celebrating the equality of all men on the occasion of the Dionysian Trieterika, moreover, is unmistakably ironic as it marks the dramatic time during which the two high-bred Athenian women plot their unspeakable crime. The willful assimilation of the Athenian princesses to the "barbarism" of their surroundings is thus rendered all the more horrific. The natural savagery and senseless violence (cf. ἄνους, fr. 589 Radt) of Sophokles' *Tereus* is echoed by Accius (fr. 639–42 Warmington):[51]

> Tereus, a man of ways untamable   fr. 639–42
> and savage heart, did turn his gaze upon her;
> senseless with flaming love, a man laid low.
> the foulest deed he fashioned from his madness.   (tr. Warmington)

Prokne's and Philomela's revenge, on the other hand, elicits the severe judgment of fr. 589 (Radt) cited above. An impetuous erotomaniac, Tereus is "senseless," to be sure, but the slaughter of Itys and macabre feast are acts of vengeance and, as such, are even more senseless and inexcusable. The other choral fragments (592 and 593 Radt: nine verses in all), though metrically interesting,[52] are harder to place since their commentary on the dangers of presumption and the mutability of human fortune does not mention specific people or events and can be applied only to the final crisis of the play. It is worthwhile noting, however, that the chorus is not blindly loyal to Tereus and, as we would expect, comments on the events with some degree of detachment.

In the following scene, Prokne returns with her sister disguised as a maenad and relates Tereus' crimes to the chorus (fr. 648–49 and 639–42 Warmington).[53] *Non est lacrimis hoc agendum*, Ovid has Prokne exhort her sister *sed ferro, sed siquid habes, quod vincere ferrum possit!* "Now is not the time for tears but for the sword; for something indeed, if you have it, even more powerful than the sword!" (*Met.* 6.611–13). As the women plan their revenge, Itys appears, suggesting himself quite naturally as their victim. At this point, someone (a nurse?) contemplates rescuing the boy from the queen in such a way as to elude Tereus at the same time (fr. 652–53 Warmington). The sacrifice and cooking take place during the following choral song (third stasimon), which, if Welcker is correct, was a poignant lament for Itys.

The fourth episode involved an attempt on the part of the chorus to dissuade Prokne from carrying out the final act of her revenge. Her answer may have been the hybristic exclamation of scorn: *Alia hic sanctitudo est, aliud nomen et numen Iovis*, "Here holiness is different, different here the name and nod of Jupiter" (fr. 650 Warmington). Realizing that their words have had no effect, the chorus observe: *Struunt sorores Atticae dirum nefas*, "The Athenian sisters are plotting dire wickedness" (fr. 651 Warmington). Tereus, who must have entered by this point, speaks with Prokne, who "seduces him into the palace with the pretext that she has prepared a sacred ancestral meal which he must consume alone.... One recalls the carpet scene in Aeschylus, *Agamemnon*."⁵⁴ The chorus sings another song.

As the final stasimon comes to its conclusion, we hear Tereus' cry of horror (off-stage) as he realizes what has been done: Ἥλιε, φιλίπποις Θρηξὶ πρέσβιστον σέλας, "Sun, most august light for horse-loving Thracians" (fr. 582 Radt). The exodos must have unfolded in at least three stages: confrontation and pursuit, metamorphosis, and epiphany. First, Tereus, armed with a javelin (ἀκόντιον) or a similar weapon, confronts the two sisters and pursues them across the stage. This moment is recalled by Aristophanes at *Lysistrata* 563–64: ἕτερος δ' αὖ Θρᾷξ πέλτην σείων κἀκόντιον, ὥσπερ ὁ Τηρεύς, / ἐδεδίσκετο τὴν ἰσχαδόπωλιν, "and another, a Thracian, brandishing a light shield and a javelin, just like Tereus, frightened the fig vendor," an allusion suggesting that the original performance (as, subsequently, the script and iconography) of *Tereus* was impressive enough to be remembered and quoted decades after its production. All three exit by one of the *eisodoi*.

Iconographic evidence for Sophokles' play attests several scenes that must have been especially memorable.⁵⁵ The general impression conveyed by these images is that *Tereus* was not only an unusual and thorough reworking of traditional material, as a script, but that it deeply impressed its spectators as a violent and original spectacle. Memory of the latter, possibly the pursuit and final tableau, were obviously the motivation for Aristophanes' hoopoe character in *Birds*. Another striking feature of the several possible illustrations of *Tereus* is the wealth and detail of the tragic costumes. It is almost certain that *Birds* contained further imitation or parody of this aspect of the Sophoklean performance.

It is conceivable that the moment of metamorphosis was illustrated by the display of Tereus, Prokne, and Philomela on the *ekkyklêma* in a superimposition of the death-tableau of the *Khoephoroi* exodos and the familiar Euripidean deus ex machina. The rapid succession of events would seem to preclude a full costume change.⁵⁶ We might imagine this moment marking the conclusion of the tragedy as an arrangement of three characters (Tereus in pursuit?) in which their metamorphosis is marked symbolically by certain prominent signs—a token change of clothing or headdress, perhaps. The death wish implicit in the desiderative metaphor of lyric and tragic poetry "Would that I were a bird" (i.e., the desire to flee from life and the human condition) is well known⁵⁷ and would make quite natural the association of this desperate tableau of metamorphosis-in-crisis with the scenes of death that had already been presented on the *ekkyklêma*. Thus Sophokles would achieve a counterpoint of sorts between this final image of the unfortunate "birds" and his audience's expectation of a death scene. Such a visual representation of the lyric metaphor would certainly have been an innovative and powerful moment of theatrical symbolism. The compelling suggestion (note 21) that Tereus was "costumed in the Thracian manner of hair-style (*akrokomoi*) and headgear" would contribute to the effectiveness of the final tableau and constitute part of the "outrage" (λυμαίνεται) that the comic Tereus says has been inflicted on him by Sophokles. The final stage of the exodos involved the appearance of a *deus*, perhaps Hermes, who reproaches the Athenian women as foolish and their revenge as a "remedy worse than the illness" applied by a foolish doctor (fr. 589 Radt).[58] To this final *rhêsis* belongs the famous fragment (581 Radt) that has been attributed to Sophokles' *Tereus* since Welcker's time:[59]

> And this hoopoe, an initiate into his own misfortunes,   fr. 581
> he (Zeus) has embroidered, having manifested him
> as a bold bird, living among rocks, in full armor.
> When spring comes, he will ply the wing of a hawk
> with white feathers, for he will display two forms
> from a single womb, both the fledgling's and his own.
> Whenever the stalks of grain grow yellow in early July,
> a spotted wing will guide him anew.
> But, driven by hatred for these [women], he will always fly
> to another place, inhabiting lonely thickets and crags.   (Kiso tr. adapted)

This passage suggests strongly that the tragic poet innovated Tereus' metamorphosis into a crested hoopoe, choosing the supposedly strange and harsh-tempered bird to represent the alien, warlike Thracian. The similarity of ἔποψ and ἐπόπτης along with the apparent uncertainty about the hoopoe's appearance and behavior no doubt conspired to encourage this innovation.[60] Sophokles, moreover, seems to be at pains to reconcile an older version of the myth in which Tereus becomes a common hawk with his dramatic metamorphosis of a barbarian into a correspondingly strange bird. Motivation for this epiphany must be sought in the unusual resolution of the final crisis: the metamorphoses, unlike suicide or murder, have a supernatural cause and, as such, must be reported by a messenger, most likely Hermes, capable of revealing the will of Zeus. This *rhêsis* no doubt prompts the sententious strophe (fr. 590 Radt) that resembles the closing words of the chorus in several other Sophoklean plays (e.g., *Aias* and *Trakhiniai*):[61]

> Men of mortal race must think mortal thoughts.   fr. 590
> Knowing this full well, that there is none
> but Zeus to dispose of what is to come
> in the way that it must be accomplished.

It is hard not to detect an anti-Thracian sentiment in Sophokles' spectacle of two high-bred Athenian women driven to commit crimes that exceed their barbarian host's "natural" savagery. Prokne and Philomela are said to have become "even more senseless" than Tereus, which suggests that the foreign context and xenophobic rhetoric coupled with the cheerful occasion of the Dionysiac festival only serve to highlight the depravity of the two sisters. The Atheno-Thracian antithesis thus contributes to the ironic undermining of Athenian superiority (cf. *Andromakhe* 168–77) in the spectacle of Pandion's daughters outdoing their host and ally in savagery.[62] This complex interplay of "natural" and willful savagery is quite clearly the product of Sophokles' dramatic design, which imparted to the legend of Tereus and Prokne its definitive shape. It is hardly an exaggeration to say that after the production of this tragedy, mention of Tereus and the others was made, more often than not, in reference to Sophokles' play.

Although dating the play on the basis of the anti-Thracian theme cannot be precise, it is reasonable to follow Webster, William Calder, and many other scholars in regarding the *Medeia* (431) as the *terminus ante quem*.[63] The context of the first years of the Peloponnesian War calls to mind Thoukydides' polemic (2.29.3) in which the historian asserts vehemently that Teres (father of the Athenians' Thracian ally Sitalkes) has nothing to do with the Tereus who married Pandion's daughter Prokne.[64] Marcel Detienne has recently illustrated that the Athenians were contemptuous of Thracians as barbarians hostile to the art of writing and education.[65] Sophokles' *Tereus* is a striking example of the "war" between Thracians and writing. The tragedy was especially powerful since it involved the double spectacle of a Thracian attempting to suppress communication by means of mutilation and the cunning victory of (Athenian) writing over Thracian violence. The subversion of this theme lies at the heart of Aristophanes' comic Tereus in *Birds*.

Tereus Comicus

It is safe to conclude that "the canonical form of the [Tereus] myth was clearly fixed by Sophocles" and that the influence of the tragic performance was deep and long-lasting.[66] Even from the incomplete picture that we have of the lost play it is obvious that the tragedian's contribution was extensive. *Birds*, produced in March 414, stands as an elaborate testament to the profound impression made by Sophokles' *Tereus*. We may admire the power of memory required of both the comic poet and spectator for the explicit parody of a tragedy produced well over a decade before to be intelligible and effective.[67] It is, nevertheless, not unusual for a comedy and a "target" tragedy (tragic model) to be separated by a number of years. Euripides' *Telephos*, as we have seen, was produced in 438, that is, thirteen years before its extended parody as "the old play" in *Akharnians* (line 415). There can be little doubt, moreover, that memorable tragedies (or excerpts thereof) were kept alive and circulated as texts for private use. Aristophanes himself makes this clear in passages such as *Clouds* 1371 (a *rhêsis* from Euripides) and *Frogs* 52–54 (Dionysos as reader of Euripides' *Andromeda*). The comic Tereus of *Birds* identifies Sophokles' play as his place of origin, thereby inviting us to investigate how Aristophanes has transformed the tragic character into a central player in his comedy.

A major thematic moment of *Birds* is the comic subversion of the desiderative lyric metaphor "would that I were a bird!"[68] The unusual climax of Sophokles' *Tereus* was unquestionably the most elaborate and memorable tragic enactment of this metaphor: the oblique death-in-metamorphosis served as an innovative conclusion to a series of equally innovative dramatic events. In designing the literary synthesis that is *Birds*, Aristophanes clearly fastened on Sophokles' dramatic intersection of language and spectacle: the poetic flight from the human condition in a crisis (possible only in language) becomes a comic flight from the Athenian condition, with the ultimate "flight" of Athenians in droves from their city to the bird polis. While the tragic trio of Tereus, Prokne, and Philomela pass, in metamorphosis, out of an explicitly horrible past into an indeterminate animal state that preserves old hostilities, Peisetairos and Euelpides flee from rather vague social problems into what turns out to be a complex and harmonious avian future in Nephelokokkygia. Tereus, himself a refugee from tragedy, undergoes an important secondary transformation before our very eyes: first an active guide whom the Athenians approach as suppliants, he assumes a passive role in which he serves as the living blueprint for Peisetairos' Great Idea. From the moment of Peisetairos' inspiration with the bird life, Tereus becomes the Athenian's assistant, taking instructions and learning from him. Tereus' catalytic role in the contrafact connects the various thematic strands of the comedy in a flexible and dynamic fashion that derives much of its force from Aristophanes' systematic response to the Sophoklean invention that had so impressed the spectators of the *Tereus*. In this respect, Aristophanes succeeds in matching the creativity of his older contemporary by producing a innovative comic countercharacter. Thus a skeletal overview of the contrafact, point by point:

Thrace in the Tragedy

The setting of *Tereus* has been removed from Phokis to Thrace with attendant emphasis on an Atheno-Thracian antithesis: Prokne and Philomela reunite far from home among barbarians with whom they can have nothing in common. From nearby Daulis, the women have been exiled to the quintessentially barbaric Thrace.[69] Sophokles thus sets up a stark polarity between literate Athenians and the antiliterate Thracians across which the spark of Philomela's epistle flashes to ignite the final crisis. The violent effort to suppress language by means of mutilation, a feature invented by Sophokles for his play, fits quite naturally in the context of this polarity.

Thrace in the Comedy

Tereus' behavior in *Birds* is far from that of a violent Thracian erotomaniac. The tragic Tereus was made especially strange by being placed far from Athens in an entirely foreign and barbaric country. Contradicting Sophokles' removal of the king from Daulis to Thrace, Aristophanes makes his character comically familiar, as we have seen. He speaks a colloquial Attic (of course), has a servant, and, much like an Athenian, eats Phalerian whitebait and pea-soup using a bowl, pot, and stirring spoon. The name of Tereus seems to have occurred naturally to Philokrates, the Athenian vendor who recommended him to Peisetairos and Euelpides. Throughout the scenes featuring the hybrid Epops, his Thracian past and ethnic character are rejected. At *Birds* 1363–69, for example, Peisetairos says to the young patraloias who wishes to settle in Nephelokokkygia:[70]

> Don't hit your father; just take this wing
> and this spur in your other hand,
> imagine that this comb you've got is a cock's,
> and do garrison duty, serve on expeditions, maintain yourself
> by earning pay. Let your father live. In fact, as you're a fighting type,
> fly off to the Thracian Coast and fight there.

Far from being ignorant, threatening, or strange, Tereus is a widely traveled bird (line 118) who inspires laughter and sympathy. The most striking aspect of Aristophanes' neutralization of the tragic Atheno-Thracian antithesis is his promotion of Tereus to the forefront as an articulate intermediary, coupled with the virtual banishment of Sophokles' Athenian protagonist: Prokne has no speaking part in the comedy and, as Frank E. Romer has pointed out, does not even appear onstage as a bird.[71] This is an impressive and ironic spectacle: the Athenian princess, famous as the eloquent protagonist who laments the lot of women and punishes her husband for his erotic crimes, is trotted out by Tereus as a silent character (more accurately, a flute girl) to be the butt of Peisetairos' and Euelpides' lusty jokes (lines 665–74). Peisetairos finds her "a lovely birdie . . . fair, and tender" while Euelpides says that he would have "great pleasure in spreading her legs" and "peeling her like an egg."

In *Birds*, Prokne's exile amidst violent foreigners is translated into a political allotopia[72] (Nephelokokkygia), an important aspect of which is its gradual familiarization: the city in the air, which is located essentially "nowhere," comes to look and sound more and more like Athens. Although Tereus explicitly identifies the birds as having been barbarians (lines 199–200) whom he had to teach Greek(!), the hostility of the bird mob is short-lived and is mollified by Peisetairos' *rhêsis* and concluding treaty. Unlike Thracians, the "natural" community of birds lacks a strong and ancient tradition and submits easily to the creative *didaskalia* (teaching, choreography) of Peisetairos. This comic portrayal of the persuasion of the Athenian demos by members of the sociopolitical elite influenced by the activist sophists (e.g., Alkibiades)[73] is a far cry from an encounter between Athenians and Thracians. Beginning with their "parodos" as a new chorus in the parabasis, the birds speak with authority and comically deny any external influence even as they enact Peisetairos' teachings in every detail. Thus, along with Prodikos (line 692), the newly civilized citizens of Nephelokokkygia dismiss all sophists—rivals of their city planner and chief—with an explicit allusion to Sophokles' *Tereus*. No longer "tongueless" barbarians, they denounce this new race of "Tongue-to-Belly Men," criminal abusers of language who "mutilate" Athenians Tereus-style (lines 1694–1705, cf. θερίζειν and φιλίππων, a pun on fr. 582):[74]

And found in Accusatia, near
the Klepsydra, is the villainous
race of Tongue-to-Belly Men,
who reap and sow
and gather vintage with their tongues—
and also figs;
they are barbarian stock,
Gorgiases and Philips.
And it is because of these
philippic Tongue-to-Belly Men
that everywhere in Attica
the tongue is cut out.

If we consider the result of Peisetairos' city-planning activities (Athenians flock to the bird city) it is clear that the relationship between Athens and Nephelokokkygia is the polar opposite of the Sophoklean hostility between Athens and the royal house of Tereus. Peisetairos and Euelpides voluntarily flee from Athens to establish a successful colony by manipulating a natural community of bird-barbarians to reverse Sophokles' ethnic schema at every moment of the comedy. Tereus' prominent role in *Birds* serves to keep this reversal in the dramatic foreground. In this respect, *Birds* represents the culmination of an evolving comic idea: the El Dorado scenarios of early comedy (cf. Telekleides' *Amphiktyones*, *PCG* fr. 1) involved refugees from culture passing their time blissfully in a natural paradise. Pherekrates' *Agrioi* (*PCG* fr. 5–20) challenged this topos by showing how two such refugees would come to grief, sharing the hardships of cultureless savages in the wilderness. *Birds*, however, presents the spectacle of inevitable civilization: frustrated by what they find in "nature," the refugees from city and culture proceed to organize, civilize, and build. "Nature" and "barbarians" yield as Athens comically reproduces itself in the air!

Metamorphosis in the Tragedy

That Sophokles innovatively transformed his Tereus into a hoopoe (instead of a hawk) "rests on unimpeachable evidence."[75] The *rhêsis* with the suggestive play on the word ἔποψ and an odd representation of the bird's natural history (fr. 581 Radt) is an addition to the earlier form of the legend attested, for example, by Aiskhylos (*Hiketides* 63), who mentions the nightingale "pursued by a hawk," κιρκηλάτου τ᾽ ἀηδόνος. The metamorphosis of Tereus into a crested hoopoe both thematically and visually motivated. Exhibiting behavior and an appearance that were popularly seen as strange and even repugnant (e.g., hostile to women, smears its nest with human excrement), the hoopoe suits the tragedian's barbarized king. This point is emphasized at line 280 when Euelpides expresses surprise that Tereus is not the *only* representative of his species.[76] The resemblance between the hoopoe's crest and the Thracian hairstyle (*akrokomos*) was most likely exploited in the final tableau. Sophokles enacted the lyric topos "I wish I were a bird" as a visual metaphor for death on the *ekkyklêma*. Heinz Hofmann correctly points out that while, in the pre-Sophoklean version of the legend, metamorphosis was a simple punishment, in Tereus "the metamorphosis . . . was, for the first time, reinterpreted by Sophokles as a solution. Aristophanes employed this positive conclusion, with further elaboration, as the fundamental idea of his play."[77]

Metamorphosis in the Comedy

Griffith explores Aristophanes' play with the name ἔποψ, "hoopoe." Since Old Comedy thrives on exuberant wordplay, it is natural that Sophokles' choice of species (and play therewith) would have been cheerfully exploited and greatly extended by Aristophanes in *Birds*. Griffith discerns a variety of puns from the obvious "pooping" cries (ἐποποῖ, lines 58 and 227) to a subtle play on ἐπί, ὀπ- (εἶδον), and πετ- at line 48: Peisetairos says that he is seeking Tereus the Hoopoe to find out from him "if he's seen a city of that [trouble-free, ἀπράγμων] kind anywhere he's flown over," εἴ που τοιαύτην εἶδε πόλιν ᾗ 'πέπτατο. Since this bird "is the very same character that Sophocles staged in his Tereus," Griffith notes, it is "singularly appropriate that the pun which Aristophanes makes on the Hoopoe's name had almost certainly been made by Sophocles in this very play, the *Tereus*."[78] This is a comic extension of the wordplay cited above (in fr. 581 Radt): from Sophokles' allusion to Eleusinian ἐποπτεία (and perhaps to Zeus Epopeus), Aristophanes has created a rich network of jokes that collectively characterize the comic Tereus' function as initiator of Athenians into birdhood (we might say ὀρνιθαγωγός) with an implicit "parody of religious worship in which the birds cast themselves in the role of those gods who could best be called παν(τ)όπται," (Zeus and Helios, cf. Aiskhylos, *Eum.* 1045 and *Prom.* 91).[79]

In addition to the punning strategies mentioned above, Aristophanes has undermined Sophokles' dramatic point. Whereas the metamorphosis into a hoopoe in tragedy represents the Thracian king's strange and savage nature, the peculiar appearance of the comic Epops is made the object of several aggressive jokes. "Are you a bird or a peacock?" asks a bewildered Peisetairos in line 102. Failing to identify Tereus' species, he reaches for the most alien and exotic ornithoid he can think of, the ταῶς (peacock), a name that in *Birds* is used to denote a marginal or entirely unfamiliar species (cf. line 269).[80] This use of ταῶς to comically extend the hoopoe's strangeness illustrates well how Aristophanes abuses and distorts what one might call the "popular ornithology" to suit his purposes (indeed, the serious ornithologist will be frustrated at times by Aristophanes' text). The metamorphosis of the comic Epops, moreover, appears to be incomplete and elicits Euelpides' comment that he looks "as though the Twelve Gods had blasted" him (lines 95–96). Tereus' attempt to excuse his funny appearance ("all birds shed their feathers in winter") suggests that the Aristophanic costume exceeded the "Sophoklean indignities" (line 100) to make the Epops perfectly ridiculous. The dangerously sparse coat of the second hoopoe is given an even more hilarious explanation (lines 285–86): the poor fellow, like Kallias, son of Hipponikos, has been plucked bare by prosecutors and females! Thus Aristophanes marks his comic commentary on the strangeness of the Sophoklean hoopoe innovation by extending the tragic wordplay (ἔποψ ~ ἐπόπτης, "hoopoe" ~ "initiate") and distorting the tragic costume so as to adapt Tereus to his new role as guide and catalyst in *Birds*. This transformation of the hoopoe's dramatic effect is linked with Aristophanes' neutralization of the Atheno-Thracian antithesis: fr. 581 describes the result of Tereus' metamorphosis in terms of a bitter *apoikia* of a solitary bird in a rocky terrain. This exile, connected with hatred for Prokne and Philomela, contrasts with the happy life of Tereus and his wife in *Birds*: *apoikia* becomes an Athenian desideratum, a place that attracts *apragmones* (cf. line 44) to a new involvement in public life, in comic contradiction to Perikles' famous criticism of such men.[81]

The Name "Tereus" in the Tragedy

There can be little doubt that Sophokles established the Thracian king's name as Τηρεύς (as opposed to Zethos, Polytekhnos, etc.), alluding, perhaps, to the Teres who united the kingdom of the Odrysians in the first half of the fifth century.[82] The *redende Name* of Prokne's grim "custodian" (cf. τηρέω) thus expresses a general anti-Thracian feeling as well as specific disapproval of the Athenians' alliance with Teres' son Sitalkes (reigned 440–24) at the beginning of the Peloponnesian War.

The Name "Tereus" in the Comedy

Aristophanes' choice of Tereus, it has been argued, was inspired by Sophokles' innovative treatment of metamorphosis as a solution (as opposed to a punishment, see
note 67). Birdhood does, indeed, turn out to be a practical solution for Peisetairos
and Euelpides, but Tereus' mock-tragic entrance at line 92 engages Sophokles' significant name suggestive of vigilance and guarding: "this understanding of the name
[i.e., from τηρέω] is consonant with Tereus' unexpected appearance: having heard
of a human dining with ladle and pot (76–79), we meet a bird battened on myrtles
and gnats (82); having searched for the 'Watcher,' we find him asleep (82)."[83]

Language and Recognition in the Tragedy

In addition to the incarceration of Philomela, Sophokles has Tereus cut out her
tongue in order to set up the recognition by means of the "voice of the shuttle." The
passage in *Poetics* mentioned above (16.1454b 30–37) set alongside the peculiar doubly determined suppression of Philomela (incarceration *and* mutilation) strongly
suggests that Sophokles invented the tongue cutting to set up another dramatic innovation: the destruction of Tereus by an act of writing (i.e., the recognition scene
involving Philomela's textum). Occurring nowhere else in Greek legend as a means
of preventing communication, this "lingual castration" is highly marked and serves
to emphasize Tereus' singular savagery. His role as violent suppressor of language is
thereby dramatized in the foreground.[84]

The revelation of Tereus' crimes by means of a written message woven and sent
by the mutilated Philomela is a remarkable device designed specifically for the tragic
stage by Sophokles, as Aristotle makes clear. The immediate result is the victory of the
Athenian women with their literate cunning over their oppressive and crude Thracian
environment. An irony implicit in the sophisticated strategy surfaces: Philomela becomes a swallow capable only of χελιδονίζειν, "swallow twittering." She is deprived
of intelligible (Greek) speech and her song becomes proverbial for unintelligible foreign chatter.[85] The spectacle of Tereus exposed and destroyed by means of writing seems
to have been especially memorable (cf. note 47, on the Lucanian bell-krater).

Sophokles has Prokne and Philomela use the occasion of the Trieterika to carry
out their revenge. The vivid Dionysiac element in Ovid (*Met.* 6.587–600) most likely
reflects Sophokles' *Tereus*, an inference based both on Ovid's frequent use of tragedy (especially here) and on the absence of this element in other versions of the Tereus
myth. Particularly important is the tragedian's metatheatrical deployment of this
element. The cult context provides the costume and setting for the Athenian sisters'
mise en abyme. The maenad disguise, the sacred meal, and the gift of a special *peplos*,
as well as the elements of violence and sacrifice, are nicely integrated, dramatically
and thematically, in the Dionysiac context.

Language and Recognition in the Comedy

Tereus is first engaged by the Athenian refugees as a natural bridge between their
past and a desired, if uncertain, future. Peisetairos appeals to him in a passive mode,
employing the language of supplication as he asks for guidance (lines 114–22):[86]

It is because you were originally a man, once upon a time, like us;
and you owed people money, once upon a time, like us;
and you liked to avoid paying them, once upon a time, like us.
Then later you changed to the shape of a bird,
and you've flown over land and sea in every direction;
and you have all the knowledge that a man has and that a bird has.
That's why we've come here to you [as suppliants],
to beseech you if you could tell us of some city that's nice and fleecy,
soft as a woolly mantle to go to sleep in.

The wisdom of the feathered guru, however, amounts to little more than a series of weak puns on proper names (Aristokrates, Melanthios, Opuntios) surrounding Peisetairos' and Euelpides' lusty scenarios of the good ἀπράγμων life (lines 128–42). The chief suppliant, apparently disappointed, begins to study Tereus himself; "What's this life here with the birds like?" he asks (line 155). "You'll know all about it." As Peisetairos "reads" Tereus—his living blueprint for the future—he is suddenly struck by the Great Idea that clarifies his own *redende Name* (lines 162–64):[87]

PEISETAIROS. Yow!
I see in the race of birds what could be a grand design
and a mighty power, were you to be persuaded by me.

TEREUS. What do you want us to be persuaded of?

PEISETAIROS. What should you be persuaded of [you ask]? Well, first of all . . .

Aristophanes marks this important moment etymologically by a triple repetition of the morpheme πιθ-, which anticipates the comic name of the as yet unnamed protagonist (see line 644): Peisetairos now assumes leadership as "persuader of friends" and fellow members of ἑταιρίαι, "clubs."[88] His plan of a bird rebellion and boycott unfolds so rapidly that Tereus, now his student, has difficulty following it. When the meaning of Peisetairos' vigorous speech (lines 180–83), the kernel of which is the pun πόλος ~ πόλις ("firmament" ~ "state"), finally dawns on Tereus, he unwittingly hints at the significant name of the future city (Νεφελοκοκκυγία, cf. line 819) as Peisetairos' "trap" (νεφέλη) for "fools" (κόκκυγες). This passage (lines 194–204) is a turning point in the play:[89]

TEREUS. Wowee!
Holy Earth! Holy snares, gins, and nets,
but I've never heard a cleverer idea!
So much so that I'll found this city with you,
should the other birds agree.

PEISETAIROS. Then who's going to explain the idea to them?

TEREUS. You. They used to be inarticulate [barbarians],
but I've lived with them a long time and I've taught them language.

PEISETAIROS. So how are you going to call them together?

TEREUS. Easily. I'll go into my thicket here right away,
and wake up my nightingale,
and we'll summon them.

The reversal of Sophokles' *Tereus* is complete: in the tragedy the Atheno-Thracian antithesis provides the context for Tereus' efforts to suppress communication by means of the incarceration and "lingual castration" of Philomela. When the latter's *textum* defeats these efforts, Prokne avenges her sister in the most horrible way possible. Connecting two salient innovations, Sophokles has the barbarian suppression of language trigger the Athenian sisters' Dionysiac theater of revenge. In Sophokles' mise en abyme, Tereus, a Thracian "full of scorn for writing," in Detienne's phrase, seeking "to destroy in fury everything which concerned the intellectual sphere," is himself destroyed by writing and the superior intellectual abilities of the Athenians. Tragedy reacts, as it were, to the Thracian's war on language by complicating its own discourse and embedding one performance (Prokne and Philomela disguised as maenads simulate Trieteric ritual) in another. The bloody conclusion of Sophokles' play may have presented to the audience a symbolic tableau in which Tereus, Prokne, and Philomela were represented as having passed out of the human condition following a series of unspeakable crimes. Even in this metaphorical death-as-solution the hoopoe shuns all women, nurturing an eternal hatred for them (fr. 581 Radt).

Aristophanes makes his Tereus a benevolent teacher and disseminator of language, and not any language, at that, but Greek! The comic counterinnovation provides Peisetairos with a linguistic context for his city-planning activities. This "Thracian" has taught his fellow barbarians Greek and so unleashes a new wave of Athenian cunning and creativity that surfaces as a comedy within a comedy, with the parabasis the opening of Aristophanes' new political drama mise en abyme starring the birds as citizens of Nephelokokyggia. The persuasive speeches of the agon (lines 451–638) represent a fascinating metatheatrical moment in Aristophanic drama in which Peisetairos as *khorodidaskalos* trains a hostile bird *taxis* for their solemn "parodos" as a new chorus in the parabasis. Assimilating the Athenian's clever lessons and "constitution," the birds assume a new identity to deliver an authoritative comic cosmogony. Peisetairos, representing the comic poet, stands aside, as the birds perform with an impressive air of autonomy. The comic polis, Nephelokokkygia, emerges as a play written and directed by Peisetairos, who supervises the many entrances and exits of various (often quite literate) characters in his comedy. Tereus' activities of disseminating language are catalytic for this metacomedy, allowing Peisetairos' political career to mirror, among other things, the improvisational creativity of the playwright.

From Tongue to Wing: λέγων πτερῶ σε

Whereas the tragic Tereus' war on language precipitated a crisis that forced the participants to escape an intolerable human condition into birdhood (symbolic of death), the comic Tereus' linguistic pedagogy opens for the Athenians a political future marked by wings that Aristophanes uses as signs of rhetorical prowess and comic freedom. The multidirectional governing metaphor of this contrafact in which men assimilate to birds and birds to men, and so forth, springs directly from the presence onstage of Tereus, the incarnate comic countercharacter. "The apotheosis of Peisetaerus is only the climax of a persistent pattern," writes A. H. Sommerstein,[90] running through the play from start to finish, of subversion (both in word and in deed) of the established hierarchy of the universe with its unbridgeable gulfs between immortals and mortals, and between man and the lower animals. Over and over again, men are spoken of as birds, gods as birds or as men, birds as men or as gods. Tereus, his wife, and his servant, are birds who were once human; Peisetaerus and Euelpides acquire wings and feathers during the play; while before himself becoming the new supreme god, Peisetaerus has offered to make a god (Heracles) "sovereign of the birds." All boundaries and categories seem to be obliterated, just as Cloudcuckooville itself defies logic and nature, this walled and gated city which somehow floats in mid-air, which Iris can fly through without realizing it exists, which visitor after visitor from earth can reach before being equipped with wings . . . . Nowhere, even in Aristophanes, are the laws of the universe so utterly set aside for the hero's benefit. He has but to will, and it is so. His power is total.

This essentially linguistic power (cf. the central pun in line 184) drives the series of theatrical innovations that produce Nephelokokkygia. The comic Tereus has restored the severed tongue and Aristophanes celebrates a bizarre possible future.[91] Metamorphosis into birds represents a comic solution of a very different kind. Wings signify rhetorical prowess coupled with the freedom to escape "tragedy" in precisely the same way as Tereus, bird-man par excellence, escaped from Sophokles' play to *Birds*. The chorus invite the spectators to join them in their bird comedy (lines 785–89):[92]

> There's nothing more advantageous or more agreeable than to grow wings.
> For instance, if one of you spectators were winged,
> and if he were hungry and bored with the tragic performances,
> he could have flown out of here, gone home, had lunch,
> and when he'd filled himself up, flown back here to see us.

The spectators are invited to fly, with the birds, from the annoyances of tragedy and the constraints of the theater to enjoy the usual carnal pleasures celebrated in Old Comedy: food, sex, and the relief of defecation. As Peisetairos disburses wings to newcomers, the creative power of speech is expressed in a number of winged metaphors of "taking wing," ἀναπτερῶ / ἀνεπτερῶσθαι (lines 1437–39, 1445, 1449), the most vivid of which is λέγων πτερῶ σε, "I render you winged through speech." This brave new world of birds is not one of undifferentiated bliss, however. Peisetairos' apotheosis and tyrannical rule over Aristophanes' utopia suggest that, latent in the subversion of the barbaric and tragic (i.e., Sophokles' *Tereus*) is the potential for a return to the same. The outrageous success of Peisetairos' aggressive attack on the established order appears, in the end, to be a return to a terrifying pre-Olympian monarchy in which he, like Kronos (and like the tragic Tereus), eats his own "children."

At the heart of Aristophanes' complex design in *Birds* is the systematic contrafact of Sophoklean innovation. *Birds* is not merely a concatenation of general mythical travesties but a sophisticated synthesis of reactions to specific people, events, dramatic performances, and texts. As in the case of the Prometheus scene, which Herington has shown to be a contrafact of the *Prometheia*,[93] so the first half of *Birds* arises from an exuberant improvisation on the themes and situations of one of the most memorable tragedies of the fifth century. This improvisation, moreover, engages the mechanism of metamorphosis that works throughout *Birds* as a poetic program informing the contrafact, that is, a comic poetics of transformation. Characters, situations, dramatic *Bauformen*, and themes are subjected to an exuberant series of metamorphoses, the sum of which is the conversion of the inchoate world of the prologue into Nephelokokkygia, a fantastic polis occupying an explicit position between gods and men. Each of the manifold transformations catalyzed by Tereus is interesting in itself and deserves much fuller treatment than can be given here. The metamorphosis of the chorus, for example, from a natural community of birds into a self-aware *politeia* of Nephelokokkygians has important metatheatrical implications for the enactment of the polis after the parabasis. An equally significant metamorphosis is that of Peisetairos from a disaffected exile seeking a τόπος ἀπράγμων, first into an energetic and opinionated sophist-choreographer, and then into the supreme tyrant and anti-Zeus. Sophokles' *Tereus*, refracted through the comic poet's metafictional prism, informs the design of *Birds* on many levels, from the governing metaphor of transformation to the definition of "Athenian" and "polis" against a barbarian Other. In creating his own masterpiece by transforming and distorting a product of Sophokles' dramatic genius, Aristophanes was, quite clearly, honoring his older contemporary with the highest praise.

Euripides' *Helene* and the Metafictional μηχανὴ σωτηρίας

Two years after Aristophanes crafted his escape from Athens to the "barbarian" world of Tereus and the birds, Euripides staged an equally metafictional escape from Egypt back to Greece in *Helene*, a melodrama that has long intrigued scholars with its comic elements and pointed allusion to *Birds*. Just as *Bakkhai* exhibits much in common with comedy, both formally and aesthetically, so *Helene* points to Aristophanes as an inspiration in contriving metafictional stratagems of escape, μηχαναὶ σωτηρίας. Next to *Bakkhai*, Euripides' *Helene* has received more attention than any other play for its self-reflexive study of representation and its searching fusion of rationalism and moralism. The trend in recent scholarship has been to read Greek culture through and against the various "Helene documents" from Homer to Euripides (and beyond).[94] Related to the current preoccupation with synoptic analysis is the specific problem of genre noted above: What is the significance of the allusion to *Birds* at lines 1107–13? Why does Euripides explicitly connect his metatheatrical extravaganza with that of Aristophanes? As we have come to appreciate, the study of detail reveals much about the "big picture," which, in this case, is one of the most extensive and explicitly metafictional experiments of the fifth century.

The choral ode in question signals Euripides' response to Aristophanes in a way that points up the tragedian's metafictional challenge to, and redefinition of, tragedy. In *Helene*, Euripides "is not simply dancing on the grave of the genre he has outraged, but looking for a new mode of expression for another kind of thought."[95] This new mode of expression is less reluctant to acknowledge comedy directly, especially as practiced by a playwright who has been engaging Euripides for well over a decade. *Helene* practices tragic reinvention of myth in a particularly literary and aggressive manner for which Helene—the female *aition* incarnate of the Trojan War—is ideally suited. "Uniquely among mortal women in Homeric epic," notes Ingrid Holmberg, "she is represented as capable of constructing a poetic narrative, of acting as a type of poet. In the *Iliad* her well-known poetic activities include weaving the story of Troy in her tapestry, describing the Greeks in the *Teichoscopia*, and commenting upon her own position within the epic tradition." Similarly, Eric Downing foregrounds the boldness with which Euripides has his protagonist assert her authority in composing a hybrid counterfiction, a play within the play that she calls her *mêkhanê sôtêrias*.[96]

Euripides improvises along the lines of Stesichoros' *Palinode*[97] to create an exciting intrigue in Egypt that maintains the Homeric narrative as a backdrop. This is neither negation of epic nor simple revision, but rather a reinscription of the older narrative in a secondary plane. Like a theatrical prop, the epic construction of events at Troy is rendered artificial by the problematic presence/absence of the phantom Helene. The scenarios of epic (*Iliad, Cypria, Little Iliad,* and *Iliou Persis*) are bleached of substance and exist at a distinct remove from the "live" action in front of us, starring a Helene who is the ethical antithesis of the archaic figure. Those, like Menelaos, who "read" the epic narrative seriously are deceived and are bound for trouble; salvation shall be contrived by the new Helene in a formally comic manner in the free manipulation of fictions. This split between a discredited tradition and tragic revelation of truth allows Euripides simultaneously to continue his criticism of the heroic ethos and to construct Helene as a virtuous subject whose words and actions undermine the heroic ethos and its narratives.

The centerpiece of *Helene* is a mise en abyme composed and directed by the protagonist, who appropriates the authority of comic *poiesis* to invent a contemporary scenario of *sôtêria*,[98] in this case a sham Hellenic burial ritual. This minidrama will be initiated by a fiction imported from abroad (lines 1032–34):[99]

> We are safe, Menelaos, as far as the maiden is concerned.
> Now it is yours to supply the narrative, so that we
> can compose a plot-device of escape.

With its insistence on *sôtêria*,[100] Helene's theatrical stratagem bears a strong resemblance to the comic utopianism of plays such as *Peace* and *Birds* in that it is a unique mechanism for escape from an intolerable social situation. Like Peisetairos' inspiration, Helene's Great Idea, though anticipated since at least line 813, comes to her in a flash (lines 1049–50): "Listen!" she says to her husband, "If a woman can say something clever . . . Would you have it reported that, though not dead, you are in fact dead?" The next fifty lines present her plan of "salvation" (lines 1055, 1060) in explicitly theatrical terms that fit quite naturally into a script otherwise preoccupied with mimesis and the related dichotomies between presence and absence, appearance and reality, sign and signified.[101]

The plot device is soon carefully laid out in terms of story, props, and cast. A remarkable feature of this little play is the way in which Helene, whose story has been complicated by the *eidôlon* at Troy, writes the script for her husband by separating sign and signified: the "corpse" will be an effigy, a phantom Menelaos, which frees the real Menelaos to play a supporting role. In a sense, the entire mise en abyme emerges as the ultimate *eidôlon*, a phantom double of reality. The plan immediately reframes the situation, players, costumes, and so forth, at an aesthetic remove from the main mythos as these are made strange in preparation for the mise en abyme. In a marvelous play with the tragic funeral-as-wedding topos, Euripides shows us that this mock-funeral is, in fact, a symbolic wedding, the reunion and reconciliation of

the long-estranged Helene and Menelaos. The mythos of Helene's minidrama might
be outlined as follows:

1. Menelaos has perished at sea and must be buried (in effigy);
2. Greek custom requires that victims of the sea be buried at sea with sacrifice,
   armed or dressed according to their station in life;
3. Helene's resultant devotion to Theoklymenos shall distract him into planning
   their marriage;
4. the ritual will be managed by women performing traditional laments (Helene
   will cut her hair and otherwise assume the demeanor of grief);
5. Menelaos will play the part of Menelaos' companion (sole survivor; and bearer
   of the bad news); he must return to Greece to tell Helene's "true" story;
6. his men will enter the action to be recognized as fellow Greeks, also shipwrecked;
7. the Greeks will help in the work of the funeral (and will fight when discovered);
8. the mise en abyme shall be defined by submission of the internal audience
   (Theoklymenos, locals, and crew aboard the ship) to the dramatic illusion.
   Revelation of the ruse will end in violence as the Greeks secure the ship.

"This shall be a great agon," asserts the protagonist (lines 1090–92), "that will
have one of two outcomes: death, if my *tekhne* is discovered, otherwise homecoming
and your salvation." "The *apatê* and *dolos* of Hera," notes Downing, "and her *technai*
and *mêchanai* which are responsible for the tragedy of the Trojan War (930, 610),
are answered by the *technai* and *mêchanai* of Helen (1091, 1621, 813, 1034), which are
responsible for the 'comedy' of their escape, or rather for the *dolos* by which they win
their *agôn*."[102] This comparison with comedy is not unwarranted and we have, in lines
1079–80, the first hint of intertextual reciprocity between genres when Menelaos "re-
cycles" language from *Telephos*[103] to make a comment about his "costume":[104]

> Yes, and these rags thrown around my body
> will attest to my recent rescue from a shipwreck.

An important effect of this auto-allusion may have been to evoke the extensive play
in *Akharnians* with *Telephos*, especially fr. 697 N² containing the phrase ἀμφίβληστρα
(or ἀμφίβλητα) σώματος ῥάκη — and all the associated language of costume and disguise. Euripides cleverly makes double use of Menelaos' appearance: the ῥάκη resulting from the Spartan king's recent misfortune shall now be redefined as the costume of a new, fictional character within the mise en abyme composed by Helene.
As in *Akharnians*, a typically pathetic Euripidean outfit is appropriated for an internal scenario of deceptive playacting. The internal audience, in the person of
Theoklymenos, responds accordingly (line 1204) by expressing horror at Menelaos'
appearance. Helene details her own plans for sham lamentation that requires a special costume: "I shall cut my curls and change the white clothing that I wear for black,
and drag my nails across my cheek leaving a red furrow there" (lines 1087–89). She
exits giving stage instructions— "Stay here ," and so forth (line 1085) — and uttering a
powerful prayer to two of the goddesses associated with the Judgment of Paris. She
concludes with a reproach, a bold ψόγος Ἀφροδίτης — enumerating the evils of the
goddess. This prayer, of course, is central to Euripides' ethical revision of Helene's
"epic" reputation. In keeping with the reversal of the Judgment of Paris discerned by
Austin, these verses are a negation of all that Aphrodite represents (lines 1102–1106):[105]

Why this thirst for evil things?
Why do you work in passions, lies, devices full
of treachery, love-magics, murder in the home?
Were you only temperate, in all else you are found sweet
to us beyond all other gods. This I confess.

This comment and the immediately following choral response have in common the theme of damage done when deception is motivated by male eros. The abduction of Helene by Paris and subsequent complications are in the foreground, of course, but the chorus answers with a striking quotation from Aristophanes—specifically his adaptation of Sophokles—to remind us of Tereus, another "barbarian" whose Aphrodite-inspired eros was devastating to Greeks, a male eros particularly destructive to women (lines 1107–21):[106]

On you who dwell in halls of the Muses
in the dense cover of the trees,
on you will I cry,
most melodious singing bird,
the tearful nightingale;
come, trilling through vibrant throat
to join with me in lamentation,
as I sing the hard sorrows of Helen, for all the suffering,
from spears held by Achaeans,
all from the time when with outland oar he swept over
the water-flats, came, came, and his coming was sorrow
in marriage for Priam's people, moving
from Lakedaimon, from you, Helen: Paris, dark lover
brought there by Aphrodite.

In the juxtaposition of *Birds* and *Tereus* above the Hoopoe's song was shown to preserve the only hint of the slaughter of Itys (and, implicitly, Tereus' *teknophagia*) as the old *aition* for the nightingale's song. Otherwise, as we have seen, Tereus has been allowed to escape from tragedy (as the spectators are invited to do at *Birds* 785–89) and his tragic history has been thoroughly revised. Euripides zeroes in on this most vulnerable passage in Aristophanes' script to make his metafictional connection. In his only gesture to Prokne, Tereus sings for her a song that has been characterized as "one of the most exciting things in Greek poetry"[107] (*Birds* 206–14):

PEISETAIROS. Dearest of birds, don't just stand there now!
Come on, I beg you, as fast as you can, go into the thicket
and wake up the nightingale!

TEREUS. Come, my consort, leave your sleep
and let forth the melodies of sacred song
with which from your divine lips you lament
your child and mine, the much-bewailed Itys,
trilling with the liquid melodies
of your vibrant throat.

The implicit connection between Prokne and Helene as victims of (barbarian) male eros is made quite clear in Euripides' presentation. The comic escape from Athens

(Peisetairos' and Euelpides' *mêkhanê sôtêrias*) is boldly constructed as the meta-fictional negative of tragedy in which Tereus is no longer a savage barbarian and Prokne is acknowledged in loving terms (despite her haunting silence and the reference to "your child and mine, the much-bewailed Itys"). Both texts construct Prokne at a remove, a voice of female lament that is quoted, never heard. Her song reminds us of Itys and the Trojan women, that is, women and children as the most pathetic victims of male eros and aggression. But the act of quotation reassures us that in the principal plane of dramatic fiction, things are better, and that the internal "poet" is composing a brighter future.

In *Birds*, tragic dystopia is manipulated to become a comic utopia in a way that invests the protagonist with an omnipotent authority to adapt the poetics of his sources to his own purposes. Helene, similarly, is given the authority to revise her dismal epic reputation and she does so before our very eyes, fearlessly reproaching the gods and, with them, the rejected epic tradition. Euripides has his chorus answer her hybrid prayer-*psogos* with a transgressive allusion that points up this moment. An important aspect of the melodramatic or "comic" quality of *Helene* is bound up with the free exercise of authority that pushes the envelope of tragic poetics. An intolerable narrative is rejected and new fictions developed in its stead. As composers, both Peisetairos and Helene are given ideal conditions, of course, by their respective playwrights. Peisetairos is free to draw inspiration for his utopia from an already converted Tereus while Helene constructs her minidrama against the background of an alternate history involving her phantom double. We might redefine the famous term "Euripidaristophanize" to signify a convergence of method between two genres of Athenian State Theater that, in its maturity, displays its confident powers of self-representation by transforming the poetics of the old (Homer, Sophokles) into a new theatrical poetics that, on some level, must always be metafictional.

Epilogue: *Thesmophoriazousai*

Aristophanes was certainly the best qualified critic ever to "publish" on Euripides, and there is little reason to be surprised that he brings the tragedian onstage a year after the production of *Helene* to star in his most overtly metatheatrical play, *Thesmophoriazousai*. There could be no more vivid response to the Euripidean experiment with authority (Helene as playwright) than to bring the poet himself on the comic stage to improvise a plot and manage the stage business. This play is a splendid example of literary criticism in action, a dramatization that simultaneously shows off and redefines its own poetics. As many have pointed out, the plot of *Thesmophoriazousai* is deeply concerned with Euripidean technique, the escape plot in particular.[108] This comedy is a demonstration of the comic poet's prowess, with special emphasis on an emerging theory of mimesis.[109] Aristophanes moves beyond his earlier contrafacts, for example, in *Peace* and *Birds*, to create a Euripidean medley unified by a focus on an explicitly theatrical element—the *mêkhanê sôtêrias*. Played for different internal audiences, the series of contrafacts from *Telephos*, *Palamedes*, *Helene*, and *Andromeda* suggests both a chronological progression—for the first three at least with dates of 438, 415, and 412 BC, respectively—and an evolution toward the tragicomic hybrid of the poet's later phase.[110] Having followed the exchange between Euripides and Aristophanes thus far, we now consider the final entry in the dialogue where the comic poet reconfigures *Helene* (*Thesmo.* 840–928). This study in the failure of tragic mimesis and *sôteria* is simultaneously a celebration by Aristophanes of a victory in his ongoing "imaginary" rivalry with Euripides.

Aristophanes imparts to his little contrafact the illusion of completeness by beginning with a recitation of the opening lines. This strategy would be especially effective for the literate spectators accustomed to identifying a papyrus roll from the first accessible text. The play with authority is amplified by having "Euripides" play Menelaos, and Euripides' Kinsman (and main transvestite) play Helene, while Kritylla is inserted as a comic voice reminding us of the utter nonsense of it all. It is as if the comic poet enters to participate in his own invention, complicating the humor with his straight-faced and stupid *bômolokhia*. "In this brief and absurd scene," writes Froma Zeitlin,

> all the issues which characterized the novelty of the original play are present, but wonderfully deflected through the comic travesty as a dissonance between two levels of reference—the comic fiction of the play and the paratragic rendition. In the counterpoint of the text which sets the recognition scene from the *Helen* against Critylla's misrecognition of the identity of the parody, the questions of illusion and reality, of truth and falsehood, of mimesis and deception, are reframed in metatheatrical terms.

"Let me imitate [μιμήσομαι] Euripides' brand new *Helene*," begins the Kinsman (line 850),[111] setting this most innovative play against *Palamedes*, judged "frigid" on account of the failure of the reference to it before the parabasis. "I'll be Helene since I'm already costumed as a woman." His custodian (Kritylla) is not amused and begins a crude commentary as "Helene" prepares to speak. The comparison between the predicaments of Euripides' Kinsman tied to a plank and the tragic Helene languishing in Egypt is hilarious and identifies "salvation" as the theme on which new fictions shall be improvised.

The Kinsman thus announces his main activity as mimesis, the very skill that distinguished Euripides' Helene a year earlier. Lest he be thought a slavish imitator, the comic actor distorts his opening quotation to mark it as comic verse with a silly pun. Throughout the contrafact, however, s/he is the "straight man" intent on his/her purpose, putting up with interminable interference from Kritylla, who remains on another plane, that is, entirely ignorant of the internal fiction. Kritylla is the bad spectator in whose person the playwright simultaneously analyzes and satirizes this mode of play. *Bômolokhia* is here extended to include ignorance of theatrical convention. The literary ruses of Euripides and his Kinsman may be growing in length and sophistication, as it were, but all is lost on a stupid (female) audience. A particularly funny moment in this transaction comes when the Kinsman announces that he is Helene (lines 862–63):[112]

KINSMAN. I am called Helene.

KRITYLLA. What, you've become a woman again?
You haven't even been punished for the first time you played a woman!

Several more authentic lines from the tragedy alternate with Kritylla's commentary until "Helene" strikes out on her own to compose a brief soliloquy that achieves a wild mixture of tragic and comic styles (lines 866–70). At this point, Euripides-Menelaos enters and responds with similarly clever speech that leans more strictly toward tragic mimesis, as befits the tragic poet. Kritylla methodically intervenes to derail the dialogue and manages to generate a metatheatrical confusion at line 888 with a sharp instance of surface play. She is outraged that, as often happens in tragic fiction, the central altar has been redefined (in this case, as the tomb of Proteus). "How dare you call this altar a tomb!" she shrieks. "Helene" and "Menelaos" are noticeably frustrated by Kritylla's intrusions and try valiantly to incorporate her presence into their internal scenario. In answer to her husband's inquiry, "Helene" identifies her as Theonoe. Though she refuses to play along, Kritylla is quiet during the climactic recognition.

Aristophanes briefly disrupts his contrafact even without Kritylla's help by referring to the matrix fiction of *Thesmophoriazousai*: in line 903 "Helene" momentarily remembers that "she" is Euripides' relative who has just shaved and singed himself in order to infiltrate the women's festival; in line 910, similarly, "Helene" distorts the tragic script to insert a stock joke that can refer only to Euripides: "I see from the vegetable greens, that you must be . . . Menelaos." Otherwise, however, line 906–12 are pure Euripides (*Helene* 558, 561–66). The reading of tragedy then gives way to an ecstatic "song" of sorts in which "Helene" pleads with her husband to rescue her from the Egyptian dystopia. With the entrance of the *prytanis* and Scythian archer the wishful reenactment of tragic salvation is quashed before it has a chance to develop further. The author of the fiction is shown to be a coward lacking in the qualities he has tried to represent. "I'd better slip away for a little while," he says, adding a weak promise "never to betray [his Kinsman/ "Helene"] as long as s/he lives" (lines 924–26).

Aristophanes' play with *Helene*, of course, participates in a large-scale rivalry between tragic and comic *sôtêria* played here in terms of gender conflict. Euripidean fiction is the source of trouble—in particular, his all-too-realistic representation of women (this, of course, with a comic "spin"). The repeated attempts to wriggle out of the predicament by tragic means fail—Euripides' Kinsman is discovered, and the various *mêkhanai* drawn from recent plays are thwarted by people far inferior to the tragedian in craft and intellect. A happy ending becomes possible only when Euripides abandons tragedy and agrees to play by the rules of comic discourse. With the failure of *Andromeda*, he drops the tragic mask to address the women directly as contemporaries in the polis with whom he shall conclude a treaty (lines 1160–63). Only this way can he finally save his relative and demonstrate his competence as an agent of comic salvation.[113] We thus come to a pause in a long dialogue between tragedy and comedy in which a fundamental interactive opposition has been explored and finally "resolved" in a symbolic treaty across the lines of gender and genre.

8

Herakles

Euripides' Peirithous
and Aristophanes' Frogs

I mmediately after the parabasis (lines 738 ff.), Aristophanes' *Frogs* starts over with a
new "prologue" symptomatic of the play's double plan that has long troubled critics.
First, there is the retrieval of Euripides played out in two sequences involving katabasis
and comic business at the door to Hades. Second, there is the poetic agon that is
already in progress and for which Dionysos is recruited as judge. Considerable attention has been paid recently to the problem of why and how Dionysos imperson-
ates Herakles.[1] Going beyond the acknowledgment of Herakles' qualifications as a
paradigm of traditional heroic virtue,[2] this chapter presents the more concrete argument that *Frogs* exhibits a metafictional relation to an earlier tragedy. In terms applied above to *Akharnians*, *Peace*, and *Birds*, *Frogs* is presented here as a contrafact
of Euripides' *Peirithous*, a tragic script that Aristophanes uses to undergird his comic
katabasis and to set up the central agon. Dionysos, who is enlisted to represent comedy, interacts with the tragic Herakles as *sôtêr*, "savior," and judge to preside over a
dramatic festival-in-miniature.

As in *Peace*, Aristophanes mingles "low" and "high" elements in a composite
protagonist who creatively fuses genres to suggest a type of drama beyond tragedy
and comedy. The linear and evolutionary schemes proposed in earlier scholarship—
for example, the "conversion" or "education" of Dionysos[3]—are set aside in favor of
a thoroughgoing counterpoint between the comic-Dionysiac (relativism, politics of
the present), on the one hand, and the tragic-Heraklean (traditional heroism, aristocratic ideals of the past), on the other. The comic Dionysos' delight in Euripides
motivates the action and endures throughout the play, marking comedy as the discourse of the present. Within the frame, however, nostalgic fictions of social concord and the "good old days" of tragedy prevail in the Heraklean rescue of Athens'
past (Aiskhylos). Thus, although *Frogs* is preoccupied with Euripides from the outset,
there can be no place for him in the final utopian "time warp," which, of course, is
not coextensive with the entire play. It is comedy, represented by Dionysos, that crosses
boundaries between worlds and genres to accomplish the "salvation" of the city con-
templated in the tragic agon. In other words, the nostalgic rescue of Aiskhylos is a

utopian fiction orchestrated by comedy in a show of its superior abilities and value to society. The vehicle for this demonstration is a contrafact whereby *Frogs* trans-forms Euripides' katabasis play to celebrate the end of an era—and the end of Old Comedy as well—in an expansive and idealizing review of the dramatic genres, their "imaginary rivalry," and their status as influential media in the polis.

The presentation of the possible connection between *Peirithous* and Aristophanes' *Frogs* builds on the suggestions of many scholars from the time of Welcker to the present.[4] Instead of the commonly assumed burlesque of katabasis-myth, *Frogs* will be read as a sustained involvement with the Euripidean production in which Herakles descended to Hades to fetch Kerberos and that featured a conflict between Herakles and Aiakos, a chorus of Eleusinian initiates, an innovative relationship between Theseus and Peirithous in the underworld, and the formal release of both Theseus and Peirithous. Furthermore, the tragic script is brilliantly altered and exploited by Aristophanes throughout the full extent of *Frogs*. Konstan's sequence of movements emphasizing different modes of transcending death—individual heroism, mystic communion, and civic competition (all being types of *sôtêria*)—is introduced, sus-tained, and informed by the ongoing contrafact of *Peirithous*. This demonstration by the comic poet of his mastery over tragedy confirms the argument that the famous poetic agon implicitly reveals comedy alone to be capable of a comprehensive *sôtêria* uniting the powers and social values represented by both Euripides and Aiskhylos.[5]

Hercules Tragicus

Wilamowitz appears to have been the first to argue that *Frogs* involves explicit refer-ence to *Peirithous*, though in attributing the play to Kritias he departed from the influential work of scholars such as Welcker and Nauck on the question of author-ship.[6] We have more to work with since the publication of the sixteen-line exchange between Herakles and Aiakos, along with several papyrus fragments.[7] Given the promi-nent position of *Frogs* in current scholarship on Greek drama, it is time to take a fresh look at this potential connection between Aristophanes and Euripides.[8]

For many years, two focal issues here have been those of authorship and the presence of a paratragic connection between *Frogs* and *Peirithous*. Taking his cue from J. Kuiper, Dana Sutton has reviewed the evidence and argued convincingly in Euripides' favor.[9] The second issue has been equally divisive, with a number of au-thorities on either side.[10] Since the outline of the tragic model for this contrafact is particularly tenuous, there is much room for disagreement. "Speculative reconstruc-tion of such plays," notes C. Collard, "is wholly justifiable, indeed an almost irresist-ible challenge, and each attempt either narrows the possibilities or adds new ones; speculation, however, it must remain."[11] As with the contrafact of Sophokles' *Tereus* in Aristophanes' *Birds*, there is not much in the way of demonstrable verbal borrow-ing—although there are some clear points of contact—and we must rely more on situational and thematic similarities.[12]

Recent studies of the connection between Theseus and Peirithous, especially in the work of Euripides,[13] reveal that his play possesses a number of extraordinary and innovative features. Though working with a legend of venerable antiquity, Euripides once again found clever ways to manipulate tradition, this time making a rather serious drama from material that elsewhere showed comic potential.[14] An important aspect of Aristophanes' contrafact, as we shall see, was to reclaim the Peirithous-Theseus episode for comedy. In fact, here the manipulation of myth and innovative stagecraft collude nicely as Theseus is spared confinement to a seat (and the embarrassing consequences of being torn away). This freedom facilitates the development of the plot in what would otherwise be a rather static situation. In order to set up the overview of the play, the testimonia and fragments are distilled into the following outline:

> *Dramatis locus*: Upper world, most likely Eleusis (prologue and parodos) with a change of scene to Hades (the palace of Aiakos has been suggested).
>
> *Dramatis Personae*: Herakles, Aiakos, Theseus, Peirithous, and Plouton (perhaps Persephone).
>
> *Chorus*: Eleusinian initiates (cf. language of the choral fr. 2).
>
> *Prologue*: Narrative (expository monologue) or action that presents the initiation of Herakles at Eleusis in preparation for his mission to fetch Kerberos.
>
> *Parodos*: A band of initiates performs a chthonic sacrifice (to summon ghost[s]?); They engage Herakles and escort him to the underworld.
>
> *Scene A*: A confrontational meeting between Herakles and Aiakos.
>
> *Scene B*: An interview between Herakles and Peirithous in the presence of the chorus. Peirithous is in a sort of trance (i.e., the "chair of forgetfulness") and is shown gradually recovering from his dazed condition. He begins to explain things to Herakles by invoking the example of his father, Ixion.
>
> *Scene C*: A conversation in which Theseus offers to help Herakles with Kerberos. We learn that Peirithous has been imprisoned there for his attempt to abduct Persephone. He is bound to an immovable stone chair guarded by serpents. His accomplice, Theseus, remains with him voluntarily.
>
> *Narrative* (messenger ?) of how Herakles overcame Kerberos.
>
> *Scene D*: A debate (?): Peirithous. who is enduring a "fitting punishment," encourages Theseus to depart with Herakles. Theseus refuses, "considering it shameful to abandon a friend." This motivates Herakles to rescue both.
>
> *Scene E*: Herakles successfully persuades Plouton to release Peirithous and, with him, Theseus. How the Kerberos issue fit in with the release of Peirithous is not known (at the very least it provided dramatic interest). It is clear, however, that the voluntary imprisonment of Theseus as well as the rescue through persuasion by Herakles of both Peirithous and Theseus are innovations on the part of Euripides.

This sketch relies on the so-called Logothetes hypothesis[15] for these critical details: (1) Theseus asserts his loyalty to Peirithous and *voluntarily* stays with him in the underworld throughout his imprisonment in an "immobile seat" (apparently in an incapacitating trance); and (2) Herakles subsequently wins the "favor of the chthonic gods" and rescues *both heroes* from Hades. This latter feature is confirmed by Tzetzes, who notes that "in Euripides' play both are rescued (as Theseus explains to Herakles)."[16]

It is most likely that the action began in the upper world, as Wilamowitz suggested,[17] in order to avoid the impossible situation of a chthonic sacrifice in the underworld performed by initiates who refer to the night sky above them. Most of the action, however, took place in Hades, making *Peirithous*, in more ways than one, a "tragedy of *opsis* (spectacle)" — Aristotle's fourth category that includes underworld settings.[18] Unless we regard fr.1 as the opening lines of the play (and this is unlikely),[19] we do not have any text of the prologue, so that the attestation of *Peirithous* begins with the parodos. Hyginus, who commonly follows the Greek tragic plot,[20] mentions a *descent* to Hades via Tainaron, and it is certainly attractive to see *Frogs* as reflecting a bold scene change innovated by Euripides.[21] Tzetzes (Scholion on *Frogs* 142a) relates the following:

> Being [Peirithous'] accomplice but not a thief himself, Theseus was caught and tied down. In Euripides' play Theseus subsequently narrates everything accurately to Herakles when the latter arrives to fetch Kerberos.

This comment would seem to place the katabasis of Herakles and his meeting with Aiakos after some introductory material, most certainly the prologue and the entrance of the chorus.

Given the coincidence of initiates with Herakles' mission to Hades, it seems quite likely that the prologue involved narration, or even partial enactment, of Herakles' well-known purification (from his slaughter of the Centaurs) and initiation at Eleusis just before the Kerberos labor.[22] If so, *Peirithous* emerges quite naturally as not only the model for *Frogs* but as a tragic script that was influential in shaping subsequent katabasis narratives down to Apollodoros and Virgil. As *Medeia* and *Bakkhai* did for their respective "myths," Euripides' *Peirithous* would appear to have played a critical role in mediating between the later reception of the Greek katabasis story (stories) and the common epic source postulated by Eduard Norden and Hugh Lloyd-Jones.[23]

The solemn sequence of purification and initiation constitutes a fine preface to the dramatic representation of katabasis. The pseudo-Platonic *Axiokhos* (371 E), for example, relates that "those descending to Hades with Herakles and Dionysos are said to have been initiated beforehand, borrowing from the Eleusinia the courage for the journey there." This harmonizes well with Herakles' comment to Amphitryon at Euripides' *Herakles* 613 that he overpowered Kerberos by force (as opposed to divine aid), "having been fortunate to behold the rites (*orgia*) of the initiates." Hans-Joachim Mette has argued persuasively from the close thematic connections between *Herakles* and *Peirithous* that the latter is undeniably Euripidean and that the two probably were part of the same trilogy (dated somewhere between the late 430s to the early 420s?) with knowledge of *Peirithous* indeed a prerequisite for appreciation of *Herakles*.[24] "The entire drama (*Herakles*)," notes Mette, "proceeds from the situation with which *Peirithous* concludes." The emphasis in *Herakles* on the bond of friendship, for example, shows a great affinity with the way, in Schmid's words, the plot of *Peirithous* was also "stark ethisiert."[25] The reminiscence of the *orgia* at Eleusis, on this reading, points to a prominent Eleusinian episode in *Peirithous* and indicates a continuity between the two plays.

Euripides' *Herakles* connects the protagonist intimately with Attica as a result of his rescue of Theseus.[26] The striking attraction of Herakles to Attica that runs through both plays began in *Peirithous* where he is featured in an Eleusinian context. While we cannot be certain how the initiation was represented, there is evidence that the chorus encounters Herakles in the upper world during their sacrifice.[27] Were they

to serve as his escort and give directions—as do the "nether" initiates in *Frogs*[28]—
they would be present in Hades for the rest of the play. It might be useful to consider
this role (for the chorus of *Peirithous*) in the context of the evolving and related functions of "katabasis sponsor" and "prophet-guide."[29] The former assures the success
of the katabasis by means of his or her special "chthonic" credentials, as it were, while
the latter advises and gives the Harrower of Hell special information. There is evidence
that the tradition before Euripides had Eumolpos and Hermes in these capacities, respectively.[30] *Peirithous* (and, following it, *Frogs*) would then represent a dramatic
economy of sorts in which a chorus, that is, a representative body, of Eleusinians unite
the credentials of Eumolpos with the guidance function of Hermes:

1. *Odyssey*: Kirke "sponsors" Odysseus' visit to the underworld and assumes some
   of the "guide" function (though, of course, Odysseus does not have an escort to
   Hades nor does he enter the underworld proper). Teiresias also participates in
   the function of "prophet-guide."
2. *Sixth-century epic of Herakles, Fifth-century lyric (Pindar, Bakkhylides)*: Eumolpos,
   first hierophant and founder of the mysteries, "sponsors" Herakles, thereby en-
   suring a kindly reception from Persephone. Hermes (cf. his epithets Psykho-
   pompos and Khthonios) acts as the "guide."
3. *Peirithous*: Eleusinian initiates combine the functions of "sponsor," authorized
   by their Eleusinian connection, and "guide" (cf. the necromancy of fr. 912 N²).
4. *Frogs*: Dionysos is certainly qualified to conduct a katabasis, but Herakles acts
   as both "sponsor" and "guide" with the nether initiates completing the function of "guide" in Hades itself.
5. *Virgil's Aeneid*: Sibyl (as priestess of Hekate) "sponsors" the katabasis of Aeneas;
   Anchises acts as "prophet and guide." The blessed inhabitants of Elysium are
   an echo of the initiate choruses of drama whose role has been taken over by
   figures particular to the given narrative. Thus Deiphobe and Anchises once again
   split the functions that had been united in Greek drama in the person of the
   chorus.

The anapestic fragments 2–4 represent a moment early in the play when the
chorus of initiates perform their parodos. There is evidence that they engage Herakles
at this point (see fr. 913 N² later). Furthermore, it appears from fr. 912 N² that the
initiates may already be preparing for the katabasis, thus placing the chthonic sacrifice at the juncture between changes of scene. If so, we can imagine a prologue in
which Herakles explains why he has come to Eleusis and what he now must do. A
group of fellow initiates then enters and says, in effect, "we are ready to go, but must
first offer prayer and sacrifice to the nether gods." In the first of the fragments relating to this moment, the initiates pour a libation from their *plêmokhoai*, earthenware
vessels associated with Eleusinian ritual:[31]

That we pour forth this offering from our vessels   fr. 2
into the chthonic opening with words of good omen

Fr. 868 N² may also belong to this point in the action that addresses the "chthonic
gods who hold the dark realm of the dead, the lake of Acheron, from which there is
no return."[32]

In an arresting image reminiscent of Aias' deception speech,[33] Euripides has his
chorus express the cyclicity of time in visual terms. With an upward gesture, the ini-

tiates regard the heavens, noting the motion of the constellations on the celestial sphere by way of illustration. We are clearly in the upper world at this point:[34]

> Tireless Time whirls about, complete in   fr. 3
> the eternity of his flow, ever begetting
> himself of himself. The Twin Bears
> guard the firmament of Atlas with
> rapidly fluttering wings.

> You, born of yourself, who have interwoven   fr. 4
> the nature of all things with the rotation of the heavens;
> You, about whom the light of day, black spangled night,
> and the innumerable throng of stars
> moves constantly in measured dance.

Although we cannot be certain, it is plausible to assume that Time again is the addressee of the second fragment (4), given the theme of self-begetting and the image of rotation in both passages.[35] As Kuiper notes, the chorus' sustained natural imagery, especially ὀρφναία νύξ, "black night," of fr. 4, appears to have inspired the opening of the mock-Euripidean monody at *Frogs* 1331, ὦ Νυκτὸς κελαινοφαὴς ὄρφνα, "O black-bright dark of Night."[36] It has been suggested that we also place Euripides fr. 913 N[2], which one ancient source attributes to Herakles, in this context.[37] This important connection simultaneously links fr. 913 N[2] with *Peirithous* and proves that Herakles interacted with the chorus during their parodos:[38]

> [HERAKLES] Who, beholding this, does not contemplate god,   fr. 913 N[2]
> firmly rejecting the twisted deceptions
> of the astronomers? Possessing no understanding at all
> they wag their ruinous tongues at random
> about things that lie beyond the evidence of sense.

In fact, over the years, three or four other fragments have been associated with the parodos of the play, especially frr. 910, 912, and 913 N[2] (above). The latter two, if they indeed belong to *Peirithous*, add considerable color and detail to the sacrifice. The prayer to Hades of fr. 912 N[2], which seems most natural in an upper-world context, involves necromancy in which shades are summoned for interrogation. In seeking a sort of "sneak preview" of the afterlife, the chorus may be anxious specifically about the challenges of negotiating passage to the underworld as Herakles' escort. The high moral tone of fr. 910 N[2], critical of atheism on ethical grounds, is quite consistent with what we would expect of Eleusinian initiates. The intellectual objection to atheism in fr. 913 N[2] (Herakles) would seem to fit in close conjunction with fr. 910 N[2], though as Sutton has argued, the objection here may be more to the abuse of science (i.e., the glib promotion of atheism) rather than to science itself.[39] Finally, the reference to political life in fr. 910 N[2] hints at an Athenian context, a connection made explicit later in the play (fr. 7, lines 8–9):[40]

> Fortunate is he who has learned   fr. 910 N[2]
> from inquiry,
> intent neither on causing pain to his fellow citizens
> nor on committing wicked deeds,

but rather, contemplating the
unaging order of immortal nature,
to understand to what end, whence,
and how it arose.
The practice of shameful deeds
is never found near those such as this.

To you, guardian of all, —whether you   fr. 912 N^2
prefer to be called Zeus or Aidês —
I bring this libation and meal [*pelanos*].
Accept from me this fireless offering
of all kinds of fruits poured forth in abundance.
Among the gods, the descendants of Ouranos, it is you
who hold the sceptre of Zeus and you who
share in power of the nether gods in Hades.
Send the shades of those below up to the light,
to us who wish to learn in advance what
struggles [await us], whence they arise,
what is the root of evil, and to which of the
blessed gods we should sacrifice in order to
find relief from suffering.

Following the events at Eleusis suggested above, the scene shifts to the underworld. How was the journey represented? Noting the similar patterning of Apollodoros' katabasis narrative and that of *Frogs*, Lloyd-Jones outlines what appears to be the sequence of the sixth-century epic source:[41]

1. Herakles goes to Eleusis where he is purified and initiated by the Eumolpids. He has, in particular, the blessing of Eumolpos which will ensure a friendly reception from Persephone (whose cult he represents).
2. Herakles then descends via Tainaron guided by Hermes.
3. At the entrance to Hades he encounters ghosts (Medousa and Meleagros).
4. Inside the gates of the underworld he encounters Theseus, Peirithous, and a certain Askalaphos (whose story is not related to that of the other two).
5. Herakles sacrifices one of the cattle of Hades and wrestles with the herdsman Menoites.
6. Herakles faces Plouton and negotiates the abduction of Kerberos. This he must do (and does successfully) with his bare hands.
7. Herakles ascends via Troizen.
8. Herakles shows Kerberos to Eurystheus and then returns the hound.

"We cannot help suspecting," notes Lloyd-Jones, ". . . that a standard account of the descent of Heracles was in [Aristophanes'] mind."[42] As noted above, while there was no doubt an epic source of greater antiquity than *Peirithous* (so Norden and Lloyd-Jones), a very influential presentation of this narrative was Euripides' katabasis play, which is most immediately the script informing the metafictional design of *Frogs*.

We pick up the action of the play at the fourth item of the sequence above. Herakles arrives to engage the doorkeeper Aiakos in a lively exchange (fr. 1). The tradition of Herakles as Harrower of Hell, supported by the great play made of this moment in *Frogs*, makes it quite likely that Aiakos challenged Herakles' right to invade his domain and abduct so important a fixture as Kerberos. In fact, the adjective *eutolmos* in line 2 probably has a negative value, that is, "audacious," and the following line has a defensive tone, that is, "you had better have a good reason for being here!" In other words, it is only *dikaion* for him to explain his bold request to violate Hades' realm. This trouble at the gate may be a dramatic transformation of the more elaborate episode with Menoites. Instead of theft and confrontation, Herakles must simply negotiate his right to enter at the door.[43]

AIAKOS. Now, what is this? I see someone   fr. 1
hastening this way, very bold [audacious] in spirit.
It is only right for you to [you had better] say, Stranger,
who you are and why you have come to these parts.

HERAKLES. I shall not delay to reveal the whole story.
My fatherland is Argos, my name Herakles,
born of Zeus, father of all the gods.
Zeus entered my mother's modest chambers,
as the tale is truthfully told.
I have come here under compulsion, obedient to
the command of Eurystheus who sent me for Hades' hound
and bade me bring him alive to Mykenae's gate.
Not that he has any desire to see the creature, but rather
he believes he has invented for me a task impossible to
accomplish.
Pursuing this deed, then, I have come all round
into the recessess of Europe and all of Asia.

If fr. 1 does not represent Herakles' first entrance, where does it occur and how does it fit with the parodos and role of the chorus? Sutton has convincingly connected several Euripidean fragments *incertae sedis* (frr. 910, 912 and 913 N²) with other significant evidence to suggest some possibilities.[44] The most plausible scenario would have the initiates meet Herakles in the upper world during their parodos ritual performed in preparation for the katabasis.[45] We can imagine them continuing from the threshold of Hades, as it were, observing the action, commenting on it, but not actively participating. Evidence for what this action might have been is furnished by several papyrus fragments (5A, 5, and 7). Particularly interesting is the question of staging. How was the (presumably stationary) Peirithous presented? How did Theseus move about in the limited sphere to which he had restricted himself? "The general idea," summarizes Sutton, "is that in F 5A Peirithous begins to recuperate from some kind of spell he has been under and Herakles, in the presence of the chorus, asks him how he came to be in his present predicament." Fr. 5 would naturally be Peirithous' answer to this question. For the first of these (Sutton fr. 5A = P.Oxy. 3531 [not in Snell]), consider the following reconstructions drawing on the translations and supplements of Cockle and Parsons:[46]

serpent(s) . . .   fr. 5A
I know the wrath [of the gods].

[CHORUS.] having understood too late . . .
. . . honor the gods .. .

[HERAKLES.] Son of Ixion, often I have seen
and heard by report [many sufferings]
but have not [known] anyone approaching
even close to your misfortune.
On what pretext [are you enduring this . . .]
of blindness unexpectedly?

[PEIRITHOUS.] [The sound] is no longer indistinct
[nor] like a dream; [it is a voice,] and Greek.
But as for seeing the [speaker],
I was [not] able for a mist
floats before my [eyes]. Are you
asking how I fell into this misfortune?
The sound of your voice is [now audible].

[HERAKLES.] It is no wonder for one to
be deprived of [the ability to recognize]
voice and shape. Many [a day] has
gone by since you and I [last met].
But I shall remind you . . .

[PEIRITHOUS.] Silence . . .
Sound . . .

The physical and mental fog engulfing Peirithous may well be a special feature
promoted (if not invented) by Euripides and reflected in contemporary iconography and remembered later as a "chair of forgetfulness."[47] Thus Herakles has arrived to disturb Peirithous' trancelike gloom with a conversation thematically organized around the contrast between seeing and hearing. This emphasis appears
quite Euripidean and brings to mind the fun poked at the tragedian for a similar
sophistic distinction in the opening lines of *Thesmophoriazousai*. Fr. 5 (P.Oxy. 2078,
fr. 1) appears to follow, physically (as papyrus) and thematically, with a narrative
by Peirithous of his own misfortunes. He begins with the story of his father's notorious crime and punishment.[48]

tripped up . . . / going . . . / Greek . . .   fr. 5
altar . . . / God . . . madness
sent blindness . . .
a cloud woman . . .
sowed in the midst of the [gods] . . .
he should mingle with the daughter . . .
of such boasts . . .
he paid the penalty to the gods . . .
to the wheel of insanity . . .
gadfly-driven . . .
unheard of by men . . .
he concealed, but the north[-wind] . . .

was torn to pieces with . . .
my father, having sinned against the gods . . .
Now I [take pattern by] his sufferings . . .

The logical sequence would then lead to Peirithous' own misdeeds with emphasis on the way the assaults on a goddess by both father and son are punished by confinement in the underworld. Housman conjecturally restored the last line to yield an etymology of Peirithous' name based on Ixion's punishment: *thous*, "swift" and *peri*, "circling": "Now a similar fate has befallen me, whose name, Peirithous, is a riddle of his sufferings."[49]

This first encounter is then followed at some point by a more expansive dialogue between Herakles and Theseus attested by fr. 7 (P.Oxy. 2078, frr. 2 and 3). The fifth-century iconography of the given legend sometimes features the detail that Theseus, holding two swords (or spears)—his own and that of his friend—stands by an apparently feeble (or "forgetful") Peirithous.[50] It is possible that in Euripides the Athenian also comes *verbally* to the rescue using his greater energy and unimpaired mental faculties to converse with Herakles. An important function of this interview is to clarify the role and motivations of Theseus. Euripides has created for him a compromise between the other attested versions involving either punishment for both men on an equal basis or—what looks like an Attic innovation—separate fates for Peirithous (eternal imprisonment) and Theseus (rescue).[51] In our play Theseus does indeed stay with Peirithous but does so voluntarily and will not abandon his friend, "yoked to him," in the words of an important fragment, "by fetters of shame/respect [*aidôs*], that are not forged of metal" (fr. 6).[52] Not only does Theseus' loyalty make for better theater, freeing at least one of the two heroes to move about, but it also innovates an important Heraklean parergon, that is, the project of securing the release of *both* Theseus and Peirithous.

In this exchange, Herakles politely declines Theseus' offer of help in capturing Kerberos. At a later point in the play, as the Logothetes hypothesis suggests, this exciting episode was narrated (by a messenger perhaps) in order to spice up an otherwise static plot. Only the more intelligible portions (lines 4–19) of this papyrus are translated, in which the conversation turns to the interaction between Herakles and Theseus:[53]

. . . it now seems pleasant to you.   fr. 7

[THESEUS.] . . . Herakles, I shall blame [you]
. . . for, to betray . . . a trustworthy man and
a friend . . . held in thrall by an enemy.

[HERAKLES.] Theseus, you have spoken words befitting both
[yourself] and the Athenian polis, for you
are ever an ally to those in distress. It would
be unseemly for me, however, to return home
with false show [of accomplishment].
How gladly do you think Eurystheus will claim
—if he learns that you assisted me—
that the effort to perform this labor was fruitless.

[THESEUS.] But that which you need . . . you have
my favor, [in which attitude I am] not capricious but
openly hostile to my enemies and kind to my friends.
Before, to me you . . . an account;
Now you should speak . . . words.

One other fragment, fr. 964 N², identified by Cicero as "spoken by Theseus in Euripides" (Tusc. Disp. 3.14.29), has been connected with this moment in the play:[54]

[THESEUS.] Having learned this from a certain wise man,　　　　　　　　　fr. 964
I cast my mind into worries and misfortunes,
imagining to myself exile from my homeland,
scenarios of untimely death, and other manners of evil,
so that, should I experience any of these things which I imagined
mentally, the pain of a sudden calamity might be muted.

Mette[55] and others have pointed out that this is apparently another reference by Euripides to his "teacher" Anaxagoras. As such, it fits with the quotation of frr. 4, 912 N², and 913 N² by Satyrus in his discussion of Anaxagorean influence on Euripides. This coincidence simultaneously brings the fragments together thematically, as Sutton argues, and identifies them as extracts from the same play, *Peirithous*.[56]

There is little direct evidence for the rest of the play beyond the final points in the outline. Thus there can be no doubt that Herakles performed his assignment for Eurystheus and rescued both Theseus and Peirithous from imprisonment in Hades. The bond of friendship emphasized in the hypothesis is clearly an innovation on the part of Euripides, for whom this would not be a solitary exercise in representing "male bonding" (cf. the *philia* of Orestes and Pylades). Plutarch (*Moralia* 7.96 C) gives the sentiment of fr. 6 to Theseus as a retort "to the bound and tormented Peirithous." It is not unreasonable to assume an argumentative context in which the latter urges Theseus to leave with Herakles, to which Theseus says, in effect, "[by no means shall I abandon you as I am] bound by fetters of shame, that are not forged of metal." Looking forward to *Frogs*, it is tempting to think that the famous contest of the poets was inspired by a tragic agon that was, in theme, its diametric opposite.

Finally, there was some mechanism by which Herakles managed to free both Peirithous and Theseus. Hyginus (Fab. 79) says that he "secured their release by entreating Plouton and led them safely away." Force is out of the question and we are left to imagine a scene in which Herakles prevails upon Plouton by means of his distinction and rhetoric. If we accept the sketchy evidence of the anonymous papyrus fragment 658 (Kannicht-Snell)[57] Persephone may have also had a speaking part here. Among the tatters of sense preserved in the first part of this fragment (fr. a) we find "Spartans [Sown Men?]," "unflinching hound," "struggle . . . not in battling with a beast," "mighty struggle," "I shall destroy you utterly." In the second, following a mention of "the land, together with Herakles" there are several suggestive phrases: "he shall go to the underworld . . . he shall appear as a helper . . . the boundary of no return," "Gorgon-mask, of/from eyes . . . terrible with threats." Most intriguing is the phrase, "he shall prevail upon my husband" (κρ]ατήσει τὸν ἐμὸν εὐνέτην). If these lines indeed belong to *Peirithous* as Mette and Carlini suggest, it would appear that Persephone was present at the agon (if we may call it that) involving Herakles and Plouton. This scene is certainly behind the statements in the hypothesis that Herakles "enjoying the favor of the chthonic gods, freed Theseus and his friend" and having "won divine favor, showed mercy towards his friends."

The last three book fragments (frr. 10–12) are sententious in nature and impossible to order. Fr. 10 yields little more than the modified proverb that "fortune helps those who are sensible,"[58] but the other two suggest more interesting connections with the play as we know it. The sentiment of fr. 11 could fit in the exchanges between Peirithous and Theseus or Herakles and Plouton. The contrast here is between different determinants of behavior (character, law) and their vulnerability to rhetoric:[59]

> Sterling character is more secure than law [*nomos*].   fr. 11
> No orator will be able to pervert the former, while
> the latter he will often abuse, battering it back and forth
> with his words.

Fr. 12 is most appropriate in the mouth of Theseus: "Is it not better to die than to live a coward?"[60] Finally, we might have a last fragment (936 N^2) regarding the paradox of katabasis: "No, rather Hades received me though still alive." Welcker suggests that this was a response to a question such as "Are you one of the dead, a permanent dweller in the underworld?"[61]

Hercules Comicus

We now return to the introductory question concerning the Dionysos-Herakles hybrid and the function of Euripides' katabasis play as a model for *Frogs*. How and why does Dionysos engage the role of Herakles in his mission to retrieve Euripides? What light can a metafictional reading of *Frogs* as a contrafact of *Peirithous* shed on the relationship between the two great "movements" of the comedy and its outcome? We must begin by inquiring how *Frogs* fuses the two dramatic types, that is, the comic Dionysos and the tragic Herakles. In elaborating a comic script from *Peirithous*, Aristophanes intertwines the wide-ranging *sôtêria* and civic usefulness of the tragic Herakles with the character of the comic Dionysos to produce a protagonist who not only crosses the boundary between the upper and lower worlds but who transgresses generic boundaries to suggest a theatrical realm *beyond*, an imaginary agon in which tragedy and comedy compete. The metafictional interaction of the two plays is inscribed in the counterpoint between the Dionysiac and Heraklean aspects of the protagonist throughout *Frogs* up to the parabasis (and, to a considerable degree, into the agon). An appreciation of this counterpoint provides insight into how *Frogs* works on formal and thematic levels. Rather than find evolution or conversion within the lead character, the Dionysiac and Heraklean components will be seen ultimately to register their impact on different levels: the Heraklean rescue of the past in Aiskhylos is a utopian fiction framed by the activities and powers of comedy represented by Dionysos. In other words, comedy of the present assumes a tragic mask to imagine a nostalgic, if impossible, recapitulation of the past. Marking the death of Euripides, *Frogs* concludes the vigorous "imaginary rivalry" between Aristophanes and the tragedian followed in this study from its inception in *Akharnians* a full two decades earlier.

As comedy had long known various amorous and cowardly versions of Dionysos, *Frogs* appears self-consciously nostalgic both in its allusion to earlier plays[62] and in its inclusion of an honorary (i.e., subsidiary) chorus of "real" animals. The *alazoneia* of Dionysos, his effeminacy, and his experimentation with disguise identify him clearly as the figure within the primary fiction who, while explicit about performing comedy (lines 1–18), is only a spectator and critic of tragedy. In other words, he is formally outside the sphere of tragic competition. As yet another Aristophanic protagonist who appears to "improvise" the comic plot, that is, to "write" the script as he goes along, Dionysos unambiguously represents the genre in which he is currently a player (*pace* Heiden).[63] As we learn early in the play from the god himself, however, Dionysos will lead us to Euripides.

Frogs is, of course, preoccupied with Euripidean theater and Euripides himself, whose recent death offered Aristophanes the irresistible combination of celebrity news with one last opportunity to engage his favorite (tragic) counterpart and rival. Each of the "big three" tragedians was now dead, making a "scenario in Hades" a natural choice for a drama involving them. There is also the recent debut of the specifically Euripidean Dionysos in *Bakkhai*. As we have seen, Euripides' play, most likely performed before *Frogs*,[64] was definitive in articulating the relationship between Dionysos and tragedy with unprecedented clarity and vigor. Now it was comedy's turn. As did Euripides for his genre, Aristophanes reinvents the role of Dionysos by making him the lead figure in a metafictional experiment, a god who asserts his function as representative of comic poiesis.[65] Whereas *Bakkhai* had worked with the Theban episode, Aristophanes naturally fastened on katabasis as a mechanism for bringing together Dionysos and the society of dead poets. In the foreground of *Frogs*, moreover, is the strong bond between comedy (as Dionysos) and the figure of Euripides, who represents "new-fangled rhetoric, class confusion, relativism, and innovative poetry and music."[66] It was certainly a masterstroke on the part of Aristophanes to integrate all these elements with superb economy in a comic essay on Euripides, drama, and society based on a katabasis script written by Euripides himself! The absurdity whereby Euripides is, in a sense, to the comic Dionysos what Kerberos was to the tragic Herakles enhances the humor of the initial situation.

Euripidean drama had also presented a new Herakles who was ethically and politically assimilated to traditional Attica. He emerges from *Herakles* and *Peirithous* as an Eleusinian initiate, effective orator, social critic, arbiter of virtue, and *sôtêr*, "savior,"[67] of Theseus (and, by implication, Athens) in a way that amplifies this important cultic epithet. Not only is Herakles willing to rescue Theseus, but he modifies his mission to the underworld and confronts Plouton to support his friend's commitment to *philia*. Participation in the abduction of Persephone was not, after all, a particularly honorable or defensible mission, so Herakles' actions constitute a strong endorsement, even rehabilitation, of the Athenian hero's character. Implicit in the double rescue of *Peirithous* is Herakles' function as judge who awards the bond of *philia* an even higher priority than respect for the gods. A powerful dramatic expression of this priority in *Peirithous*—which has important implications for *Frogs*—is the unexpected emergence of Theseus as a focal figure whose rescue all but eclipses the Kerberos labor. The resultant bond of friendship and gratitude between Herakles and Theseus is politically significant as well: Herakles is celebrated in Athens formally by the transfer to him of Theseia, and he will now enjoy the status of special guest-friend there. The motivation for the rescue gains force from Theseus' own virtues, which Herakles admires. "Theseus," he says in fr. 7 of *Peirithous*, "you have spoken words befitting both [yourself] and the Athenian polis, for you are ever an ally to those in distress." From the context we see that Theseus had offered Herakles assistance with Eurystheus' assignment, but it is just as likely that Theseus' refusal to "betray . . . a trustworthy man and a friend . . . held in thrall by an enemy" refers to his reason for being in Hades, that is, his loyalty to Peirithous.

Herakles' initiation at Eleusis strengthens the Athenian connection and suggests a rather striking acculturation of the Peloponnesian hero to Attica, with Theseus performing his well-known function as host.[68] Aristophanes acknowledges this connection by making Herakles, like the Atticized Tereus in *Birds*, a handy reference point in a comic prologue (note his familiarity with the current tragic "scene," lines 73–106) and modeling the procession of his initiate chorus on that of the Lesser Mysteries at Agrai.[69] It is curious, however, that the comic Dionysos does not draw a parallel between the initiation of Herakles and his own.[70] Instead, the Eleusinia of the tragic past yields to the Lenaia of the present, where the onstage Dionysos emphasizes his love for Euripides and the immediacy of participating in the comic competition. Once again, a productive tension manifests itself between the ethical and political Atticization of Herakles and that of Dionysos, which is evidently more aesthetic and intellectual.

The bond of *philia* between Herakles and Theseus was amplified in Euripides' plays into a vivid cultural reciprocity. Herakles was aggressively assimilated into Athens while the juxtaposition of Theseus and Herakles highlighted the latter's well-known status as the paradigm for Theseus' ever-evolving heroic "career." Aristophanes invests his Aiskhylos with the social and ethical qualities of the tragic Theseus to set up a clear relationship between their respective rescues. *Frogs*, of course, complicates things by substituting fierce dramatic competition for the bond of friendship celebrated in *Peirithous*. This is not only a natural transgressive gesture on the part of comedy but an important by-product of the metafictional process. The interweaving voices of the tragic past (Herakles-Aiskhylos) and the comic present (Dionysos-Euripides) cannot collapse into a single harmony, but maintain distinct melodies that often collide and, ultimately, make very different impressions. Rather than look for "enlightenment" or "education" on the part of Dionysos, the double perspective implicit in a metafictional reading of *Frogs* will suggest a different approach to the final verdict. As "Herakles," on the one hand, the protagonist participates in a nostalgic reach for the past that imagines renewed social concord set to the words and music of Aiskhylos. As a representative of comedy, on the other hand, Dionysos demonstrates the superior power of his genre in securing *sôtêria* for the polis. The "soundtrack" for the latter exploit is, of course, "Euripidaristophanic."

Katabasis

In his capacity as a professional player of comedy, Dionysos is contemptuous of unworthy practitioners of his own craft (*Frogs* 3–4, cf. 13–14). His initial desire for

Euripides, however, and his disdain for lesser composers (e.g., lines 92–93) recall mock-sophistic enthusiasm in the mouths of characters such as Strepsiades (*Clouds* 260, 445–51) and the bird chorus (*Birds* 429–30): "I am in need of a clever poet," says Dionysos, "a real one of the sort who dared to come up with lines like 'Aither, house of Zeus,' or 'the Foot of Time' . . . " (lines 71, 99–100). We recognize here a caricature of the common spectator who fancies himself a keen critic of tragedy (lines 71–103).[71] From this perspective it is not surprising to hear Dionysos announce his purpose to be the rescue of Euripides. After the great exploit of the tragic Herakles in *Peirithous* there could be no doubt that this particular katabasis yields the rescue of a beloved figure, hence a context for Dionysos' "fond yearning" and "desire" for Euripides (*Frogs* 53, 59). *Peirithous*, however, presents a sharp disjunction between the initial reason for the katabasis (Kerberos) and its result, a twist in the plot that Aristophanes exploits with wonderful comic effect. What Dionysos believes he is doing and what he actually ends up doing will be very different indeed.

The opening of *Frogs* shares with *Birds* introductory banter and wandering that lead up to an interview with a figure from the tragic stage—a key player, in fact, from the model informing the contrafact. Just as the interview with Tereus clarified the relationship between *Birds* and Sophokles' play, the Herakles scene in *Frogs* establishes the connection between that comedy and *Peirithous*, without explicitly naming the source.[72] Dionysos explains his purpose to Herakles as follows (lines 108–15):

> Well, the reason why I've come wearing this costume,
> impersonating [*mimesis*] you, is so that you might tell me
> what friends received and entertained you
> when you descended to fetch Kerberos, in case I need them.
> And tell me too the harbors, bread-shops, brothels, resting places,
> turnings, fountains, roads, cities, accommodations, and hostesses
> with the fewest bugs.

Like *Peace*, however, *Frogs* has its protagonist appropriate the role of the tragic lead *kata mimêsin*, "by impersonation." Dionysos thus enjoys the best of both fictional worlds: He first interviews the tragic figure in a way that puts the metafictional process on display and then proceeds to enact the transformation himself. The theme of a social revival linked to the revival of tragedy is developed as Dionysos literally re-performs *Peirithous*, that is, enacts a revival of Euripides.

With a dramatic model ready to hand, the comic Dionysos, like Peisetairos in *Birds*, seeks out his tragic counterpart to authorize his imitation. Unlike Peisetairos, however, he is able to fulfill the intention signaled by his costume, which, we notice, he has put on in advance of the interview. "I can't help laughing," guffaws Herakles, "at the sight of the lion-skin slung over your saffron gown. What's the meaning of this? Why have your shoes and my club come together?" The juxtaposition of *kothornoi* worn by Dionysos (here as in vase paintings of the period) and Herakles' club is emblematic of the composite protagonist. Dionysos explains that he was smitten with yearning for Euripides while reading *Andromeda* on naval duty. We could add a joke about stagecraft to the sexual sense of this reference, discussed by Richard Moorton.[73] *Peirithous*, after all, is remarkable for its stationary character who must remain awkwardly onstage, Prometheus-like, until the final rescue. As we begin to recognize that *Frogs* is replaying the katabasis sequence of *Peirithous*, the reference to *Andromeda* emerges as a preview of Dionysos' involvement in this type of scenario, that is, a tragedy "starring" a bound figure waiting to be rescued. The difference between *Andromeda* and *Peirithous* is explicitly relevant to the development of *Frogs* in that Dionysos starts out thinking more in terms of an *Andromeda* but ends up enacting a reversal of *Peirithous*. That is to say, a rescue involving desire between the hero (himself) and a beautiful captive (Euripides) becomes a katabasis in which the rescuing hero (Dionysos) is faced with two "captives" whose rescue is not a matter of desire but successful argument. The added twist is that the *philia* of *Peirithous* mutates to become the competition of *Frogs*.

The extended interaction between *Frogs* and *Peirithous* begins with the Herakles scene and comes into full view with the katabasis and bold change in the *dramatis locus*. The latter feature, as we have seen, was a memorable innovation in *Peirithous* that made creative use of the Eleusinian connection. Beyond the explicit interview with Herakles, Aristophanes is careful to make his contrafact intelligible as the comic scenario evolves. Rejecting Herakles' first, lurid suggestions, Dionysos insists on mimesis. "I want to follow the precise path you did," he says at line 136, "on *that* occasion," that is, on the occasion of the performance of *Peirithous*. To give another example, Herakles informs Dionysos that the ferry across the lake of Akheron will cost not one obol (the traditional price) but two, and there has been considerable discussion of the exact point of the joke, for example, is it the cost of the journey from the Piraeus to Aigina (i.e., Athens to Aiakos)? a reference to the "theoric" fund (i.e., the price of admission to the theater)?[74] In light of the latter possibility the doubling of the "cost" of the katabasis emerges as a marker of its metafictional reduplication, that is, the superimposition of comic and tragic katabaseis performed by the composite Dionysos-Herakles. In this connection we have also the reference to the *tragic* Theseus (so Dover) as the one who instituted the new fee, presumably, on his way back with Peirithous and Herakles. Moreover, the traditional topography and katabasis sequence outlined earlier in this chapter include a blessed spot where initiates sing and dance. "They shall tell you everything you want to know," explains Herakles, "as they live near the very road you will travel, right by Plouton's gate" (lines 161–64). Theatrically, of course, this is no doubt a pointed reminder of how the Euripidean chorus escorted Herakles to the underworld and performed, symbolically, at the boundary between worlds. We will pick up with them, that is to say, where the tragedy left off. So Dionysos sets out, performing, indeed juggling, his double role in the grim crossing. In answer to Kharon's cry (line 187), "who wants to go to Kerberos-country, or Tainaron, or to Birdition?" he replies, "I do."

The passage of the hybrid Dionysos-Herakles to Hades is accompanied by the appropriately hybrid "swan frogs" who provide the comic color and song that the initiates, as a tragic import, cannot replicate (not, at least, in their "pure" form at the beginning of their performance).[75] Since we have been warned that the initiates are waiting at Plouton's gate, Dionysos is given a substitute escort, one that is explicitly linked to his own genre. The metafictional significance of this first chorus that sings to "Dionysos of the marshes" is to represent comedy as a nostalgic counterweight to the tragic-styled initiates. Given the explicit reference to the comic Phrynikhos in the opening lines of the play (cf. the comic etymology from *phrynê*, "toad," = "toad-man" or "croaker"), it is likely that we have in the victory of Dionysos over the frog chorus an extension of the god's comic function, that is, a symbolic victory of Aristophanes over his rival at this very Lenaia of 405.[76] Thus *Frogs* continues to experiment with doubling along lines dictated by its dynamic as a contrafact. We are given to enjoy, for a brief space, a genuine animal chorus in an authentic Athenian setting (the "marshes") as a preface to the performance of the borrowed tragic chorus in the underworld. First, however, our protagonist must disembark and encounter some of the traditional frights awaiting him at the entrance to Hades.[77] Here Dionysos is made to remind us again of what is going on by indirectly blaming Euripides as the author of the scenario in which he has been so frightened: "Which god shall I blame for my perdition? Air, the house of Zeus, the foot of Time?" that is, Euripidean poiesis (lines 310–11). Following the encounter with a monster in which Dionysos' cowardice is comically contrasted with the assumed Heraklean identity (lines 282, 298), the main chorus enters for the parodos.

While we cannot, unfortunately, directly compare the choral songs from *Peirithous* and *Frogs*, there can be no doubt that, along with the Aiakos scene, the choral entrance is one of the most vivid scenic points of contact, "taken by Aristophanes not from popular legend," in Wilamowitz's words, "but from the work of a [tragic] composer."[78] In his cogent analysis of the semantics of the numerous references to play (*paizo, paidia,* etc.) in the parodos, Kenneth Dover has shown how this fundamental concept is deployed by Aristophanes to illustrate the interaction of the chorus' serious (tragic) persona as initiates and its function as a *comic* chorus in *Frogs*.[79] The layering of dramatic texts is made especially clear as we observe Dionysos in the role of a spectator of a ritual from which he is conspicuously excluded by a wall of theatrical illusion, as it were. Despite the ease with which Dionysos could be (and often was) connected with the epithet Iakkhos[80] and the mysteries of Demeter in general, the lyric portions of the parodos, true to their tragic source, make no mention of his name or cult and, of course, ignore the god on stage. The liminality of the initiate chorus positioned between genres is given clear metrical expression as well: The ionic rhythm of the lyrics hark back to archaic tragedy[81] while the anapestic meter of lines 354–71 advertises this passage as a bit of pure comedy spliced into the ritual context.

A third of the way through the parodos, Aristophanes makes his chorus deliver *parabatic* anapests, that is, what traditionally was the most direct and nonmimetic portion of the comedy, its thematic and programmatic center.[82] Here is another example of how *Frogs* manipulates comic form, this time surprising us with an intrusion that marks a radical shift in tone. The hymns to Iakkhos and Demeter are punctuated by the miniparabasis in a way that enacts the promise at lines 389–90 to "say much that is hilarious and much that is serious." The Eleusinian procession and poetry frame a Dionysiac interlude celebrating comedy as the "rites of the real (γενναίων) Muses" and "Bacchic rites of bull-eating Kratinos' tongue." Kratinos, the father of what might be called the political satire school of comedy, is an appropriate model figure to invoke here as the ritual abuse (cf. Eleusinian *gephyrismos*) colludes with the *iambike* idea of comedy.[83] Anyone who is ignorant of these things is enjoined to be silent or depart. In keeping with the interactive dynamic of the parabasis, which aggressively links comedy and political life, the qualifications for participation extend beyond the theater of Dionysos to include conscientious citizenship as well. The banishment of individuals who promote strife, or who are greedy or ill-tempered, and so on (lines 359–62), interestingly recalls the choral fragment 910 N^2 associated with *Peirithous*.

This "parabasis," however, calls for and delivers specific names and events, thus breaking the colorless surface of tragic generalization to deliver ad hominem attacks. The repeated association of Dionysos and comedy (e.g., line 368: comedy as the god's "rites") propels the counterpoint between the Herakles persona supported by the initiate chorus and derived from tragedy, on the one hand, and the persona of Dionysos, player and representative of comedy, on the other. Explicit, parabatic reference to poetics and form continue in the anapestic interjection at lines 383–84 where the chorus announces that it will praise Demeter "in another genre of song" (ἑτέραν ὕμνων ἰδέαν). What follows is, in fact, radically new ("another genre") as it blends the preceding elements of the parodos, the archaic and tragic-style hymn and the parabatic anapests, into a hybrid. The end of the parodos thus turns out to be an astonishing tissue of cultic song (e.g., the refrain to Iakkhos) imbricated with all manner of comic business. The apparent departure of the chorus leader at this point (with part or all of the chorus) is a notorious problem.[84] In light of the metafictional reading developed here, this moment turns out to be simply the conversion of the tragic (initiate) persona to a more generic comic one. In other words, no one actually departs but rather the text and performance signal the conclusion of their close narrative dependence on *Peirithous*.

As we approach the parabasis proper by way of the Aiakos scene and costume-changes, it is appropriate to confront the issue of comic structure and its manipulation in *Frogs*. First of all, in themselves and in their syntax the Bauformen of comedy have a great deal to do with how a given play conveys its meaning. The innovative parabasis of *Birds* discussed above is one example of many that could be invoked.[85] While there can be no doubt that these Bauformen—prologue, parodos, symmetrical scenes, parabasis, and so on, and their various parts—were modules that could be assembled into a wide variety of sequences, there are certain fundamental patterns that *Frogs* clearly violates. The most important formal distortions may be listed as follows:

1. The parabatic anapests have been transposed to the parodos, leaving a rather reduced parabasis at lines 674–737.
2. The usual postparabasis "revue" featuring incidental characters and comic business has been transposed to come *before* the parabasis to conclude the katabasis sequence.
3. The chorus of initiates appears to depart formally with the song at lines 449–59.
4. A "new" comedy featuring the tragic competition begins with a formal prologue, immediately after the parabasis, in which two slaves are bantering and setting the scene for the spectators.

Thus the parabasis emerges as a pivot around which the expected sequence of elements has been rearranged, a reflective and programmatic interlude between two movements that participate in the contrafact of *Peirithous* quite differently. The function of the latter as a paradigm and narrative scaffolding is thus manifested in two ways. Up to the parabasis, as we have seen, *Peirithous* is featured as the narrative pattern that *Frogs* retraces in the katabasis adventure and counterpoint between Herakles and Dionysos. Subsequently the action turns to a comic metaphor of the tragic competition that no longer relies on the close tracking of a tragic script. Although the narrative control of *Peirithous* attenuates after the parabasis, it continues to be operative on a thematic level. The opposition between Euripides and Aiskhylos, for example, as well as in the structure and outcome of the agon, has been set up and continues to be informed by the tragic model. The effect of the formal transposition of elements is to articulate two distinct revivals of tragedy, the first mimetic—a "remake" of Euripides' katabasis play—the other on the level of the comic mythos, that is, a fiction of determining (and rescuing) the most authentic author of the genre.

The sustained mimesis of *Peirithous* culminates in the Aiakos scene and the playful studies of costume and role that follow.[86] The comic Dionysos must be reminded of his commitment to playing the tragic Herakles (line 463), a role that Aiakos, unfortunately, remembers all too well (467–68). It is important to note here that the counterpoint between personae (Herakles/Dionysos) and genres is sustained, for the moment, by reference to Herakles' tragic exploit, that is, the formidable last labor, and not his comic reputation. The Aristophanic reenactment of the encounter between Aiakos and Herakles is a delightful exercise in exaggeration motivated by the incongruity of the tragic disguise superimposed on a character (Dionysos) drawn from the comic tradition. As keeper of the gate to Hades, Aiakos simply cannot countenance the return of the hero famous for violating the boundaries and defying the constraints that it is his duty to enforce. His rhetoric spills over the top with tripledecker invective and colorful threats a là Hades. It is significant that Aiakos goes out of his way to address his "guest" in explicitly tragic language. The ring of the "foreign" idiom at this point is striking and led Wilamowitz and others to suggest that portions of the Aiakos scene (e.g., lines 470–73) involve direct quotation from *Peirithous*.[87] This possibility should be tempered, however, by an admission that the most obvious candidate (lines 470–78) appears to be no more than "an accumulation of bombastic and not always entirely coherent tragic motifs and phrases."[88] At any rate, the desired effect is achieved and Dionysos responds in an appropriately comic fashion by soiling himself.

The impersonation by Dionysos of the tragic Herakles and his reception as such by Aiakos is followed by a scene featuring a new intruder, the Heracles-Xanthias of line 499. The shift in genre—that is, the transition from tragic to comic reference—requires a shift in gender, so Xanthias is greeted by a woman[89] who, in a willful "misreading," invokes the *comic* Herakles and invites him to satisfy his various appetites at dinner with Persephone, the lady of the royal house. Dionysos is outraged and objects that he was merely "playing" (line 523) when he suggested the costume change. He takes back the disguise only to get into deep trouble with two other women, the "metic" innkeepers who are not nearly so amused by Herakles' return.

It is striking that the traditional postparabasis sequence of intruders occurs at this point in *Frogs* with the additional twist that the intruders are "recycled" from the characters already onstage. The pace is quick and there is yet another costume change (back to Xanthias) as the chorus engages the characters in a lively internal discussion of the action. Again, changes are rung on the comic/tragic dichotomy with a thematic reversal of sorts: When he plays Herakles, Dionysos is a *comical* Theramenes who seeks to position himself to greatest advantage (lines 534–41), while Xanthias is exhorted to play *seriously* and convincingly the part of a dignified Herakles who is referred to as "the god" (lines 590–97). In anticipation of the parabasis with its forward-looking program, the chorus now emerges as a fully self-conscious comic chorus, that is, "simply the chorus necessary to an Old Comedy, divested of any distinctive character,"[90] to contribute a metatheatrical commentary on the complex proceedings. In a clever resolution of this game with gender, genre, and identity, the two players end up in a physical agon, a contest of endurance in which both are stripped of their clothing (costumes and disguises) and whipped on an equal basis. The narrative of the tragic katabasis ends with a celebration of ambiguity in which categories—Dionysos/Herakles, tragic/comic, master/slave, divine/human—are suspended. The last word in this preliminary comedy, that is, the contrafact of the tragic katabasis, belongs to Aiakos (lines 668–71):

> I cannot, by Demeter, in any way determine
> which one of you is a god. Get out of here!
> It will be up to our Master himself and Persephone,
> inasmuch as they are gods themselves, to figure out who is who.

Tragic Agon and Comic Victory

When it comes to the contest between Euripides and Aiskhylos, our reconstruction of *Peirithous* has little to offer in the way of a clear narrative pattern or model. We are beginning to see that the broad outlines of the tragedy are relevant to the second movement of *Frogs*, which is self-consciously configured as an independent play. In fact, it would be natural to expect that, as *Frogs* turns to a discussion of tragic technique and the value of tragic composers to the polis, the situational and narrative contrafact studied above would yield to freer comic invention. From the "departure" of the initiates with the song at 440–59 to the breakdown of the tragic disguise after the costume changes, Aristophanes signals the disentanglement of his narrative from that of the tragedy. Thus the close reading of Euripides appears to conclude with the flogging scene, leaving the agon dependent on *Peirithous* more in terms of theme and agonistic dynamics. This dependence might be broken down into three broad areas. First, as we have seen, the leitmotif of *sôtêria* in *Frogs* is informed by Herakles' rescue of Theseus and its political consequences. Second, the keen rivalry between tragedians in Hades preserves the scenic pattern—two "prisoners" of Hades, a mediator, and Plouton—while subverting the tragic philia between Peirithous and Theseus. Finally, the ethical contrast between Aiskhylos and Euripides draws on a similar contrast between Theseus and Peirithous.[91]

The deconstruction of categories in the flogging scene provides a fine scenic metaphor to introduce the parabasis with its message of political redemption. Master and slave are both naked and subjected to a "democratic" punishment that puts an end to their complex metatheatrical power play. This idea is picked up in the parabasis at line 694 where the slaves emancipated after Arginusai are referred to as "masters rather than slaves."[92] In general, the conclusion of the explicit *Peirithous* sequence appears to launch the most serious and specific political recommendation in *Frogs*, that is, the plea of the epirrhema (lines 687–99) to restore citizen rights to those who had taken part in the oligarchic revolution of 411.[93] A broader theme is implicit in the famous coinage metaphor—traditional silver versus modern bronze—which deplores the contrast between old and new leadership of Athens. This image participates in a more general and fanciful project of "saving" the city. "The recurrent political theme of the play is a familiar one," writes Dover, "old ways good, new ways bad . . . . The heroic ideals of Aeschylean tragedy will preserve the city, the unsettling realism of Euripidean tragedy will subvert it."[94] Just as the first movement of *Frogs* is based on a love for Euripides expressed in an aggressive imitation of his katabasis play, so the second movement drags a caricature of him onto the comic stage, transforms him into an object of ridicule, and, at the "trial," delivers a verdict against him. Thus from an object of personal pleasure in the prologue Euripides emerges after the parabasis as a stage figure who represents all that is "new" and "bad." Rescue of Euripides, in other words, mutates to become rescue of the city at Euripides' expense as Dionysos redefines what it is that "his soul desires" in terms of unexpected political insight. The profound formal division between movements of the comedy reinforces a thematic shift.

After the parabasis, the action begins anew with a standard prologue scenario involving two slaves. There is no memory of the tragic dramatis personae (Herakles, initiates) or katabasis, and we must accept the new setting in Hades as a given, the new locus of a fiction that has just begun. What is more, the role that Dionysos is to play as arbiter of the agon is simply an accident of his being in Hades, a feature of *Frogs* that has puzzled critics. However, the second movement of the comedy is ignorant of the first only in a superficial sense. On a deeper, thematic, level there is continuity in that Euripidean invention informs both movements of *Frogs*, albeit in different ways. That is to say, Dionysos' "accidental" involvement in the contest is modeled on the "accidental" involvement in a rescue by Herakles performing the Kerberos labor. Just as Herakles found himself arbiter of Theseus' and Peirithous' destinies, so Dionysos stumbles into his role as critic and judge in the agon.

We have seen that in *Peirithous* the role of Theseus was invested with considerable dignity and moral force. His decision to endure Hades voluntarily with his friend and his forthcoming attitude toward Herakles reveal him to be a stalwart, indeed archaic, paradigm of loyalty and civic virtue (as Herakles himself points out in fr. 7). Peirithous, on the other hand, is portrayed as a (potential) usurper, criminal, and somewhat of a fool. His punishment is represented as well deserved ("fitting") and he himself articulates his destiny as parallel to that of his father, Ixion, whose crimes of hybris were proverbial. This opposition between the just Theseus and criminal Peirithous informs the evolving and contrasting portrayal of Aiskhylos and Euripides in the second movement of *Frogs*. Whereas the tragedy innovated an unexpected bond between the righteous man and the villain, comedy makes common sense of it all and sets them in opposition to one another. Thus from a glancing allusion to Euripides as *panourgos*, "villainous," at line 80, the term is repeated later in reference to Euripides (line 1520), those who admire him (line 781), and those whom he had influenced (line 1015). In the new prologue the local slave[95] explains that Euripides is a usurper whose craft caters to the "underworld" (pun intended, lines 771–78):

> But when Euripides arrived down here, he put on performances
> for garment-thieves, purse-cutters, beaters of fathers,
> and burglars, of which there is an abundance in Hades.
> They, listening to his arguments and twists and turns of logic,
> went crazy for him and judged him to be the first and finest craftsman.
> Aroused by this, Euripides then claimed the throne upon which
> Aiskhylos was seated.

Aiskhylos, on the other hand, is a stern and righteous figure whose reputation is secure. "My poetry survived me," he claims with some justification in line 868, "but [Euripides'] died with him."[96] The comparison with tragic Theseus is striking. Like Aiskhylos, this hero, as featured in Euripides' *Herakles* and *Peirithous* (and much local lore), is the one whom Herakles, having arrived and discovered, naturally chose for rescue on the basis of his reputation. Both Aiskhylos and Theseus symbolize on artistic and sociopolitical levels, respectively, the good old days of Athens with its prosperity, power, and aristocratic values. Accordingly, the few "good" (χρηστοί) supporters of Aiskhylos are contrasted with the many disreputable fans of Euripides. It is important to point out, however, that Dionysos does not cease to be a comic player and representative of his genre, as it were.

In this capacity Euripidean poetry continues to delight him throughout the contest as a modern discourse somewhat akin to comedy, whereas Aiskhylean tragedy was already a "classic," that is, potentially austere, alienating, with its composer certainly not a pleasant person.[97] The dissonance between the thematic alliance of the good Aiskhylos and the "salvation" theme, on the one hand, and Dionysos' pleasure in the villainous realist Euripides, on the other, culminates in the striking quandary at lines 1411–13:

> Dear gentlemen, I will not decide on my own,
> and shall not, thereby, make an enemy of either one.
> I consider one wise, the other pleases me.

When he is forced to decide, however, he is made to suppress his original mission abruptly and to offer a revised alternative. We learn that he set out to fetch a poet "in order that the city might be saved and continue to produce plays. Whichever of the two shall offer the city the best advice, him shall I decide to take back with me" (lines 1418–21). Does Dionysos suddenly change or evolve as he mysteriously passes from the pleasures of the private citizen to discover his "political self," in the sense argued by Anton Bierl?[98] An important clue is provided by Dionysos' answer to the angry Euripides, who asks if the judge "can do this shameful deed" and still dare look him in the eye. "What is so shameful about it, if the spectators approve?" he replies (line 1475), distorting a verse from Euripides' own *Aiolos*. This is clearly the voice of comedy, self-aware and confident in its critical abilities (e.g., the difference between the "wisdom" of Aiskhylos and Euripidean pleasure) and in its ability to save the city.

The "political self" of the protagonist emerges as the result of *theatrical* self-realization achieved at this moment, after enacting the Euripidean katabasis and presiding over the agon. Aristophanes' metafictional reading of *Peirithous*, as we have seen, associated Dionysos vividly with the culture of comedy, while the Heraklean (tragic) role was added to set up a counterpoint between genres. A prominent feature of the contrafacts presented in earlier chapters (*Akharnians, Birds, Peace*) has been a demonstration of the superior power of comedy to provide solutions in desperate situations derived from tragedy or defined in tragic terms. The conclusion of *Frogs*, I submit, has Dionysos realize this power and assume responsibility for it in his capacity as "judge." In *Frogs*, tragedy provided both the narrative for the hero's journey as well as a metaphor of the current political crisis (all good poets are dead). Dionysos' specific role up to this point expands to comprehend the full range and significance of the relationship between tragedy and comedy latent in the metafictional prologue and brought into full view in the agon. As a traditional comic figure, comic player, and representative of comic invention, Dionysos finds himself in a position of ironic power over tragedy. Comedy will "save" Athens by returning one of her tragedians! His *sôtêria* differs, however, from that of protagonists in other contrafacts in several important details. Whereas Trygaios' reenactment of Euripides, for example, was unequivocal in its mission, Dionysos has been charged with managing a miniature tragic competition involving two candidates for rescue. Similarly, Dionysos, unlike Peisetairos or Dikaiopolis, is not obviously a member of the demos in search of help for himself and his peers. Rather, he must operate as an "honorary" Athenian from his position as a representative, indeed embodiment, of comedy. Once realized—and this takes time—this position makes him recognizable as belonging to the same dramatic category as Dikaiopolis and Trygaios.

Dionysos realizes that his decision will define the salvation of Athens as represented within the framework of the given performance. The utopian "good-old-days" theme had been stated quite clearly in the parabasis, leaving little doubt about which of the two poets fits the program. These are bad times (the best poets are dead) so we must go back in time to the figures of the past. As noted earlier, the rescue of Aiskhylos is accordingly informed by Herakles' rescue of the upright, quintessentially Athenian Theseus in *Peirithous*. But it is the Dionysos persona who, from the broadest perspective of *Frogs* as a contemporary performance, demonstrates comedy's ability to manipulate and surpass tragedy to provide a powerful remedy for the city's troubles. The fictional agon between tragedians is, moreover, critically dependent upon the real comic competition in which Aristophanes was always intent on pleasing his audience and winning the prize. In this connection, the poet's "advice" in the parabasis and the decision to revive Aiskhylos cater to public opinion and are transparently self-serving. At the same time, we cannot easily dismiss the possibility that, following the installation of the Thirty, the poet was manipulated by being commended and allowed to restage *Frogs* (in 404).[99] Not only does Aiskhylos participate in the "silver coinage" metaphor but he remained ever-popular, an established classic a half century after his death (unlike Euripides, who was too contemporary and too close in technique to comedy). The utopian vision of *Frogs*, in other words, has an especially intense agonistic focus.

Aristophanes' extended experiment with Euripides concludes, appropriately, with the assistance of Plouton—a figure from *Peirithous*—who escorts Aiskhylos to the door, as it were. The utter erasure of Euripides at the end is astonishing and belies the way in which he has dominated *Frogs* from the beginning. After a feeble retort to Dionysos (line 1476) he is not heard from again and Aiskhylos leaves his chair to Sophokles. Plouton's presence, however, with its connection to the wider frame of the action (and its dependence on *Peirithous*), reminds us of the clever way Aristophanes has managed to involve tragedy in a nostalgic return to the past while remaining intent on his favorite rival in the imaginary contest that began at least as far back as 425 with *Akharnians*.

The metafictional strategy employed in *Frogs* has allowed Aristophanes to involve Euripides on every conceivable level, as author of the literary model, the ostensible goal of the katabasis, a dramatis persona, and its explicit subject (Euripidean poetry). In the ongoing imaginary contest between Aristophanes and Euripides, there is a clear sense of closure at the point when, for his final demonstration of the superior powers of comedy and comic *sotêria*, Aristophanes conducts an agon between the past and present personified by tragedians. The great contest between tragedy and comedy is represented and settled once and for all by means of a tragic competition. Utopia is "nowhere," as noted at the outset, so Aiskhylos' return is a token of the impossibility on the part of the demos (or a certain sector thereof) of realizing its collective nostalgia; and, despite the passionate beginning, Euripides must remain in Hades. This is the bitter, realistic downside of the dream. At the very least, this paradoxical contrafact stands as a vivid parable of the great influence and importance Euripides was to "enjoy" only after his death.

Conclusion

The last three chapters (with chapter 3) have outlined in some detail the workings of Aristophanes' remarkable "imaginary rivalry" with Euripides. As in any love affair, disagreement and criticism are necessarily mixed with affection and, as in any love affair, there is no secure shelter from the ravages of time. Being the last extant Old Comedy, *Frogs* stands portentously at the end of a century and at the end of a literary era. Even in the first two decades of the fourth century we see the clear emergence of a different type of comedy. Nesselrath has established with great care in his book on Middle Comedy that there was scarcely a single aspect of the genre that did not undergo reexamination and change: plot, character, language, presentation of myth, and so forth. The evidence, alas, is too fragmentary for us to appreciate and compare the more elusive aspects of comic discourse studied here. However, with the conclusion of the Euripidaristophanic contest things were never the same. To put it simply, there never was, nor could there be, another *Frogs*.

Conclusion

σκηνὴ πᾶς ὁ βίος καὶ παίγνιον· ἢ μάθε παίζειν,
τὴν σπουδὴν μεταθείς, ἢ φέρε τὰς ὀδύνας.

Palladas AP 10.73

All of life is a stage and a game. Either learn to play, laying seriousness
aside, or endure the pain.

This study has explored how, in different ways, the composition and production
of Greek drama were fundamentally metafictional, and therefore reflexive, pro-
cesses: one fiction into another, yesterday's narrative absorbed and metabolized into
something new today. The invention of tragedy and its prominence at the dramatic
festivals reflect an impulse to transform traditional material into a "live" performance
with immediate relevance to the evolving polis. Comedy's approach was more complex, involving a secondary transformation in which the comic performance "pro-
cessed" a contemporary narrative or script. The very difference implicit in such transformations—an archaic narrative into tragedy, tragedy into comedy—prompted
composers of both genres to problematize received and normative aspects of the social
order; tragedy in its reexamination of tradition and norms, comedy in its caricature of the same and in its reevaluation of various tragic scenarios. Greek dramatic
metafiction emerges here as a process of questioning and scrutiny that has great
critical potential. The juxtaposition of genres is productive not simply for the purpose of demonstrating a commonality per se but to suggest that the self-conscious
poetics of both participated—albeit differently—in an equally self-conscious festival program informed by a wider, reflexive, and agonistic cultural poetics.

To build on Bertolt Brecht's well-known dictum, Greek theater became theater
only when it separated from ritual in the sense of unreflective protodrama; that is to
say, when its deep structure and the themes were freed from the confines of religious
practice to study contemporary society in public performance at the festival competitions. Religion and ritual continued to be important in drama, of course, but mainly
as they were featured in the "modern" polis, not as a "mystical past" haunting the
stage. The narrative patterns underlying pre-dramatic ritual—the Dionysiac cycle,
for example—gave way to freedom of choice and invention on the part of the composers who focused on the crises and complexities of *human* society. This transformation of myth into drama, as we have seen, is necessarily metafictional.

Despite its obvious roots in the metafictional process, tragedy pretends to maintain the myth of its originality and hides the seams of its textuality, thereby giving its transformational and critical project a different "feel." To us as readers (spectators) of tragedy, it is tempting to be lulled into accepting this originality as having to do with a sort of tragic essence, an authority having no need for sources. Comedy turns this implicit tragic self-definition on its head and pretends to be nothing but a parasite whose characters, plots, and very words are always from somewhere else: the streets of Athens, the old poets, Euripides. Aristophanes exemplifies this in play after play where good old-fashioned myths and characters are featured only as figures imported from tragedy with extensive situational and verbal parody into the bargain. Unlike tragedy, which denies any heteroglossia, comedy pretends to have no language of its own as it slips from style to style, register to register. We have seen, however, that tragedy is neither as authentic as it claims to be, nor is comedy as derivative or parasitic.

What distinguishes genres is the relationship of the script and performance to the metafictional process itself. In practice, the phenomenology of this process is metatheatrical. Tragedy habitually reshapes and manipulates epic narratives to produce a new fable that is recognizably modern and aware of itself as theatrical performance. Recent scholarship is revealing this metatheatricality as an important dimension long overlooked because of tragedy's covert modus operandi. The direct references to Homer, for example, at points such as Aias' advice to his son or the conclusion of his last speech are seamlessly woven into the fabric of the tragic text with no disruption of language or narrative flow. Comedy, of course, flaunts its sources and borrowings. Both the covert allusiveness of tragedy as well as the overt quoting of comedy are symptoms of interpretation through performance. The opposition between genres has much to do with a difference in the *dramatis tempus*. Tragedy is resolutely the discourse of the past; comedy, of the present. The past affords tragedy some shelter from responsibility for contemporary language, technology, and culture—a mask that fits rather poorly and often slips (the so-called anachronisms of tragedy are essential to its contemporary relevance). Comedy's present time frame harmonizes with its mask of an overt appeal, whether aesthetic or political, to the body politic. And yet comedy, too, has a long memory and can be quite nostalgic.

Tragedy operates more as an interrogative discourse in which closure is suspended or deferred while comedy adopts the forms of a public appeal with the pretense of a decisive conclusion. Thus, as readers of *Aias*, we are left to contemplate the contrast between Aias and Odysseus for ourselves with all the attendant tensions and ambiguities. The conclusion of *Frogs*, on the other hand, would have us believe in a clearcut resolution. Rhetorical surface is one thing, but theatrical, three-dimensional realities quite another, and we have seen a great deal of ambiguity and open-ended questioning in comedy, utopian teleology notwithstanding. Tragedy, similarly, is quite capable of focused persuasion and "selling" an idea. What is important to emphasize here is that the reflexive aspects of both genres identify them as engaging the body politic in an implicit dialogue similar to that observed in the law courts and popular assembly with the important difference that, as representations with high mimetic and aesthetic priorities (as entertainment), tragedy and comedy operated at a comfortable remove from the "real" political process. Herodotos' anecdote about the punishment of Phrynikhos' for his *Capture of Miletos*, however, and the well-known conflict between Aristophanes and Kleon suggest that the buffer zone insulating drama was not always very secure and that the composers of both genres had to face the consequences of their public "statements" as would any speaker in a court or the Pnyx.

The general concept of "metafiction" was limited in this study to several "figures of play"—broad, phenomenologically distinct, modes of representation employed by both genres to mark their contribution and to foreground the problematic of a given drama. In a dramatic context it is natural that reflexive play with fiction be manifested metatheatrically. The device of a theatrical inset, or mise en abyme, was studied in various contexts with a focus on tragedy. These remarkable quasi plays-within-plays emerge as vivid moments in which the genre exploits its own particular powers of representation in a display of a transformational poetics. It is clear from the metafictions of Sophokles' *Philoktetes* and *Aias*, for example, that the mise en abyme contributes powerfully and productively to the ongoing study of the interplay between norm and transgression. Remarkably, both scenarios featured a hero isolated by pathology of body or mind. The prologue of *Aias*, in particular, works to set Aias and his enemy, Odysseus, in a relation of spectacle and spectator, thereby involving the actual spectators in the representation of a clash between value systems that, vis-à-vis the fifth-century context, is very modern indeed. The interplay between persuasion and violence, virtue and expediency, divine and mortal, is viewed from a perspective of spectatorial fear and pity that has important consequences for the second half of the play.

Bakkhai, similarly, transforms the conflict between Dionysos and Pentheus into a metatheatrical contest of fictions in which the well-known ambiguity of the god is used to express the constitutive ambiguity of the genre and its elusive textuality. Euripides quite literally invented Dionysos at the end of the century as the god of tragedy and tragic fiction. It is no coincidence that the explicit presentation of the divine figure as theatrical patron and god of dramatic illusion is carried out in a play notorious for its aggressive and overlapping metafictional strategies. In both *Aias* and *Bakkhai*, the interplay between madness and dramatic illusion, mortal and divine, truth and fiction, reveals a deep reflexive awareness on the part of the playwrights of the powers and limits of their craft.

Comedy's part in the festival context has been less appreciated and it is in the comic reworkings of tragedy that we find the clearest example of how Aristophanes problematized traditional values and social norms. An important phenomenon that emerges here is the "imaginary rivalry" between tragedy and comedy studied over the course of several chapters, that is, a competition in which tragedy was reread and rewritten by a genre that was "younger" (as a festival event) and more ostentatiously reflexive. A distinctive aspect of this rivalry is the emphasis on the temperamental and "ideological" differences between genres. Comedy claims to inhabit a different world with different rules under which the impasses and crises of tragedy find easy solution. We have seen that Aristophanes repeatedly fastened on a tragic problematic in order to resolve it with the greater resources available to him. The results are well known: comedy always prevails and offers sure rescue in the person of a reinvented tragic figure such as Tereus, Bellerophontes, Herakles, and so on. Reaching beyond the frame of the strict festival competitions, this rivalry across generic lines exemplifies a new stage in the self-definition of comedy and on the part of a playwright who becomes concerned not only with rivals at eye level (fellow comics) but in a larger, citywide, contest for power as maker of culture and shaper of public opinion. So prominent is this openly reflexive "imaginary" rivalry that it has tended to eclipse the metatheatrical aspects of tragedy and the significant complementary distribution of comedy's criticism of the two genres. Tragedy was incorporated into the fabric of comic mimesis while rival comedy was addressed largely in the nonmimetic parabasis and parabasislike passages.

The well-known example of Euripides' *Telephos* and Aristophanes' *Akharnians* was used to introduce the metafictional mode of the "contrafact," a term drawn from music theory to replace "parody" in articulating the relationship between Greek comedy and tragedy. Aristophanes' fifth-century utopian plays, *Birds*, *Peace*, and *Frogs*, are built to a large extent on the alien scaffolding of a tragic script and an acknowledgment of these comedies as extended metafictions reveals important new dimensions of meaning. Thus the social and political thematics of *Birds* are informed by Sophokles' *Tereus*, whose protagonist appears as a "guest artist" in the comedy; *Peace* reenacts the *Bellerophontes* of Euripides while *Frogs* is a "remake" of Euripides' *Peirithous*. It is not sufficient to say that comedy "subverts" or "inverts" the themes and plots of tragedy. Rather, each contrafact is seen to be an intelligent rereading of tragedy with a response motivated by the particular nature of the object. Aristophanes was especially interested in innovative moments, and much of what we see in his contrafacts highlights and comments on such innovations (e.g., the hostage scene in *Telephos*). The contrafacts of Euripides in *Akharnians* and *Peace* turn out to have exactly the opposite approach to representing the relationship of the "hero" to society. In the former, the Euripidean happy ending and social integration become a comic *stasis* that only finds closure at the level of the individual (at the expense of society), while *Peace* transforms tragic despair and isolation into a Panhellenic rescue effort. The upshot of the imaginary rivalry between Aristophanes and Euripides, in particular, is that comedy has the resources to offer a powerful solution (*sôtêria*) for the scenarios of social disintegration in tragedy. Dikaiopolis' separate peace, Trygaios' flight to Olympos, Peisetairos' city in the air, and the comic Dionysos' rescue of tragedy all have in common a display of comedy's superior power to resolve problems of society as represented in tragedy. The clever juxtaposition in *Frogs* of a tragic contest and the "imaginary rivalry" between genres is the climactic expression of this power in the work of Aristophanes.

These "figures of play"—both in the phenomenological sense as surface play, mise en abyme, contrafact, and literally as the stage figures Aias, Pentheus, Tereus, Bellerophontes, and Herakles—are important markers of the pervasively metafictional poetics of Greek drama. Even within the limitations of the framework used here, much remains to be done. The full range of Aristophanic intertextuality is only beginning to receive adequate discussion as are the various ways in which later tragedy rereads Aiskhylos and his contemporaries. Richard Seaford's challenge to acknowledge a greater intertextual potential in the satyr-play deserves a careful investigation of its own. Finally, with the great advantage of Rudolph Kassel and Colin Austin's edition of the Greek comic texts, the rivalry among comic poets and its literary manifestation is ready to be updated and reevaluated. The current crop of scholarship on various metafictional aspects of Greek drama by Margalit Finkelberg, Mark Ringer, Niall Slater, and others is encouraging. In this collective effort to understand and explicate the poetics of ancient art and culture, we ourselves inevitably engage in construction and projection as we self-consciously transform our tradition and rewrite the myths of the past.

Notes

1. Drama and Metafiction

1. E.g., Richard Seaford's *Reciprocity and Ritual* and Mihai Spariosu's *Dionysus Reborn*, respectively.

2. For an interesting discussion of the positive aspects of lying on the part of the epic tricksters Hermes and Odysseus see "Odysseus and Other Tricksters: Lying *Kata Kosmon*," the second chapter of Pratt, *Lying and Poetry*. "Hermes is the figure who marks transition and exchange, whether it be the transition of a soul from life to death (he is portrayed on tombs), or the exchange and transition of money between people (hence he is the patron of merchants and thieves), or the communicational exchange of words (when silence fell in a conversation, the Athenians said that Hermes was passing; Hermes is a witness to oaths). Hermes travels always in the middle, marking the boundary to be crossed. 'Nothing about him is settled, stable, permanent or restricted or definite. He represents in space and in the human world movement and flow, mutation and transition, contact between foreign elements.' Hermes marks the liminal process of crossing" (Goldhill, *Reading Greek Tragedy* 71).

3. For this issue with regard to Athenian drama see Green, *Theatre in Society* 2 (esp. note 4).

4. See Girard, *Violence and the Sacred*. *Contra* see Vernant, "God of Tragic Fiction" (in Vernant and Vidal-Naquet, *Myth and Tragedy*). In his *Interpretation of Cultures*, Clifford Geertz characterizes ritual performances as "metasocial commentaries" and "texts within texts" that are received and interpreted by the performers and outside observers alike.

5. Vernant and Vidal-Naquet, *Myth and Tragedy* 33.

6. See the essays in Dobrov, *City as Comedy*.

7. In *Mimesis as Make-Believe* (e.g., 95–102), Kendall Walton sheds light on the way an individual or society may engage myths and other narrative forms that are not strictly held to be "true" and yet that hold a central position in various modes of representation. Of his position Walton notes that it "avoids postulating that the 'enlightenment' of a person or culture effects a radical transformation in the nature of his or its interest in legend or tales. If that were the case, it would be hard to explain why the stories often have such strong appeal both before and after. The possibility of continuity across the enlightenment is likely to remain unnoticed if we fail to distinguish clearly between fiction understood in terms of make-believe and what is not true or not believed or not asserted" (98).

8. Gregory Nagy in his introduction to Batchelder, *Seal of Orestes* ix, notes that the dramatic illusion authorized by the metatheatrical protagonists of tragedy "has the effect of transforming the poetics of epic into the poetics of theater, much as Athenian State Theater historically transformed the sum total of epic traditions into its own authorized repertoire."

9. "If self-awareness is a sign of the genre's disintegration, then the novel began its decline at birth," notes Hutcheon, *Narcissistic Narrative* 18. See 9–10 for a review of this and related suggestions to which the author replies by noting that "one might choose to see the origins of this phenomenon in the parodic intent of the novel, in the unmasking of dead conventions, by a mirroring of them."

10. "Tragedy," notes C. P. Segal, "deliberately call[s] into question all social institutions, including the institution of tragedy. Hence an increasing concern in the plays over the course of the fifth century with examining the conventions of the theater is not just an aberration of late Euripides but *a development inherent in the form itself*" (emphasis added; Segal, "Review of Goldhill" 234).

11. *Eumenides* lines 526, 571–73, 996–97, 1038.

12. "From the point of view of the play," notes Sommerstein, *Eumenides* 186, "they are the Athenians *of the future* whom Athene thrice says she is addressing."

13. The will of the goddess, her "voice," in both plays is associated with the powerful and penetrating sound of the Etruscan trumpet that highlights her metatheatrical presence.

14. As have other metatheatrical moments in tragedy such as the choral exclamation in Sophokles' *Oidipous* τι δεῖ με χορεύειν. Cf. αἰνέσῃς (line 528), σοι (line 538), ἀτίσῃς (line 541) in the stasimon, and the choral exclamation χαίρετε χαίρετ᾽ ἐν αἰσιμίαισι πλούτου, / χαίρετ᾽ ἀστικὸς λεώς, "farewell, farewell to you amidst the wealth you deserve; farewell people of the city" (lines 996–97). The words of the final song that appeal to the whole demos to be discriminating in speech (line 1038) are also striking: εὐφαμεῖτε δὲ πανδαμεί. On the passage from *Oidipous Tyrannos* (line 895) cf. the comments of Dodds, "On Misunderstanding" 186: "The meaning is surely 'Why should I, an Athenian citizen, continue to serve in a chorus?' In speaking of themselves as a chorus they step out of the play into the contemporary world, as Aristophanes' choruses do in the *parabasis*."

15. See N. Slater, "Space, Character, and ΑΠΑΤΗ" 399: "As others have noted, the theatre audience must represent the assembly of citizens on the Pnyx. No tiny group of extras on the stage could successfully represent this essential element."

16. See Sommerstein, *Eumenides* 34.

17. Vernant and Vidal-Naquet, *Myth and Tragedy* 242.

18. "The interest in the theatrical experience itself," writes Goldhill in his chapter on *Bakkhai* (*Reading Greek Tragedy* 274), "and the self-reflexive concern with representation . . . cannot be separated from the question of self and other, of self-projection and self-definition within social norms and their transgression."

19. On this point see Foley, *Ritual Irony* 20.

20. Taplin, *Comic Angels*, 67, note 1.

21. Works such as Kitto, *Greek Tragedy*, and Lesky, *Greek Literature*, do, however, offer much that implicitly supports a metatheatrical interpretation of individual passages. Lesky, *Greek Literature* 371, for example, speaks of Dionysos' theatrical entrapment of Pentheus as "a horrible grotesque" achieved by means of disguise. The current proliferation of "meta-" terms might obscure the relatively early emergence of "metatheater" in the title of Abel, *Metatheatre*.

22. Thus Slater, *Plautus in Performance*, uses Abel, *Metatheatre*, as a point of departure; C. P. Segal, *Dionysiac Poetics*, begins with Calderwood, *Shakespearean Metadrama*; and Goldhill's work (*Reading Greek Tragedy*, *Poet's Voice* 167–222) is a digest of critical views

within classical studies and beyond (e.g., Turner, Bakhtin). For work that draws on a variety of contemporary critical discourses see the collections edited by Winkler and Zeitlin, *Dionysos*, Sommerstein et al., *Tragedy, Comedy and the Polis*, and Dobrov, *City as Comedy*. Criticism of other ancient genres is situated in an ever-widening context exemplified by works such as Pratt, *Lying and Poetry* (archaic poetry), and Gill and Wiseman, *Lies and Fiction*.

23. Seminal works are Bain, *Actors and Audience*; Pucci, *Aristofane ed Euripide*; Rau, *Paratragodia*; Russo *Aristophanes*; and some of the essays reprinted in Zeitlin, *Playing the Other*. Other work of an interpretive nature includes Batchelder, *Seal of Orestes*; Chapman, "Dramatic Illusion"; Foley "Tragedy and Politics"; Hubbard, *Mask of Comedy*; Muecke, "Playing with the Play"; Taaffe, "Metatheater and Gender" and *Aristophanes and Women*; and Taplin, *Comic Angels*.

24. Strict generic separation would appear to deny tragedy explicit self-consciousness that belongs properly only to comedy. Consider Taplin, "Greek Tragedy" 164: "It might be argued that, from their shared setting, the two genres oppose each other, and even to some extent build up mutually exclusive characteristics. And this is what I shall maintain: that to a considerable degree fifth-century tragedy and comedy help to define each other by their opposition and their reluctance to overlap." (He turns out to allow, however, for considerably more "interference" that this statement would suggest.) See also Saïd, "Travestis et travestissements" 217–23, whose exploration of the semiotics of costume is not much hampered by her adherence to Taplin's doctrine of generic separation.

25. Foley, *Ritual Irony*, and C. P. Segal, *Dionysiac Poetics*. For comic elements in tragedy see Knox, "Euripidean Comedy," and Seidensticker, "Comic Elements," and *Palintonos Harmonia*. In her *Townsend Lectures* at Cornell University (Spring 1990) entitled "Play Worlds," Patricia Easterling argued against viewing the distinguishing features of *Bakkhai* and its metatheatrics simply as turn-of-the-century ("death of tragedy") anomalies.

26. For examples of work on tragic metatheater in plays other than *Bakkhai* see C. P. Segal, *Poetics of Sorrow* (especially chapter 1) and *Sophocles' Tragic World*; Henrichs, "Why Should I Dance"; Bierl, *Dionysos*; and Zeitlin, "Closet of Masks" and "Playing the Other"; Batchelder, *Seal of Orestes*; Ringer, *Empty Urn*.

27. Lissarague "Satyrs," 235–36: "None of this [undermining of dramatic illusion] appears in satyric drama. . . . The play stays at one remove from the audience, which observes without being called to account. Satyric drama as far as we know never parodies tragedy, and the principal characters, such as Odysseus, maintain their epic stature without any caricature or burlesque. (Note the dignity of the three actors on the Pronomos Vase.) Nor does it contain any political allusions. The 'comedy' of satyric drama lies somewhere else. In fact, it resides in the constitutive element of the genre: the presence of satyrs required by the nature of the chorus. It works by playing with myth, by taking a well-known story and overlaying it with a group of satyrs who react to the situation in their own peculiar fashion. The recipe is as follows: take one myth, add satyrs, observe the result." A similar point was made a while ago by Bain, "Audience Address" 23–25 and *Actors and Audience* 72, note 2.

28. See J. R. Green, "On Seeing and Depicting the Theatre" 47–49. Green translates lines 5–21 of fr.1: "Look and see whether this image could be more like me, this Daedalic likeness: it only lacks a voice. Look at them. Do you see? Come, yes, come. I bring this offering to the god to decorate his house, this finely painted votive. It would give my mother trouble. If she could see it, she would certainly turn and shriek, thinking it me, the son she brought up. He is so like me. Look, then, upon the house of the Lord of the Sea, the Earth-shaker, and each of you fasten up the likeness of his handsome form (face: Lloyd-Jones), a messenger, a voiceless herald to keep off travellers . . . it will halt strangers on their way by its terrifying look." See Sutton, *Satyr Play* 29–33, and Zeitlin, "Artful Eye."

29. Seaford, *Cyclops* 16. There are, however, arguments (Lloyd-Jones, Zimmermann) in favor of ascribing the Pratinas fragment to late fifth-century dithyramb. See Zimmermann "Überlegungen" and Nesselrath, *Mittlere Komödie* 243. We simply do not have sufficient evidence to fully assess the degree of self-presentation and intertextuality in the satyr-play.

30. Seaford, *Cyclops* 19–20, discusses the possibility of a paratragic and topical assimilation on the part of satyr-play to comedy. An interesting bit of possible paratragedy occurs as *Kyklops* 706–707 in which a verbal echo of *Philoktetes* (the phrase δι' ἀμφιτρῆτος [αὐλίου], line 19) signals a borrowing from Sophoklean stagecraft, i.e., a cave from which there is a rear exit allowing a character to be led into the cave and then to leave the cave without reappearing.

31. There is no attempt to rival the work of Rau in cataloguing all paratragic moments in comedy, nor much interest in glancing self-referentiality in tragedy of the sort so competently treated by Henrichs and Bierl. See Henrichs, "Why Should I Dance?" (cf. Sophokles' *Oidipous*, line 895), and Bierl, *Dionysos*.

32. Note, for example, the plausible connection between the establishment of the Kleisthenic democracy and the establishment of tragedy suggested by Connor in "City Dionysia and Athenian Democracy" 7–32.

33. See Lonsdale, *Dance and Ritual Play*.

34. For an eloquent articulation of the difference between the strictly semiotic and phenomenological approaches see States, *Great Reckonings* 20–30. "Throughout," he notes, "I use the adjective *phenomenal* in the sense of pertaining to phenomena or to our sensory experience with empirical objects. The adjective *phenomenological*, of course, refers to the analytical or descriptive problem of dealing with such phenomena" (21, note 5). Paul Ricoeur is cited by States (24, note 10) with this definition: "One can present phenomenology as a generalized theory of language. Language ceases to be an activity, a function, an operation among others: it is identified with the entire signifying milieu, with the complex of signs thrown like a net over our field of perception, our action, our life."

35. Influential contributions to theater semiotics include Elam, *Semiotics*; Helbo, *Sémiologie*; Kowzan, *Littérature et spectacle*; Pavis, *Problèmes*; Ruffini, *Semiotica*; and Ubersfeld, *Lire le théâtre*. The thirty or so papers from the 1990 conference at Montpellier are edited by Laroque in *The Show Within*.

36. It is important to emphasize that "metatheater" and "metafiction" are placed in a hierarchical relationship with "metatheater" a theatrical species of "metafiction." This is not to be confused with the more specialized usage in which "metafiction" refers merely to the reflexive aspects of the modern novel (with "fiction" representing a genre).

37. Waugh, *Metafiction* 2, and Hutcheon, *Politics of Postmodernism* 61 (The subject of the latter comment is novelistic fiction of the last twenty years).

38. Heeding Green's accusation of literary critics who are "blinkered" by their bookishness (*Theatre in Society* xii).

39. Over the last few decades the study of the latter has grown on the foundations laid by scholars such as Pickard-Cambridge and Webster to become an impressive sub-field. See Green, "Theatre Production."

40. Judd Hubert, *Metatheater* 2, concentrates on the duplicity inherent in theatrical discourse as "combining overt mimetic representations of the story with covert performative and metadramatic clues pointing to its own operations at the risk of undermining or at the very least problematizing the fable." In the simplest cases metatheater involves "linguistic signs that, in addition to communicating developments in plot and characterization, explicitly designate the art of stagecraft and entertainment." (The subsequent discussion shows, however, that he does not intend to exclude ambiguity or polysemy of the linguistic sign from his metatheatrical inventory.) Going beyond the notion of a dramatic "anti-form" in

which the barrier between art and life is dissolved, Calderwood, *Shakespearean Metadrama* 5, intends "metadrama" in broader terms to comprehend the fact that Shakespeare's plays are about "dramatic art itself—its materials, its media of language and theater, its generic forms and conventions, its relationship to truth and the social order." Such observations are common in metatheatrical criticism; cf. Gruber, "Systematized Delirium" 99: "Aristophanes' real subject is drama, for his plays may be best understood as forming an ongoing self-conscious discourse on theatre."

41. This is an adaptation to the theater of Richards's "meaning triangle," which locates linguistic signifier, signified (as "sense," "thought," "Vorstellung"), and referent (real-world object, "signified" only in a qualified sense) at the apexes of an equilateral triangle (see Lacan, *Speech and Language* 223–24). The various relationships between the three terms are then illustrated along the triangle's legs: a relationship of signification between signifier and signified; a causal relationship between signified and referent; and only an imputed relationship of "substitution" between signified and referent. With the exception of controversial "analog" phenomena such as comic portrait-masks (see Dover, *Greek and the Greeks* 266–78) or the use of living rock in *Prometheus Bound* ("Hammond's rock"; see Conacher, *Prometheus Bound* 181, note 12), items in the theatrical inventory bear a clear, but still arbitrary relationship to what they are supposed to represent. As with linguistic signs, it is convention that allows items of the theatrical vocabulary to signify.

42. Cf. Hornsby's "axioms for relating drama to reality" (*Drama, Metadrama* 17):
1. A play does not reflect life; instead, it reflects itself.
2. At the same time, it relates to other plays as a system.
3. This system, in turn, intersects with other systems of literature, nonliterary performance, other art forms (both high and low), and culture generally. Culture, as it centers on drama in this way, I shall refer to as the "drama/culture complex."
4. It is through the drama/culture complex, rather than through individual plays, that we interpret life.

Stam, *Reflexivity* xv, noting the centrality of language in the work of thinkers as different as Wittgenstein, Bakhtin, and Derrida, points out that "a corollary of this 'linguistic turn' has been an awareness that concepts and representations cannot be transparent; they are inevitably caught up in discourse, power, intertextuality, dissemination, and *differance*." For an important corrective to semiotic extremes see States, *Great Reckonings* 20.

43. What metafictional narrative does "in flaunting, in baring its fictional and linguistic systems to the reader's view," notes Linda Hutcheon, *Narcissistic Narrative* 20, "is to transform the process of making, of *poiesis*, into part of the shared pleasure of reading." Her exploration of how metafiction exposes the very process of poetic production is anticipated by (Russian formalist) Shklovskii's concepts of "defamiliarization" (*ostranenie*) and "laying bare the process" (*obnazhenie priema*), which he set forth in the 1920s in essays on Cervantes and Sterne.

44. "If we cannot know reality directly," notes Charles Segal, *Dionysiac Poetics* 222, anticipating this moment, "if all reality is, on one view, a function of our way of viewing it, and if perception shades into illusion and illusion into madness, then the poet's task is to provide a stage for the simultaneous projection of the multiple planes of reality." In the figure of Dionysos the poet finds both the power to accomplish this and a "screen on which each of us can project his own world views, his different selves." See also Muecke, "'I Know You.'"

45. For the mimetic dimension of late fifth-century drama see Matthews, "Euripides and Mimesis." Similarly, Muecke "'I Know You,'" contains valuable discussion of costume, disguise, and character in Aristophanes.

46. Elam, *Semiotics* 156, who defines a metalanguage as "a semiotic whose content plane is a semiotic."

47. States, *Great Reckonings* 20.

48. Stam's work, for example, while quite interested in narrative and performative genres from Homer to Hollywood, passes over Athenian tragedy and comedy in silence, while others notice only the comic parabasis. See, for example, Pfister, *Theory and Analysis* 79. It would appear that Greek drama did not even come to mind at moments such as the discussion of the "covert" play-within-the-play (229) or interaction between stage figure and fictionalized "poet" (77–78).

49. "When the audience become relatively immune to the tensions through which the old dramatist has had sport with it, the new playwright, rising arrogantly from the audience once again challenges it 'to play', to be reengaged, . . .a new game at last" (States, *Irony and Drama* 69). Burnett, *Catastrophe Survived* 16, implies a caveat against oversimplifying this sequence: "Euripides' 'deviant' plays must thus be read against the 'norms' of tragic action . . . , but those norms of course are never to be found in their pure form. Every written tragedy is a variant." See E. Segal, "φύσις of Comedy" 129–36.

50. As Manfred Pfister has documented in his *Theory and Analysis of Drama*. See, for example, his discussion of the polyfunctionality of dramatic language and the dramatis personae in *Theory and Analysis* 105–18 and 160–83.

51. Along similar lines, Frances Muecke, in "Playing with the Play" 5, notes, "Drama demands a twofold reaction from the spectator, who must on the one hand be imaginatively involved in the fiction which is being presented, and on the other hand detached enough to allow him to 'read' or 'decode' the play according to the rules of theatrical discourse." Muecke approaches the notion of a reader/spectator's competence in the linguistic sense. For competence as applied to the generalized reader of the modern novel see Culler, *Structuralist Poetics* 113–30. See also Hernadi, *Interpreting Events* 150–86, for a formal approach to the layering of roles. Pfister, *Theory and Analysis* 105–18, outlines a spectrum of linguistic functions including "referential," "expressive," "apellative," "phatic," "metalingual," and "poetic."

52. This is not to minimize the gulf separating genres in many respects, but the case has been overstated: see Taplin, "Greek Tragedy." For examples of comic "infiltration" of tragedy, with a selective review of relevant scholarship see 163–65. Since the article's publication in 1986, however, Taplin appears to have backed down a great deal from the more austere position set forth there.

53. "Usurpation of tragic form" comprehends various strategies in which the comic poet incorporates tragic language, character, costume, plot, situation, etc., into the fabric of his play. This broad conception of paratragedy constitutes a continuum ranging from interjections of a single word such as χαιρηδόνος at *Akharnians* line 4 to the extended involvement with Euripides' *Telephos* in the same play.

54. This agreement depends on the spectators' willingness to "accept the claim of the actor to be person A or B" and to understand that "a bare stage, whether or not it has on it a merely symbolic piece of scenery or stage property, is place so and so" (Sifakis, *Parabasis* 10–11). Cf. Walton, *Mimesis as Make-Believe* 38: "Props function only in a social, or at least human, setting. The stump in the thicket makes it fictional that a bear is there only because there is a certain convention, understanding, agreement in the game of make-believe, one to the effect that wherever there is a stump, fictionally there is a bear. I will call this the *principle of generation*. This principle was established by explicit stipulation: 'Let's say that stumps are bears.' But not all principles are established thus. Some, including most involving works of art, are never explicitly agreed on or even formulated, and imaginers may be unaware of them, at least in the sense of being able to spell them out." See McLeish, *Theatre of Aristophanes* 79, where the author distinguishes between the "theatre of illusion" and the "theatre of convention": "In the theatre of illusion the effects *simulate* reality; in the theatre of convention the effects *symbolize* reality." The term "illusion," however, is remarkably prominent in *Theatre of Aristophanes* despite the book's apparent rejection of it (e.g., 85, 86, 91, and passim).

55. "Illusion as a psychological phenomenon was entirely alien to Greek theatrical audiences . . . the use of the term with reference to Greek drama is an anachronism" (Sifakis, *Parabasis* 7). Bain, "Audience Address" 13, note 1, objects that "G.M. Sifakis . . . thinks the term [dramatic illusion] completely inappropriate for Greek drama. I believe he is fudging a distinction that is still valid and confusing 'realism' with 'illusionism'. . . . What is unsatisfactory about the term applied to any form of drama is the suggestion it carries that an audience may be in some way *deceived* so as to confuse stage fiction with reality." Interestingly, as de Romilly, "Gorgias," Bierl, "Dionysos, Wine, and Tragic Poetry," and others have argued, the evolving notion of poetry in the fifth century did, in fact, include deception, ψεῦδος or ἀπάτη, which appears in this context as a positive aesthetic dimension quite unlike the "deception" and "confusion" in Bain's comment. The discussion of illusion in Greek drama has many entries including McLeish, *Theatre of Aristophanes* (e.g., 79–91), and Gruber, "Systematized Delirium" (97–99).

56. So Bain, *Actors and Audience* 6–7.

57. See Walton, *Mimesis as Make-Believe*, for an exploration of this concept.

58. With Sifakis's extreme views compare Styan's comments (cited in N. W. Slater, *Plautus in Performance*, 10–11): "Illusion is the province of all theatre: a spectator goes to the playhouse in the expectation that he will be free to indulge it. In an introduction to Pirandello's *Six Characters in Search of an Author*, Lionel Trilling wrote, 'The word *illusion* comes from the Latin word meaning "to mock" (*illudere*), which in turn comes from the word meaning "to play" (*ludere*), and a favourite activity of the theatre is to play with the idea of illusion itself, to mock the very thing it most tries to create—and the audience that accepts it.' The term *illusion* is obviously an embarrassment for criticism, and has been for years."

59. It is interesting, in this connection, to note the way vase paintings "see" the theater: "Attic artists generally ignored drama's signifiers in direct contemplation of what it signified: it is the impact of the dramatic illusion, not the performance, that one can detect on many hundreds of mythological scenes in Attic art" (Csapo and Slater, *Context* 53).

60. Hutcheon, *Narcissistic Narrative* (cover text.)

2. *Figures of Play, Part 1*

1. Metz, *L'enonciation impersonelle*.

2. Cf. Pfister, *Theory and Analysis* xv.

3. See Chapman, "Some Notes." Strategies belonging to the category of surface metatheater would include familiar phenomena, e.g., "ruptures of dramatic illusion": audience address, commentary on the circumstances of production, explicit mention and micro-manipulation of dramatic convention, reference to extradramatic phenomena, parody, quotation, etc.

4. Taplin, *Comic Angels* 68, note 2, 67–78, calls attention to metatheatrical instances of πρόσωπον in comedy as well as a variety of surface play with aspects of performance such as costume and the *aulos*. Denniston, "Technical Terms" 113–21 identifies other words as *termini technici* in comedy (ἐσβολαί, βιβλίον, etc.). Despite the relative lingustic conservatism of tragedy, it is difficult to follow Bain in his extreme skepticism, *Actors and Audience* 209.

5. "Reflexive regression" or, more accurately, "inescutcheon."

6. See Ron, "Restricted Abyss" 418, for a throrough articulation of the theory of the mise en abyme.

7. Patrick, "Charlie Parker" 3: "Thus, George Gershwin's 'I Got Rhythm' (1930) may be transformed into Sidney Bechet's 'Shag' (1932) or into Charlie Parker's 'Dexterity' (1947). Similarly, new blues compositions may be created by fitting a newly-composed melodic line to a basic I–IV–I–V–I harmonic scheme. By analogy to text substitution in medieval music,

I call this general technique the 'melodic contrafact' (*contrafactum*)." The genre of modern jazz (beginning with early bebop) does much more than parody or respond to its model. It uses a significant aspect of its structure to produce an entirely new composition. For improvisation in other contexts see Greenblatt, *Renaissance Self-Fashioning* 22–28 (the European Renaissance) and N. Slater, *Plautus in Performance* 16–18.

8. For a recent attempt to broaden the range of the term see Rose, *Parody* 59, who defines parody as "the critical quotation of performed literary language with comic effect." For a postmodern response see chapters 1 and 2 (pp. 1–49) of Hutcheon, *Theory of Parody*. In particular, Hutcheon reminds her readers that there is nothing, philologically, "in *parodia* that necessitates the inclusion of a concept of ridicule, as there is, for instance, in the joke or *burla* of burlesque. Parody, then, in its ironic 'trans-textualization' and inversion, is *repetition with difference*" (emphasis added). This approaches the poetics of the contrafact.

9. For a philological review of the terms "parody" and "travesty" see Rau, *Paratragodia* 7–18 and Dover, *Frogs* 24–28. For paratragedy as distinct from parody see Pucci, *Aristofane ed Euripide* 277–78. The concept of the "remake" is implicit in Pucci, "Gods' Intervention" 25: "[an] 'allusion' names a 'remake' that text B would produce of text A (see, e.g., Pasquali's "Arte allusiva") and assumes that a certain intention of rivalry or admiration animates the author of that imitation." Note also Niall Slater's suggestion ("Space, Character, and ΑΠΑΤΗ" 403) of "recycling" to capture the true spirit of the Aristophanic contrafact. Silk, *Aristophanes and the Definition of Comedy*, also promises to contribute to this inquiry.

10. In "Maculate Music" Urios Aparisi and I explore the curious contrafact of a well-known dithyramb, Philoxenos' *Kyklops*, in Aristophanes' last play *Wealth*.

11. In *Palimpsestes* Genette develops a typology of transtextual relations, including "intertextuality," "paratextuality," "metatextuality," etc., that elaborates on the ways in which different texts collude and collide. "Hypertextuality" involves the interaction of two texts, one anterior (model, or hypotext), the other posterior (hypertext). The latter interacts with, restructures, and transforms the hypotext in ways that apply directly to the relationship between a contrafact and its model. The approach taken here differs from Genette's hypertext, however, primarily because of the inherent focus and coherence of a dramatic performance in "real time" interacting with another such performance, i.e., a species of dramatic transtextuality that is ill-served by the exceedingly broad and vague notion of two or more interacting "texts." For a classic study of these issues see Pasquali, "Arte allusiva."

12. N. Slater, *Plautus* 14: "Metatheatre has recently been defined as a quite different concept by Bruno Gentili [*Theatrical Performances*]: plays constructed from previously existing plays [i.e., Plautus from Menander]. He distinguishes this definition based on the history of a text's creation sharply from a literary critic's definiton of a play-within-the-play motif in a text. The two definitions are indeed hermeneutically distinct, but a central thesis of this work will be that, at least in Plautus, they are phenomenologically related."

13. The importance of recognizing extended situational "parody" (as opposed to the merely verbal) is noted by Herington, "*Birds* and *Prometheia*" 242, and Sutton, *Two Lost Plays* 67–68.

14. To the views of Hutcheon cited above might be added the more comedy-specific observation of Dover, *Frogs* 25, where he distinguishes between two different levels of parody: "Sometimes [parody] is extensive. . . . More often a motif, a short passage, a line, or a phrase is taken from tragedy." The province of the contrafact is, of course, the former, "extended" type of parody. See the discussion in Silk, "Aristophanic Paratragedy" 479–80: "By way of a working definition, let me suggest that *paratragedy* is the cover term for all of comedy's intertextual dependence on tragedy, some of which is parodic, but some is not; and that *parody* is any kind of distorting representation of an original, which in the present context will be a tragic original. All Aristophanic parody of tragedy, then, is paratragic; but not all Aristophanic

paratragedy is parodic. . . . Parody is essentially negative: it works by recalling a more or less specific original and subverting it. Non-parodic paratragedy is not necessarily subversive or negative at all. Parody, in the second place, commonly exists within a comprehensive identificatory frame; non-parodic paratragedy does not."

15. The items listed in the bibliography look forward to a book-length treatment of this topic that Sidwell has termed, appropriately, "parcacomedy."

16. "We find autoreferential cross-reference at home in Greek tragedy," notes Hubbard, *Mask of Comedy* 39. He goes on to observe that "the verbal, thematic, imagistic, and structural links between plays of a connected trilogy are familiar to any student of Aeschylus. More significantly any such links can from time to time be shown to exist between plays of the same author on related mythological themes, even when separated by many years, as is familiar from the case of Sophocles' *Oedipus Tyrannus* and *Oedipus at Colonus*. There must also have been some such relation between Sophocles' *Ajax* and *Teucer*, given the prominence assigned Teucer in the second half of the *Ajax* and the particular emphasis placed on his fear of coming home to Telamon in Salamis (*Aj.* 1006–20). Equally the introduction of Ajax' young son Eurysaces as a mute personage (*Aj.* 574–77) does not seem to be motivated by internal considerations nearly so much as by allusion to Sophocles' *Eurysaces.*"

17. This issue sports a formidable modern bibliography that begins with Lloyd-Jones's response to Eduard Fraenkel ("Alleged Interpolations"). See Goldhill, *Reading Greek Tragedy* 248, and the papers in the *Bulletin of the Institute of Classical Studies* by West, Bain, Donzelli, Gellie, and Kovacs. See Kovacs, "Euripides, *Electra*, 518–44" 67, note 1.

18. [Πρ.] σκέψαι δὲ χαίτην προστιθεῖσα σῇ κόμῃ, / εἰ χρῶμα ταὐτὸν κουρίμης ἔσται τριχός· / φιλεῖ γάρ, αἷμα ταὐτὸν οἷς ἂν ᾖ πατρός, / τὰ πόλλ᾽ ὅμοια σώματος πεφυκέναι. / [Ηλ.] οὐκ ἄξι᾽ ἀνδρός, ὦ γέρον, σοφοῦ λέγεις, / εἰ κρυπτὸν εἰς γῆν τήνδ᾽ ἂν Αἰγίσθου φόβῳ / δοκεῖς ἀδελφὸν τὸν ἐμὸν εὐθαρσῆ μολεῖν. / ἔπειτα χαίτης πῶς συνοίσεται πλόκος, / ὁ μὲν παλαίστραις ἀνδρὸς εὐγενοῦς τραφείς, / ὁ δὲ κτενισμοῖς θῆλυς; ἀλλ᾽ ἀμήχανον. / πολλοῖς δ᾽ ἂν εὕροις βοστρύχους ὁμοπτέρους / καὶ μὴ γεγῶσιν αἵματος ταὐτοῦ, γέρον. κ.τ.λ.

19. Thus, for example, Goff, "The Sign of the Fall" 259: "By 573, Elektra has rejected all the Aeschylean tokens of recognition that are offered to her by the old man, and the play threatens to depart ever more wildly from its prescribed mythical course."

20. See Dover, *Frogs* 12–24.

21. Comic poets did, on occasion, play intertextual games with each other. See chapter 7 for the prologue of *Birds* as a contrafact of Pherekrates' *Agrioi* and chapter 8 on the allusions to various comic poets in *Frogs*. In addition to Hubbard's attention to this phenomenon (*Mask of Comedy*, passim), we can expect a sustained treatment from Keith Sidwell.

22. Vernant and Vidal-Naquet, *Myth and Tragedy* 28: "The link with legendary tradition is now so stretched that it is no longer felt necessary to engage in a debate with the 'heroic' past. The dramatist can continue to write plays in which he invents the plot himself, following a model that he believes to be in conformity with the works of his great predecessors, but for him, his public, and the whole of Greek culture, the mainspring of tragedy has snapped."

23. See Hubbard, *Mask of Comedy* 40, who notes that "entire dramatic scenes [in tragedy] may be designed with an eye to . . . intertextual coordination. It has been argued that the Io scene in the *Prometheus Bound* is intimately connected with the motif of Io in Aeschylus' *Suppliants* and acts to imply that trilogy's conception of Zeus as a developed, compassionate god and a *telos* toward which the *Prometheia* will move, even as Io did. Similarly the burial scene at the end of Aeschylus' *Seven Against Thebes*, which has seemed to many critics awkward and out of place, makes better sense if regarded as a device coordinating the drama with Aeschylus' other trilogy on the Argive war, in which we know that burial of the Argive dead was a major issue."

24. Stam, *Reflexivity* 5.

25. οἴμ᾽ ὡς δέδοικα, κοὐκέτι σκώπτων λέγω. / ὦ μηχανοποιὲ πρόσεχε τὸν νοῦν ὡς ἐμέ. / ἤδη στρέφει τι πνεῦμα περὶ τὸν ὀμφαλόν, / κεὶ μὴ φυλάξει, χορτάσω τὸν κάνθαρον.

26. See Sommerstein, *Peace* 142.

27. I cite MacDowell's text: [Ξα.] νόσον γὰρ ὁ πατὴρ ἀλλόκοτον αὐτοῦ νοσεῖ, / ἣν οὐδ᾽ ἂν εἷς γνοίη ποτ᾽ οὐδ᾽ ἂν ξυμβάλοι, / εἰ μὴ πύθοισθ᾽ ἡμῶν· ἐπεὶ τοπάζετε. / [Σω.] Ἀμυνίας μὲν ὁ Προνάπους φῆσ᾽ οὑτοσὶ / εἶναι φιλόκυβον αὐτόν· [Ξα.] ἀλλ᾽ οὐδὲν λέγει. / μὰ Δί᾽, ἀλλ᾽ ἀφ᾽ αὑτοῦ τὴν νόσον τεκμαίρεται. /[Σω.] . . . . / [Ξα.] οὔκ, ἀλλὰ "φιλο" μέν ἐστιν ἀρχὴ τοῦ κακοῦ.

28. Rau, *Paratragodia* 185–218 (20 percent of the book).

29. Hubbard, *Mask of Comedy* ix.

30. For a discussion of audience address in New Comedy see Bain, *Actors and Audience* 186–207.

31. See Bain, "Audience Address" 15, who notes "the commonplace of ancient criticism . . . that Euripides indulges in extra-dramatic digressions and disrupts the illusion." Bain documents the historicizing interpretation of Euripides in Aelius Aristides, Pollux, and the scholia as suggestive of something like a tragic parabasis.

32. An influential discussion of tragic poetics is Winnington-Ingram's *Poietes Sophos*: "Here we have Euripides, one of the world's greatest tragedians, and he seems to spend his time making sophisticated jokes at the expense of gods, of Aeschylus, and of stage conventions." (p. 132). For satyr-play see Sutton, *Greek Satyr Play* 159–79; Seaford, *Cyclops* 10–33; Bain, "Audience Address" 23–25; and Taplin, "Greek Tragedy" 166, note 16., and 170–71.

33. [Ηλ.] σφαγὴν ἀϋτεῖς τήνδε μοι· τί μέλλομεν; / [Χο.] ἔπισχε, τρανῶς ὡς μάθῃς τύχας σέθεν. / [Ηλ.] οὐκ ἔστι· νικώμεσθα· ποῦ γὰρ ἄγγελοι; / [Χο.] ἥξουσιν· οὗτοι βασιλέα φαῦλον κτανεῖν.

34. See Bain, "Audience Address" 17–21. It is surely too dismissive to call εἴδετε a "passing second-person plural" as does Taplin, "Greek Tragedy" 166. Even in comedy, a significant moment of audience address is marked by a single word such as θεαταῖσιν at *Knights* 36. Bain, whom Taplin cites to support his argument, is in fact more liberal (Bain, "Audience Address" 21).

35. Lines 128–29: εἴδετε παρ᾽ ἄκρας ὡς ἀπέθρισεν τρίχας, / σῴζουσα κάλλος; ἔστι δ᾽ ἡ πάλαι γυνή.

36. For a discussion of play with convention in Euripides' *Alkestis* see Kraggerud, "Apollon als Regisseur," and C. P. Segal, *Poetics of Sorrow*. Classic works in this area include Winnington-Ingram, "Poietes Sophos"; Arnott, "Euripides and the Unexpected," "Red Herrings," "Off-Stage Cries," and "Tensions, Frustrations"; Jens, *Bauformen*; Seidensticker, "Comic Elements" and *Palintonos Harmonia*. For other examples of metatheatrical interest in tragedy compare the direct audience-address in the prologues of Aiskhylos' *Septem* and Sophokles' *Oidipous*, and the much-discussed intertextual potential of Euripides' *Phoinissai*, lines 751–53 and *Elektra*, lines 524–33.

37. In Euripides, argues Zeitlin, "Closet of Masks" 54, there are "instances when one allusion conceals another and perhaps another, and we find a *palimpsestic* text, where one layer can be deciphered under another; each makes its own contribution but the total effect is one of bewildering and cumulative complexity that establishes a series of new if often contradictory relations between the primary level of the text and the oscillating substratum that shifts beneath it." She illustrates her point by tracing the relationship between Aiskhylos' *Eumenides*, Sophokles' *Philoktetes*, and the first part of *Orestes*, which emerges as a "chaos of forms."

38. Dover, *Aristophanic Comedy* 149, notes that "it would seem that at the same time as comedy plundered tragedy for parodic purposes, a tragic poet was not above borrowing from a comedian." See also Sommerstein and Dunbar ad loc.

39. The modern bibliography on the subject begins with Stoessl, "Die Phoinissen." See Hall, *Persians*.

40. See Bain, *Actors and Audience* 208–12. The Roman poet, by contrast, does not seem to have been bothered by such anachronism, and the details of theater construction are prominent in the description of Carthage at *Aeneid* 1.426–28.

41. A few refreshing exceptions are *Lilly in Love*, *Farewell My Concubine*, and *The End of Violence*.

42. Printed in Laroque, *The Show Within*, 461–68.

43. Cf. Taplin, "Greek Tragedy" 171: "There is no surviving example even in comedy of a fully fledged play within a play; but the use of *Telephus* in *Acharnians*, or of *Helen* and *Andromeda* in *Thesm.*, is half-way there. The nearest that tragedy approaches to this is in certain uses of contrived disguise such as the 'merchant' in *Philoctetes* and the escape scene in *Helen*. Such scenes seem to occur in the 'outer periods' of fifth-century tragedy." For a detailed characterization of the modern play-within-the-play see Pfister, *Theory and Analysis* 223–30 and Laroque, *The Show Within*. For *Thesmophoriazousai* in the context of other plays that engage in a metatheatrical dialogue see chapter 7.

44. Kleon appears to have been preparing to prosecute Lakhes for some misdeed as general in Sicily in the autumn of 427 (Aristophanes assumes embezzlement).

45. Cf. Hubbard, *Mask of Comedy* 132: "Inasmuch as we have seen an identification between Bdelycleon and the poet built up throughout the *Wasps*, we should find in Bdelycleon's stage-management of this mock trial a reflection on the nature and function of Aristophanes' own dramatic art. We are struck by the equation between the legal and dramatic agons as the two kinds of spectacle presented for the entertainment and enjoyment of the audience." See also Russo, *Aristophanes* 121–32.

46. So MacDowell, *Wasps* 164. "The power of Comedy," concludes Hubbard, *Mask of Comedy* 132–33, "is the power to manipulate public imagination into new modes of perception and, it is hoped, new modes of judgment."

47. For studies of important problems specific to *Birds* see Hofmann, *Mythos und Komödie*; Dobrov, "Language, Fiction, and Utopia"; and Hubbard, *Mask of Comedy* 158–60. The unique position of the play in the Aristophanic corpus is well analyzed in Newiger, "Die *Vögel* und ihre Stellung" 266–82.

48. The revival of Droysen's hypothesis concerning the Law of Syrakosios (Sommerstein, "Decree of Syrakosios" followed by Hubbard in *Mask of Comedy*, and others) seeks to find an external, legislative constraint on comedy, ὀνομαστὶ κωμῳδεῖν. *Contra* see Halliwell, "ὀνομαστὶ κωμῳδεῖν." See also Carey, "Comic Ridicule and Democracy," and Atkinson, "Curbing the Comedians."

49. "There is a plague of books in Νεφελοκοκκύγια," in the words of Denniston, "Technical Terms" 117.

50. That is to say, choral and military service were mutually exclusive for young men of ephebic age. See Winkler, "Ephebes' Song" 20–62. For the connection between sophistry and comic poiesis in *Clouds* see chapter 5, "Misunderstood Intellectuals and Poets," pp. 88–112 of Hubbard, *Mask of Comedy* (p. 95, note 22, in particular).

51. See Dobrov, "Winged Words" 111–65. It is important that Peisetairos reaffirms his status as choreographer and director in the later episodes. Note, for example, his clement dismissal of the poet with whom he apparently sympathizes as with a competitor (cf. line 947), i.e., a rival choral didaskalos (line 912).

52. See Gelzer, *Epirrhematische Agon* 22, 130, 135, and "Some Aspects" 9; also Händel, *Formen und Darstellungsweisen* 317.

53. See Sifakis, *Parabasis* 62, who is arguing against the work of scholars such as Francis Cornford who held the parabasis to be a cultic remnant of sorts that first replaced the parodos

and to which dramatic scenes were added. Although certainly not identical to the so-called "marching anapests" of tragedy, the anapestic tetrameter in combination with a new persona (bird-god citizens of Nephelokokkygia) cannot have failed to allude to the convention of a first choral entrance. On this question see Harsh, "Position of the Parabasis."

54. ἄγε δή, φύσιν ἄνδρες ἀμαυρόβιοι, φύλλων γενεᾷ προσόμοιοι, / ὀλιγοδρανέες, πλάσματα πηλοῦ, σκιοειδέα φῦλ᾽ ἀμενηνά, / ἀπτῆνες ἐφημέριοι, ταλαοὶ βροτοί, ἀνέρες εἰκελόνειροι, / πρόσχετε τὸν νοῦν τοῖς ἀθανάτοις ἡμῖν, τοῖς αἰὲν ἐοῦσιν, / τοῖς αἰθερίοις, τοῖσιν ἀγήρως, τοῖς ἄφθιτα μηδομένοισιν, / ἵν᾽ ἀκούσαντες πάντα παρ᾽ ἡμῶν ὀρθῶς περὶ τῶν μετεώρων, / φύσιν οἰωνῶν γένεσίν τε θεῶν ποταμῶν τ᾽ Ἐρέβους τε Χάους τε / εἰδότες ὀρθῶς, Προδίκῳ παρ᾽ ἐμοῦ κλάειν εἴπητε τὸ λοιπόν. / Χάος ἦν καὶ Νὺξ Ἔρεβός τε μέλαν πρῶτον καὶ Τάρταρος εὐρύς. / γῆ δ᾽ οὐδ᾽ ἀὴρ οὐδ᾽ οὐρανὸς ἦν. Text and translation from Sommerstein, *Birds*.

55. For an extended treatment of the self-reflexive aspects of *Ekklesiazousai* see Taaffe, "Metatheater and Gender" and *Aristophanes and Women* 103–33. For a discussion of gender boundaries in a recent production of the play see Maitland, "Tripping the Light Fantastic" 212–21.

56. See Taaffe, *Aristophanes and Women* 123–29. For the interplay between grammatical gender and the dramatic construction of gender (in *Thesmophoriazousai*) see Sommerstein, *Thesmophoriazousai* 7–10.

57. *Ekklesiazousai* is roughly datable to the late 390s, the last extant play, *Plutus*, to 388. After this we know of only two other plays (*Aiolosikon* and *Kokalos*), now lost, that were produced by one of Aristophanes' sons.

58. γυναῖκα δ᾽ εἶναι πρᾶγμ᾽ ἔφη νουβυστικὸν / καὶ χρηματοποιόν· κοὔτε τἀπόρρητ᾽ ἔφη / ἐκ Θεσμοφόροιν ἑκάστοτ᾽ αὐτὰς ἐκφέρειν, / σὲ δὲ κἀμὲ βουλεύοντε τοῦτο δρᾶν ἀεί. . . . / καὶ ταῦτ᾽ ἀποφέρειν πάντα κοὐκ ἀποστερεῖν· ἡμῶν δὲ τοὺς πολλοὺς ἔφασκε τοῦτο δρᾶν. . . . / οὐ συκοφαντεῖν, οὐ διώκειν, οὐδὲ τὸν / δῆμον καταλύειν, ἀλλὰ πολλὰ κἀγαθά. / ἕτερά τε πλεῖστα τὰς γυναῖκας εὐλόγει.

59. For example, *The Crying Game* and *M Butterfly*.

60. Compare to the starkly tragic mise en abyme of *Aias*, "written and directed" by Athene (see chapter 4).

61. See Roberts, "Different Stories" 171. The prophecy is presented through several sources, some of whom are in potential conflict with the standard of prophetic truth.

62. "Sophocles' purpose in evoking the Odyssey so consistently," notes Davidson, "Homer and Sophocles' *Philoctetes*" 35, "would appear to highlight the ironic perversity of Odysseus' mission to Lemnos and his alienating behavior in the course of it."

63. καὶ δεῦρ᾽, ἐάν μοι τοῦ χρόνου δοκῆτέ τι / κατασχολάζειν, αὖθις ἐκπέμψω πάλιν / τοῦτον τὸν ἄνδρα, ναυκλήρου τρόποις / μορφὴν δολώσας, ὡς ἂν ἀγνοίᾳ προσῇ· οὐ δῆτα, τέκνον, ποικίλως αὐδωμένου / δέχου τὰ συμφέροντα τῶν ἀεὶ λόγων. Text that of Lloyd-Jones and Wilson. Ussher's translation (based on R. D. Dawe's second Teubner edition [Leipzig, 1985]) is given here with some modification. Greengard's *Theatre in Crisis* approaches a metatheatrical reading of the play (e.g., pp. 23–26) inasmuch as the narrative allows for the blending of truth and fiction in a way that has Neoptolemos create his own myth. Along similar lines see also Taplin, "Significant Actions" 37 and *Tragedy in Action* 154. For a critical bibliographical survey of the play see Easterling, "*Philoctetes* and Modern Criticism." The reading here is informed also by the essays of Dolores O'Higgins, Pietro Pucci, Mary Whitlock-Blundell, Deborah Roberts, Oliver Taplin, and Meredith C. Hoppin.

64. The ancient testimonium for the three Philoktetes plays is Dio Chrysostom, who notes at 52.12–13 that "[Odysseus] then clearly and accurately sets forth the play's plot. He explains why he has come to Lemnos and says that he has been disguised by Athena so as not to be recognized by Philoktetes when he encounters him. In this Euripides imitated

Homer." (Euripides' *Philoktetes* was produced with *Medeia* and *Diktys*.) See also Dio's para-phrase of the prologue at 59.7.

65. To this we might compare Odysseus' second sudden entrance and exit (lines 1291–1303). Though such intrusion on the part of a character in hiding is hard to parallel in trag-edy (cf. Euripides *Iphigeneia at Aulis* 855), it is more common in comedy (*Clouds* 1145, *Lysistrata* 430, and a few times in Menander).

66. This includes an expedition to Lemnos to fetch Neoptolemos as well as Odysseus' and Diomedes' search for Philoktetes.

67. [Νε.] πρὸς ποῖον αὖ τόνδ' αὐτὸς Οὐδυσσεὺς ἔπλει; [Εμ.] ἦν δή τις—ἀλλὰ τόνδε μοι πρῶτον φράσον / τίς ἐστίν· ἂν λέγῃς δὲ μὴ φώνει μέγα. / [Νε.] ὅδ' ἔσθ' ὁ κλεινός σοι Φιλοκτήτης, ξένε. / [Εμ.] μή νύν μ' ἔρῃ τὰ πλείον', ἀλλ' ὅσον τάχος / ἔκπλει σεαυτὸν ξυλλαβὼν ἐκ τῆσδε γῆς. / [Φι.] τί φησιν, ὦ παῖ; τί δὲ κατὰ σκότον ποτὲ / διεμπολᾷ λόγοισι πρός σ' ὁ ναυβάτης.

68. It is interesting that in Aiskhylos and Euripides, Odysseus (or Diomedes) takes the bow from Philoctetes during such a bout of pain. Sophokles has clearly changed this and placed an emphasis on the suffering hero's debility as a boundary between him and his world. Philoktetes' illness is even characterized in terms of madness (line 815), a strategy that has something in common with the rewriting of myth in *Aias* and *Bakkhai*.

69. Ussher, *Philoctetes* 134. For a fuller discussion of the stasimon see Ussher, *Philoctetes* 15 (note 14).

3. *Figures of Play, Part 2*

1. *Akharnians*, lines 375–82 and 500–506.

2. αὐτὸς τ' ἐμαυτὸν ὑπὸ Κλέωνος ἄπαθον / ἐπίσταμαι διὰ τὴν πέρυσι κωμῳδίαν. / εἰσελκύσας γάρ μ' εἰς τὸ βουλευτήριον / διέβαλλε καὶ ψευδῆ κατεγλώττιζέ μου / κἀκυκλοβόρει κἄπλυνεν, ὥστ' ὀλίγου πάνυ / ἀπωλόμην μολυνοπραγμονούμενος.

3. οὐ γάρ με νῦν γε διαβαλεῖ Κλέων ὅτι / ξένων παρόντων τὴν πόλιν κακῶς λέγω. / αὐτοὶ γάρ ἐσμεν οὑπὶ Ληναίῳ τ' ἀγών, / κοὔπω ξένοι πάρεισιν·

4. A representative sampling of entries in the current discussion would include Goldhill, *Poet's Voice* 191, Hubbard, *Mask of Comedy* 45–47, Fisher, "Multiple Personalities" 31–33, Bowie, *Aristophanes* 44, and Sidwell, "Aristophanes' *Acharnians*."

5. For a fuller discussion of the categories below in their literary-historical context see Dobrov, "Poet's Voice."

6. See Dover, "The Style of Aristophanes" and "Language and Character in Aristophanes" in *Greek and the Greeks* 224–48; Arnott, "Comic Openings" 19–22; and Dobrov, "Poet's Voice" 73–77.

7. See, for example, *Birds* 462 ff.

8. *Poetics* 1449a9–10: γενομένη δ' οὖν ἀπ' ἀρχῆς αὐτοσχεδιαστικῆς–καὶ αὐτὴ [τραγῳ δία] καὶ ἡ κωμῳδία, "both tragedy and comedy had their first beginnings in improvisation."

9. Thus Xanthias, Dionysos' sidekick in *Frogs*, undergoes a progressive characteriza-tion through a series of manipulative utterances and actions (so Dover, *Frogs* 196).

10. Hubbard, *Mask of Comedy* 137.

11. E.g., *Birds* 92.

12. See *Wasps* 54–67.

13. *Akharnians* lines 6 and 300–301 (that is, the play *Knights*).

14. "No other characters in a Greek drama are so bookish, so learned," notes Zeitlin "Closet of Masks" 53, of this phenomenon in tragedy—and she could well have been de-scribing Dikaiopolis or Trygaios—"although they themselves are marvelously unaware of their erudition."

15. Hubbard, *Mask of Comedy* 33.

16. So at some length Hubbard, *Mask of Comedy* 16–40.

17. As the genre evolves through the Middle Period, comedy loses the fictional persona of the poet "behind" the players and addressing the spectators. There arises between stage and theatron a formidable wall of illusion or distance. Fourth-century comedy does not continue with the intensely topical and political satire exhibited in early Aristophanes. Finally, comic language and action are brought into conformity with "the probable." Cf. T. B. L. Webster's discussion (*Later Greek Comedy* 114–16) of Aristotle's τὸ εἰκός. "[New] comedy is a 'combination of probable incidents'; the important word is 'probable' and it can be interpreted in three ways." These are: 1. "A probable sequence. In this sense 'probable' refers to the technique of plot-construction, to the unity of action and the preparation and motivation of exits and entrances"; 2. "the sort of things which do happen every day . . . . The realities of time and place are also carefully observed"; 3. "'probable' can be used in the sense of 'suitable to the character in this particular situation.' . . . Most of the characters of New Comedy are realistically drawn."

18. Compare Taplin, "Greek Tragedy," who separates the world of the play from the world of the audience in an attempt to sharpen the contrast between fifth-century tragedy and comedy (against the rapprochement implicit in the work of Seidensticker and others).

19. Barthes, "l'ancienne rhétorique" 174, note 1.

20. Compare with this the account given by Hyginus (101), who appears to have followed Euripides closely: *"Telephus Herculis et Auges filius ab Achille in pugna Chironis hasta percussus dicitur. ex quo vulnere cum in dies taetro cruciatu angeretur, petit sortem ab Apolline, quod esset remedium; responsum est ei neminem mederi posse nisi eandem hastam qua vulneratus est. hoc Telephus ut audivit, ad regem Agamemnonem venit et monitu Clytaemnestrae Orestem infantem de cunabulis rapuit, minitans se eum occisurum, nisi sibi Achivi mederentur. Achivis autem quod responsum erat sine Telephi ductu Troiam capi non posse, facile cum eo in gratiam redierunt et ab Achille petierunt ut eum sanaret. quibus Achilles respondit se artem medicam non nosse. tunc Ulixes ait, Non te dicit Apollo sed auctorem vulneris hastam nominat. quam cum rasissent, remediatus est. a quo cum peterent ut secum ad Troiam expugnandam iret, non impetrarunt, quod is Laodicen Priami filiam uxorem haberet; sed ob beneficium, quod eum sanarunt, eos deduxit, locos autem et itinera demonstravit; inde in Moesiam est profectus."*

21. See the discussion in Collard, Cropp, and Lee, *Euripides* 19–20.

22. This incorporates fr. 696 and 884 N²: ὦ γαῖα πατρίς, ἣν Πέλοψ ὁρίζεται, / χαῖρ᾽, ὅς τε πέτραν Ἀρκάδων δυσχείμερον / Πὰν ἐμβατεύεις, ἔνθεν εὔχομαι γένος· / Αὔγη γὰρ Ἀλέου παῖς με τῷ Τιρυνθίῳ / τίκτει λαθραίως Ἡρακλεῖ· σύνοιδ᾽ ὄρος / Παρθένιον, ἔνθα μητέρ᾽ ὠδίνων ἐμὴν / ἔλυσεν Εἰλείθυια, γί<γ>νομαι δ᾽ ἐγώ. / καὶ πόλλ᾽ <ἐ>μόχθησ᾽, ἀλλὰ συντεμῶ λόγον. / ἦλθον δὲ Μυσῶν πεδίον, ἔνθ᾽ ε<ὑ>ρὼν ἐμὴν / μητέρα κατοικῶ, καὶ δίδωσί μοι κράτη / Τεύθρας ὁ Μυσός, Τήλεφον δ᾽ ἐπώνυμον / καλοῦσί μ᾽ ἀστοὶ Μυσίαν κατὰ χθόνα· / τηλοῦ γὰρ οἰκῶν βίοτον ἐξιδρυσάμην. / Ἕλλην δὲ βαρβάροισιν ἦρχον ἐκπονῶν / πολλοῖς σὺν ὅπλοις, πρὶν <γ᾽> Ἀχαϊκὸς μολὼν / στρατὸς τὰ Μυσῶ[ν πε]δί᾽ ἐπ[ι]στρωφᾷ <ποδί>. Unless stated otherwise the account of *Telephos* here relies on the text as presented by John Rea in Handley and Rea and the various reconstructions by Welcker, Nauck, Handley, Heath, and others. The presentation, translation, and commentary in Collard, Cropp, and Lee, *Euripides* 17–52, has also been most useful.

23. Cf. fr. 705a N²: "chasing the raiders with his spear."

24. Fr. 705 N²: κώπης ἀνάσσων κἀποβὰς εἰς Μυσίαν / ἐτραυματίσθην πολεμίῳ βραχίονι. Fr. 707N²: καλῶς ἔχοι μοι, Τηλέφῳ δ᾽ ἀγὼ φρονῶ.

25. Accius fr. I, XIV, XV, and XIII (text and numbers as presented by Handley and Rea); Webster, *Euripides* 45.

26. Ennius Telephius fr. I notes Webster, *Euripides* 45, "adds that he had left home in disguise," while fr. III attests "that his disguise was to avoid being killed, *caedem caveo* . . . . The story of a Greek reconciliation with Telephos before they left Mysia is therefore excluded. Telephos expects hostility; he therefore arrives disguised as an Arcadian beggar."

27. fr. 697: πτώχ' ἀμφίβλητα [ἀμφίβληστρα Burges] σώματος λαβὼν ῥάκη / ἀλκτήρια τύχης. fr. 698: δεῖ γάρ με δόξαι πτωχὸν [εἶναι τήμερον] / εἶναι μὲν ὅσπερ εἰμί, φαίνεσθαι δὲ μή.

28. *Akharnians* 440–41

29. ἐνσκευάσασθαί μ᾽ οἷον ἀθλιώτατον, line 384.

30. See the passage from Apollodoros quoted in note 20.

31. Handley and Rea, *Telephus* 30. The evidence for this include Tzetzes' claim that Telephos assumed the humble position of gatekeeper at Agamemnon's court (with its mention of a painless life of modest means), σμίκρ᾽ ἂν θέλοιμι καὶ καθ᾽ ἡμέραν ἔχων / ἄλυπος οἰκεῖν μᾶλλον ἢ πλουτῶν νοσεῖν; and a line (fr. 2 N²) from the *Telephos* by (late tragic poet) Moskhion, στυγνὸν ἢ κατ᾽ αὐχένων ἡμῶν ἐρείδεις τῆσδε λατρείας ζυγόν, "you who push this hateful yoke of service upon my neck."

32. ἄνασσα πράγους τοῦδε καὶ βουλεύματος.

33. τόλμα σὺ κἄν τι τραχὺ νείμωσιν θεοί.

34. Tzetzes makes this comment on *Clouds* 922: μετὰ πηρίου ἐλθόντα προσαίτην εἰς τὴν Ἑλλάδα καὶ τῆς Ἀγαμέμνονος αὐλῆς μόλις πυλωρὸν γεγονότα. See Collard, Cropp, and Lee, *Euripides* 19.

35. The corrupt Rylands papyrus that appears to contain the name of Telephos (line 3) does not contribute much to a reconstruction. If we could be certain that this excerpt belongs to Euripides' play, something might be made of the reference to "sailors and captains" in line 4 (an actor referring to the chorus?).

36. See Collard, Cropp, and Lee, *Euripides* 20.

37. Though he is not the first to suggest two speeches, Heath, *Telephus* 275, is certainly correct to emphasize in Dikaiopolis' argument two separate defenses: "There are signs of conflation within the speech itself; the shift from 'they'—the Spartans, representing the Trojans of the original—to 'Telephus' at the end is a marked discontinuity." While others (e.g., Webster, *Euripides* 46) consider the possiblity of two speeches, Heath suggests that the second speech in self-defense is spoken by the beggar "in character" and that the recognition occurs at the altar, after the seizure of Orestes.

38. Fr. 720 N²: κακῶς ὀλοίτ᾽ ἄν· ἄξιον γὰρ Ἑλλάδι (the text of Collard, Cropp, and Lee, who point out, *Euripides* 52, that the conjecture of Dobree, ὀλοίατ᾽, printed by Nauck, is not really needed as the singular makes good sense).

39. Fr. 975 N²: χαλεποὶ πόλεμοι γὰρ ἀδελφῶν.

40. Fr. 722 N²: ἴθ᾽ ὅποι χρήζεις οὐκ ἀπολοῦμαι / τῆς σῆς Ἑλένης εἵνεκα. fr. 723 N2: Σπάρτην ἔλαχες, κείνην κόσμει· / τὰς δὲ Μυκήνας ἡμεῖς ἰδίᾳ.

41. μή μοι φθονήσετ᾽, ἄνδρες Ἑλλήνων ἄκροι, / εἰ πτωχὸς ὢν τέτληκ᾽ ἐν ἐσθλοῖσιν λέγειν.

42. Ἀγάμεμνον, οὐδ᾽ εἰ πέλεκυν ἐν χεροῖν ἔχων / μέλλοι τις εἰς τράχηλον ἐμβαλεῖν ἐμόν, / σιγήσομαι δίκαιά γ᾽ ἀντειπεῖν ἔχων.

43. Heath, "Telephus" 278. Fragments 708–10 may belong to this speech (in the translation of Collard, Cropp, and Lee, *Euripides* 30): (fr. 708) "Someone will say, 'it was not right'"; (fr. 708a) "Come now, suppose < > had sailed out in a bark . . ."; (fr. 709) "Would you have sat quiet at home? Nay, far from it!"; (fr. 710) ". . . and do we think that Telephos (should) not (have done it)?"

44. εἶτα δὴ θυμούμεθα / παθόντες οὐδὲν μεῖζον ἢ δεδρακότες (cf. *Thesmophoriazousai* 517–19).

45. Thematic and verbal echoes of this moment are found in *Akharnians* 557 ff., 576–78 and *Thesmophoriazousai* 520–30.

46. τῆδε θἠμέρα κριθήσεται, εἴτ᾽ ἔστ᾽ ἔτι ζῶν εἴτ᾽ ἀπόλωλε Τήλεφος.

47. [ἰ]δόντες αὐτὸν . . . πόλιν μαστεύωμεν . . . μαστεύειν χρή. Odysseus is mentioned in fr. 10 of P.Oxy 2460 and the first word of fr. 14 is μαστήρ. "Odysseus," explains Webster, *Euripides* 46, "perhaps prompted by the discomfited Menelaos, assumes that Telephos is a spy: 'a bad man is abusing your hospitality' (fr. 721 N²); 'All Argos is inflamed against him' (Ennius VI R). A series of fragments from Accius (III–V, X) mention an unknown stranger whose ragged clothes contrast with his personality; this is Agamemnon, answering Odysseus' questions about Telephos."

48. Heath, "Telephus" 278.

49. Fr. 704 N²: οἶδ᾽ ἄνδρα Μυσὸν Τήλεφον . . . εἴτε δὲ / Μυσὸς <γεγὼς> ἦν εἴτε κἄλλοθέν ποθεν, / πῶς . . . Τήλεφος γνωρίζεται; So Nauck, who includes all of *Akharnians* 430 in the fragment. *Contra*, see Collard, Cropp, and Lee, *Euripides* 46.

50. If Klytaimnestra is not onstage, Telephos may have to run into the palace to get the child. This awkward moment may be avoided either by bringing the queen onstage (Heath) or relegating the abduction and flight to a messenger speech.

51. Of the eighteen or so known examples, Webster, *Euripides* 302, lists the following important items: Attic kalyx-krater (Berlin 3974), a Campanian hydria (Ixion painter, Naples, RC141), an Apulian vase (published by L. Sechan in 1926, now lost), a Campanian bell-krater (Naples 2293), an Etruscan column-krater (Berlin inv. 30042), Attic relief, Squat lekythos (New York, Metropolitan Museum 28.57.9), and an Attic pelike (Thessaloniki 34.263). "Metzger," he notes, *Euripides* 46, "has rightly connected this with the Attic kalyx krater on which Telephos with the child Orestes sits on an altar in a sanctuary of Apollo. The Campanian hydria shows Klytemnestra set out with Orestes and her women to pray to the Lycian Apollo in an earlier scene, probably the prologue. The Attic pelike shows two bearded men discussing together while Telephos holds the baby (probably he is sitting on a high altar, but the lower part of this vase has been broken away): they will be Agamemnon and Odysseus. (The young man who is separated from the rest on both the Attic red-figure vases is Achilles, whom the painter added because, although he had not arrived at this moment, he was essential to the story.)" For a list of relevant iconography, see Collard, Cropp, and Lee, *Euripides* 17 and 22. For work on comedy and iconography see Csapo, "A Note" and Taplin, *Comic Angels* 17, 37–38, 80.

52. P. Berol. 9908, col. ii, 1–10: ἢ νότ[ου ἢ] ζεφύροιο δίνα / πέμψ[ει Τ]ρωάδας ἀκτάς, / σύ τε π[ηδ]αλίῳ παρεδρεύῳ[ν / φράσει[ς τ]ῷ κατὰ πρῷραν / εὐθὺς Ἰλ[ίο]υ πόρον / Ἀτρεΐδα[ις] ἰδέσι̣θαι. / σὲ γὰρ Τε[γ]εᾶτις ἡμῖν, / Ἑλλάς, οὐχὶ Μυσία͵, τίκτει / ναύταν σύν τινι̣ δὴ θει̣ῶν / καὶ πεμπτήρ᾽ ἁλίων ι̣ἐ̣ρι̣ετμῶν. The text here and in note 54 from Collard, Cropp, and Lee, *Euripides* 38–39. Translation adapted from the same.

53. Webster, *Euripides* 47.

54. P. Berol. 9908, Col. ii, 11–23: [Α.] μῶν καὶ σὺ καινὸς ποντίας͵ ἀπὸ χι̣θονὸς / ἥκεις, Ὀδυσσεῦ; ποῦ ᾽στι σύλλογος φι̣[ί]λων; / τί μέλλετ᾽; οὐ χρῆν ἥσυχο͵ν κεῖσθαι ι̣π[ό]δα. / [Ο.] δοκεῖ στρατεύειν καὶ μέλει̣ τοῖς ἐν τέλει / τάδ᾽· ἐν δέοντι δ᾽ ἦλθες, ὦ̣ παῖ Πηλέως. / [Α.] οὐ μὴν ἐπ᾽ ἀκταῖς γ᾽ ἐστι κωπήρι̣ης στρατός, / οὔτ᾽ οὖν ὁπλίτης ἐξετάζεται παρών. / [Ο.] ἀλλ᾽ αὐτίκα· σπεύδειν γὰρ ἐν καιρῷ χρεών. / [Α.] αἰεί ποτ᾽ ἐστὲ νωχελεῖ̣ς καὶ μέλλετε / ῥήσεις θ᾽ ἕκαστος μυρίας͵ καθήμενος / λέγει, τὸ δ᾽ ἔργον [ο]ὐδαμοῦ̣ περαίνι̣εται. / κἀ̣[γ]ὼ μέν, ὡς ὁρᾶ[τ]ε, δρᾶνι̣ ἕι̣τι̣οιμος̣ ὢν / ἥκω, στρατός τε Μ[υρ]μιδ͵ων, καὶ πι̣λεύσ[ομαι / τὰ ι̣[τ]ῶν Ἀτρειδ[ῶν οὐ μένω]ι̣ μελλι̣ήμ[ατα.

55. σὺ δ᾽ εἰκ᾽ ἀνάγκη καὶ θεοῖσι μὴ μάχου· / τόλμα δὲ πι̣ρι̣οσβλέπειν με καὶ φρονήματος / χάλα. τά το͵ι μέγιστα πολλάκις θεός / ταπείν᾽ ἔ̣θηκι̣ε καὶ συνέστειλεν πάλιν.

56. See Collard, Cropp, and Lee, *Euripides* 21, 24–25.

57. Heath, "Telephus" 280.

58. "In this play," notes Foley, "Tragedy and Politics" 31, "Aristophanes goes out of his way to give the audience clues for recognizing his major tragic source and for interpreting his use of it."

59. See Handley and Rea, *Telephus* 23–25; Rau, *Paratragodia* 10–18, and Silk, "Aristophanic Paratragedy" 479–80.

60. In this respect it is hard to follow Silk, "Aristophanic Paratragedy" 494–95, who denies that the adaptation of fr. 703N^2 at *Akharnians* 497–98 is intelligibly framed. Aristophanes' lines may not be parody, but they are most certainly framed in a way that their intertextuality may be effective.

61. The deme Akharnai in particular: see Thoukydides 2.14–17, 20–22.

62. Though not used explicitly in *Akharnians*, see the parallel contexts in *Clouds* 74, 243; *Wasps* 71, 76, 87, 114, 651; *Birds* 31; *Lysistrata* 1085, 1088; *Thesmophoriazousai* 1116, etc.

63. See N. Slater, "Space, Character and ΑΠΑΤΗ" 397–99, Hubbard, *Mask of Comedy* 41–59.

64. For this force of ἀμφι- in composition cf. ἀμφιγενής, ἀμφίγλωσσος, ἀμφιγνωμονεύω, ἀμφιδοξέω, ἀμφικλινής, and many other similar terms.

65. Lines 119–21: ὦ θερμόβουλον πρωκτὸν ἐξυρημένε, / τοιόνδε γ᾽ ὦ πίθηκε τὸν πώγων᾽ ἔχων / εὐνοῦχος ἡμῖν ἦλθες ἐσκευασμένος;

66. Thus the woman "from the ape" in Semonides 7 (lines 71–82) is said to be ἄπυγος, "lacking a rump."

67. E.g., lines 384 and 436: ἐνσκευάσασθαί μ᾽ οἷον ἀθλιώτατον.

68. Cf. ἐξαπατώμεθ᾽, line 114; and lines 634, 636.

69. ἕπου, δίωκε, πυνθάνου, ξυλλαβεῖν, μοι μηνύσατε, εἴ τις οἶδ᾽ ὅποι τέτραπται γῆς, ἐκπέφυγ᾽, οἴχεται φροῦδος, διωκόμενος ἐξέφυγεν, ἐλαφρῶς ἀπεπλίξατο, διωκτέος δε, ἐκφυγών, κοὐκ ἀνήσω, δεῖ ζητεῖν τὸν ἄνδρα καὶ βλέπειν Βαλληνάδε / καὶ διώκειν γῆν πρὸ γῆς, ἕως ἂν εὑρεθῇ ποτέ, etc.

70. Cf. πολιτοφθόρος at Plato, *Laws* 854c.

71. Cf. his ironic appeal to the choice rowers as σωσίπολις λεώς, line 163.

72. See Zimmermann, *Untersuchungen* I 34–41.

73. See Handley and Rea, *Telephus* 33 and 36.

74. λαβέ, "seize," at *Eumenides* 130 becomes βάλλε, βάλλε, βάλλε, βάλλε, etc.

75. E.g., *Thesmophoriazousai*, and the Telephos plays of Rhinthon, Ennius, Accius.

76. See Collard, Cropp, and Lee, *Euripides* 20, 22.

77. Lines 355–57: ἐμοῦ ᾽θέλοντος ὑπὲρ ἐπιξήνου λέγειν / ὑπὲρ Λακεδαιμονίων ἅπανθ᾽ ὅσ᾽ ἂν λέγω· / καίτοι φιλῶ γε τὴν ἐμὴν ψυχὴν ἐγώ. Lines 366–69: ἰδοῦ θεᾶσθε, τὸ μὲν ἐπίξηνον τοδί, / ὁ δ᾽ ἀνὴρ ὁ λέξων οὑτοσὶ τυννουτοσί. / ἀμέλει, μὰ τὸν Δί᾽ οὐκ ἐνασπιδώσομαι, / λέξω δ᾽ ὑπὲρ Λακεδαιμονίων ἁμοὶ δοκεῖ. See Rau, *Paratragodia* 26–27, and Collard, Cropp, and Lee, *Euripides* 46.

78. "The serious," notes Hubbard, *Mask of Comedy* 44, of the transformational poetics at work here, "can be communicated only through the ridiculous, the higher through the lower mimetic."

79. Long ago A.-W. Schlegel noted that it was "eine von den Hauptformen des Aristophanischen Scherzes, *eine Metapher buchstäblich zu nehmen*." In Newiger, *Metapher und Allegorie* 181. "I label [this aspect of comic representation] visual presentation," writes Handley in Handley and Rea, *Telephus* 24, "as when Socrates in the *Clouds* is made to raise himself physically in order to think about τὰ μετέωρα, or when scales are brought on to test the weight of verses in the *Frogs*."

80. For another explanation of Dikaiopolis' "multiple personalities" see the provocative piece by Keith Sidwell, "Aristophanes' *Acharnians* and Eupolis." Sidwell supports

E. Bowie's identification of Dikaiopolis with Eupolis and argues, among other things, that caricature of real individuals was much more pervasive in comedy than is usually acknowledged. See also his "Poetic Rivalry" on a similar identity between Philokleon (*Wasps*) and Kratinos.

81. Foley, "Tragedy and Politics" 47.

82. E.g., the rather serious [epic/tragic] ἀτάρ in his first address to the tragedian.

83. For a similar tragic/comic diglossia, see below on the Aiakos scene in *Frogs* (chapter 8).

84. ἀναβάδην ποιεῖς, / ἐξὸν καταβάδην; οὐκ ἐτὸς χωλοὺς ποιεῖς./ ἀτὰρ τί τὰ ῥάκι᾽ ἐκ τραγῳδίας ἔχεις, / ἐσθῆτ᾽ ἐλεινήν; οὐκ ἐτὸς πτωχοὺς ποιεῖς. / ἀλλ᾽ ἀντιβολῶ πρὸς τῶν γονάτων σ᾽ Εὐριπίδη, / δός μοι ῥάκιον τι τοῦ παλαιοῦ δράματος. / δεῖ γάρ με λέξαι τῷ χορῷ ῥῆσιν μακράν· / αὕτη δὲ θάνατον, ἢν κακῶς λέξω, φέρει.

85. δεῖ γάρ με δόξαι πτωχὸν εἶναι τήμερον / εἶναι μὲν ὅσπερ εἰμί, φαίνεσθαι δὲ μή. / τοὺς μὲν θεατὰς εἰδέναι μ᾽ ὅς εἰμ᾽ ἐγώ, / τοὺς δ᾽ αὖ χορευτὰς ἠλιθίους παρεστάναι, / ὅπως ἂν αὐτοὺς ῥηματίοις σκιμαλίσω.

86. "The staging [of this moment]," notes Foley ("Tragedy and Politics" 40), "reinforces the verbal point. For although Dikaiopolis immediately before this passage dons the attire of Telephus, his own comic costume remains visible through the multiple holes in the rags (435)—visible to the audience if not to the chorus or to Lamachus who both swallow the dramatic illusion produced by the tragic beggar costume (558, 578)."

87. μή μοι φθονήσετ᾽ ἄνδρες οἱ θεώμενοι, / εἰ πτωχὸς ὢν ἔπειτ᾽ ἐν Ἀθηναίοις λέγειν / μέλλω περὶ τῆς πόλεως, τρυγῳδίαν ποιῶν. / τὸ γὰρ δίκαιον οἶδε καὶ τρυγῳδία. / ἐγὼ δὲ λέξω δεινὰ μὲν δίκαια δέ.

88. On this word see Taplin, "Tragedy and Trugedy."

89. Henderson, "Comic Hero" 309.

90. πολίτης χρηστός, line 595.

91. Henderson, "Comic Hero" 313. "Dikaiopolis tries first to work within the system and strikes a separate peace only after he finds that the system has been co-opted by the political élite (as represented by Kleon, Lamakhos and the officers of Assembly and Council). His ambition . . . was one surely shared by the collectivity of Athenians, as was his attitude that the money wasted on self-seeking leaders should be used to keep ordinary people like himself in well-earned luxury."

92. See Collard, Cropp, and Lee, *Euripides* 45.

93. The source of the reciprocal abductions theme has been much debated. See Heath, "Telephus."

94. ταῦτ᾽ οἶδ᾽ ὅτι ἂν ἐδρᾶτε· τὸν δὲ Τήλεφον / οὐκ οἰόμεσθα; νοῦς ἄρ᾽ ἡμῖν οὐκ ἔνι.

95. Bowie, *Aristophanes* 30–31.

96. Foley, "Tragedy and Politics."

97. "Nothing can offer a more bewildering illustration of dramatic illusion," explains Hubbard, *Mask of Comedy* 59, "than the spectacle of a beggar who is really the disguised Mysian king Telephus who is really the Euripidean character 'Telephus' as acted by the comic character 'Dicaeopolis,' who clearly speaks for the comic poet, known to most of the play's audience as Callistratus, who is however really fronting for the little known Aristophanes."

98. See, for example, Fisher, "Multiple Personalities," and Sidwell, "Aristophanes' *Acharnians* and Eupolis."

4. Aias

1. This chapter was first presented as "Metatheatrical Madness in Greek Tragedy" on February 17, 1991, at "Madness in Drama: the Twelfth Annual Themes in Drama Conference" at the University of California at Riverside.

2. This is not to imply a monolithic form of "myth." See subsequent chapters on the contrafact (6, 7, and 8) for further discussion. For a judicious statement of the issues see March, "Euripides' *Bakchai*" 34–45.

3. See the essays by Vernant and Vidal-Naquet, *Myth and Tragedy* 23–28 and 29–48, for eloquent exploration of this aspect of dramatic fiction.

4. Pucci, "Gods' Intervention"; see also Vernant and Vidal-Naquet, *Myth and Tragedy* 29–48.

5. See Goldhill, "Character and Action" 109–10, esp. note 28.

6. Zeitlin, "Playing the Other" 85, notes the "feminization" of Aias in the play that involves the paradox "that the theater uses the feminine for the purpose of imagining a fuller model for the masculine self, and 'playing the other' *opens that self to those often banned emotions of fear and pity*" (emphasis added).

7. See Janet Lloyd's translation of Detienne and Vernant's 1974 monograph *Les ruses de l'intelligence: La Mêtis des grecs*.

8. Bradshaw, "Ajax Myth" 114 (also 121–25): "In the Homeric Ajax, moreover, Athenians of the mid fifth century might see qualities which, without willful distortion, they could associate with virtues of their own historic-heroic past, the period of the Persian wars."

9. Foley, *Ritual Irony* 158. Somewhat later she draws an interesting comparison: "In the *Ajax* the hero goes mad while contemplating violent action, and the gods substitute animals for the intended human victims. But in the *Heracles* Euripides creates a sane and modest hero without an explicit record, like that of Sophocles' Heracles or Aeschylus' Agamemnon, of illegitimate violence" (161).

10. Aias exhorts Tekmessa (line 586), for example, to ask no further questions: μὴ κρῖνε, μὴ 'ξέταζε· σωφρονεῖν καλόν.

11. Thoukydides 3.82: "To fit in with the change of events, words, too, had to change their usual meanings. What used to be described as a thoughtless act of aggression was now regarded as the courage one would expect to find in a party member; to think of the future and wait was merely another way of saying one was a coward; any gesture of moderation was taken to be a facade of cowardice; ability to understand a question from all sides meant that one was totally unfit for action" (Warner tr. adapted).

12. Cf. lines 677–83: ἡμεῖς δὲ πῶς οὐ γνωσόμεσθα σωφρονεῖν; / ἔγωγ'· ἐπίσταμαι γὰρ ἀρτίως ὅτι / ὅ τ' ἐχθρὸς ἡμῖν ἐς τοσόνδ' ἐχθαρτέος, / ὡς καὶ φιλήσων αὖθις, ἔς τε τὸν φίλον / τοσαῦθ' ὑπουργῶν ὠφελεῖν βουλήσομαι, / ὡς αἰὲν οὐ μενοῦντα. τοῖς πολλοῖσι γὰρ / βροτῶν ἄπιστος ἐσθ' ἑταιρείας λιμήν.

13. "We might compare," notes Hornblower, *Thucydides* 119, "the exploration by Jocasta of the words *philotimia*, ambition, and (especially) *isôtes*, equality, in Euripides' *Phoenissae*; the whole relevant section is in effect about *pleonexia*, greed, a thoroughly Thucydidean preoccupation."

14. Cf. the comments of Mielziner, *Designing for the Theatre* 183, on his innovation of a thrust stage for the 1955 Broadway production of *Cat on a Hot Tin Roof*: "This design and subsequent studies of the relationship between audience and actor led me into a great deal of thinking about the thrust stage in the design of new theatres. Looking back on the past twenty-five or thirty years, I find that I have been repeatedly trying to push the forestage out in order to break the rigid, restricting line of the aprons of our twentieth-century theatres."

15. Ron, "Restricted Abyss" 427–28.

16. Cf. Sophokles, *Philoktetes* 129, μορφὴν δολώσας.

17. ὅ τ' ἀπατήσας δικαιότερος τοῦ μὴ ἀπατήσαντος καὶ ὁ ἀπατηθεὶς σοφώτερος τοῦ μὴ ἀπατηθέντος; Plutarch, *Moralia* 384c.

18. See Bierl, "Dionysos, Wine, and Tragic Poetry" 365–68, for a discussion of ἀπάτη as dramatic illusion. "It has been shown recently," he notes, "that this definition is based on

the archaic concept of δίκη [justice] as a relationship of equilibrium between action and reaction. In this purely theoretical sense ἀπάτη means not only fraud, trick, or deceit, but also theatrical illusion or 'suspension of disbelief.'" For another Gorgian passage ("On Non Being" MXG 980a9) referring to the ἀπάτη of tragedy see Guthrie, *Sophists* 198. This passage is of particular metatheatrical interest in connection with *Prometheus Bound*.

19. See Walton, *Mimesis as Make-Believe* 38.

20. For ἀπάτη in comedy see *Tractatus Coislinianus* 6.

21. In connecting ἄτη with ἀπάτη I am not arguing, of course, for actual etymology (for no such connection exists), but for the "folk" etymology operative throughout Greek poetry, e.g., the Aiskhylean play with the names Helene (*Agamemnon* 688–89) and Apollon (*Agamemnon* 1080–82). For a theoretical discussion of this issue in its application to Latin poetry see Ahl, *Metaformations*, especially the notion of the "Varronian declension."

22. Padel, *In and Out of Mind* 157. For an interesting discussion of the tragic madness of Aias see also Davis, "Politics and Madness" 142–56.

23. δέδορκα [1], ὁρῶ [3], ἴδῃς [6], παπταίνειν [11], εἰδυίας [13], εὐμαθές [15], ἄποπτος [15], ἀκούω καὶ ξυναρπάζω φρενί [16], ἐπέγνως [18], ἄσκοπον [21], ἴσμεν γὰρ οὐδὲν τρανές [23], ὀπτήρ, εἰσιδών [29], φράζει τε κἀδήλωσεν [31], σημαίνομαι [32], κοὐκ ἔχω μαθεῖν [33], ἔγνων [36], etc. See Davis, "Politics and Madness" 146–47; Pucci, "Gods' Intervention" 15–22; Massenzio, "Cultura e crisi" (for related terminology in *Bakkhai*); Seale, *Vision and Stagecraft* 144–76; C. P. Segal, *Sophocles' Tragic World* 16–25; Padel, *Whom the Gods Destroy* 65–77.

24. καὶ σ᾽ οὐδὲν εἴσω τῆσδε παπταίνειν πύλης / ἔτ᾽ ἔργον ἐστίν, ἐννέπειν δ᾽ ὅτου χάριν / σπουδὴν ἔθου τήνδ᾽, ὡς παρ᾽ εἰδυίας μάθῃς.

25. ὦ φθέγμ᾽ Ἀθάνας, φιλτάτης ἐμοὶ θεῶν, / ὡς εὐμαθές σου, κἂν ἄποπτος ᾖς ὅμως, / φώνημ᾽ ἀκούω καὶ ξυναρπάζω φρενί / χαλκοστόμου κώδωνος ὡς Τυρσηνικῆς.

26. Kamerbeek, *Plays of Sophocles* 22, observes that "as a rule the dramatis personae are not supposed to see the gods when they appear on the scene but to become aware of their presence by their voice or fragrance: cf. Hippolytus and Artemis in the final scene of Eur.'s *Hipp.*: it does not appear from 1440 that Hippolytus sees Artemis (cf. also 85 sq.). But she is visible to the spectators (probably on the θεολογεῖον: cf. Pollux IV 129–30: he cites Aeschylus for making use of it in the *Psychostasia*)." For a review of divine epiphanies across the epic-tragic boundary see Pucci, "Gods' Intervention."

27. See also lines 218, 754, 796, and 985.

28. See Broneer, "Tent of Xerxes." There is explicit mention by Aristophanes of σκηναί as "theater-building" at *Peace* (421 BC) 729–32: ἀλλ᾽ ἴθι χαίρων· ἡμεῖς δὲ τέως τάδε τὰ σκεύη / παραδόντες / τοῖς ἀκολούθοις δῶμεν σῴζειν, ὡς εἰώθασι μάλιστα / περὶ τὰς σκηνὰς πλεῖστοι κλέπται κυπτάζειν καὶ κακοποιεῖν. / ἀλλὰ φυλάττετε ταῦτ᾽ ἀνδρείως·

29. Davis, "Politics and Madness" 143.

30. See Winkler, "Ephebes' Song."

31. There is a sense in which every speaker of an expository prologue touches on this function.

32. Zeitlin, "Closet of Masks" 71.

33. See Batchelder, *Seal of Orestes* (e.g., 65), Kraggerud, "Apollon als Regisseur," and the extended presentation of the Euripidean Dionysos as *chorodidaskalos* in Foley, "Masque of Dionysus," and *Ritual Irony* 218–34.

34. εὐθέως δ᾽ ἐγὼ / κατ᾽ ἴχνος ᾄσσω, καὶ τὰ μὲν σημαίνομαι, / τὰ δ᾽ ἐκπέπληγμαι, κοὐκ ἔχω μαθεῖν ὅπου. / καιρὸν δ᾽ ἐφήκεις· πάντα γὰρ τά τ᾽ οὖν πάρος / τά τ᾽ εἰσέπειτα σῇ κυβερνῶμαι χερί.

35. Falkner, "Making a Spectacle" 36.

36. ἁρπάσαι θηρώμενον (line 2), κυνηγετοῦντα καὶ μετρούμενον ἴχνη (lines 5–6), εὖ δέ σ᾽ ἐκφέρει κυνὸς Λακαίνης ὥς τις εὔρινος βάσις (lines 7–8), βάσιν κυκλοῦντα (line

19), κατ' ἴχνος ᾄσσω (line 32), τῇ σῇ πρόθυμος εἰς ὁδὸν κυναγίᾳ (line 37). Kamerbeek, *Plays of Sophocles* 20, and others have pointed out this metaphor in connection with the parallels to the tracking satyr chorus in *Ikhneutai*. The difference between genres, no doubt, accounts for the difference between the concrete use of language in the satyr-play and the metaphor in tragedy.

37. ἐγώ σφ' ἀπείργω, δυσφόρους ἐπ' ὄμμασι / γνώμας βαλοῦσα τῆς ἀνηκέστου χαρᾶς, / καὶ πρός τε ποίμνας ἐκτρέπω . . . / ἐγὼ δὲ φοιτῶντ' ἄνδρα μανίασιν νόσοις / ὤτρυνον, εἰσέβαλλον εἰς ἕρκη κακά.

38. "It is important to note," specifies Falkner, "Making a Spectacle" 36, "that it is not the fact of Ajax's madness that renders him unseeing of Odysseus but a particular kind of sight with which Athena will endow him that will prevent him from seeing one who is otherwise present."

39. γένοιτο μέντἂν πᾶν θεοῦ τεχνωμένου. "The increasing concern in the plays over the course of the fifth century with examining the conventions of the theater," writes C. P. Segal, "Review of Goldhill" 234, "is not just an aberration of late Euripides but a development inherent in the form itself. The self-consciousness about the dramatic illusion of Athena's invisibility in the prologue to Sophocles' *Ajax* bears this out."

40. See Goldhill, *Reading Greek Tragedy* 183.

41. Knox, "*Ajax*" 20, and Winnington-Ingram, *Sophocles* 18–19.

42. I.e., on the choral exclamation "τί δεῖ με χορεύειν" at *Oidipous Tyrannos* 896: Dodds, "Misunderstanding" 186.

43. ἐποκτίρω δέ νιν / δύστηνον ἔμπας, καίπερ ὄντα δυσμενῆ, / ὁθούνεκ' ἄτῃ συγκατέζευκται κακῇ, / οὐδὲν τὸ τούτου μᾶλλον ἢ τοὐμὸν σκοπῶν. / ὁρῶ γὰρ ἡμᾶς οὐδὲν ὄντας ἄλλο πλὴν / εἴδωλ', ὅσοιπερ ζῶμεν ἢ κούφην σκιάν.

44. On the partial identity between poet and protagonist see Hubbard, *Mask of Comedy* 29–31, 45–47, 136–38.

45. "Making a Spectacle" 38.

46. See lines 586 and 677, which lend themselves to sarcastic delivery (especially in the latter example from the Deception Speech).

47. For a discussion of the dynamics of ἐχθρός and φίλος see Goldhill, *Reading Greek Tragedy* 84–88, and, in general, Whitlock Blundell, *Helping Friends*.

48. ἡμεῖς δὲ πῶς οὐ γνωσόμεσθα σωφρονεῖν; / ἔγωγ'· ἐπίσταμαι γὰρ ἀρτίως ὅτι / ὅ τ' ἐχθρὸς ἡμῖν ἐς τοσόνδ' ἐχθαρτέος, / ὡς καὶ φιλήσων αὖθις, ἔς τε τὸν φίλον / τοσαῦθ' ὑπουργῶν ὠφελεῖν βουλήσομαι, / ὡς αἰὲν οὐ μενοῦντα. τοῖς πολλοῖσι γὰρ / βροτῶν ἄπιστος ἔσθ' ἑταιρείας λιμήν.

49. φιλεῖν ὡς μισήσοντας, μισεῖν ὡς φιλήσοντας. Diogenes Laertius 1.5.87; Aristotle *Rhetoric* 1389 b 24–25; Cicero, *De Amicitia* 16.59. Jebb, *Sophocles* (vol. 6) 231–32, collects several ancient and modern interpretive references to the maxim.

50. [Αγ.] τί ποτε ποήσεις; ἐχθρὸν ὧδ' αἰδῇ νέκυν; / [Οδ.] νικᾷ γὰρ ἀρετή με τῆς ἔχθρας πλέον. / [Αγ.] τοιοίδε μέντοι φῶτες οὔμπληκτοι βροτῶν. / [Οδ.] ἦ κάρτα πολλοὶ νῦν φίλοι καὖθις πικροί.

51. The story of Aias is related in scholia drawing on epitomes of the lost epics *Aithiopis* (Σ Pindar *Isthmian* 3.53) and *Mikra Ilias* (Σ Aristophanes' *Knights* 1056).

52. Cf. Vernant, "God of Tragic Fiction," in Vernant and Vidal-Naquet, *Myth and Tragedy* 187: "The 'presence' embodied by the actor in the theater was always the sign, or mask, of an *absence*, in the day-to-day reality of the public. Caught up by the action and moved by what he beheld, the spectator was still aware that these figures were not what they seemed but illusory simulations—in short, that this was mimesis." Cf. the self-conscious allusion to this at Euripides *Elektra* 391–92.

53. Bradshaw, "Ajax Myth" 123. Cf. his comments on 115: "The Ajax whom Sophocles

introduced onto the tragic stage, then, would have been regarded as a protective *daimôn* of the polis, a figure revealing an admirable balance of physical prowess and intellectual discretion, and, above all, a hero distinguished by his consistent espousal of the honor one secures and maintains through loyalty to one's allies."

54. See Garnison, *Groaning Tears* 78: "Ajax reflects aristocratic values (corroborates them) but shows an individual caught between tradition and change." In a similar vein C. P. Segal, "Review of Seaford" 654, notes that "in the *Ajax* . . . where hero-cult is firmly in the background (as Burian and more recently Henrichs have emphasized), civic solidarity is far from complete . . . . Although the Athenian audience is surely reminded of Ajax's eventual power as a hero (especially in 1171–81), the ending itself places no clear emphasis on 'benefit to the polis.'"

55. Thoukydides 5.89.

56. Zeitlin, "Playing the Other" 82–85.

5. Pentheus

1. For different approaches see Dodds, *Greeks and the Irrational* and *Bacchae*; Blaiklock, *Male Characters*; Grube, *Drama of Euripides* 378–420; Winnington-Ingram, *Euripides and Dionysos* (esp. 6–13); Diller, "Die *Bakchen*"; Rohdich, *Euripideische Tragödie* 162–68; Rosenmeyer, *Masks of Tragedy* 105–52; and Arthur, "Choral Odes."

2. A representative sampling would include Seaford, "Dionysiac Drama" and *Reciprocity and Ritual*; Foley, *Ritual Irony*; Henrichs, "Loss of Self"; Easterling, "Tragedy and Ritual," and Wise, *Dionysus Writes*.

3. Seaford, *Reciprocity and Ritual* 318.

4. See the distillation of his views in the introduction to his edition of *Bakkhai*.

5. Else, *Origin and Early Form* 63.

6. Vernant, "God of Tragic Fiction" in Vernant and Vidal-Naquet, *Myth and Tragedy* 185.

7. The title of an important article by Vernant in Vernant and Vidal-Naquet, *Myth and Tragedy* 181–88 (first published in *Comédie française* 98 [April 1981] 23–28).

8. C. P. Segal, *Dionysiac Poetics* 233. Thus, for example, Zeitlin, "Staging Dionysus" 148, agrees with Bierl that "each naming of Dionysus and related words plays a definite function in the course of the action of that tragedy which stands in a direct relation to the essence of the god."

9. See Bierl, *Dionysos* (on *Frogs*) 27–44, and 115–19. It should be noted, however, that Bierl's approach and that taken here are fundamentally different. For Bierl, Dionysos is the focus and motivation for any discussion of metatheater, whereas I regard dramatic metafiction in all its phenomenological variety without special concern for the involvement of a specific god or character.

10. "From this point of view," observes Vernant, "God of Tragic Fiction" 185, "tragedy could be said to be a manifestation of the city turning itself into theater, presenting itself on stage before its assembled citizens."

11. C. P. Segal, "Tragedy and Society" 59.

12. The first attestations of the "theatrical" Dionysos are no earlier than *Bakkhai* and, most likely, somewhat later: e.g., the well-known "actors' relief" from the Peiraeus and the Pronomos Vase (ARV² 1336).

13. March is virtually ignored by Seaford. I find nothing in *Reciprocity and Ritual* and only brief mention in the commentary on *Bakkhai* (p. 27, note 16): "Even if (and it is not impossible) Eur. did make these innovations, both kin-killing . . . and transvestism . . . were traditional Dionysiac themes. In general, modern critics tend to assume that the first appear-

ance of a theme is the same as innovation, even though what survives may always represent no more than a tiny portion of the versions that once existed (written, visual, oral)." Fair enough, but this very point has more serious implications for Seaford's own hypotheses (e.g., "Dionysiac sacrifice" in the fifth century) where there is no evidence at all.

14. See Bierl, *Dionysos* 1–20, 67–75.

15. *Pace* Bierl, *Dionysos*.

16. See March, "Reconsideration" 33–35, for thoughts on reading an ancient text in an environment of many competing theoretical points of view (inspired by C. P. Segal, *Tragedy and Civilization*).

17. On this point see especially Seidensticker, *Palintonos Harmonia*. In this monograph, as in the earlier article "Comic Elements," Seidensticker illustrates, using ancient and modern examples, how certain comical moments can sublimate unbearable horror and leaven an otherwise very serious script.

18. P. Slater, *Glory of Hera* 228. Cf. also the comments of Goldhill, *Reading Greek Tragedy* 273: "The inherent self-reflexiveness of a theatrical chorus in a festival to honour Dionysus playing a chorus of Dionysiac worshippers is also to be seen within this wider series of men playing women, adopting another role, the role of the other (as 'woman' is fragmented into a variety of male representations)."

19. Zeitlin, "Thebes" 65–66.

20. Cited in March, "Reconsideration" 50, note 59.

21. [Δι.] βούλῃ σφ᾽ ἐν ὄρεσι συγκαθημένας ἰδεῖν; / [Πε.] μάλιστα, μυρίον γε δοὺς χρυσοῦ σταθμόν. / [Δι.] τί δ᾽ εἰς ἔρωτα τοῦδε πέπτωκας μέγαν; / [Πε.] λυπρῶς νιν εἰσίδοιμ᾽ ἂν ἐξῳνωμένας. / [Δι.] ὅμως δ᾽ ἴδοις ἂν ἡδέως ἅ σοι πικρά; / [Πε.] σάφ᾽ ἴσθι, σιγῇ γ᾽ ὑπ᾽ ἐλάταις καθήμενος.

22. οἰκεῖα ἡδονή. Poetics 1448b16–17, and especially 1453b12–13. Cf. Malcolm Heath on "emotive hedonism," in *Poetics of Greek Tragedy* 11–12.

23. C. P. Segal, *Dionysiac Poetics* 220–21.

24. On the language of vision in the play see Massenzio, *cultura e crisi*. Cf. the comments of C. P. Segal, *Dionysiac Poetics* 221: "The repeated words for 'seeing' in the so-called miracle call attention to dramatic illusion *per se* and the possible discrepancy between what is actually there and what appears to be there but may not be . . . . Expressions like *dokein*, 'seems,' *phainesthai*, 'appears,' *phasma*, the 'seeming image,' *hos eoike*, 'as seems likely,' all keep in the foreground this concern with the power of Dionysiac illusion (605, 616, 629–30, 638, 646)." See also the comments of Vernant, "Masked Dionysos" 393–94.

25. Symptomatic of how forced is Seaford's "initiatory" approach is his translation of ἐν τέλει θεός (line 860) as "born to be a god in initiation ritual" (Seaford, *Bacchae* 113).

26. March, "Reconsideration" 55–56.

27. See the comments of E. R. Dodds on Sophokles' *Oidipous* in the classic essay "On Misunderstanding" (esp. 187–88).

28. Scolnicov, "Theatre Space" 14–15: "The theatrical space without adds an extra dimension to the performance. For, whereas the visible theatrical space is wholly within the given theatre space, the theatrical space without extends as far as the playwright wills it to, thus demanding an imaginative response on the part of the spectators . . . . [F]ar from being accidental or arbitrary, the articulation of the theatrical space is, at its best, an expression of the playwright's philosophical stance. As such, it becomes of thematic and structural importance to the play. An analysis of the spatial conception of a play, especially of the theatrical space without, can thus lead us directly to a consideration of its innermost problems."

29. Cf. March, "Reconsideration" 61: "The rational world of Agave and Pentheus was not enough. For both of them Kithairon was waiting, Kithairon which becomes in the play

the symbol for the kingdom of Dionysos." For an interesting alternative see Vernant, "Masked Dionysos" in Vernant and Vidal-Naquet, *Myth and Tragedy* 402–3, who discusses the encounter between Pentheus and Dionysos as one between sophistic rationalism and religious experience.

30. March, "Reconsideration" 62.

31. Vernant, "God of Tragic Fiction" 187.

32. Βάκχαις ἐστρατήγησεν θεός. *Eumenides* 458.

33. March, "Reconsideration" 36 has the following discussion (with references to Brommer, *Vasenlisten*, and Philippart, "Iconographie," etc.): "On a red-figure pyxis about contemporary with the *Bakchai* we see Pentheus setting out from his palace with net and hunting spears to hunt the maenads [Brommer 485 B6; Philippart no. 132]. . . . An Italiote kalpis of a similar date shows an armed Pentheus hiding between two trees, presumably about to leap out and attack the maenads [Munich 3267; Brommer 486 D8; Philippart no. 137]. . . . Several illustrations from around the end of the fifth century show Pentheus in armed combat with the maenads: an Italiote cup shows a named Pentheus, armed with spear and sword, attacked by two maenads, one of whom has a sword [Naples H.2562; Brommer 486 D6; Philippart no. 138] . . . ; a red-figure fragment has again a named Pentheus, armed and fighting [Brommer 486 D7; Philippart no. 139] . . . ; another Italiote cup shows Pentheus armed with sword and two spears in combat with three maenads, one of whom fights with a sword, another with a thyrsos [Ruvo, Jatta 1617; Brommer 486 D5; Philippart no. 133]. . . . The lid of a large red-figure pyxis of the second half of the fifth century shows Pentheus about to be torn apart: one maenad has him by the leg, another by an arm and a leg [Louvre G 445; Brommer 485 B5; Philippart no. 142]. . . . Again, as in all the other illustrations, Pentheus is armed: his sword is at his side." See also chapter 7 of Carpenter, *Dionysian Imagery*.

34. March, "Reconsideration" 37.

35. See Evans, *God of Ecstasy*, and Henrichs, "Male Intruders."

36. See the comments of Zeitlin, "Thebes" 65–66, cited above on the feminine aspects of Aias' suicide. The inversion of power in the *sparagmos* is suggestive of a similar feminization. Pentheus is vulnerable, helpless, and his body pathetically "permeable," to use Zeitlin's term.

37. Lines 325–27: κοὐ θεομαχήσω σῶν λόγων πεισθεὶς ὕπο. / μαίνῃ γὰρ ὡς ἄλγιστα, κοὔτε φαρμάκοις / ἄκη λάβοις ἂν οὔτ᾽ ἄνευ τούτων νοσεῖς.

38. E.g., lines 367: οὐδ᾽ ὁρᾶν ἵν᾽ εἶ κακοῦ.

39. John 18:28–19:16.

40. εἶδος, μορφή; he also has assumed the nature (φύσις) of a man.

41. ταῦτα καὶ καθύβρισ᾽ αὐτόν, ὅτι με δεσμεύειν δοκῶν / οὔτ᾽ ἔθιγεν οὔθ᾽ ἥψαθ᾽ ἡμῶν, ἐλπίσιν δ᾽ ἐβόσκετο. / πρὸς φάτναις δὲ ταῦρον εὑρών, οὗ καθεῖρξ᾽ ἡμᾶς ἄγων, / τῷδε περὶ βρόχους ἔβαλλε γόνασι καὶ χηλαῖς ποδῶν, / θυμὸν ἐκπνέων, ἰδρῶτα σώματος στάζων ἄπο, / χείλεσιν διδοὺς ὀδόντας· πλησίον δ᾽ ἐγὼ παρὼν / ἥσυχος θάσσων ἔλευσσον.

42. Cf. the perceptive comments on theatrical presence and absence in Vernant, "God of Tragic Fiction" 187.

43. The chorus say that he was led to his death by a ταῦρος προηγητήρ (line 1159).

44. θύσω, φόνον γε θῆλυν, ὥσπερ ἄξιαι, / πολὺν ταράξας ἐν Κιθαιρῶνος πτυχαῖς.

45. Cf. Dodds' complaint *ad loc.*: "L.S. s.v. θῆλυς surprisingly mistranslates φόνον θῆλυν as 'murder *by* women.'" Dodds and others, moreover, incline to read ἄξιον instead of ἄξιαι, which would reinforce the ambiguity: "as is right."

46. Line 810; cf. March, "Reconsideration" 41: "Here, at this significant point, there comes a dramatic break in the action, emphasized by a break in the metre with the single response of Dionysos: 'ἅ' he cries; the sign of readjustment: and makes a complete change

of direction to a quite different and unexpected revenge, on a Pentheus suddenly transformed from military strength to womanish weakness."

47. Taplin, *Tragedy in Action* 121 (with an interesting discussion of the performative aspects of this moment).

48. See C. P. Segal, *Dionysiac Poetics* 223–32 with the relevant bibliography.

49. See above pp. 46–50.

50. γυναῖκες, ἀνὴρ ἐς βόλον καθίσταται, / ἥξει δὲ βάκχας, οὗ θανὼν δώσει δίκην. / Διόνυσε, νῦν σὸν ἔργον· οὐ γὰρ εἶ πρόσω· / τεισώμεθ᾽ αὐτόν. πρῶτα δ᾽ ἔκστησον φρενῶν, / ἐνεὶς ἐλαφρὰν λύσσαν· ὡς φρονῶν μὲν εὖ / οὐ μὴ θελήσῃ θῆλυν ἐνδῦναι στολήν, / ἔξω δ᾽ ἐλαύνων τοῦ φρονεῖν ἐνδύσεται. / χρῄζω δέ νιν γέλωτα Θηβαίοις ὀφλεῖν / γυναικόμορφον ἀγόμενον δι᾽ ἄστεως / ἐκ τῶν ἀπειλῶν τῶν πρίν, αἷσι δεινὸς ἦν. / ἀλλ᾽ εἶμι κόσμον ὅνπερ εἰς Ἅιδου λαβὼν / ἄπεισι μητρὸς ἐκ χεροῖν κατασφαγείς, / Πενθεῖ προσάψων· γνώσεται δὲ τὸν Διὸς / Διόνυσον, ὃς πέφυκεν ἐν τέλει θεός, / δεινότατος, ἀνθρώποισι δ᾽ ἠπιώτατος.

51. Seidensticker, "Comic Elements" 305–6, distinguishes elements that are formally characteristic of comedy from the claim that a given element is humorous, i.e., the former he terms "comedy element," the latter "comic element." For a full discussion of this issue see *Palintonos Harmonia*, and C. P. Segal, *Dionysiac Poetics* 255–56. See also Segal's recent discussion in the afterword, pp. 369–78.

52. "We can speculate . . . ," writes Foley, *Ritual Irony* 228, "that Euripides was inspired by Aristophanes to invent the toilet scene of the Bacchae . . . to borrow Old Comedy's ludicrous transformations of the body to express an equivalent ambiguity in the human soul. Euripides' gesture is in any case outrageous, since Aristophanes' parody seems clearly directed at addressing the limits that tragedy must respect in relation to costume."

53. In this play Dionysos is disguised as Paris and plays his part in a sexually charged version of the Trojan prince's famous "judgment." For a reasonable reconstruction see Heath, "Aristophanes and His Rivals" 144–47; Dover, *Frogs* 38–39; and Bierl, *Dionysos* 27–44. For a sampling of Dionysos in comedy see the testimonia and fragments of Kratinos *Dionysalexandros*, Eupolis' *Taxiarkhoi*, Aristophanes' *Babylonians*, *Dionysos Nauagos* and, perhaps, *Gerytades* along with Kratinos' *Arkhilokhoi*, and Platon's *Adonis*. On the comic Dionysos, see chapter 8, below.

54. (πρόθυμον) σπεύδοντα τ᾽ ἀσπούδαστα; see Dodds, *Bacchae* ad loc.

55. Cf., for one example of many, the ταῦρος προηγητήρ of line 1159.

56. Foley, *Ritual Irony* 243, notes that "Pentheus' terrifying transformation from spectator to spectacle shows in an extraordinarily theatrical form what it means to act or imitate without full knowledge. The god, unlike the tragic hero, never confuses representation with reality; instead he controls reality through representation." For a review of various stage-types in their relation to self-knowledge see Hubbard, *Mask of Comedy* 2–8.

57. In the sense of Belifore's analysis, "ΠΕΡΙΠΕΤΕΙΑ" 193–94: "An understanding of Aristotle's philosophy of action allows us to be more precise and to avoid the inaccuracy of those who translate περιπέτεια as 'reversal of intention.'" Περιπέτεια is the kind of discontinuous action that occurs when the action of an agent is prevented from achieving its intended result and instead arrives at an actual result that is the opposite of the one intended. Περιπέτεια breaks up the simple plot's linear motion between the endpoints of the tragic change and forces it to turn back in the opposite direction. Thus, περιπέτεια is neither a 'reversal of intention' nor a 'reversal of fortune' but a turning back (ἀνάκαμψις) of the action from its straight course."

58. Dodds, *Bacchae* 924–26, ad loc.

59. The verb is commonly used intransitively to mean "to take leave" of one's senses; in the active it can mean "to drive" mad, as in the phrase ἔκστησον φρενῶν cited earlier (line 850). The connection with the nominal form ἔκστασις is obvious.

60. Dodds, *Bacchae* 934, ad loc.

61. Dodds, *Bacchae* 927–29, ad loc: "Eur. allows such breaches of symmetry especially towards the beginning of a stichomythic passage . . . . [T]hey seem to occur chiefly at places where the actor may be expected to pause and make a gesture."

62. ἦ πού με τῶν σῶν πρῶτον ἡγήσῃ φίλων, / ὅταν παρὰ λόγον σώφρονας βάκχας ἴδῃς.

63. Πε. ἆρ᾽ ἂν δυναίμην τὰς Κιθαιρῶνος πτυχὰς / αὐταῖσι βάκχαις τοῖς ἐμοῖς ὤμοις φέρειν; / Δι. δύναι᾽ ἄν, εἰ βούλοιο· τὰς δὲ πρὶν φρένας / οὐκ εἶχες ὑγιεῖς, νῦν δ᾽ ἔχεις οἵας σε δεῖ.

64. See March, "Reconsideration" 43.

65. E.g., κρύψῃ κρύψιν, κρυφθῆναι (line 955), λήψῃ, ληφθῆς (line 960), μόνος, μόνος (line 963).

66. Cf. the comments of Foley, *Ritual Irony* 20: "Does man, then, disguise in his worship of the gods a worship of himself and his own need for order? So the poets seem to imply in many dramas in which the city itself becomes a source of salvation alternative to the gods (see, for example, Euripides' *Suppliants, Heracleidae*, or *Heracles*)."

67. Δι. μόνος σὺ πόλεως τῆσδ᾽ ὑπερκάμνεις, μόνος· / τοιγάρ σ᾽ ἀγῶνες ἀναμένουσιν οὓς ἐχρῆν. / ἕπου δέ· πομπὸς [δ᾽] εἰμ᾽ ἐγὼ σωτήριος, / κεῖθεν δ᾽ ἀπάξει σ᾽ ἄλλος. Πε. ἡ τεκοῦσά γε. / Δι. ἐπίσημον ὄντα πᾶσιν. Πε. ἐπὶ τόδ᾽ ἔρχομαι. / Δι. φερόμενος ἥξεις . . . Πε. ἁβρότητ᾽ ἐμὴν λέγεις. / Δι. ἐν χερσὶ μητρός. Πε. καὶ τρυφᾶν μ᾽ ἀναγκάσεις. / Δι. τρυφάς γε τοιάσδε. Πε. ἀξίων μὲν ἅπτομαι. / Δι. δεινὸς σὺ δεινὸς κἀπὶ δείν᾽ ἔρχῃ πάθη, / ὥστ᾽ οὐρανῷ στηρίζον εὑρήσεις κλέος.

68. See March, "Reconsideration" 58–59, for the interesting debate about when exactly Pentheus regains his senses; is it 1101 (March) or 1115 with the discarding of the *mitra* (Dodds)?

69. Offstage, of course, within earshot of the audience. See the discussions in McDermott, *Incarnation of Disorder* 47, and Michelini, "Neophron and Euripides' *Medea*."

70. March, "Reconsideration" 57–59.

71. ὤφθη μᾶλλον ἢ κατεῖδε μαινάδας. / ὅσον γὰρ οὔπω δῆλος ἦν θάσσων ἄνω, / καὶ τὸν ξένον μὲν οὐκέτ᾽ εἰσορᾶν παρῆν, / ἐκ δ᾽ αἰθέρος φωνή τις, ὡς μὲν εἰκάσαι / Διόνυσος, ἀνεβόησεν· Ὦ νεάνιδες, / ἄγω τὸν ὑμᾶς κἀμὲ τἀμά τ᾽ ὄργια / γέλων τιθέμενον· ἀλλὰ τιμωρεῖσθέ νιν.

72. "When the god has withdrawn from the level of human action to the machine or *theologeion*," observes Foley, *Ritual Irony* 233, of this moment, "Euripides' tragedy frames and changes the audience's emotional response to the divine drama. The final scenes restore . . . the traditional boundaries between genres, drawing a sharp and specifically tragic line between man and god, the individual and his heroic aspirations, audience and protagonist, and between laughter and tragic pity."

73. Dodds, *Bacchae* ad line 1116: "The removal of the μίτρα—which was, as the vase-paintings show, a mere headband—would not in itself much assist recognition. Did it hold the wig . . . in place, so that the latter would drop off when it was removed?" Loss of the wig at this point, however, makes difficult another feature popular with modern directors—to have the unbound wig unfurl to resemble the lion's mane of Agave's delirium.

74. In the iconographic record Pentheus' head is carried by the hair. See Philippart, "Iconographie."

75. The earliest literary approximation to this idea that I am able to find is in a fragment of the fourth-century poet Amphis (*Erithoi* fr. 17 K.-A.): "Isn't solitude golden? / The countryside is Father of Sustenance for us; / only the country knows how to conceal poverty. / The city, on the other hand, is a theater, a full house before whom your misfortune is on display."

76. Vernant, "God of Tragic Fiction" 187–88.

77. Foley, *Ritual Irony* 239.

78. Foley, *Ritual Irony* 220.

6. Bellorophontes

1. See Bowie, *Aristophanes* 134–35.

2. In "Aristophanes' *Wasps* and the Sociopolitics of Aesop's Fables," Kenneth Rothwell, Jr., has argued for a nuanced understanding of the role that *ainoi* play in Aristophanes. He suggests that *ainoi*, as "a common mode of expression for the lower classes or the disadvantaged" (253), "could highlight power relations" in the complex discourse of comedy. In the present contrafact, the Aisopic element is, among other things, a metaphor of comedy's parasitic usurpation of tragedy.

3. Di Gregorio, "Bellerofonte I" 160, note 3; Riedweg, "Atheistic Fragment" 48; and Collard, Cropp, and Lee, *Euripides* 101. For a Middle-Comic Bellerophontes, see Euboulos fr. 15 K.-A. in which a flying character likens himself to a tall kottabos-shaft.

4. [Eu.] ἀλλ᾽ ἦ τὰ δυσπινῆ θέλεις πεπλώματα, / ἅ Βελλεροφόντης εἶχ᾽ ὁ χωλὸς οὑτοσί; / [Δι.] οὐ Βελλεροφόντης· ἀλλὰ κἀκεῖνος μὲν ἦν / χωλὸς προσαιτῶν στωμύλος δεινὸς λέγειν.

5. See Riedweg, "Atheistic Fragment" 48.

6. Especially Di Gregorio, "Bellerofonte I," which I follow here. This impressive study reviews, synthesizes, and updates a number of reconstructions undertaken in the course of the last hundred and fifty years—from Welcker to Rau. He was not able to incorporate the (nearly worthless) P.Oxy. 3651, however. See also Aélion, *Quelques grands mythes* 192–96.

7. See Collard, Cropp, and Lee, *Euripides* 98–101. In his presentation of the fragments of *Bellerophontes*, Collard is somewhat critical of Di Gregorio's first, long study ("Bellerofonte I"). The main results of this piece, however, as well as of Di Gregorio's reconstruction ("Bellerofonte II") are taken seriously.

8. ἀλλ᾽ ὅτε δὴ καὶ κεῖνος ἀπήχθετο πᾶσι θεοῖσιν, / ἤτοι ὁ κἀπ πεδίον τὸ Ἀλήϊον <οἶος> ἀλᾶτο, / ὃν θυμὸν κατέδων, πάτον ἀνθρώπων ἀλεείνων. See also the preceding narrative from lines 155–99 (note that Schol. A on line 155 [=Asklepiades *FGH* 1.12 fr. 13] and Schol. Pindar *Ol.* 13.91–92 curiously place the wandering of Bellerophontes after his fall).

9. *Theogony* 319–25 and frr. 43a and 129 MW. See Gantz, *Early Greek Myth* 313–14.

10. θνάσκομεν γὰρ ὁμῶς ἅπαντες· / δαίμων δ᾽ ἄϊσιος· τὰ μακρὰ δ᾽ εἴ τις / παπταίνει, βραχὺς ἐξικέσθαι χαλκόπεδον θεῶν / ἕδραν· ὅ τοι πτερόεις ἔρριψε Πάγασος / δεσπόταν ἐθέλοντ᾽ ἐς οὐρανοῦ σταθμούς / ἐλθεῖν μεθ᾽ ὁμάγυριν Βελλεροφόνταν / Ζηνός. τὸ δὲ πὰρ δίκαν / γλυκὺ πικρότατα μένει τελευτά. Nisetich, tr.

11. This epigram, as others in this series (e.g., see Collard, Cropp, and Lee, *Euripides* 122, on *Kresphontes*), appears to reflect Euripides' presentation and reworking of a given myth. The salient plot element here reflects an innovation into tradition. See Di Gregorio, "Bellerofonte I" 199.

12. Βελλεροφόντης ὑπὸ τοῦ παιδὸς Γλαύκου σωζόμενος, ἡνίκα κατενεχθεὶς ἀπὸ τοῦ Πηγάσου εἰς τὸ Ἀλήϊον πέδον, ἔμελλεν ὑπὸ Μεγαπένθους τοῦ Προίτου φονεύεσθαι. The cryptic epigram is thus rendered by W. R. Paton from his Loeb text: "No longer could Bellerophontes stay the murderous hand of this son of Proitos, nor the death designed for him by his father. Glaukos, in vain thou fearest for him (?); he shall escape the plot of Iobates, for thus the Destinies decreed. Thyself, too, then didst shield thy father from death, standing near him, and wast an observant witness to the truth of the glorious story."

13. See Collard, Cropp, and Lee, *Euripides* 102–3. I cite Collard's translation: P.Oxy 4017: "disaster . . . Stheneboia . . . Bellerophontes (?)"; P.Oxy. 3651: "having determined . . . to ( ) . . . going to . . . (his) own ( ) and brother (*or* sister) . . . Bellerophontes . . . the fitting . . . he himself . . . corpse . . . from the (Taurus ?) . . . Bellerophontes . . . river . . . (Isander ?) . . . the country . . . the springs . . . Bellerophontes . . . of Lycia . . . the ship . . ." See the discussion by Luppe (*Eikasmos* 1 [1990] 171–77), cited by Collard, which includes an entirely separate, though unattested, subplot in which Bellerophontes seeks revenge for a seduced daughter-in-law.

14. See Rau, *Paratragodia* 91; Di Gregorio "Bellerofonte II" 368–69; and Riedweg, "Atheistic Fragment" 50, note 60. On the earliest lines we have from the play (fr. 285N²) Collard, Cropp, and Lee, *Euripides* 112, rightly note that "the style and length are not those of an orientatory prologue-speech."

15. ἐγὼ τὸ μὲν δὴ πανταχοῦ θρυλούμενον / κράτιστον εἶναι φημὶ μὴ φῦναι βροτῷ· / τρισσῶν δὲ μοιρῶν ἐγκρινῶ νικᾶν μίαν, / πλούτου τε χὤτῳ σπέρμα γενναῖον προσῇ / πενίας τ᾽ ἀριθμὸν γὰρ τοσόνδε προυθέμην. / . . . οὕτως ἄριστον μὴ πεπειρᾶσθαι καλῶν. / ἐκεῖνο γὰρ μεμνήμεθ᾽, οἷος ἦν ποτε / κἀγὼ μετ᾽ ἀνδρῶν ἡνίκ᾽ ηὐτύχουν βίῳ. I cite Collard's translation of lines 6–17: "The very wealthy man, but without the fortune of birth, is miserable, yes, miserable—but it is a splendid misery when his hand opens up his treasure-house for his delight; yet when he goes outside it, despite his wealth during the time before, he falls under folly's yoke and suffers hard. Then, the man with proud and noble blood who lacks a living, has the fortune of his birth but poverty makes him inferior; †his thoughts inside are misery† and shame makes him reject manual work. The absolute nobody, however, in misfortune to the end, is superior in as much as he is unaware that he lacks well-being, since he is always in misfortune and distress."

16. Fr. 287 N²: τοῖς πράγμασιν γὰρ οὐχὶ θυμοῦσθαι χρεών. / μέλει γὰρ αὐτοῖς οὐδέν· ἀλλ᾽ οὑντυγχάνων / τὰ πράγματ᾽ ὀρθῶς ἢν τίθῃ, πράσσει καλῶς. "There is no point in getting angry at difficult circumstances as they care nothing [for your feelings]. If a man handles matters correctly as they occur, he prospers." Fr. 292 N²: πρὸς τὴν νόσον τοι καὶ τὸν ἰατρὸν χρεών / ἰδόντ᾽ ἀκεῖσθαι, μὴ ἐπιτὰξ τὰ φάρμακα / διδόντ᾽, ἐὰν μὴ ταῦτα τῇ νόσῳ πρέπῃ. / νόσοι δὲ θνητῶν αἱ μέν εἰσ᾽ αὐθαίρετοι, / αἱ δ᾽ ἐκ θεῶν πάρεισιν, ἀλλὰ τῷ νόμῳ / ἰώμεθ᾽ αὐτάς. ἀλλ᾽, ὅ σοι λέξαι θέλω, / εἰ θεοί τι δρῶσιν αἰσχρόν, οὐκ εἰσὶν θεοί. See the discussion in Collard, Cropp, and Lee, *Euripides* 116, which examines the fragment in the context of contemporary medical theory and practice (thus, for example, ἐπιτὰξ can mean both "summarily" and "continuously").

17. Riedweg, "Atheistic Fragment," 46–47, who plausibly connects Aristophanes' reaction to Euripidean atheism (e.g., *Thesmophoriazousai* 450–51 and 667–74) with this fragment. See also Collard, Cropp, and Lee, *Euripides* 114–15.

18. φησίν τις εἶναι δῆτ᾽ ἐν οὐρανῷ θεούς; / οὐκ εἰσίν, οὐκ εἴσ᾽, εἴ τις ἀνθρώπων θέλει / μὴ τῷ παλαιῷ μῶρος ὢν χρῆσθαι λόγῳ. / σκέψασθε δ᾽ αὐτοί, μὴ ἐπὶ τοῖς ἐμοῖς λόγοις / γνώμην ἔχοντες. φήμ᾽ ἐγὼ τυραννίδα / κτείνειν τε πλείστους κτημάτων τ᾽ ἀποστερεῖν / ὅρκους τε παραβαίνοντας ἐκπορθεῖν πόλεις· / καὶ ταῦτα δρῶντες μᾶλλόν εἰσ᾽ εὐδαίμονες / τῶν εὐσεβούντων ἡσυχῇ καθ᾽ ἡμέραν. / πόλεις τε μικρὰς οἶδα τιμώσας θεούς, / αἳ μειζόνων κλύουσι δυσσεβεστέρων / λόγχης ἀριθμῷ πλείονος κρατούμεναι. / οἶμαι δ᾽ ἂν ὑμᾶς, εἴ τις ἀργὸς ὢν θεοῖς / εὔχοιτο καὶ μὴ χειρὶ συλλέγοι βίον, / . . . . . . / τὰ θεῖα πυργοῦσιν αἱ κακαί τε συμφοραί. There is clearly a lacuna after συλλέγοι βίον in line 14. The last clause appears to consist of a verb, its direct object, and half of a conjoined subject: "'X' and misfortunes build up religion like a tower." For a discussion of the text see Riedweg, "Atheistic Fragment" 40, whose translation I have adapted here, and Collard, Cropp, and Lee, *Euripides* 115.

19. Riedweg, "Atheistic Fragment" 43.

20. For example, fr. 295 N² gives the example of honorable *parastatai* (= συνήγοροι), "supporters at a trial," overcome by the evil of envy (see Collard, Cropp, and Lee, *Euripides* 117). A more general example is 297 N²: ὡς ἔμφυτος μὲν ἀνθρώποις κάκη· / ὅστις δὲ πλεῖστον μισθὸν εἰς χεῖρας λαβὼν / κακὸς γένηται, τῷδε συγγνώμη μὲν οὔ, / πλείω δὲ μισθὸν μείζονος τόλμης ἔχων / τὸν τῶν ψεγόντων ῥᾷον ἂν φέροι λόγον. "Wickedness is indeed an inborn quality of humankind. Whoever becomes evil on account of having amassed much wealth enjoys little indulgence [from others]. But the greater his wealth and audacity, the easier it is for him to endure criticism and blame."

21. On the absence of Glaukos at the beginning of the second episode see Di Gregorio, "Bellerofonte I" 204.

22. Here belongs fr. 305 N², which relates that someone "stood upon the dressed-stone tribunal of the Danaids, he stood in the midst of the heralds and said . . . ." See Di Gregorio, "Bellerofonte II" 371.

23. Di Gregorio, "Bellerofonte I" 199–200, 211–12, has convincingly reclaimed this and fr. 666 N² for our play. On the text and interpretation of these passages, see Collard, Cropp, and Lee, *Euripides* 88, 95, 100, 112, 120.

24. Fr. 293 N²: τιμή σ' ἐπαίρει τῶν πέλας μεῖζον φρονεῖν. / θνήσκοιμ' ἄν· οὐ γὰρ ἄξιον λεύσσειν φάος / κακοὺς ὁρῶντας ἐκδίκως τιμωμένους. Fr. 296 N²: ἀνὴρ δὲ χρηστὸς χρηστὸν οὐ μισεῖ ποτε, / κακὸς κακῷ δὲ συντέτηκεν ἡδονῇ· / φιλεῖ δὲ θοὐμόφυλον ἀνθρώπους ἄγειν. Such a context for these fragments solves some of the problems identified by Collard, Cropp, and Lee, *Euripides* 116 (e.g., who is "you" of fr. 293 N², line 1?).

25. Wecklein, "Fragmentarisch erhaltene Tragödien" 104.

26. Webster, *Tragedies of Euripides* 109. If we imagine Bellerophontes taking off inside his house, we avoid an awkward entrance between the beginning of the third episode (with its heated debate between Iobates and Megapenthes) and the hero's flight.

27. ἄγ', ὦ φίλον μοι Πηγάσου ταχὺ πτερόν (fr. 306) / ἴθι χρυσοχάλιν' αἴρων πτέρυγας (fr. 307) / πάρες, ὦ σκιερὰ φυλλάς, ὑπερβῶ / κρηναῖα νάπη· τὸν ὑπὲρ κεφαλῆς / αἰθέρ' ἰδέσθαι σπεύδω, τίν' ἔχει / στάσιν εὐοδίας (fr. 308). For the text, see Di Gregorio, "Bellerofonte II" 379, note 38. With this fragment the scholia to *Wasps* 757 transmit a half-line—σπεῦδ' ὦ ψυχή, "hasten, O my soul"—which Aristophanes picks up in his adaptation. This may have been separated from the text of fr. 308 N² by only a few lines. I have, with Di Gregorio (and now Collard and Kannicht), retained the transmitted reading εὐοδίας instead of Nauck's Εἰνοδίας (emendation proposed by Heath and Valckenaer).

28. Fr. 309a K was first published by H. Hunger. See Di Gregorio, "Bellerofonte II" 379, note 40; and Collard, Cropp, and Lee, *Euripides* 110–11.

29. ἦσθ' εἰς θεοὺς μὲν εὐσεβής, ὅτ' ἦσθ', ἀεὶ / ξένοις τ' ἐπήρκεις οὐδ' ἔκαμνες εἰς φίλους.

30. τοιοῦτόν τινα καὶ τὸν Βελλεροφόντην ἡρωικῶς καὶ μεγαλοψύχως εἰς θάνατον παρεσκευασμένον ὁ Εὐριπίδης ὑμνεῖ· πεποίηκε γοῦν πρὸς τὴν ἑαυτοῦ ψυχὴν λέγοντα αὐτόν 'ἦσθ' – φίλους.'

31. For an interesting solution to the textual problem presented by this fragment see Wecklein, "Fragmentarisch erhaltene Tragödien" 108–9.

32. Or, perhaps, with Collard, "A man won't produce a wound if he whittles in marshy thickets, etc." (since *thamnos* seems limited to the meaning "marsh"). Welcker's suggestion, *Griechischen Tragödien* 789, that we assign fr. 1059 N² (fr. inc. 53 for Welcker) to a context such as this is plausible and would connect Bellerophontes' misogyny and poverty with the "atheism" theme prominent in the play. Thus in the last lines of this ψόγος γυναικῶν, the speaker says: "and if [woman] is a creature of one of the gods, then he should know that he is a craftsman of wickedness, inimical to mankind."

33. Welcker, *Griechischen Tragödien* 799. For other possibilities see Di Gregorio, "Bellerofonte II" 382, and Collard, Cropp, and Lee, *Euripides* 120 (Athena).

34. κομίζετ᾽ εἴσω τόνδε τὸν δυσδαίμονα.

35. ἐκεῖνο τήρει, μὴ σφαλεὶς καταρρυῇς / ἐντεῦθεν, εἶτα χωλὸς ὢν Εὐριπίδῃ / λόγον παράσχῃς καὶ τραγῳδία γένῃ. Text and translations are those of Sommerstein, *Peace*.

36. Cf. Athenaios 65A. "It is conceivable," observes Denniston, "Technical Terms" 116, "that in Aristophanes [the term ἐπύλλια] may be used to describe the elaborate messenger-speeches that are so prominent a feature in Euripides' plays."

37. On Euripidean echoes in *Peace* see Rau, *Paratragodia* 92–95. On the autobiographical interpretation see Collard, Cropp, and Lee, *Euripides* 101.

38. Sommerstein, *Peace* 140–41. There is some disagreement between the fable in Aesop (*Fab.* 3 Perry) and the variant given ad loc. by the scholiast. See also *Wasps* 1448 and *Lysistrata* 695.

39. Rothwell, "Aristophanes' *Wasps*" 239–44. Cf also 233–34: "[Fables] frequently served as a mode of expression for peasants and slaves. Significantly Aesop (sixth century BC) and the fable writers Phaedrus (first century AD) and Babrius (second century AD) were all said to have been ex-slaves." After cautioning against exaggeration of this point, Rothwell continues: "In practice, however, there was a recurrent tendency for fables to be used by [the lower classes], and Phaedrus' claim that fables were a form of servile protest cannot be discounted altogether." See also Rosen, *Old Comedy* 30–35.

40. Hubbard, *Mask of Comedy* 144. See in general the chapter "The Flight of the Dung Beetle" pp. 140–56.

41. See lines 54, 65, 90, 95, 66; for the anti-Zeus theme, see lines 42, 62, and 361–455.

42. ὁ δεσπότης μου μαίνεται καινὸν τρόπον, / οὐχ ὅνπερ ὑμεῖς, ἀλλ᾽ ἕτερον καινὸν πάνυ. / δι᾽ ἡμέρας γὰρ εἰς τὸν οὐρανὸν βλέπων / ὡδὶ κεχηνὼς λοιδορεῖται τῷ Διὶ / καί φησιν· "ὦ Ζεῦ, τί ποτε βουλεύει ποιεῖν; / κατάθου τὸ κόρημα· μὴ ᾽κκόρει τὴν Ἑλλάδα."

43. [Οι.β] οὐκοῦν ἂν ἤδη τῶν θεατῶν τις λέγοι / νεανίας δοκησίσοφος· "τὸ δὲ πρᾶγμα τί; / ὁ κάνθαρος δὲ πρὸς τί;" [Οι.ᵃ] κᾆτ᾽ αὐτῷ γ᾽ ἀνήρ / Ἰωνικός τίς φησι παρακαθήμενος· / "δοκέω μέν, ἐς Κλέωνα τοῦτ᾽ αἰνίσσεται, / ὡς κεῖνος ἐν Ἀΐδεω σπατίλην ἐσθίει."

44. On this issue I would synthesize the views of Reckford, *Aristophanes' Old-and-New Comedy* 10–11, who sees the passage as critical of symbolic interpretation, and Hubbard, *Mask of Comedy* 141, for whom "Kleon" symbolizes the "repulsive, dirty, invective, low-comic world the dung beetle embodies." The joke is funny precisely because the Ionian's stupid interpretation suggests that Kleon is a dung-eating insect (a genuine Aristophanic sentiment indeed).

45. This direction is fully realized in *Birds*, a sustained experiment with established conventions and forms. On this see Gelzer, "Some Aspects."

46. νῦν ἐστιν ἡμῖν, ὦνδρες Ἕλληνες, καλὸν / ἀπαλλαγεῖσι πραγμάτων τε καὶ μαχῶν / ἐξελκύσαι τὴν πᾶσιν Εἰρήνην φίλην, / πρὶν ἕτερον αὖ δοίδυκα κωλῦσαί τινα.

47. εἰς ἄντρον βαθύ ... εἰς τουτὶ τὸ κάτω ... ὅσους ἄνωθεν ἐπεφόρησε τῶν λίθων (lines 223–25). For a discussion of the staging of this scene, see Russo, *Aristophanes* 137–41.

48. See Radt, *Tragicorum Graecorum Fragmenta*, vol 4, 388. The sole interesting fragment of this play is fr. 482, καὶ πρῶτον ἄρχου πηλὸν ὀργάζειν χεροῖν, "and first begin working the mud with your hands," which suggests the Hesiodic version of the Pandora story (Athene speaking to Hephaistos?). Iconography suggests a very different version, which is ultimately more compelling in the absence of textual evidence to the contrary.

49. Steffen, "Der Hilferuf" 35–45.

50. Sutton, *Satyr Play* 55. Relevant iconographic evidence: "London neck amphora F 147 (Trendall, LCS 667); Attic r. f. volute krater of ca. 450, Oxford G 275 (V525)." See also Sutton, "Vase Paintings" 119–26 and "Staging of *Anodos* Scenes" 356–64.

51. Sutton, *Two Lost Plays* 68: "Here is where Aristophanes got the nuclear idea for his plot."

52. τοιαῦτ᾽ ἀφελὼν κακὰ καὶ φόρτον καὶ βωμολοχεύματ᾽ ἀγεννῆ / ἐποίησε τέχνην μεγάλην ἡμῖν κἀπύργωσ᾽ οἰκοδομήσας / ἔπεσιν μεγάλοις καὶ διανοίαις καὶ σκώμμασιν οὐκ ἀγοραίοις. Cf. the marked usage of κἀπύργωσ᾽ here and the tragic πυργοῦσιν of fr. 286 N².

53. Sommerstein, *Peace* xviii: "They are introduced, very explicitly, as representatives of the whole Greek people and every class within it (292–98), they call themselves Panhellenes (302). Yet quite early on they speak as if they were Athenian (349–57). In the hauling scene they are again Panhellenes, classified now, for the most part, politically instead of socially (464–507); then at 508 we are told that only the peasants remain (whether the peasants of Greece or of Attica is not made clear), and from then on, whenever the chorus have a dramatic identity at all, they are Attic peasants."

54. A weak thematic candidate is the confrontation between Trygaios and Hermes, but this is conducted in a rudimentary iambic syzygy that does not much resemble the epirrhematic agon of a play such as *Wasps*. See Gelzer, *Epirrhematische Agon* 169–72 and 251. See also Pickard-Cambridge, *Dithyramb, Tragedy, and Comedy* 221–22.

55. For an even bolder experiment with a satyr chorus, cf. Kratinos' *Dionysalexandros* which may have featured the god in the company of choristers imported from this genre.

56. Bowie, *Aristophanes* 142–50.

57. Bowie, *Aristophanes* 149, relating the views of Cassio.

58. As there was not a cult of Eirene in Attica until 374, "Aristophanes' representation of a cult of Peace would have been somewhat novel, but it did not start a fashion" (Bowie, *Aristophanes* 142, note 51).

59. [Τρ.] ὦ κάνθαρ᾽, οἴκαδ᾽ οἴκαδ᾽ ἀποπετώμεθα. [Ερ.] οὐκ ἐνθάδ᾽, ὦ τᾶν, ἐστι. [Τρ.] ποῖ γὰρ οἴχεται; / [Ερ.] ὑφ᾽ ἅρματ᾽ ἐλθὼν Ζηνὸς ἀστραπηφορεῖ.

7. *Tereus*

1. He enters at 92 and exits at 675. The traditional assignment of lines in the prologue (e.g., in Coulon, *Aristophane*) is improved in Sommerstein's *Birds*, the text followed here (see Dunbar, *Birds* ad loc.). Peisetairos' role as protagonist is thereby made more coherent as he is in control from the very beginning. Sommerstein's text is influenced by Marzullo, "L'interlocuzione" 181–91 (also Fraenkel, *Beobachtungen* 61–65). For a contrary view see Nesselrath, "Sprecherverteilung." Translations given are also Sommerstein's (with minor changes), unless otherwise noted. The first section of this chapter appeared as "The Tragic and the Comic Tereus."

2. Cf. Zannini Quirini, *Nephelokokkygia* 41, who notes that "molte delle componenti del personaggio mitico vengono funzionalmente utilizzate nella commedia." He points out, in particular, Tereus' warlike character, skill in various crafts (cf. the Boios version of the myth featuring a Polytekhnos=Tereus), the Hoopoe's characteristic song, and his "savage (barbarian)" context. Zannini-Quirini seeks the broadest possible thematic implications of the Tereus myth. See also Hofmann, *Mythos und Komödie* 72–78, and Alink, *De Vogels* 50–65.

3. So in the better-known literary treatments of the legend (e.g., Sophokles and Ovid). Important secondary literature on this myth includes Hiller von Gärtringen, *De Graecorum fabulis*; Mayer, "Mythistorica"; Robert, *Griechische Heldensage* 154–62; Halliday, *Indo-European Folk-Tales* 85–112; Chandler, "Nightingale"; Cazzaniga, *La saga di Itis*; Mihailov, "La lègende de Térée"; Fontenrose, "The Sorrows of Ino and Prokne"; Schroeder, "ΠΡΟΚΝΗ"; Zaganiaris, "Le mythe de Térée"; and C. P. Segal, "Philomela's Web."

4. Sommerstein, *Birds* 5, who notes that "it is symptomatic of this [optimism] that every time an allusion is made in the play to current, recent, or projected military operations, the tone adopted is one of almost cheerful bellicosity."

5. Whitman, *Aristophanes* 167–200; Arrowsmith, "Aristophanes' *Birds*" 71–102; and Zannini Quirini, *Nephelokokkygia*, highlight different aspects of the terrors and dangers implicit in the play. The latter, for example, speaks of the "monstrous and ambiguous" inhabitants of Nephelokokkygia (*Nephelokokkygia* 86), whose rejection of the present entails a "dangerous" return to mythical origins (p. 150). See also Pozzi, "Polis in Crisis."

6. In his twelfth lecture, for example, A. W. Schlegel (*Lectures* 166) dismisses the possibility that *Birds* is somehow *engagé* and suggests that the play is "a harmless display of merry pranks, which hit alike at gods and men without any particular object in view." That the problem was recognized in antiquity is clear from *Hypothesis II* (to *Birds*). Hofmann, *Mythos und Komödie* 79, notes of the latter that "Sie berichten von einer Kontroverse unter antiken Philologen (ohne daß wir die Beteiligten genauer eingrenzen könen) über die Methoden aristophanischer Handlungsgestaltung." See the discussion of this problem in Dobrov, "Aristophanes' *Birds*."

7. οἱ μὲν γὰρ οὖν τέττιγες ἕνα μῆν᾽ ἢ δύο / ἐπὶ τῶν κραδῶν ᾄδουσ᾽, Ἀθηναῖοι δ᾽ ἀεὶ / ἐπὶ τῶν δικῶν ᾄδουσι πάντα τὸν βίον. / διὰ ταῦτα τόνδε τὸν βάδον βαδίζομεν· / κανοῦν δ᾽ ἔχοντε καὶ χύτραν καὶ μυρρίνας / πλανώμεθα ζητοῦντε τόπον ἀπράγμονα, / ὅποι καθιδρυθέντε διαγενοίμεθ᾽ ἄν. / ὁ δὲ στόλος νῶν ἐστι παρὰ τὸν Τηρέα, / τὸν ἔποπα, παρ᾽ ἐκείνου πυθέσθαι δεομένω, / εἴ που τοιαύτην εἶδε πόλιν ᾗ 'πέπτατο.

8. Sommerstein, *Birds* 1. Similar observations are made by Henderson (*Maculate Muse* 83) and many other students of the play. The difference between *Birds* and the earlier extant comedies certainly suggests a process of gradual evolution. For activity between *Peace* and *Birds* see Geissler, *Chronologie* 50.

9. For the many specifically theatrical aspects of the comic polis see N. Slater, "Performing the City in the Birds," and Dobrov, "Language, Fiction and Utopia," in Dobrov, *City as Comedy*.

10. Henderson, *Maculate Muse* 82. The maturity and complexity of *Birds* has been often noted and is well analyzed by Newiger, "*Die Vögel* und ihre Stellung," and Gelzer, "Aristophanes' Dramatic Art."

11. οὐκ τῶν ὀρνέων / ὁ πινακοπώλης Φιλοκράτης μελαγχολῶν, / ὃς τῶδ᾽ ἔφασκε νῶν φράσειν τὸν Τηρέα, / τὸν ἔποφ᾽, ὃς ὄρνις ἐγένετ᾽ †ἐκ τῶν ὀρνέων.†

12. The crux (line 16, ἐκ τῶν ὀρνέων) no doubt conceals a phrase that anticipates Peisetairos' explanation (lines 46–48) of his interest in Tereus. A compelling solution is offered by Koenen, "Tereus in den *Vögeln*" 83–87, who emends to ἐκ τῶν ὀργίων, restoring an allusion to the Dionysian cult-context of Tereus' metamorphosis. We should then translate "Tereus, the hoopoe, who became a bird from the rites (of Dionysos)." In this case ἐκ + genitive would denote both a causal and a temporal connection between the Dionysian Trieterika and Tereus' metamorphosis. Dunbar, *Birds* ad loc., on the other hand, sees here an interpolation, a gloss on the preceding line.

13. Thompson, *Greek Birds* 95–100. Sacred in Egypt and in Islamic tradition (as one of the four creatures it is forbidden to kill), the hoopoe is associated with the sun by virtue of its rayed crest. The lore of this bird involves odd behavior and magic. It was believed, for example, to use the herb ἀδίαντον to liberate its imprisoned young (cf. the magic root introduced at lines 654–55 to transform men into birds). Thompson, *Greek Birds* 98, notes that this "is a version of the well-known Samir legend (the 'open Sesame' of the Forty Thieves), and is told also of the Hoopoe in connexion with Solomon . . . . Hence used in magic to reveal secrets or discover treasure." See also Kanellis, *Catalogus Faunae Graeciae*; Lamberton and Rotroff, *Birds of the Athenian Agora*; and (for bibliography especially) Arnott, "Some

Bird Notes." For the hoopoe in particular see Oder, "Der Wiedehopf"; Dawson, "The Lore of the Hoopoe"; and Griffith, "The Hoopoe's Name."

14. [Τη.] μῶν με σκώπτετον / ὁρῶντε τὴν πτέρωσιν; ἦ γάρ, ὦ ξένοι, / ἄνθρωπος. [Πε.] οὐ σοῦ καταγελῶμεν. [Τη.] ἀλλὰ τοῦ; / [Πε.] τὸ ῥάμφος ἡμῖν σου γελοῖον φαίνεται. / [Τη.] τοιαῦτα μέντοι Σοφοκλέης λυμαίνεται / ἐν ταῖς τραγῳδίαισιν ἐμὲ τὸν Τηρέα. / [Πε.] Τηρεὺς γὰρ εἶ σύ; πότερον ὄρνις ἢ ταῶς.

15. Griffith, "Hoopoe's Name" 60 (emphasis added).

16. Kock, *Die Vögel* 36. On the four dancers see Lawler, "Four Dancers" 58–63; Carrière, "La choréographie des *Oiseaux*" 211–35; Dover, *Aristophanic Comedy* 145.

17. [Ευ.] τί τὸ τέρας τουτί ποτ' ἐστίν; οὐ σὺ μόνος ἄρ' ἦσθ' ἔποψ, / ἀλλὰ χοὖτος ἕτερος; [Τε.] οὑτοσί μέν ἐστι Φιλοκλέους / ἐξ ἔποπος, ἐγὼ δὲ τούτου πάππος, ὥσπερ εἰ λέγοις / "Ἱππόνικος Καλλίου κἀξ Ἱππονίκου Καλλίας." / [Ευ.] Καλλίας ἄρ' οὗτος οὔρνις ἐστίν. ὡς πτερορρυεῖ. / [Τε.] ἅτε γὰρ ὢν γενναῖος ὑπό τε συκοφαντῶν τίλλεται, / αἵ τε θήλειαι πρὸς ἐκτίλλουσιν αὐτοῦ τὰ πτερά.

18. See Sommerstein, *Birds* 216.

19. Schol. 281 informs us that Philokles, the son of Philopeithes and Aiskhylos' sister, was known as Ἁλμίωνος, "son of Briny," for his harsh style. See, for example *Wasps* 461–62 and *Thesmophoriazousai* 168 with scholia. Sommerstein, *Birds* 215–16, points out that the phrase Φιλοκλέους ἐξ ἔποπος could also mean "Philokles the hoopoe," in which case the allusion would be to Philokles personal appearance (so in *Thesmophoriazousai*). It is best to let the ambiguity stand, since the reading "from Philokles' hoopoe [i.e., his Tereus]" is suggested by the lineage: the Philokles-hoopoe is the "son" of Sophokles' Tereus. The reading "from Philokles the hoopoe," on the other hand, supplies the necessary intermediate name, giving the sequence Tereus-Philokles-Tereus necessary for the parallelism to work (i.e., to match Kallias-Hipponikos-Kallias). Merkelbach, *Kritische Beiträge* 26–27, emends the text in a way that makes Aristophanes' dancer identical with Philokles' tragic character, yielding parallelism between the Sophoklean Tereus and the "Philoklean Hoopoe." The text makes good sense, however, without emendation.

20. Koenen, "Tereus in den *Vögeln*" 86–87. (The unfortunate typographical error at this point in Koenen's argument is corrected in Merkelbach, *Beiträge* 26.) Regarding the *Baptai* see (with caution) Edmonds, *Fragments of Attic Comedy*, vol. 1, 330–31, and Kassel and Austin, *Poetae Comici Graeci*, vol. 5, 331–43, fr. 76–98. The indirectness of this reference to Alkibiades (cf. a similar strategy at *Birds* 145–47) would seem to support Sommerstein, "Decree of Syrakosios" 101–8, in his revival of J. Droysen's hypothesis that the so-called Decree of Syrakosios forbade ὀνομαστὶ κωμῳδεῖν, "explicit lampoons (involving the name)" of the hermokopid *atimoi*. Many studies of *Birds* spanning the century and a half from Süvern's *Essay* to Katz's "The *Birds* and Politics" detect satire of Alkibiades of one sort or another. Few will be convinced, however, by the more recent attempts in Vickers, "Alcibiades on Stage" and *Pericles on Stage*.

21. Schol. 100, ἐν γὰρ τῷ Τηρεῖ Σοφοκλῆς ἐποίησεν αὐτὸν ἀπωρνιθωμένον καὶ τὴν Πρόκνην· ἐν ᾧ [i.e., quam ob causam] ἔσκωψε [ὁ Ἀριστοφάνης] πολλὰ τὸν Τηρέα (White, *Scholia* 32). Sommerstein, *Birds* 205, and others have built upon the dismissal of this scholion by Welcker, *Griechischen Tragödien* 386, to reject the possibility of there having been physical representation of the metamorphosis in Sophokles' play. The dubious authority of Horace (*Ars Poetica* 187) is usually invoked in this connection. The tragic λύμη referred to by the comic Tereus is assumed to be merely verbal (i.e., the contents of a messenger speech). Kiso, *Lost Sophocles* 144, note 74, reports the interesting suggestion of E. K. Borthwick, no doubt inspired by the Arkhilokhean epithet, that the tragic Tereus was "costumed in the Thracian manner of hair-style (*akrokomoi*) and headgear" so that his metamorphosis into a hoopoe would seem more appropriate. See Peisetairos' suggestion, (lines 1363–66) that the young

Patroloias forsake father-beating and go fight instead on the Thracian coast. The appropriate equipment for this involves a spur and *cock's* comb, items that invoke the imagery of a cockfight in a distinctly Thracian context.

22. The semantics of λυμαίνεσθαι are those of physical outrage (cf. Liddell and Scott, *A Greek-English Lexicon*, p. 1065: 1. outrage, maltreat, harm, injure, spoil, ruin; 2. inflict indignities or outrages upon, cause damage, etc.). Tereus' use of the verb to defend his funny beak suggests that the outrage inflicted on him by Sophocles involved being brought onstage in a striking bird-costume. So Kock, *Die Vögel:* "Und eben die als ein λυμαίνεσθαι (100) empfundene 'Befiederung,' die ἀπωρνέωσις überhaupt, hat ihm Sophokles angetan, der sie in seiner Tragödie (fr. 523 ff N²) . . . auf die Bühne gebracht hat."

23. Welcker, *Griechischen Tragödien* 374–88.

24. In addition to Welcker, *Griechischen Tragödien*, see Pearson, *Fragments of Sophocles*, vol. 2, 221–38 (fr. 581–95); Buchwald, *Studien zur Chronologie* 33–42; Bacon, *Barbarians* 86–88; Johansen, "Sophocles" 286–87; Webster, *Introduction to Sophocles* 4, 176–77; Calder, "Sophocles' *Tereus*"; Radt, *Tragicorum Graecorum Fragmenta*, vol. 4, 435–45 (fr. 581–95); Sutton, *Lost Sophocles* 127–32; Kiso, *Lost Sophocles* 51–86; Hourmouziades, "Sophocles' *Tereus*"; and Lloyd-Jones, *Sophocles: Fragments*.

25. Tzetzes on Hesiod, *Works and Days* 566 (Radt, *Tragicorum Graecorum Fragmenta*, vol. 4, 435), and a scholion on Aristophanes' *Birds* 212; see Mihailov, "La lègende de Térée" 94–95, and Mayer, "Mythistorica" 490. I give Parsons' translation: "Tereus, the *hypothesis:* Pandion, the ruler of the Athenians, having (two) daughters, Procne and Philomela, united the elder, Procne, in marriage with Tereus the king of the Thracians, who had by her a son whom he named Itys. As time passed, and Procne wished to see her sister, she asked Tereus to travel to Athens to bring (her back). He, after reaching Athens and receiving the girl from Pandion and making half the return journey, fell in love with the girl. And he disregarded his trust from Pandion and violated her. But, as a precaution in case she should tell her sister, he cut out the girl's tongue. On arriving in Thrace, and Philomela being unable to speak her misfortune, she revealed it by means of a piece of weaving. When Procne realized the truth, driven mad by jealousy . . . she took Itys and killed him and after cooking him served him up to Tereus. He ate the meal without realizing. The women took flight and became, one of them a nightingale, one a swallow, and Tereus a hoopoe."

26. Adapted from Hourmouziades, "Sophocles' *Tereus*" 135.

27. *Odyssey* 19. 518–23; Hesiod, *Works and Days* 564–70 and fr. 125; Sappho, fr. 135 Page; Aiskhylos, *Agamemnon* 1140–49 and *Hiketides* 60–67; Pseudo-Euripides, *Rhesos* 550 and fr. 773 N²; Philokles, *Pandionis* (Radt, *Tragicorum Graecorum Fragmenta*, vol. 1, 140–41). See also Sophokles, *Elektra* 107, 148–49. "The legend," observes Kiso, *Lost Sophocles* 57, "must have included both the husband's crime and the wife's vengeance when Sophocles found dramatic material in it. No other great tragedian except Sophocles seems to have dramatized it." Mihailov, "La lègende de Térée" 88, points out that the passage in *Agamemnon* suggests that the story of Prokne and Tereus must have been quite familiar to the Athenian audience for the allusion to be effective.

28. Accius, fragments 639–55 in Warmington, *Remains*, vol. 2, 543–49. The fragments of Livius' *Tereus* seem less dependent on Sophokles (so Warmington, *Remains*, vol. 2, 10 and 542).

29. Welcker, *Griechischen Tragödien* 376. So Warmington, *Remains*, vol. 2, 543, who says concerning Accius that "the model was, it seems, chiefly Sophocles." For a contrary view see Bömer, *Metamorphosen*, vol. 3, 115–19. Mihailov, "La lègende de Térée" 88, emphasizes the fundamental place of Sophokles' play in the literary tradition of the Tereus story.

30. Prokne's isolation (fr. 583 Radt), the suppression of her grief (Ovid, *Met.* 6.581–86 and Accius fragments 643–64 Warmington), and the deceit involved in the recognition and revenge suggest that Prokne had to contend with a hostile chorus. The choral fragments seem more appropriate to a male chorus, as Kiso, *Lost Sophocles* 61, points out (see fragments 590–93 Radt). Hourmouziades, "Sophocles' *Tereus*" 137, extends the potential similarities between the Tereus and Sophokles' *Trakhiniai* (a connection made by Webster, Welcker, and others) and argues for a *female* chorus.

31. Dissenting from Welcker, *Griechischen Tragödien* 383–84, who suggests Hermes as the *deus*, Calder, "Sophocles' Tereus" 88, nominates "the father of the belligerent, reigning monarch, the Thracian Ares." Since the status of fr. 581 Radt is vital for identifying the deus ex machina in the play, it seems more sensible to shy away from assigning this fragment, with its neutral tone of admonition and σωφροσύνη, "soundness of mind," "discretion," to so partisan and violent a god as Ares.

32. Welcker, *Griechischen Tragödien* 376, on the basis of Ovid, *Met.* 6.587, Accius fr. 647 Warmington, and Libanius, *Narr.* 18, makes much of the festival element in the play. Since Hiller von Gärtringen, *De Graecorum fabulis* 41, first made the connection, the striking parallels between the Tereus myth and Plutarch's account (*Quaest. Gr.* 38) of the Dionysian Agrionia (Orkhomenos) have been much discussed. See, for example, Mihailov, "La légende de Térée" 100–103. A Campanian fragment of Caivano Painter (Dresden PV 2891 ca. 350–320) seems to show Tereus armed with a πέλεκυς, a prehellenic Thraco-Phrygian cult implement (see Apollodorus 3.14.8). The much-discussed ἐν ποικίλῳ φάρει, "in an embroidered cloak," of fr. 586 Radt may refer to maenad dress, Philomela's *textum*, or both. Koenen, "Tereus in den *Vögeln*" 84, cites M. Bieber's identification of a Paestan potsherd depicting Tereus: "hängen von dem Gürtel des Tereus, der die Schwestern verfolgt, die dionysischen Wollfäden herab." The specifics of the cult as represented by Sophokles, however, are irretrievable. What seems certain, however, is that the play was set on the day of a Dionysian festival, that the festival involved a sacrificial meal, and that Prokne and Philomela exploited their freedom as maenads to get revenge on Tereus.

33. So Welcker, Calder, and most. Hourmouziades, in order to incorporate the Dryas episode, posits five "epeisodia." In light of the scant remains of the choral element of the play, certainly in this matter is not possible.

34. Webster, *Introduction to Sophocles* 177. Hourmouziades, "Sophocles' *Tereus*," makes even more of the similarity between *Trakhiniai* and *Tereus*, positing a friendly female chorus, a "Likhas and Iole scene," etc.

35. Gelzer, "Sophokles' *Tereus*" 191. Calder, "Sophokles' *Tereus*" 89, for example, suggests that during the first stasimon "one year of dramatic time passes (Ovid, *Met.* 6. 571)." While this is not impossible, it is safer to assume that the action of the *Tereus* takes place within the typical Sophoklean dramatic day. "Was vor diesem Tag geschehen war," argues Gelzer, "muss irgendwann im Verlauf des Stücks erzählt worden sein."

36. Hyginus (*Fab.* 45): *Procne cognita sorore et Terei impium facinus, pari consilio machinari coeperunt regi talem gratiam referre. interim Tereo ostendebatur in prodigiis Ity filio eius mortem a propinqua manu adesse. quo responso audito, cum arbitraretur Dryantem fratrem suum filio suo mortem machinari, fratrem Dryantem insontem occidit.*

37. In response to Gelzer, "Sophokles' *Tereus*" 191: "Von entscheidender Bedeutung muss die Rolle der Prokne gewesen sein. Schon Welcker hat sich die Frage vorgelegt, warum das Stück nicht nach ihr benannt wurde." Hourmouziades, "Sophocles' *Tereus*" 138, argues that Tereus, as a victim of misinterpreted omens, becomes "a tragic figure in the Sophoclean sense of the term, a hero, in fact, not very different from Heracles or even Oedipus." In light

of the fact, however, that no source except Hyginus (not even Ovid!) mentions Dryas, it is highly unlikely that this striking episode was represented by Sophokles only to be subsequently forgotten or suppressed. The tragic Tereus, moreover, clearly impressed posterity as an unusually savage character. The very "problem" with which Hourmouziades begins his argument—that Tereus redundantly sequesters Philomela *and* cuts out her tongue—suggests that Sophokles made his Tereus more violent that he had been traditionally, innovating the preventive glossectomy (a feature otherwise unknown in Greek legend) in order to set up the recognition by means of a written message. It is this aspect of dramatic innovation to which Aristotle reacts at *Poetics* 1454b 30-37.

38. νῦν δ' οὐδέν εἰμι χωρίς. ἀλλὰ πολλάκις / ἔβλεψα ταύτῃ τὴν γυναικείαν φύσιν, / ὡς οὐδέν ἐσμεν. αἳ νέαι μὲν ἐν πατρὸς / ἥδιστον, οἶμαι, ζῶμεν ἀνθρώπων βίον· / τερπνῶς γὰρ ἀεὶ παῖδας ἀνοία τρέφει. / ὅταν δ' ἐς ἥβην ἐξικώμεθ' ἔμφρονες, / ὠθούμεθ' ἔξω καὶ διεμπολώμεθα / θεῶν πατρῴων τῶν τε φυσάντων ἄπο, / αἱ μὲν ξένους πρὸς ἄνδρας, αἱ δὲ βαρβάρους, / αἱ δ' εἰς ἀγηθῆ δώμαθ', αἱ δ' ἐπίρροθα. / καὶ ταῦτ', ἐπειδὰν εὐφρόνη ζεύξῃ μία, / χρεὼν ἐπαινεῖν καὶ δοκεῖν καλῶς ἔχειν.

39. Since it is assumed that Tereus has already returned from Athens, the words πολλά σε ζηλῶ βίου, "I am envious of your life," cannot be addressed to Philomela, whom Prokne already believes to be dead. Prokne seems to be speaking in general of the woman fortunate enough to marry close to home. The fragments of Accius that may belong here (645–46, 655 Warmington) are less informative.

40. Kiso, *Lost Sophocles* 65.

41. ἀλγεινά, Πρόκνη, δῆλον· ἀλλ' ὅμως χρεὼν / τὰ θεῖα θνητοὺς ὄντας εὐπετῶς φέρειν.

42. Cf. Libanius, *Narr.* 19: "Taking advantage of a feast during which it was the custom for Thracian women to send gifts to the queen, Philomela sent [Prokne] a robe embroidered with writing describing the violence which she had experienced."

43. Such an epistle is not unique in tragedy: In *Trakhiniai*, for example, Herakles leaves behind an inscribed tablet (δέλτον ἐγγεγραμμένην ξυνθήμαθ', lines 157–58) while Iphigeneia's letter (*Iphigenia in Tauris* 725–94) and "dictation" are well-known features of Euripidean invention that Aristotle implicitly equates with Philomela's epistle in *Tereus*. In his classification of εἴδη ἀναγνωρίσεως, "types of recognition," Aristotle ranks such dramatic devices next to last in terms of intellectual and technical skill. See Cazzaniga, *La saga di Itis* I 50, with most scholars, on the following evidence: Ovid, *Met.* 6.577–81, *purpureasque notas filis intexuit albis . . . carmen miserabile legit*; Apollodorus 3.14.8, ἡ δὲ ὑφήνασα ἐν πέπλῳ γράμματα, "having embroidered the robe with letters"; Schol. *Birds* 212, ὑφαίνουσα διὰ γραμμάτων ἐδήλωσε, "made manifest by embroidering with letters." Similar language is found in other accounts (Libanius, *Narr.* 18, and Achill. Tat. 5.5).

44. *Concita per silvas turba comitante suarum / Terribilis Procne furiisque agitata doloris, / Bacche, tuas simulat.*

45. Cultic disguise as a metatheatrical strategy seems to have played a part also in Euripides' *Peliades* (where Medeia was disguised as a priestess) and *Ino*, in which the heroine participates in a bacchic ceremony on Parnassus. See Mihailov, "La légende de Térée" 101.

46. McDermott, *Incarnation of Disorder* 47, and Michelini, "Neophron." Cf. also the cryptic description of Itys' death as φόνον θυόμενον Μούσαις, "murder, sacrifice to the muses" (*Herakles* 1021–23). In *Medeia* the chorus fails to make the metafictional connection before they are interrupted by Jason (lines 1282–89); they can think only of Ino, despite the more obvious Athenian exemplum!

47. Kiso, *Lost Sophocles* 80. Mihailov's unconvincing conclusions, "La légende de Térée" 103, detract somewhat from his interesting discussion, 98–103.

48. Calder, "Sophocles' *Tereus*" 89.

49. ἓν φῦλον ἀνθρώπων, μί' ἔδειξε πατρὸς / καὶ ματρὸς ἡμᾶς ἁμέρα τοὺς πάντας· οὐδεὶς / ἔξοχος ἄλλος ἔβλαστεν ἄλλου. / βόσκει δὲ τοὺς μὲν μοῖρα δυσαμερίας, / τοὺς δ' ὄλβος ἡμῶν, τοὺς δὲ δουλεί— / ας ζυγὸν ἔσχεν ἀνάγκας.

50. A parallel passage (*Orphic Hymns* 37.1) cited by Pearson ad loc. is instructive in this connection: Τιτῆνες, Γαίης τε καὶ Οὐρανοῦ ἀγλαὰ τέκνα, ἡμετέρων πρόγονοι πατέρων, "Titans, illustrious children of Gaia and Ouranos, our parents' forebears." Peisetairos refers jokingly to this Titan lineage in his speech promoting the priority of the birds over the gods (*Birds* 468–69). The many references to cosmogony and the titanomachy/gigantomachy are discussed in considerable detail by Hofmann, *Mythos und Komödie* 177–96. For the Pythagorean and Orphic utopianism see Foley, *Ritual Irony* 35.

51. *Tereus indomito more atque animo barbaro / conspexit in eam; amore vecors flammeo, / depositus, facinus pessimum ex dementia / confingit.*

52. Kiso, *Lost Sophocles* 73, cites Buchwald's *Studien zur Chronologie* on the strong similarity between these verses and the dactylo-epitrites at *Oidipous Tyrannos* 1086 and *Aias* 172. Although this observation has potential value for dating the play it is less useful in reconstruction.

53. See Welcker, *Griechischen Tragödien* 380–81, and Radt, *Tragicorum Graecorum Fragmenta*, vol. 4, 437, for discussion of other fragments relating to the glossectomy that, for various reasons, have not been generally accepted.

54. Kiso, *Lost Sophocles* 70.

55. Most interesting are several Italian examples dating from the late fifth to the middle fourth centuries: there is the well-known Apulian fragment by the Painter of the (Berlin) Dancing Girl depicting the Thracian king with the inscription ΤΗΡΕΥΣ (Bibliothèque Nationale, ca. 430/420), a rendering by the Dolon Painter on a Lucanian bell-krater (CA 2193, Louvre; ca. 400–370/60) of the peplos-scene in which Prokne receives her sister's textum in the presence of the king, and a Campanian fragment by the Caivano Painter (PV 2891, Dresden; ca. 330/310) depicting the flight of Prokne and Philomela: Tereus rushes from the palace holding what appears to be a πέλεκυς and a child's bone (so Bieber). This image, which certainly illustrates Sophokles' play, is a visual correlate to the Aristophanic allusion cited above (*Lys.* 563). Finally, Simon, "Tereus" 155–61, associates with Sophokles' *Tereus* the striking polychrome Tarantine fragment (Gnathia krater: Würzburg 832; ca. 340) depicting an actor holding his mask. For discussions of the iconographic evidence and bibliography see Webster, *Monuments* 152; Mihailov, "La légende de Térée" 98–103; Gelzer, "Sophokles' *Tereus*" 188–92; Radt, *Tragicorum Graecorum Fragmenta*, vol. 4, 473; and Kiso, *Lost Sophocles* 144, note 73. *Communis opinio* (Simon, Schmidt, Bieber, and others) identifies the Lucanian bell-krater (Dolon Painter) as illustrating Sophokles' *Tereus*. Trendall's and Webster's suggestion that this painting might illustrate a scene from Euripides' *Medea* is less convincing in light of the fact that there are no children present. Kiso, *Lost Sophocles* 75, notes that the Prokne statue in the Akropolis Museum (dated to 430–20 BC by H. Knell) may have been a dedication on the occasion of a victory in dramatic competition, possibly of Sophocles' *Tereus*." For plates see Cambitoglou and Trendall, *Apulian Red-Figured Vase-Painters*, and Trendall, *Red-Figured Vases of Lucania*.

56. On the question of mask and costume change in tragedy see Foley, *Ritual Irony* 252, with note 66.

57. The yearning to become a bird is a common lyric topos, Alkman fr. 26 being perhaps the most famous (βάλε δὴ βάλε κηρύλος εἴην ὅς τ' ἐπὶ κύματος ἄνθος ἂμ' ἀλκυόνεσσι ποτῆται, etc.). See Goosen, "Die Tiere." More or less contemporary tragic examples are numerous: Euripides, *Hipp.* 732–51, *Hel.* 1478–94, *Andr.* 861–62; Sophokles, *OC* 1080–84, fr. 476 [*Oinomaos*], etc.; This desiderative metaphor often expresses an im-

plicit death wish. See, for example, Euripides, *Ion* 1238–45, *HF* 1157–62, *Hec.* 1096–1106. The song from Sophokles' *Oinomaos* is transplanted into a comic context when quoted by the young man (second sequence of intruders) at *Birds* 1337–39. For laments with an implicit or explicit death wish see the second section of Führer, *Formproblem-Untersuchungen* 130–35. For a good discussion of bird metamorphoses see Forbes-Irving, *Metamorphosis* 96–127, 248–49. Of specific interest is tragic Prokne, concerning whom Ludwig Koenen reminds me of Wilamowitz on *HF* 1022, Fraenkel on Aiskhylos' *Ag.* 1144, Easterling on Sophokles' *Tr.* 963. Prokne figures in a papyrus fragment of Euripides *Kresphontes* (P. Mich. Inv. 6973) for which see the edition by Koenen and Bonnycastle, "Euripides' *Kresphontes*."

58. ἄνους ἐκεῖνος· αἱ δ' ἀνουστέρως ἔτι / ἐκεῖνον ἠμύναντο <πρὸς τὸ> καρτερόν. / ὅστις γὰρ ἐν κακοῖσι θυμωθεὶς βροτῶν / μεῖζον προσάπτει τῆς νόσου τὸ φάρμακον, / ἰατρός ἐστιν οὐκ ἐπιστήμων κακῶν. "[Tereus] is foolish, to be sure; but [Prokne and Philomela] showed even greater folly in vindictively punishing him. A mortal who, in anger at adverse circumstances, applies a remedy worse than the disease, is a doctor ignorant of ills."

59. τοῦτον δ' ἐπόπτην ἔποπα τῶν αὑτοῦ κακῶν / πεποικίλωκε κἀποδηλώσας ἔχει / θρασὺν πετραῖον ὄρνιν ἐν παντευχίᾳ· / ὃς ἦρι μὲν φανέντι διαπαλεῖ πτερὸν / κίρκου λεπάργου· δύο γὰρ οὖν μορφὰς φανεῖ / παιδός τε χαὐτοῦ νηδύος μιᾶς ἄπο· / νέας δ' ὀπώρας ἡνίκ' ἂν ξανθῇ στάχυς, / στικτή νιν αὖθις ἀμφινωμήσει πτέρυξ· / ἀεὶ δὲ μίσει τῶνδ' †ἀπ' ἄλλον† εἰς τόπον (ἀπαλλαγεὶς τόπων· Heath) / δρυμοὺς ἐρήμους καὶ πάγους ἀποικιεῖ. Having noted a few "mistakes" of quotation in Plato and Aristotle, Welcker (*Griechischen Tragödien* 384–85) attributes this fragment (cited from "Aiskhylos" in *H.A.* 9.49b, 633a17) to Sophokles. The main arguments supporting Welcker and those who follow him (Oder, Pearson, Robert, Mihailov, Calder, and Radt, to name a few) are (1) there is no evidence of a *Tereus* by Aiskhylos; (2) the periphrasis with ἔχειν + participle as well as the adverb ἡνίκα, while attested in Sophoklean verse, are absent from Aiskhylos.

60. The rather odd picture presented in this fragment of a perennial bird that, in effect, changes species from season to season suggests that the hoopoe's natural history was less than familiar to Sophokles and his contemporaries. The strangeness of the hoopoe is comically exaggerated throughout *Birds*. The similarity between the folk etymologies of Tereus (from τηρέω) and epops (ἐποπτεύω) may have influenced Sophokles' design. Sophokles' play with words here, moreover, seems to have inspired further wordplay in the comedy. "The derivation of ἔποψ from ἐφοράω," writes Griffith ("The Hoopoe's Name" 60–61), "as though it were an apocope of ἔποψις ('panorama') is underscored by two things. The first is the close resemblance of Τηρεύς to τηρέω, a synonym for ἐφοράω. This resemblance was remarked already in antiquity, when the folk etymology deriving Τηρεύς from τηρέω, was current. The second factor is the association of the Hoopoe with two overseeing divinities, Helios and Zeus." He goes on (61) to document the folk etymology in some detail.

61. θνητὴν δὲ φύσιν χρὴ θνητὰ φρονεῖν, / τοῦτο κατειδότας ὡς οὐκ ἔστιν / πλὴν Διὸς οὐδεὶς τῶν μελλόντων / ταμίας ὅ τι χρὴ τετελέσθαι.

62. Kiso and Hourmouziades in their attempts to "humanize" Sophokles' Tereus and to represent him as a "tragic hero" and "loving father" do not succeed. Kiso, *Lost Sophocles* 81, suggests that in Sophokles' play "the presupposed distinction between civilization and barbarism turned out to be fallacious." For different reasons Hourmouziades, "Sophocles' *Tereus*" 138, argues that the Thracian "becomes the loving father, who does not refrain from committing a purposeless murder [i.e., killing Dryas] in order to protect his child."

63. Calder, "Sophocles' *Tereus*" 91, argues that "Medeia slays her children to spite the faithless Jason. Ovid already drew the parallel at *Amores* 2.14.29 sq. Medeia's infanticides were an Euripidean innovation. Before him she merely absconded with the children. The Tereus story contrarily was an aetiological legend to explain the nightingale's plaintive cry *Ityn, Ityn*. The infanticide was central and indispensable. I should not hesitate to place *Tereus* before

Medea, dated by its hypothesis to 431 BC. The plot motivation, the destructive effects of excessive sibling affection, recalls *Antigone* of March 443 BC. I should be prepared to accept a date in the early 430s roughly contemporary with *Trachiniae*." Cf. also Kiso, *Lost Sophocles* 74–76.

64. In describing the three-way conflict between Athens, Macedon, and Thrace characterized by a series of unstable agreements in the late 430s, Thoukydides defends Sitalkes as a trustworthy middleman. M. Mayer and others have argued that this passage (as well as the other mythological digressions, e.g., 2.99.3, 2.102.5–6) is a response to contemporary tragedy (See Halliday, *Indo-European Folk-Tales* 105; Cazzaniga, *La saga di Itis* 61–62; Gernet *Mélanges* 202–7; Rusten, *Thucydides* 19). The historian's polemic at this point would be especially understandable if the Athenians had been impressed by a powerful anti-Thracian play just before the outbreak of the war. "The use of Thracian allies and troops was not popular in Athens (Ar., *Ach.* 141–71)," notes Rusten, "and they were eventually responsible for one of the worst atrocities of the war (7.29). It would have been easy to believe that Sitalces was descended from the savage king whose story had been dramatized in Sophocles' *Tereus*." Mayer, "Mythistorica" 491, says, "Es scheint mir ganz unverkennbar, dass es der Tereus des Sophokles sein muss, gegen den er [Thoukydides] polemisiert." For the Thracian element in Euripides' *Hekabe* see C. P. Segal, "Violence and the Other" 127–28 (with bibliography, 109, note 1). See also Delebecque, *Euripide* 154-64, and Danov, *Altthrakien*.

65. Detienne, "Orpheus" 2–3: "The inhabitants of Thrace, Orpheus' native country, are illiterate people; even more, they are so illiterate that they consider the knowledge of writing indecent. Consequently, the works going about under Orpheus' name are, as Androtion says, 'myths,' *mûthoi*, fictions. One should see in them the work of a forger. The charge is serious, since, at that time, Thracians had the reputation of being the most bloodthirsty and wild of all barbarians. Everyone knows, as Xenophon testifies, that on the shores of the Black Sea, they will even kill each other to get hold of the effects of shipwrecked Greeks but they leave on the shore, as valueless goods, boxes full of written papyrus rolls. Even more, during an incident of the Peloponnesian War, which Thucydides (who should know) labels one of the most horrible atrocities of the war, they slaughtered with the short sword—which is not a regular weapon of the Greeks—all of the children of the city of Mykalessos gathered in the school, helpless children learning how to read and write. Obviously, the role of the Thracians, full of scorn for writing, was to destroy in fury everything which concerned the intellectual sphere: books, tools, and men. Androtion goes straight to the point: when a Thracian hears the word book, he draws his sword." This passage is published in a modified form in Detienne, *L'écriture* 110.

66. Halliday, *Indo-European Folk-Tales* 98. Hourmouziades, "Sophocles' *Tereus*" 134 (cf. also 139, note 6), distinguishes Sophocles' contribution from the older legend: "no matter how decisive the Sophoclean influence may have been for the final shaping of the myth, its later accounts, with the exception of Ovid's elaborate narrative . . . invariably fall back on some initial trend, which seems to have been that of explaining, in the form of an αἴτιον, the idiosyncratic habits of the nightingale and the swallow." Gelzer, "Sophokles' *Tereus*" 188, discusses the breadth of the influence of Sophokles' play, especially in art. For a Middle Comic *Tereus* (Anaxandrides), see Athenaios, *Deipn.* 9.373, and Nesselrath, *Mittlere Komödie* 216-18.

67. On this subject see Schlesinger, "Indications of Parody" 309–13. Slater, *Reading Petronius* 19–20, makes the point that knowledge of the model being parodied may not always be necessary for sincere enjoyment of a comic work.

68. Dobrov, "Aristophanes' *Birds*."

69. For a detailed discussion of the Daulis question see Mayer, "Mythistorica" 489–94, and Halliday, *Indo-European Folk-Tales* 104–6, who argues that Tereus was originally a Megarian hero.

70. σὺ γὰρ / τὸν μὲν πατέρα μὴ τύπτε· ταυτηνδὶ λαβὼν / τὴν πτέρυγα καὶ τουτὶ τὸ πλῆκτρον θάτέρᾳ, / νομίσας ἀλεκτρυόνος ἔχειν τονδὶ λόφον, / φρούρει, στρατεύου, μισθοφορῶν σαυτὸν τρέφε, / τὸν πατέρ᾽ ἔα ζῆν· ἀλλ᾽ ἐπειδὴ μάχιμος εἶ, / εἰς τἀπὶ Θρᾴκης ἀποπέτου κἀκεῖ μάχου.

71. Romer, "When Is a Bird Not a Bird?" 136–38. For a discussion of the relationship between language and violence against women in the post-Sophoklean (and therefore Sophokles-inspired) tradition, especially Ovid, see Joplin, "Voice of the Shuttle."

72. See Konstan, *Greek Comedy and Ideology* 29-44.

73. See Henderson, "Mass versus Elite."

74. ἔστι δ᾽ ἐν Φαναῖσι πρὸς τῇ / Κλεψύδρᾳ πανοῦργον Ἐγ- / γλωττογαστόρων γένος, / οἳ θερίζουσίν τε καὶ σπεί- / ρουσι καὶ τρυγῶσι ταῖς γλώτ- / ταισι συκάζουσί τε· / βάρβαροι δ᾽ εἰσὶν γένος, / Γοργίαι τε καὶ Φίλιπποι. / κἀπὸ τῶν Ἐγγλωττογαστό- / ρων ἐκείνων τῶν φιλίππων / πανταχοῦ τῆς Ἀττικῆς ἡ / γλῶττα χωρὶς τέμνεται. Cf. Tzetzes' "hypothesis" (Radt, *Tragicorum Graecorum Fragmenta*, vol. 4, 435) that most certainly quotes Sophokles' script: τὴν αὑτῆς γλῶτταν θερίζει. Aristophanes accomplishes this with a two-way allusion that also points to the popular song Hybrias the Cretan (*Poetae Melici Graeci* 909) to make capital of the pun of ἐγγλωττογάστορες (Tongue-to-Belly Men) from the term for manual laborers, ἐγχειρογάστορες (hand-to-belly men): "Great wealth is mine in my spear and sword and my fine leather shield . . . . With it I plough, with it I reap, with it I tread the sweet wine from the grapes" (from Sommerstein ad loc.).

75. Pearson, *Fragments of Sophocles* 224.

76. Aelian, NA 3.26: οἱ ἔποπές εἰσιν ὀρνίθων ἀπηνέστατοι . . . , etc. See Thompson, *Greek Birds* 97–98, on the behavior, nest, and habitat of the hoopoe as understood by various cultures. It is important to be on guard against the pitfall of circularity, however, and note that Aelian may have been influenced by the myth, at least as regards the misogyny.

77. Hofmann, *Mythos und Komödie* 74.

78. Griffith, "The Hoopoe's Name" 60.

79. Griffith, "The Hoopoe's Name" 61. "Finally," he concludes (63), "the words of the tragedian which line 48 calls to mind would have been resonant for an Athenian audience, for the ἐπόπτης denotes him who in the mysteries of Demeter had passed from being 'one who keeps his eyes closed' (μύστης) to the stage of 'beholding' (ἐποπτεία), and so has reached the furthest limit of vision and knowledge. Such a man by virtue of the power of flight imparted to him by his metamorphosis is Tereus, and by the application of his little root (*Av.* 654f.) he provides the men with wings and leads them to the knowledge which they seek."

80. "Probably most Athenians had heard a good deal of talk about peacocks," notes Sommerstein, *Birds* 206, "but had never seen one; they were such a rarity that the aviary of Demos son of Pyrilampes, who exhibited his peacocks to the public once a month (charging an admission fee, according to Aelian, NA 5.21), attracted visitors from as far afield as Sparta and Thessaly." In "Fowl Play," Cartledge discusses the prosopography behind Antiphon's speech *Against Erasistratos Concerning (the) Peafowl* (fr. 57–59). He reconstructs the lawsuit of one Erasistratos against Demos son of Pyrilampes with the suggestion that this suit inspired Aristophanes' *Birds*. In connection with the Athenian spelling and pronunciation of ταώς (Athenaios, *Deipn.* 9.397c–d) he remarks (*Nomos* 52) that "there could be no more graphic illustration of the peacock's irremediable foreignness, and more specifically its orientalism . . . to Athenian eyes and ears."

81. Thoukydides 2.63: "Men like these [*apragmones*] would soon ruin a state, either here, if they should persuade others, or if they should settle in some other land founding an independent state all to themselves; for retiring and unambitious men are not secure unless flanked by men of action" (tr. Rex Warner).

82. Robert, *Griechische Heldensage* 156. Although conclusive proof is lacking, the indirect evidence, especially Thoukydides' polemic (2.29.3), suggests that the name "Tereus" was established for the Thracian king by Sophokles.

83. Griffith, "The Hoopoe's Name" 61, note 11.

84. Aiskhylean drama attests a simpler pre-Sophoklean tradition: as in the case of the passage in *Hiketides* mentioned above (line 62, hawk instead of hoopoe), *Agamemnon* 1050–51 reflects an earlier version of the legend that makes no mention of shearing Philomela's tongue. Klytaimnestra says she will "persuade Kassandra [in Greek]" provided that she is not a monolingual barbarian who can only chatter like a swallow: ἀλλ᾽ εἴπερ ἐστὶ μὴ χελιδόνος / δίκην ἀγνῶτα φωνὴν βάρβαρον κεκτημένη. This is the familiar association of swallow-song and foreign languages (see below) that, if anything, foreshadows Kassandra's mantic loquacity, *not* her inability to speak. The implication here is that a talkative Philomela was transformed into a equally "talkative" bird. For a different view see Ahl, "The Art of Safe Criticism" 182–84. Ahl's argument depends on allusion by Aiskhylos to the glossectomy.

85. For the swallow's chatter as a metaphor for babble see Aiskhylos, *Agamemnon* 1050; Aristophanes, *Birds* 1680–81, *Frogs* 93, 679–81; Euripides fr. 88 N², and Ion (the tragedian) fr. 33 N². See also Thompson, *Greek Birds* 320. "Les anciens comparaient une langue barbare (étrangère) au cri de l'hirondelle," writes Zaganiaris ("Le mythe de Térée" 222). "De là le mot ὁ χελιδών (au masculin) a pris le sens de barbare et le verbe χελιδονίζω = βαρβαρίζω. Du même sens provient le proverbe χελιδόνων μουσεῖα qui désigne des mots barbares et inconcevables. Ce dicton convient aux hommes bavards et ennuyeux. L'expression est une parodie de ἀηδόνων μουσεῖα d'Euripide qui désigne les choeurs des rossignols. De même l'expression d'Aristophane χείλεσιν ἀμφιλάλοις δεινὸν ἐπιβρέμεται θρηκία χελιδών désigne son cri barbare en faisant allusion au mythe de la métamorphose qui a eu lieu en Thrace."

86. ὅτι πρῶτα μὲν ἦσθ᾽ ἄνθρωπος ὥσπερ νὼ ποτε, / κἀργύριον ὠφείλησας ὥσπερ νὼ ποτε, / κοὐκ ἀποδιδοὺς ἔχαιρες ὥσπερ νὼ ποτε, / εἶτ᾽ αὖθις ὀρνίθων μεταλλάξας φύσιν / καὶ γῆν ἐπέπτου καὶ θάλατταν ἐν κύκλῳ, / καὶ πάνθ᾽ ὅσαπερ ἄνθρωπος ὅσα τ᾽ ὄρνις φρονεῖς. / ταῦτ᾽ οὖν ἱκέται νὼ πρὸς σὲ δεῦρ᾽ ἀφίγμεθα, / εἴ τινα πόλιν φράσειας ἡμῖν εὔερον / ὥσπερ σισύραν ἐγκατακλινῆναι μαλθακήν.

87. [Πε.] φεῦ φεῦ· / ἦ μέγ᾽ ἐνορῶ βούλευμ᾽ ἐν ὀρνίθων γένει / καὶ δύναμιν, ἣ γένοιτ᾽ ἄν, εἰ πίθοισθέ μοι. / [Τη.] τί σοι πιθώμεθ᾽; / [Πε.] ὅ τι πίθησθε; πρῶτα μὲν . . .

88. Hubbard, *Mask of Comedy* 160, suggests that *Birds* (like Ameipsias' *Revellers*, which won the comic competition of 414) was directed against the ἑταιρίαι "thought to be responsible for the sacrileges [of 415]."

89. [Τη.] ἰοὺ ἰού. / μὰ γῆν, μὰ παγίδας, μὰ νεφέλας, μὰ δίκτυα, / μὴ 'γὼ νόημα κομψότερον ἤκουσά πω· / ὥστ᾽ ἂν κατοικίζοιμι μετὰ σοῦ τὴν πόλιν, / εἰ ξυνδοκοίη τοῖσιν ἄλλοις ὀρνέοις. / [Πε.] τίς ἂν οὖν τὸ πρᾶγμ᾽ αὐτοῖς διηγήσαιτο; [Τη.] σύ. / ἐγὼ γὰρ αὐτούς, βαρβάρους ὄντας πρὸ τοῦ, / ἐδίδαξα τὴν φωνὴν ξυνὼν πολὺν χρόνον. / [Πε.] πῶς δῆτ᾽ ἂν αὐτοὺς ξυγκαλέσειας; [Τη.] ῥαδίως. / δευρὶ γὰρ εἰσβὰς αὐτίκα μάλ᾽ εἰς τὴν λόχμην, / ἔπειτ᾽ ἀνεγείρας τὴν ἐμὴν ἀηδόνα, / καλοῦμεν αὐτούς.

90. Sommerstein, *Birds* 3–4.

91. In discussions of the power of language in Aristophanes, *Birds* in particular, it is important to acknowledge Whitman's fundamental work, *Aristophanes and the Comic Hero*.

92. οὐδέν ἐστ᾽ ἄμεινον οὐδ᾽ ἥδιον ἢ φῦσαι πτερά. / αὐτίχ᾽ ὑμῶν τῶν θεατῶν εἴ τις ἦν ὑπόπτερος, / εἶτα πεινῶν τοῖς χοροῖσι τῶν τραγῳδῶν ἤχθετο, / ἐκπτόμενος ἂν οὗτος ἠρίστησεν ἐλθὼν οἴκαδε, / κᾆτ᾽ ἂν ἐμπλησθεὶς ἐφ᾽ ἡμᾶς αὖθις αὖ κατέπτατο.

93. Herington, "*Birds* and *Prometheia*" (especially p. 242 on "situational parody").

94. A list of the most recent and valuable literature would include Downing, "*Apatê, Agôn*"; Suzuki, *Metamorphoses of Helen*; Foley, "*Anodos* Dramas"; Juffras, "Helen and Other Victims"; Austin, *Helen of Troy*; and Goldhill, "Failure of Exemplarity."

95. Burnett, *Catastrophe Survived* 85. Similarly Austin (*Helen of Troy*, chapter 6) regards Euripides' *Helene* as the first work of fiction in the modern sense.

96. Downing, "*Apatê, Agôn.*"

97. For a review of what is called here the "Helene documents" see the introduction to Austin, *Helen of Troy*, and Holmberg, "Euripides' *Helen.*"

98. For comic σωτηρία in a utopian context see *Peace* 301, 595; *Lysistrata* 30, 497; *Ekklesiazousai* 202, 396–97.

99. Μενέλαε, πρὸς μὲν παρθένου σεσώσμεθα· / τοὐνθένδε δὴ σὲ τοὺς λόγους φέροντα χρὴ / κοινὴν ξυνάπτειν μηχανὴν σωτηρίας.

100. Cf. lines 1055, 1060, 1086, 1092.

101. E.g., lines 74, 875. See Matthews, "Euripides and Mimesis."

102. Downing, "*Apatê, Agôn*" 7–8.

103. Telephos' account of the journey to Argos appears to include a reference to having left home already in disguise. To this context belong the important fragments 697 N²: πτώχ' ἀμφίβλητα [ἀμφίβληστρα: Burges] σώματος λαβὼν ῥάκη / ἀλκτήρια τύχης, These humble rags thrown about my body / I wear to ward off misfortune.

104. καὶ μὴν τάδ' ἀμφίβλητρα σώματος ῥάκη / ξυμμαρτυρήσει ναυτικῶν ἐρειπίων.

105. See Austin, *Helen of Troy*, chapter 6. τί ποτ' ἄπληστος εἶ κακῶν, / ἔρωτας ἀπάτας δόλιά τ' ἐξευρήματα / ἀσκοῦσα φίλτρα θ' αἱματηρὰ δωμάτων; / εἰ δ' ἦσθα μετρία, τἄλλα γ' ἡδίστη θεῶν / πέφυκας ἀνθρώποισιν· οὐκ ἄλλως λέγω. Translation by W. Arrowsmith.

106. With important correspondences emphasized: σὲ τὰν ἐναύλοις ὑπὸ <u>δενδροκόμοις</u> / μουσεῖα καὶ θάκους ἐνί- / ζουσαν <u>ἀναβοάσω</u>, / σὲ τὰν ἀοιδοτάταν <u>ὄρνιθα μελῳδὸν</u> / <u>ἀηδόνα δακρυόεσσαν</u>, / <u>ἔλθ' ὦ διὰ ξουθᾶν</u> / <u>γενύων ἐλελιζομένα</u> / θρήνων ἐμοὶ ξυνεργός, / Ἑλένας μελέας πόνους / <u>τὸν Ἰλιάδων τ' ἀει-</u> / <u>δούσᾳ δακρυόεντα πόνον</u> / Ἀχαιῶν ὑπὸ λόγχαις· / ὅτ' ἔδραμε ῥόθια πεδία <u>βαρβάρῳ</u> πλάτᾳ / ὅτ' ἔμολεν ἔμολε, μέλεα Πριαμίδαις ἄγων / Λακεδαίμονος ἄπο λέχεα / σέθεν, ὦ Ἑλένα, Πάρις αἰνόγαμος / πομπαῖσιν Ἀφροδίτας. Dover, *Aristophanic Comedy* 148–49: "When two poets both describe the singing of the nightingale and refer to the myth that she is the heroine Prokne, mourning for her son Itys, they are likely to exhibit some coincidence of language, but the coincidence in these two passages is rather large, particularly since the verb *elelísdesthai*, 'trill' is not found elsewhere in extant Greek poetry. It would seem that at the same time as comedy plundered tragedy for parodic purposes, a tragic poet was not above borrowing from a comedian."

107. [Πε.] ὦ φίλτατ' <u>ὀρνίθων</u> σύ, μή νυν ἔσταθι· / ἀλλ', <u>ἀντιβολῶ</u> σ', ἄγ', ὡς τάχιστ' εἰς τὴν λόχμην / εἴσβαινε κἀνέγειρε <u>τὴν ἀηδόνα</u>. / [Τη.] ἄγε, σύννομέ μοι, παῦσαι μὲν ὕπνου, / λῦσον δὲ νόμους ἱερῶν ὕμνων, / οὓς διὰ θείου στόματος θρηνεῖς / τὸν ἐμὸν καὶ σὸν <u>πολύδακρυν</u> Ἴτυν, / <u>ἐλελιζομένη διεροῖς μέλεσιν</u> / <u>γένυος ξουθῆς</u>. / καθαρὰ χωρεῖ διὰ <u>φυλλοκόμου</u> / μίλακος ἠχὼ πρὸς Διὸς ἕδρας . . . . Dover, *Aristophanic Comedy* 148. Translation adapted from Dover and Arrowsmith.

108. E.g., Rau, *Paratragodia* 50, and others cited in Zeitlin, "Travesties of Gender" 213, note 9.

109. Zeitlin, "Travesties of Gender."

110. Zeitlin, "Travesties of Gender" 183, notes that every one of these parodies "conveys multiple messages, including each time some reflection of its status as a theatrical artifact."

111. Sommerstein, *Thesmophoriazousai* 211, notes that "new" points up both the fact that *Helene* was a recent production and that it was strikingly innovative both in its narrative and as a tragedy. We might add that this doubly "new" play is yet further "renewed" in the given comic context.

112. [Κ.] Ἑλένη δ᾽ ἐκλήθην. [Κρ.] αὖθις αὖ γίγνει γυνή, / πρὶν τῆς ἑτέρας δοῦναι γυναικίσεως δίκην.

113. On comic salvation and its relation to tragic *sôteria* see MacMathuna, "Trickery."

8. *Herakles*

1. Konstan, *Greek Comedy* 62, notes that "Leo Strauss seems to have been the first modern scholar to ask why Dionysus chooses to assume the attire of Heracles in his attempt to rescue Euripides." Citing Strauss's suggestion that the Heraklean costume was effective camouflage, Konstan responds that "the question . . . remains an important one and invites a different kind of reply: Heracles is chosen because he was a mortal and had become a god."

2. For a stimulating presentation of this argument see Padilla, "Heraclean Dionysus." See also Hubbard, *Mask of Comedy* 199–219, who cites Eupolis' *Demoi* as a comedy with thematic parallels to *Frogs*. Other possible comic antecedents include the Dionysos of Eupolis' *Taxiarkhoi* (see Storey, "Dating Eupolis" 392), and Dionysos as arbiter in Kratinos' *Dionysalexandros* and *Arkhilokhoi*. Pherekrates' *Krapataloi* and *Pseudherakles* may also have provided Aristophanes with some ideas.

3. See, for example, C. P. Segal, "Character and Cults," and Padilla, "Heraclean Dionysus."

4. The essential bibliography includes Welcker, *Griechischen Tragödien*; Wilamowitz-Moellendorff, *Analecta*; Kuiper, "De Pirithoo"; Cockle, "Pap. Oxy. 3531"; Mette, "Perithoos-Theseus-Herakles"; Lloyd-Jones, "Heracles at Eleusis"; Merkelbach, "Πειρίθου κατάβασις"; Paoletti, "Arula di Medma"; and Sutton, *Two Lost Plays*.

5. See Heiden, "Tragedy and Comedy" 95, who takes as his starting point the apparent reticence of *Frogs* concerning comedy.

6. Wilamowitz-Moellendorff, *Analecta* 171–72: "Idem ego mihi persuasi," he notes and enumerates the points of correspondence: "utrobique mysticus chorus est, utrobique Orci minister aditum prohibens (quem Aristophanes non ex populari fabula sed a poeta quopiam fictum accepit) hic cum vero Hercule rixans luctansque, illic simulatum obiurgans et male tractans, idque verbis aperte ex tragoedia detortis," etc. "The sheer weight of the evidence," notes Sutton, *Two Lost Plays* 6, "unambiguously goes to show that these plays [*Peirithous* included] were generally deemed authentic in antiquity." Modern scholarship remains divided on this issue, though Euripides appears to be prevailing. See Sutton, *Two Lost Plays* 6–11.

7. A book fragment (1908) and several Oxyrhynchus papyri (e.g., 17.2078 [1927] and 50.3531 [1983]), respectively.

8. Twelve pages of text in Sutton, *Two Lost Plays*.

9. *Two Lost Plays* 1–81.

10. Thus, against the opinion of Diels and Kranz, Wilamowitz-Moellendorff, and Bruno Snell, who attribute the play to Kritias, we find Welcker, Nauck, Kuiper, Page, and Mette (Sutton, *Two Lost Plays* 7). Dover, who once seemed to be inclined to accept Euripidean authorship (*Greek and the Greeks* 230), is now more agnostic (*Frogs* 54). A potentially compelling piece of epigraphic evidence is supplied by IG II/III2 2363.45. This "ephebic book list" (so Kumanudes) from the Piraeus may have included *Peirithous* with the plays of Euripides.

11. Collard, Cropp, and Lee, *Euripides* 2.

12. It is for this reason, the reader will recall, that Rau ignores *Tereus* as he does *Peirithous*. Cf. the comments of the anonymous reader of this book: "Rau [*Paratragodia*] contented

himself with compiling a catalogue of instances of Aristophanic parody of individual trag-edies. Rau was a strict, old-style German philologist, and he only acknowledged as instances of paratragedy instances involving verbal echoes. In a very important paper, C. J. Herington ["*Birds* and *Prometheia*"] demonstrated that parody could be situational as well as verbal. Indeed, one could claim that the single most important function of verbal parody is to serve as a marker that more important situational parody is present, but it is not necessary, or ac-curate, to claim that a verbal echo must be present to serve as such a marker."

13. See Mette, "Perithoos" 13–14 (who cites, among other useful sources, Hans Herter's article on Theseus in the 1973 R.-E. Supplement [13.1173–89]). Euripides shows a consider-able interest in the legend throughout his work (cf. *Herakles* 1169–70, where Theseus ex-presses gratitude to Herakles for rescuing him from Hades).

14. One tradition has Herakles wrench Theseus from his seat making him literally lose part of his buttocks—or at least the "seat of his pants"—in the getaway (hence an aetiology for the small posteriors of Athenians). The spectacle of the distinguished hero on the run with exposed rump is ready-made for the comic stage (Aulus Gellius 10.16.13, Scholion Lh on Aristophanes *Knights* 1368d, Hesychius and the Suda s.v. λίσποι, and the First Vatican Mythographer [VM 148]); see Sutton, *Two Lost Plays* 53, and Gantz, *Early Greek Myth* 295.

15. "Descending with Theseus to Hades in order to woo Persephone, Peirithous received a fitting punishment: Bound to an immovable seat on a rocky crag he sat, guarded by ser-pents' jaws. Theseus, for his part, considering it disgraceful to abandon a friend, chose to stay in Hades rather than return to life above. Herakles, sent by Eurystheus to fetch Kerberos, overpowered the beast and, enjoying the favor of the chthonic gods, freed Theseus and his friend from their present straits. Thus, with this single deed, he simultaneously subdued his opponent (Kerberos), won the divine favor, and showed mercy towards his friends." For a discussion of this and other testimonia see Sutton, *Two Lost Plays* 27–31.

16. Scholia on his own *Chiliades* 4.912 and Aristophanes *Frogs* 142a. Other relevant tes-timonia include Ps. Apollodoros, *Epitome* 1.23 and Hyginus *Fab.* 79.

17. Cited by Sutton, *Two Lost Plays* 38–39.

18. *Poetics* 1455b32–1456a3: "There are four kinds of tragedy, a number corresponding to that of the constituent parts that I spoke about. There is complex tragedy, which depends entirely on reversal and discovery; tragedy of suffering, as in the various plays on Ajax or Ixion; tragedy of character, as in *The Phthiotides* and the *Peleus*; and fourthly, spectacular tragedy, as in *The Phorcides*, in the *Prometheus*, and in plays with scenes in Hades." (T. S. Dorsch tr., who accepts Bywater's conjecture of ὄψις for οης at 1456a2 [obelized by Kassel]).

19. The association of these lines (an exchange between Herakles and Aiakos) with the Logothetes hypothesis has led some to regard them as the play's opening. The term μύχους of fr.1, however, clearly shows that the scene is set in Hades. Thus a change of scene is clearly needed between frr. 2–4 and fr. 1. Since it need not introduce Herakles for the first time (only to Aiakos) this underworld encounter would appear to follow the parodos (and any other scenes set in the upper world).

20. He agrees, for example, with the Logothetes hypothesis in having both Theseus and Peirithous rescued: "Qui [Herakles] a Plutone impetravit eosque incolumes eduxit."

21. Herakles may have spoken an expository prologue himself and then joined the cho-rus for the katabasis. See Sutton, *Two Lost Plays* 97–98.

22. On the connection between Herakles and the Lesser Mysteries see F. Graf, *Eleusis* 142–50; Robertson, "Heracles' 'Catabasis'" 295–99; and Mylonas, *Eleusis* 240, note 85. On the relevant iconography Lloyd-Jones, "Heracles at Eleusis" 211–12, notes the following: "From about the end of the fifth century, this would seem to have been well known. We find it on an Attic pelike of the fourth century from the Crimea and on the red-figure crater in the

British Museum known as the Pourtalès Vase; and later, during the imperial period we find it on the Lovatelli Urn and on the Terra-Nova sarcophagus." Lloyd-Jones enumerates the most important literary references to the episode, including the pseudo-Platonic *Axiokhos*; Plutarch, *Theseus* 33; Diodoros 4.25 and 4.14.4; Apollodoros *Library* 5.12, etc.

23. Lloyd-Jones, "Heracles at Eleusis" 212, 215.

24. Mette, "Perithoos" 18–19, and Sutton, *Two Lost Plays* 70–72.

25. Cited by Sutton, *Two Lost Plays* 52.

26. "The plot of Euripides' [*Herakles*]," notes Lloyd-Jones, "Heracles at Eleusis" 214, "connects Heracles closely with Attica, for it makes him rescue Theseus from the underworld and makes Theseus in gratitude transfer to him the countless Theseia in Attica, which now became Heracleia." For the complex relationship between Herakles and the Atticized Theseus (whose "image" in many respects is modeled on the older Peloponnesian hero) see Connor, "Theseus in Classical Athens."

27. See fr. 913 N^2 below with Sutton, *Two Lost Plays* 94–96.

28. *Frogs* 158–63, 434–39.

29. See Lloyd-Jones, "Heracles at Eleusis" 224–26.

30. Lloyd-Jones, "Heracles at Eleusis" 224–26.

31. Fr. 2: ἵνα πλημοχόας τάσδ᾽ εἰς χθόνιον / χάσμ᾽ εὐφήμως προχέωμεν. *Plêmokhoai* were used in the invocation of rain and fertility, ὗε κύε, "rain! conceive!" On the Eleusinian *plêmokhoai* see Burkert, *Greek Religion* 289. The Eleusinian resonance of *plêmokhoai* may be strengthened by the use in fr. 4 of *rhumbos*, which simultaneously denotes a ritual instrument associated with the mysteries (the "bull roarer"). Where possible, the fragments are cited after Snell *TrGF* (Critias), with an eye to their presentation as Euripidean in the commentary by Sutton (*Two Lost Plays*). Mette's catalogue of Euripidean fragments in *Lustrum* is rich in information, though his numbering system has not been generally accepted (Mette fr. 807 = Snell fr.1; frr. 809–13 = Snell frr. 2–6; Mette frr. 815–22 = Snell frr. 7–14; Mette also includes fr. 936 N^2 as fr. 808 and fr. 964 N^2 as fr. 814).

32. Fr. 868 N^2: θεοὶ χθόνιοι / ζοφερὰν ἀδίαυλον ἔχοντες / ἕδραν φθειρομένων Ἀχεροντίαν λίμνην.

33. For parallels involving the image of self-begetting (hybris) see Aiskhylos, *Agamemnon* 763–66. See also *Eumenides* 534–37.

34. Fr. 3: ἀκάμας τε χρόνος περὶ γ᾽ ἀενάῳ / ῥεύματι πλήρης φοιτᾷ τίκτων / αὐτὸς ἑαυτόν, δίδυμοί τ᾽ ἄρκτοι / ταῖς ὠκυπλάνοις πτερύγων ῥιπαῖς / τὸν Ἀτλάντειον τηροῦσι πόλον. Fr. 4: σὲ τὸν αὐτοφυῆ, τὸν ἐν αἰθερίῳ / ῥύμβῳ πάντων φύσιν ἐμπλέξανθ᾽, / ὃν πέρι μὲν φῶς, πέρι δ᾽ ὀρφναία / νὺξ αἰολόχρως ἄκριτος τ᾽ ἄστρων / ὄχλος ἐνδελεχῶς ἀμφιχορεύει. These fragments, especially fr. 3, may participate in the intertextual play between *Frogs* 100 and *Bakkhai* 889. For bibliography on the topos of the cyclicity of time see Collard, Cropp, and Lee, *Euripides* 118, and Kassel, *Kleine Schriften* 303–309.

35. On this question see the review of Sutton, *Two Lost Plays* 42–44.

36. Kuiper, "De Perithoo" 171.

37. In Satyrus' *Life of Euripides* (fr. 37, col. iii), shortly after a quotation of frr. 4 and 912 N^2 and just before a quotation of fr. 913 N^2 we find the following: Ἡρακλέα· [καὶ] δὴ καὶ τὴν [. . .]την ἐπιφ[υομέν]ην τοῖς προειρημένοις [ἐπε]ὶ λέγει "τίς [ἀτι]μόθεος [κ]αὶ [πα]αραδαίμ[ων] [ὃς] τάδε λεύσσων, . . ." (with an obvious, if altered, quotation of 913 N^2). See Sutton, *Two Lost Plays* 94–96.

38. Fr. 913 N^2: τίς τάδε λεύσσων θεὸν οὐχὶ νοεῖ, / μετεωρολόγων δ᾽ ἑκὰς ἔρριψεν / σκολιὰς ἀπάτας; ὧν ἀτηρὰ / γλῶσσ᾽ εἰκοβολεῖ περὶ τῶν ἀφανῶν / οὐδὲν γνώμης μετέχουσα. See Sutton, *Two Lost Plays* 94–96, on Satyrus' quotation of this fragment.

39. Sutton, *Two Lost Plays* 93–94. If he is right to connect this passage with the psephism of Diopeithes ca. 433–32 "against those who do not honor the divine or who promote doc-

trines about heavenly phenomena" (Plutarch, *Perikles* 32), then there may be reason to accept a date for *Peirithous* in the early 430s.

40. Fr. 910 N²: ὄλβιος ὅστις τῆς ἱστορίας / ἔσχε μάθησιν, / μήτε πολιτῶν ἐπὶ πημοσύνην / μήτ᾽ εἰς ἀδίκους πράξεις ὁρμῶν, / ἀλλ᾽ ἀθανάτου καθορῶν φύσεως / κόσμον ἀγήρων, πῆ τε συνέστη / καὶ ὅπη καὶ ὅπως. / τοῖς δὲ τοιούτοις οὐδέποτ᾽ αἰσχρῶν / ἔργων μελέδημα προσίζει. Fr. 912 N²: σοὶ τῷ πάντων μεδέοντι χοὴν / πέλανόν τε φέρω, Ζεὺς εἴτ᾽ Ἀίδης / ὀνομαζόμενος στέργεις· σὺ δέ μοι / θυσίαν ἄπυρον παγκαρπείας / δέξαι πλήρη προχυθεῖσαν. / σὺ γὰρ ἔν τε θεοῖς τοῖς οὐρανίδαις / σκῆπτρον τὸ Διὸς μεταχειρίζεις / χθονίων θ᾽ Ἅιδη μετέχεις ἀρχῆς. / πέμψον δ᾽ ἐς φῶς ψυχὰς ἐνέρων / τοῖς βουλομένοις ἄθλους προμαθεῖν, / πόθεν ἔβλαστον, τίς ῥίζα κακῶν, / τίνα δεῖ μακάρων ἐκθυσαμένους / εὑρεῖν μόχθων ἀνάπαυλαν.

41. "Heracles at Eleusis" 218–20. Lloyd-Jones, however, argues for an underlying epic source.

42. "Heracles at Eleusis" 218.

43. Fr. 1: [Αι.] ἔα, τί χρῆμα; δέρκομαι σπουδῇ τινα / δεῦρ᾽ ἐγκονοῦντα καὶ μαλ᾽ εὐτόλμῳ φρενί. / εἰπεῖν δίκαιον, ὦ ξέν᾽, ὅστις ὢν τόπους / ἐς τούσδε χρίμπτη καὶ καθ᾽ ἥντιν᾽ αἰτίαν. / [Ἡρ.] οὐδεὶς ὄκνος πάντ᾽ ἐκκαλύψασθαι λόγον· ἐμοὶ πατρὶς μὲν Ἄργος, / ὄνομα δ᾽ Ἡρακλῆς, / θεῶν δὲ πάντων πατρὸς ἐξέφυν Διός· / ἐμῇ γὰρ ἦλθε μητρὶ κεδνὰ πρὸς λέχη / Ζεύς, ὡς λέλεκται τῆς ἀληθείας ὕπο. / ἥκω δὲ δεῦρο πρὸς βίαν, Εὐρυσθέως / ἀρχαῖς ὑπείκων, ὅς μ᾽ ἔπεμψ᾽ Ἅιδου κύνα / ἄγειν κελεύων ζῶντα πρὸς Μυκηνίδας / πύλας, / ἰδεῖν μὲν οὐ θέλων, ἆθλον δέ μοι / ἀνήνυτον τόνδ᾽ ᾤετ᾽ ἐξηυρηκέναι. / τοιόνδ᾽ ἰχνεύων πρᾶγος Εὐρώπης κύκλῳ / Ἀσίας τε πάσης ἐς μύχους ἐλήλυθα.

44. See Sutton, *Two Lost Plays* 91–99.

45. The introductory tone of fr. 1, on this interpretation, has more to do with Herakles' first meeting with Aiakos than with his absolute entrance into the action.

46. Fr. 5A: δρακοντ[/ τηνου[/ ὀργὴν . [/ ἐπίσταμαι / ὀψὲ ξυνεὶς [. . . .]ο . . [/ θεοὺς ϲεβεϲθ . . . οτ[/ Ἰξίονοϲ παῖ, πολλὰ δ[/ εἶδον λόγῳ τ᾽ ἤκουσα [/ οὐδ᾽ ἐγγὺς οὐδέν᾽ ημ[/ τῇ ϲῇ πελάζοντ᾽ ἀλ[λ / δυσπραξίᾳ τοὺς π[/ ϲκήψιν τιν᾽ ητι . [/ ἄτηϲ ἀπρούπτωϲ . [/ ἤδ᾽ οὐκέτ᾽ ἐϲτ᾽ ἄϲημος [οὐδὲ / ὀνειρατώδηϲ ἀλλ᾽ ο[/ Ἕλλην· ἰδεῖν δὲ τὸν λέ[γοντ᾽ / οἷός τ᾽ ἂν εἴην, πέππταϲ[αι / ἀχλὺς πάροιθε τῶν ἐμῷ[ν ὄσσων / ἄθλους ἐρωτᾷϲ τοὺς ἐμο[ὺς / γλώϲϲηϲ γὰρ ἠχὼ τῇϲδε πρ . . [/ οὐδέν τι πάντως θαῦμ[α / ἀπεστερῆϲθαί <ϲ> ἐϲτὶν α . [/ καὶ φθέγμα καὶ ϲχῆμ᾽ . [/ πολλαὶ διῆλθον τῆς ἐ[μῆϲ / καὶ ϲῆϲ· ἀναμνήϲω δὲ . [/ ϲιγηϲιναρ[/ . . . .] . [/ φωγ[/ τηϲ[.

47. E.g., Apollodoros *Epitome* 1.24. Roughly contemporary iconography seems to reflect this feature, but the significance of Peirithous' "blank expression" and brooding postures in several representations remain controversial. See Gantz, *Early Greek Myth* 292–95.

48. . . . / εϲφηλα[/ . . . . [/ κατελ . [/ ἐλθών . [/ Ἕλλην[/ βωμω . . [/ θεὸς δὲ μανια[/ ἔπεμψεν ἄτη[ν / νεφέλην γυναικ[/ ἔϲπειρεν εἰς τοὺς θ .[/ θυγατρὶ μίϲγοιτ᾽ ε[/ τοίων δὲ κόμπω[ν / ποινὰϲ θεοῖϲ ἔτειϲεν[/ μανίας τροχῶι περι[/ οἰϲτρη[λ]άτοιϲιν ωχ[/ ἄπυϲτο[ϲ] ἀνθρώποι[ϲι / ἔκρυψεν, ἀλλὰ βορε . [α / διεϲπα[ρ]άχθη ϲ[υ]ν μ[/ πατὴ[ρ ἁ]μαρτὼν εἰς θε[οὺς / ἐγὼ [δ᾽ ἐκ]είνου π[ή]ματα[/

49. Sutton, *Two Lost Plays* 49. The intertextual connection between this fragment and Pindar, *Pythian* 2, is rich with suggestions, though the emphasis is quite different in the earlier work. Mette, "Perithoos" 16, enumerates the parallels (which are quite striking).

50. See Gantz, *Early Greek Myth* 291–95.

51. See Gantz, *Early Greek Myth* 294, with note 30.

52. Fr. 6 is quoted twice by Plutarch (*Moralia* 96 C, 533 A, once with attribution to Euripides). Note the significant detail that supports the Logothetes hypothesis, i.e., that Theseus is "bound" by loyalty to Peirithous: αἰδοῦς ἀχαλκεύτοισιν ἔζευκται πέδαις.

53. . . . .] . coι τῳ . [. . . . .] ἡδὺ ν[ῦ]ν δοκεῖ / . . . .]τος, Ἡράκλεις,
[σὲ] μέμψομαι / . . . .]η, πιστὸν γὰρ ἄνδρα καὶ φίλον / . . . . . . πρ]ọδοῦναι
δυςμ[εν]ῶς εἰλημμένον. / cαυτῶι τε,] Θηςεῦ, τῇ τ᾽ Ἀθηναίων πό[λει / πρέπονт᾽ ἔλεξας·
τοῖςι δυς[τυ]χοῦςι γάρ / ἀεί ποτ᾽ εἰ cὺ cύμμαχος· cκῆψιν [δ᾽ ἐμ]οί / ἀεικές ἐcτ᾽ ἔχοντα
πρὸς πάτραν μολεῖν. / Εὐρυςθέα γὰρ πῶς δοκεῖς ἄν, ἄςμενον / εἰ μοι πύθοιτο ταῦτα
cυμπράξαντα cε, λέξειν ἂν ὡς ἄκραντος ἤθληται πόνος; / ἀλλ᾽ οὐ cὺ χρῄζεις π[.
. . . .] ἐμὴν ἔχεις / εὔνοιαν, οὐκ ἔμπλ[ηκτον, ἀλλ᾽ ἐλ]ευθέρως / ἐχθροῖςί τ᾽ ἐχθρὰν
[καὶ φίλοιςι]ν εὐμενῆ. / πρόσθεν c᾽ ἐμοὶ τ[. . . . .]ει λόγος, / λέγοις δ᾽ ἂν [.
. . .] .   [   ]ους λόγους.

54. Fr. 964 N²: ἐγὼ δὲ <ταῦτα> παρὰ coφοῦ τινος μαθὼν / εἰς φροντίδας νοῦν
cυμφοράς τ᾽ ἐβαλλόμην, / φυγάς τ᾽ ἐμαυτῷ προστιθεὶς πάτρας ἐμῆς / θανάτους τ᾽ ἀώρους
καὶ κακῶν ἄλλας ὁδούς, / ἵν᾽ εἴ τι πάσχοιμ᾽ ὧν ἐδόξαζον φρενί, / μή μοι νεωρὲς προσπεσὸν
μᾶλλον δάκοι.

55. Mette, "Perithoos" 17; Sutton, *Two Lost Plays* 89–90.

56. Sutton, *Two Lost Plays* 93–98.

57. See Sutton, *Two Lost Plays* 100–104.

58. Fr. 10: {ὁ πρῶτος εἰπὼν} οὐκ ἀγυμνάστῳ φρενὶ / ἔρριψεν, ὅστις τόνδ᾽ ἐκαίνισεν
λόγον, / ὡς τοῖσιν εὖ φρονοῦσι cυμμαχεῖ τύχη

59. Fr. 11: τρόπος δὲ χρηστὸς ἀσφαλέστερος νόμου· / τὸν μὲν γὰρ οὐδεὶς ἂν διαστρέψαι
ποτε / ῥήτωρ δύναιτο, τὸν δ᾽ ἄνω τε καὶ κάτω / λόγοις ταράσσων πολλάκις λυμαίνεται

60. Fr. 12: οὔκουν τὸ μὴ ζῆν κρεῖσσόν ἐστ᾽ ἢ ζῆν κακῶς;

61. Welcker, *Griechische Tragödien* 591, who attributes the line to Herakles. Fr. 936
N²: οὔκ· ἀλλ᾽ ἔτ᾽ ἔμπνουν Ἀίδης μ᾽ ἐδέξατο.

62. "The buffoonish Dionysus of *Frogs*," writes Heath, "Aristophanes" 156, "was a more
common and stereotyped element in comedy than the surviving works of Aristophanes suggest." Heath mentions the following Old Comic examples: Magnes' *Dionysos* (two plays),
Kratinos' *Dionysalexandros*, Eupolis' *Taxiarkhoi*, Aristophanes' *Babylonioi* and *Dionysos
Nauagos*, Aristomenes' *Dionysos Asketes* (perhaps later than *Frogs*), Ameipsias' *Apokottabi-
zontes*, and a play by Hermippos. To this list we might add Kratinos' *Arkhilokhoi*, Platon's
Adonis, and perhaps Aristophanes' *Gerytades*. See Dover, *Frogs* 38–39. See also Bierl, *Dionysos*
27–44.

63. Heiden, "Tragedy and Comedy" 97, notes that "this funny Dionysos, far from representing the spirit of comedy as many have assumed, seems rather to represent a distinctly
anti-comic spirit." Heiden appears to require a character to have a sense of humor in order
to "represent" comedy, a criterion that would disqualify many Aristophanic protagonists!

64. Despite the possibility of reference to Euripides fr. 42 (*Alexandros*), the explicit
quotation at *Frogs* 100 (χρόνου πόδα, *Bakkhai* 889) indicates that the performance of the
tragedy at Athens preceded that of the comedy. The possibility of a precirculated script is
also worth considering.

65. C. P. Segal, "Character and Cults" 208–15.

66. Padilla, "Heraclean Dionysus" 360.

67. On this epithet and its cultic associations see Padilla, "Heraclean Dionysus" 363–64.

68. On the figure of Theseus as symbolizing two rather different modes of self-
understanding on the part of the Athenians suggested by *synoikia* (integration of Attic popu-
lation) and *metoikia* (acceptance of diversity in the form of outsiders), see Connor, "Theseus
and His City."

69. See Hooker, "Topography of the *Frogs*."

70. See Dover, *Frogs* 40, with note 11.

71. See Dover, *Frogs* 10–11.

72. This reticence with regard to the model of a sustained contrafact is quite normal if we consider *Frogs* alongside earlier plays. *Akharnians* comes closest to naming a specific play (cf. reference to "an old play," *Akharnians* 415, and the catalogue of protagonists, *Akharnians* 418–30). *Birds* and *Peace* are explicit about importing their respective characters (Tereus, Bellerophontes) from tragedy while making a point of advertising the author. *Frogs* is different only in its presentation of Herakles, who is not associated (verbally) with *Peirithous* or Euripides (but he is the source of the costume and the katabasis scenario, both of which are patently *theatrical*). The many other direct connections with *Peirithous*—the insistence on Euripides, the identity of the chorus, the Aiakos scene—amply make up for anything not spelled out or named in the script.

73. Moorton, "Andromeda" 434, argues that "Aristophanes used the mention of the Andromeda to achieve two important effects: (1) the creation of a comic analogy between Perseus/Andromeda and Dionysus/Euripides employed superficially to make an obscene joke and profoundly to assert the power of art; and (2) the establishment of the theme of peril from the sea, which haunts the play and ultimately affects its outcome."

74. Dover, *Frogs* ad loc.

75. On the issues surrounding the presentation of the chorus see Dover, *Frogs* 56–57, and Marshall, "Ambiguities Answered."

76. For this argument see Demand, "Identity of the *Frogs*."

77. For the liminal function of the topography of Hades and the action of the play, see Moorton, "Rites of Passage."

78. Wilamowitz-Moellendorff, *Analecta* 171.

79. Dover, *Frogs* 57–59: "It seems, therefore, that our chorus simultaneously παίζει in its function as a comic chorus and enacts a company of initiates παίζοντες in the under-world. This ambivalence is familiar elsewhere in Aristophanes, and the balance between theatrical function and dramatic enactment shifts from one passage to another."

80. See Burkert, *Greek Religion* 287–88.

81. Dover, *Frogs* 236 quotes Zimmermann's suggestion that "the most important asso-ciation of ionics was with archaic tragedy."

82. See Hubbard, *Mask of Comedy* 18–20.

83. On ritual abuse see Fluck, *Skurrile Riten*, passim. On the connection between iam-bic poetry and comedy see Rosen, *Iambographic Tradition*, passim. On the specific instances of ridicule in the parodos see Hubbard, *Mask of Comedy* 203–10.

84. For the various approaches to the problem of the "departure" of the chorus see Dover, *Frogs* 66–68.

85. See Hubbard, *Mask of Comedy* 16–23.

86. On the identity of the doorkeeper see Dover, *Frogs* 50–55. Dover's recent inclina-tion to skepticism is not shared by other commentators, including Alan Sommerstein in his commentary on the play.

87. Cf. lines 470–73, τοία Στυγός σε μελανοκάρδιος πέτρα / Ἀχερόντιος τε σκόπελος αἱματοσταγὴς / φρουροῦσι, Κωκυτοῦ τε περίδρομοι κύνες, with discussion in Sutton, *Two Lost Plays* 99–100, and Rau, *Paratragodia* 115–18, 202.

88. Dover, *Frogs* 254–55: "The closest analogies are the parodies of messenger-speeches in Ach. 1174–89 and Av. 1706–19."

89. But see Dover, *Frogs* 257.

90. Dover, *Frogs* 68.

91. The exclusion of Sophokles from the agon is clearly motivated by the fact that he would not fit (as one of the prisoners of Hades) in a comic replica of the Theseus-Peirithous dichotomy.

92. For a skeptical review of this connection, however, see Worthington, "'Frogs' and Arginusae."

93. See Hubbard, *Mask of Comedy* 208–12.

94. Dover, *Frogs* 69.

95. On the identity of this character see Dover, *Frogs* ad loc.

96. See Dover, *Frogs* 23.

97. "The Aeschylus of the agon is a rather nasty old man," notes Dover, *Frogs* 18, "of a kind one would try to avoid meeting in real life: sulky (832), spluttering with rage (840–59, 917; cf. 993–1003), impatient, menacing, contemptuous, relentlessly abusive."

98. Bierl, *Dionysos* 27–44. While Bierl's recognition of the importance of the meta-theatrical dimension of comedy and tragedy has been invaluable for my own project, he does not take up the intertextual relationship between *Frogs* and *Peirithous* (nor the other contra-facts presented in this book). As do C. P. Segal's and N. Slater's (forthcoming) studies on metatheater, Bierl's work demonstrates the breadth and flexibility of a metafictional approach in that many separate contributions (indeed studies of the very same text) can succeed with-out interfering or overlapping.

99. On the political implications of the possible restaging of *Frogs* see Sommerstein, "Kleophon" and Dover, *Frogs* 373–76.

Bibliography

Abbreviations

AC	*L'Antiquité Classique*
AJP	*American Journal of Philology*
ASNP	*Annali della Scuola Normale Superiore di Pisa, Classe di Lettere e Filosofia*
BICS	*Bulletin of the Institute of Classical Studies of the University of London*
CA	*Classical Antiquity*
CJ	*Classical Journal*
CP	*Classical Philology*
CQ	*Classical Quarterly*
CR	*Classical Review*
G&R	*Greece and Rome*
GRBS	*Greek, Roman and Byzantine Studies*
HSCP	*Harvard Studies in Classical Philology*
ICS	*Illinois Classical Studies*
JHS	*Journal of Hellenic Studies*
LÉC	*Les Études Classiques*
MH	*Museum Helveticum*
PCG	R. Kassel and C. Austin, *Poetae Comici Graeci* (Berlin, 1983-)
QUCC	Quaderni Urbinati di Cultura Classica
RE	G. Wissowa, ed., *Paulys Real-Encyclopädie der classischen Altertumswissenschaft* (Stuttgart, 1983-)
RÉA	*Revue des Études Anciennes*
RÉG	*Revue des Études Grecques*
RhM	*Rheinisches Museum*
TAPA	*Transactions of the American Philological Association*
WJA	*Würzburger Jahrbücher für die Altertumswissenschaft*
YCS	*Yale Classical Studies*
ZPE	*Zeitschrift für Papyrologie und Epigraphik*

Abel, Lionel. 1963. *Metatheatre: a New View of Dramatic Form*. New York.

Abraham, G. 1979. *The Concise Oxford History of Music*. Oxford.

Aélion, R. 1986. *Quelques grands mythes héroiques dans l'oeuvre d'Euripide*. Paris.

Ahl, Frederick. 1984. "The Art of Safe Criticism in Greece and Rome." *AJP* 105. 174–208.

———. 1985. *Metaformations: Soundplay and Wordplay in Ovid and Other Classical Poets*. Ithaca.

Alink, M. J. 1983. *De Vogels van Aristophanes: een structuuranalyse en interpretatie*. Amsterdam.

Anderson, Graham. 1984. *Ancient Fiction: The Novel in the Ancient World*. London.

Anderson, Warren D. 1966. *Ethos and Education in Greek Music*. Cambridge, Mass.

———. 1995. *Music and Musicians in Ancient Greece*. Ithaca.

Arnott, W. G. 1972. "From Aristophanes to Menander." *G&R* 19. 65–80.

———. 1973. "Euripides and the Unexpected." *Greece and Rome* 20. 49–64.

———. 1978. "Red Herrings and Other Bait: A Study in Euripidean Techniques." *Museum Philologum Londoniense* 3. 1–24.

———. 1982. "Off-Stage Cries and the Choral Presence." *Antichthon* 16. 35–43.

———. 1983. "Tensions, Frustrations, and Surprise: A Study of Theatrical Technique in Some Scenes from Euripides' *Orestes*." *Antichthon* 17. 13–28.

———. 1989. "Studies in Comedy, I: Alexis and the Parasite's Name." *GRBS* 9. 161–68.

———. 1993. "Comic Openings." In *Drama: Beiträge zum antiken Drama und seiner Rezeption. Band 2: Intertextualität in der griechisch-römischen Komödie.* 14–32.

———. 1993. "Some Bird Notes on Aristophanes' *Birds*." *Tria Lustra: Essay Presented to the Editor of the* Liverpool Classical Monthly *on the occasion of its 150th Issue*. Ed. H. D. Jocelyn (Liverpool Classical Papers 3; Liverpool). 127–34.

Arrowsmith, William. 1973. "Aristophanes' *Birds* and the Fantasy Politics of Eros," *Arion* n.s.1. 71–102.

Arthur, Marilyn. 1972. "The Choral Odes of the *Bacchae* of Euripides." *YCS* 22. 145–79.

Atkinson, J. E. 1992. "Curbing the Comedians: Cleon Versus Aristophanes and Syracosious' Decree." *CQ* 42. 56–64.

Austin, Norman. 1994. *Helen of Troy and Her Shameless Phantom*. Ithaca.

Bacon, Helen. 1961. *Barbarians in Greek Tragedy*. New Haven.

Bain, David. 1987. "Some Reflections on the Illusion in Greek Tragedy." *BICS* 34. 1–14.

———. 1975. "Audience Address in Greek Tragedy." *CQ* 25. 13–25.

———. 1977. *Actors and Audience*. Oxford.

Barchiesi, M. 1970. "Plauto e il 'metateatro' antico." *Il Verri* 31. 113–30.

Barker, Andrew, ed. 1984. *Greek Musical Writings I: The Musician and His Art*. Cambridge.

Barthes, Roland. 1970. "L'ancienne rhetorique." *Communications* 16. 170–97.

Batchelder, Ann G. 1995. *The Seal of Orestes: Self-Reference and Authority in Sophocles' Electra*. Lanham, Md.

Belifore. Elizabeth. 1988. "ΠΕΡΙΠΕΤΕΙΑ as Discontinuous Action." *CP* 83.3. 183– 94.

Bertelli, L. 1983. "L'utopia sulla scena di Aristofane e la parodia della città." *Civiltà classica e cristiana* 9. 215–61.

Bierl, Anton. 1990. "Dionysus, Wine, and Tragic Poetry: A Metatheatrical Reading of *P. Köln* VI 242A=TrGF II F646a." *GRBS* 31. 353–91.

———. 1991. *Dionysos und die griechische Tragödie. Politische und 'metatheatralische' Aspekte im Text*. Tübingen.

Blaiklock, E. M. 1952. *The Male Characters of Euripides*. Wellington.

Bömer, Franz. 1976. *P. Ovidius Naso Metamorphosen*. Vol. 3: books 6–7. Heidelberg.

Bonanno, M. G. 1972. *Studi su Cratete comico*. Padua.

———. 1987. "Paratragodia in Aristofane." *Dioniso* 57. 135–67.

Borthwick, E. K. 1968. "Notes on the Plutarch *De musica* and the *Cheiron* of Pherecrates." *Hermes* 96. 60–73.

Bowersock, G. W. 1994. *Fiction as History: Nero to Julian*. Berkeley.

Bowie, A. M. 1993. *Aristophanes: Myth, Ritual, and Comedy*. Cambridge.

Bradshaw, D. J. 1991. "The Ajax Myth and the Polis: Old Values and New." In Pozzi and Wickersham, *Myth and the Polis* 99–125.

Brommer, F. 1973. *Vasenlisten zur Griechischen Heldensage*. 3rd ed. Marburg.

Broneer, O. 1944. "The Tent of Xerxes and the Greek Theatre." *University of California Publications in Classical Archaeology* I, 12. 305–12.

Buchwald, Wolfgang. 1939. "Studien zur Chronologie der attischen Tragödie 455 bis 431." Diss. Königsberg.

Burkert, Walter. 1985. *Greek Religion*. John Raffan tr. Cambridge, Mass.

Burnett, A. P. 1971. *Catastrophe Survived*. Chicago.

Calder, William M., III. 1974. "Sophocles' *Tereus*: A Thracian Tragedy." *Thracia* 2. 87–91.

Calderwood, James L. 1971. *Shakespearean Metadrama: The Argument of the Play in* Titus Andronicus, Love's Labours Lost, Romeo and Juliet, A Midsummer Night's Dream, *and* Richard III. Minneapolis.

———. 1979. *Metadrama in Shakespeare's Henriad: Richard II to Henry V*. Berkeley.

———. 1983. *To Be and Not To Be: Negation and Metadrama in Hamlet*. New York.

Cambitoglou, A., and A. D. Trendall. 1961. *Apulian Red-Figured Vase-Painters of the Plain Style*. N.p.: Archaeological Institute of America.

Carey, C. 1994. "Comic Ridicule and Democracy." In R. Osborne and S. Hornblower, eds. *Ritual, Finance, Politics: Athenian Democratic Accounts Presented to David Lewis*. Oxford. 69–83.

Carpenter, Thomas H. 1997. *Dionysian Imagery in Fifth-Century Athens*. Oxford.

Carpenter, Thomas H., and Christopher A. Farone, eds. 1993. *Masks of Dionysus*. Ithaca.

Carrière, Jean. 1956. "Sur la choréographie des *Oiseaux* d'Aristophane." *REA* 58. 211–35.

Carter, L. B. 1986. *The Quiet Athenian*. Oxford.

Cartledge, Paul. 1990. "Fowl Play." In Cartledge et al., *Nomos* 41–63.

Cartledge, Paul, Paul Millett, and Stephen Todd, eds. 1990. *Nomos: Essays in Athenian Law, Politics and Society*. Cambridge.

Cazzaniga, Ignazio. 1950. *La saga di Itis nella tradizione letteraria e mitografica greco-romana, I: Da Omero a Nonno Panopolitano*. Verona.

Chailley, Jacques. 1979. *La musique grecque antique*. Paris.

Chandler, A. 1935. "The Nightingale in Greek and Latin Poetry." *CJ* 30. 78–84.

Chapman, G. A. H. 1983. "Some Notes on Dramatic Illusion in Aristophanes." *AJP* 104. 1–23.

Cockle, H. M. 1983. "Pap. Oxy. 3531: Euripides (or Critias), *Pirithous*." In *The Oxyrhynchus Papyri*. Vol 50. London: Egypt Exploration Fund.

Collard, C., M. J. Cropp, and K. H. Lee. 1995. *Euripides: Selected Fragmentary Plays*. Vol. 1. Edited with Introductions, Translations and Commentaries by C. Collard, M. J. Cropp, and K. H. Lee. Warminster.

Conacher, D. J. 1980. *Aeschylus' Prometheus Bound: A Literary Commentary*. Toronto.

Connor, W. R. 1996. "Theseus and His City." in Pontus Hellstrom and Brita Alroth, eds. *Religion and Power in the Ancient Greek World*. Proceedings of the Uppsala Symposium. Uppsala. 115–20.

———. 1970. "Theseus in Classical Athens." In A. Ward et al., eds. *The Quest for Theseus*. London. 143–74.

———. 1971. *The New Politicians of Fifth-Century Athens*. Princeton.

———. 1989. "City Dionysia and Athenian Democracy." *Classica et Mediaevalia* 40. 7–32.

Coulon, Victor, ed. 1923–30. *Aristophane*. Paris. Société d'Édition "Les Belles Lettres."

Csapo, E. 1986. "A Note on the Würzburg Bell-Crater H5697 ('Telephus Travestitus')." *Phoenix* 40. 379–92.

Csapo, E., and W. J. Slater. 1995. *The Context of Ancient Drama*. Ann Arbor.

Culler, Jonathan. 1975. *Structuralist Poetics: Structuralism, Linguistics, and the Study of Literature*. Ithaca.

Danov, Khristo Miloshev. 1976. *Altthrakien*. Berlin.

David, E. 1984. *Aristophanes and Athenian Society in the Early Fourth Century B.C. Mnemosyne* Supplement 81. Leiden.

Davidson, J. F. 1995. "Homer and Sophocles' *Philoctetes*." In *Stage Directions: Essays in Ancient Drama in Honour of E. W. Handley*. Ed. by Alan Griffiths. BICS Supplement 656. 25–35.

Davis, Michael. 1986. "Politics and Madness." In Euben, *Greek Tragedy and Political Theory* 142–61.

Dawe, R. D. 1985. *Sophokles*. Teubner.

Dawson, W. R. 1925. "The Lore of the Hoopoe (Upupa Epops L.)." *Ibis* 67. 31–39.

Dean-Jones, Lesley. 1992. "The Politics of Pleasure: Female Sexual Appetite in the Hippocratic Corpus." In Stanton, *Discourses of Sexuality* 48–77.

Delebecque, Edouard. 1951. *Euripide et la guerre du Péloponnèse*. Paris.

Demand, Nancy. 1970. "The Identity of the *Frogs*." CP 65. 83–87.

Denniston, J. D. 1927. "Technical Terms in Aristophanes." CQ 21. 113–21.

de Romilly, Jacqueline. 1973. "Gorgias et le pouvoir de la poésie." *JHS* 93. 155–62.

Derrida, Jacques. 1978. *Writing and Difference*. Chicago.

de Ste. Croix, G. E. M. 1972. *The Origins of the Peloponnesian War*. London.

Detienne, Marcel. 1987. "The Voice and the Book of Orpheus," Townsend Lecture No. 4. Translated by Richard Klein. Cornell, March 10, 1987.

———. 1989. *L'écriture d'Orphée*. Paris.

Detienne, Marcel, and J. P. Vernant. 1978. *Cunning Intelligence in Greek Culture and Society*. Translated by Janet Lloyd. Brighton.

Diels, H., and W. Kranz, eds. 1951–52. *Die Fragmente der Vorsokratiker*. 3 vols. 6th ed. Berlin and Zürich.

di Gregorio, Lamberto. 1983a. "Il 'Bellerofonte' di Euripide: I. dati per una recostruzione." *CCC* 4.2. 159–213.

———. 1983b. "Il 'Bellerofonte' di Euripide: II. tentativo di recostruzione." *Civilta Classica e Cristiana* 4.3. 365–82.

Diller, Hans. 1968. "Die *Bakchen* und ihre Stellung im Spätwerk des Euripides." In Schwinge, *Euripides* 469–92.

Dillon, Matthew J. 1985. "Aristophanes' *Ploutos*: Comedy in Transition." Diss. Yale.

Dobrov, Gregory W. 1988. "Winged Words: The Aristophanic Comedy of Language." Diss. Cornell.

———. 1990. "Aristophanes' *Birds* and the Metaphor of Deferral." *Arethusa* 23.2. 209–33.

———. 1993. "The Tragic and the Comic Tereus." AJP 14.2. 189–234.

———. 1995. "The Poet's Voice in the Evolution of Dramatic Dialogism." In Dobrov, *Beyond Aristophanes* 47–97.

———. ed. 1995. *Beyond Aristophanes: Transition and Diversity in Greek Comedy*. Atlanta.

———. 1997a. "Language, Fiction and Utopia." In Dobrov, *City as Comedy* 95–132.

———. 1997b. *The City as Comedy: Society and Representation in Athenian Drama*. Chapel Hill.

Dobrov, G. W., and Eduardo Urios Aparisi. 1995. "The Maculate Music: Pherecrates and Comedy's Evolving Response to the Dithyramb." in Dobrov, *Beyond Aristophanes* 139–73.

Dodds, E. R. 1951. *The Greeks and the Irrational*. Berkeley.

——. 1960. *Bacchae*. 2nd ed. Oxford.

——. 1983. "On Misunderstanding the *Oedipus Rex*." In E. Segal, ed., *Greek Tragedy: Modern Essays in Criticism*. New York. 177–88.

Dolan, Jill. 1988. *The Feminist Spectator as Critic*. Ann Arbor.

Dover, K. J. 1968. *Aristophanes' Clouds, Edited with Introduction and Commentary by K. J. Dover*. Oxford.

——. 1973. *Aristophanic Comedy*. Berkeley.

——. 1987. *Greek and the Greeks*. Vol. 1. New York.

——. 1993. *Aristophanes' Frogs, Edited with Introduction and Commentary by K. J. Dover*. Oxford.

Downing, Eric. 1990. "*Apatê, Agôn*, and Literary Self-Reflexivity in Euripides' *Helen*." In Mark Griffith and Donald Mastronarde, edd. *Cabinet of the Muses: Essays on Classical and Comparative Literature in Honor of Thomas G. Rosenmeyer*. Atlanta. 1–16.

Dunbar, Nan. 1995. *Aristophanes' Birds, Edited with Introduction and Commentary by Nan Dunbar*. Oxford.

Dunn, Francis M. 1996. *Tragedy's End: Closure and Innovation in Euripidean Drama*. Oxford.

Düring, Ingemar. 1945. "Studies in Musical Terminology in the 5th Century Literature." *Eranos* 43. 176–97.

Easterling, Patricia E. 1978. "*Philoctetes* and Modern Criticism." *Illinois Classical Studies* III. 27–39.

——. 1993. "Tragedy and Ritual." In Scodel, *Theater and Society* 7–23.

Edmonds, J. M. 1957. *The Fragments of Attic Comedy*. Vol. 1: Old Comedy. Leiden.

Egan, Robert. 1975. *Drama within Drama: Shakespeare's Sense of His Art in* King Lear, The Winter's Tale, *and* The Tempest. New York.

Elam, Keir. 1980. *The Semiotics of Theatre and Drama*. London.

Else, Gerald. 1967. *The Origin and Early Form of Greek Tragedy*. Cambridge, Mass.

Etman, Ahmed. 1987. "The Audience of the Graeco-Roman Drama Between Illusion and Reality." In Ghiron-Bistagne, *Anthropologie et Théâtre* 261–72.

Euben, Peter, ed. 1986. *Greek Tragedy and Political Theory*. Berkeley.

Evans, A. 1988. *The God of Ecstasy: Sex-Roles and the Madness of Dionysos*. New York.

Falkner, Thomas. 1993. "Making a Spectacle of Oneself: The Metatheatrical Design of Sophocles' *Ajax*." *Text and Presentation: The Journal of the Comparative Drama Conference* 14. 35–40.

Fischer, H. A. 1851. *Bellerophon: eine mythologische Abhandlung*. Leipzig.

Fisher, N. R. E. 1993. "Multiple Personalities and Dionysiac Festivals: Dicaeopolis in Aristophanes' *Acharnians*." *G&R* 40.1. 31–47.

Flashar, Helmut. 1975. "Zur Eigenart des Aristophanischen Spätwerks." In Newiger, *Aristophanes und die alte Komödie* 425–28.

Fluck, H. 1931. *Skurrile Riten in griechischen Kulten*. Endigen.

Foley, Helene. 1980. "The Masque of Dionysus." *TAPA* 110. 107–33.

——. 1985. *Ritual Irony: Poetry and Sacrifice in Euripides*. Ithaca.

——. 1988. "Tragedy and Politics in Aristophanes' *Acharnians*." *JHS* 108.33–47.

——. 1992. "*Anodos* Dramas: Euripides' *Alcestis* and *Helen*." In Ralph Hexter and Daniel Selden, eds. *Innovations in Antiquity*. London. 133–60.

——. ed. 1981. *Reflections of Women in Antiquity*. New York.

Fontenrose, J. E. 1948. "The Sorrows of Ino and Procne." *TAPA* 79. 125–67.

Forbes-Irving, P. M. C. 1990. *Metamorphosis in Greek Myths*. Oxford.

Fraenkel, Eduard. 1962. *Beobachtungen zu Aristophanes*. Rome.

——. 1964. *Kleine Beiträge* I. Rome.

Führer, Rudolf. 1967. *Formproblem-Untersuchungen su den Reden in der frühgriechischen Lyrik*. München.

Gantz, Timothy. 1993. *Early Greek Myth: A Guide to Literary and Artistic Sources*. Baltimore.

Garnison, Elise P. 1995. *Groaning Tears: Ethical and Dramatic Aspects of Suicide in Greek Tragedy*. Leiden.

Garzya, Antonio. 1962. *Pensiero e tecnica drammatica in Euripide: Saggio sul motivo della salvazione*. Naples.

——. 1987. "Gorgias et l'apate de la tragedie." In Ghiron-Bistagne, *Anthropologie et Théâtre* 149–66.

Geertz, Clifford. 1973. *The Interpretation of Cultures: Selected Essays*. New York.

Geissler, P. 1925. *Chronologie der Altattischen Komödie*. Berlin.

Gellie, G. H. 1981. "Tragedy and Euripides' *Electra*." *BICS* 28. 1–12.

Gelzer, Thomas. 1960. *Der epirrhematische Agon bei Aristophanes. Untersuchungen zur Struktur der attischen Alten Komödie*. Munich.

——. 1976a. "Some Aspects of Aristophanes' Dramatic Art in the *Birds*." *BICS* 23. 1–14.

——. 1976b. "Sophokles' *Tereus*, eine Inhaltsangabe auf Papyrus." In *Jahresbericht der Schweizerischen Geisteswissenschaftlichen Gesellschaft*. 183–92.

Genette, Gérard. 1980. *Narrative Discourse*. Ithaca.

——. 1982. *Palimpsestes: La littérature au second degree*. Paris.

Gentili, Bruno. 1979. *Theatrical Performances in the Ancient World: Hellenistic and Early Roman Theatre*. Amsterdam.

——. 1988. *Poetry and Its Public in Ancient Greece*. Translated by A. T. Cole. Baltimore.

Gentili, Bruno, and R. Pretagostini. 1986. *La musica in Grecia*. Rome.

Gernet, Louis. 1935. *Mélanges offertes à O. Navarre*. Toulouse.

Ghiron-Bistagne, Paulette. 1987. *Anthropologie et Théâtre antique: Actes du colloque international de Montpellier 6–8 mars 1986*. Cahiers du Gita no. 3—Octobre 1987. Montpellier.

Gilbert, Sandra M. 1980. "Costumes of the Mind: Transvestism as Metaphor in Modern Literature." *Critical Inquiry* 7. 391–418.

Gill, C., and T. P. Wiseman, eds. 1993. *Lies and Fiction in the Ancient World*. Austin.

Ginouvès, Rene. 1962. *Balaneutiké: Recherches sur le bain dans l' antiquité grecque*. Paris.

Girard, René. 1977. *Violence and the Sacred*. Translated by Patrick Gregory. Baltimore.

Goff, Barbara. 1990. *The Noose of Words: Readings of Desire, Violence, and Language in Euripides' Hippolytos*. Cambridge.

——. 1991. "The Sign of the Fall: The Scars of Orestes and Odysseus." *Classical Antiquity* 10.2. 259–67.

——. ed. 1995. *History, Tragedy, Theory: Dialogues on Athenian Drama*. Austin.

Goffman, Erving. 1974. *Frame Analysis: An Essay on the Organization of Experience*. New York.

Goldhill, Simon. 1986. *Reading Greek Tragedy*. Cambridge.

——. "The Great Dionysia and Civic Ideology." In Winkler and Zeitlin, *Dionysos* 97–129.

——. 1990a. *The Poet's Voice: Essays on Poetics and Greek Literature*. Cambridge.

——. 1990b. "Character and Action, Representation and Reading Greek Tragedy and Its Critics." In Pelling, *Characterization and Individuality* 100–127.

———. 1994. "The Failure of Exemplarity." In J. F. de Jong and J. P. Sullivan, eds. *Modern Critical Theory and Classical Literature*. Leiden.

Goldhill, Simon, and R. Osborne, eds. 1994. *Art and Text in Ancient Greek Culture*. Cambridge.

Goldman, Michael. 1975. *The Actor's Freedom: Toward a Theory of Drama*. New York.

Goosen, H. 1938. "Die Tiere bei den griechischen Lyrikern." *Sudhoffs Archiv: Vierteljahrschrift für Geschichte der Medizin und Naturwissenschaften, der Pharmazie und der Mathematik* 30. Heft 6.300–40.

Graf, Fritz. 1974. *Eleusis und die orphische Dichtung Athens in vorhellenistischer Zeit*. Berlin.

Green, J. R. 1985. "A Representation of the *Birds* of Aristophanes." *Greek Vases in the J. Paul Getty Museum* 2. 95–118.

———. 1989. "Theatre Production 1971–86." *Lustrum* 31. 7–95.

———. 1991. "On Seeing and Depicting the Theatre in Classical Athens." *GRBS* 32. 15–50.

———. 1994. *Theatre in Ancient Greek Society*. London.

Greenblatt, Stephen. 1980. *Renaissance Self-Fashioning: From More to Shakespeare*. Chicago.

Greengard, C. 1987. *Theatre in Crisis: Sophocles' Reconstruction of Genre and Politics in Philoctetes*. Amsterdam.

Griffith, Mark. 1995. "Brilliant Dynasts: Power and Politics in the *Oresteia*." *CA* 14.1. 62–129.

Griffith, R. Drew. 1987. "The Hoopoe's Name: A Note on *Birds* 48." *QUCC* 55. 59–63.

Grube, G. M. 1961. *The Drama of Euripides*. 2nd ed. London.

Gruber, William E. 1981. "The Wild Men of Comedy: Transformation in the Comic Hero from Aristophanes to Pirandello," *Genre* 14. 207–27.

———. 1983. "Systematized Delirium. The Craft, Form, and Meaning of Aristophanic Comedy." *Helios* 10. 97–110.

———. 1986. *Comic Theaters: Studies in Performance and Audience Response*. Athens, GA.

Guthrie, W. K. C. 1961–81. *A History of Greek Philosophy*. Cambridge.

———. 1971. *The Sophists*. (= part I, vol. 3, Cambridge)

Hall, Edith. 1989. *Inventing the Barbarian: Greek Self-Definition through Tragedy*. Oxford.

———. 1996. *Aeschylus' Persians Edited with Introduction and Commentary by Edith Hall*. Warminster.

Halliday, W. R. 1933. *Indo-European Folk-Tales and Greek Legend*. Cambridge.

Halliwell, S. 1984. "Ancient Interpretations of ὀνομαστὶ κωμῳδεῖν in Aristophanes." *CQ* 30. 33–45.

Händel, P. 1963. *Formen und Darstellungsweisen in der Aristophanischen Komödie*. Heidelberg.

Handley, Eric W., and John Rea. 1957. *The Telephus of Euripides. BICS* Supplement 5. London.

Harriot, R. M. 1982. "The Function of the Euripides Scene in Aristophanes' *Acharnians*." *G&R* 29. 39ff.

Harrison, Jane E. 1887. "Itys and Aedon: A Panaitios Cylix." *JHS* 8. 439–45.

Harsh, P. W. 1934. "The Position of the Parabasis in the Plays of Aristophanes." *TAPA* 65. 178–97.

Hartung, I. A. 1843. *Euripides restitutus*. Vol. 1. Hamburg.

Haslam, M. W. 1975. "The Authenticity of Euripides, *Phoenissae* 1–2 and Sophocles *Electra* 1." *GRBS* 16. 149–74.

Heath, Malcolm. 1987a. "Euripides' *Telephus*." *CQ* 37. 272–80.

———. 1987b. *The Poetics of Greek Tragedy*. London.

———. 1989. "Aristotelian Comedy." *CQ* 39. 344–54.

——. 1990. "Aristophanes and His Rivals." *G&R* 37.2. 143–58.

Heiden, Bruce. 1991. "Tragedy and Comedy in the *Frogs* of Aristophanes." *Ramus* 20. 95–111.

Helbo, André. 1975. *Sémiologie de la représentation*. Complexe.

Henderson, Jeffrey. 1987. *Aristophanes' Lysistrata, Edited with Introduction and Commentary by Jeffrey Henderson*. Oxford.

——. 1990a. "The Demos and the Comic Competition." In Winkler and Zeitlin, *Dionysos* 271–313.

——. 1990b. "Peisetairos and the Athenian Elite." Paper read at the 123rd Annual Meeting of the American Philological Association (1990).

——. 1991. *The Maculate Muse: Obscene Language in Attic Comedy*. 2nd ed. Oxford.

——. 1993. "Comic Hero Versus Political Elite." In Sommerstein et al., eds. *Tragedy, Comedy, and the Polis* 307–19.

——. 1997. "Mass versus Elite and the Comic Heroism of Peisetairos." In Dobrov, *City as Comedy*, 135–48.

Henrichs, Albert. 1984. "Male Intruders Among the Maenads: The So-Called Male Celebrant." In H. D. Evjen, ed. *Mnemai: Classical Studies in Memory of Karl K. Hulley* 69–91. Chico, Calif.

——. 1984. "Loss of Self, Suffering, Violence: The Modern Views of Dionysus from Nietzsche to Girard." *HSCP* 88. 205–40.

——. 1995. "Why Should I Dance? Choral Self- Referentiality in Greek Tragedy." *Arion*, Third Series 3.1. 56–111.

——. 1996a. *Warum soll ich denn tanzen? Dionysisches im Chor der Griechischen Tragödie*. Lectio Tebneriana IV. Leipzig.

——. 1996b. "Dancing in Athens, Dancing on Delos: Some Patterns of Choral Projection in Euripides." *Philogus* 140. 48–62.

Henry, Madeleine M. 1985. *Menander's Courtesans and the Greek Comic Tradition*. Frankfurt am Main.

Herington, C. J. 1963. "A Study in the *Prometheia*, Part II: *Birds* and *Prometheia*." *Phoenix* 17. 236–43.

Hernadi, Paul. 1985. *Interpreting Events: Tragicomedies of History on the Modern Stage*. Ithaca.

Hiller von Gärtringen, Friedrich F. 1886. *De Graecorum fabulis ad Thraces pertinentibus quaestiones criticae*. Berlin.

Hofmann, Heinz. 1976. *Mythos und Komödie: Untersuchungen zu den Vögeln des Aristophanes*. Spudasmata 33. New York.

Holmberg, Ingrid. 1995. "Euripides' *Helen*: Most Noble and Most Chaste." *AJP* 116. 19–42.

Holzinger, Karl. 1940. *Kritisch-exegetischer Kommentar zu Aristophanes' Plutos*. SAWW Band 218. Vienna and Leipzig.

Hooker, G. T. W. 1960. "The Topography of the *Frogs*." *JHS* 80. 112–17.

Hoppin, Meredith C. 1990. "Metrical Effects, Dramatic Illusion, and the Two Endings of Sophocles' *Philoctetes*." *Arethusa* 23.2. 242–82.

Hornblower, Simon. 1987. *Thucydides*. Baltimore.

Hornsby, Richard. 1986. *Drama, Metadrama, and Perception*. Lewisburg.

Hourmouziades, N. C. 1965. *Production and Imagination in Euripides*. Athens.

——. 1987. "Sophocles' *Tereus*." In J. Betts, H. Hooker, J. Green, eds. *Studies in Honor of T. B. L. Webster*. Vol. 2. Bristol. 134–42.

Hubbard, Thomas K. 1991. *The Mask of Comedy: Aristophanes and the Intertextual Parabasis*. Ithaca.

Hubert, Judd D. 1991. *Metatheater: The Example of Shakespeare*. Lincoln.

Huizinga, Johan. 1949. *Homo Ludens: A Study of the Play-Element in Culture*. London.

Hunter, R. L. 1981. "P. Lit. Lond. 77 and Tragic Burlesque in Attic Comedy." ZPE 41. 19–24.

——. 1983. *Eubulus: The Fragments*. Cambridge.

——. 1985. *The New Comedy of Greece and Rome*. Cambridge.

Hutcheon, Linda. 1991. *Narcissistic Narrative: The Metafictional Paradox*. New York. (*University Paperback* edition.)

——. 1985. *A Theory of Parody: Teachings of Twentieth-Century Art Forms*. New York.

——. 1989. *The Politics of Postmodernism*. New York.

Jebb, Richard C. 1896. *Sophocles: The Plays and Fragments. Part VII. The* Ajax. Cambridge.

Jens, W., ed. 1971. *Die Bauformen von griechischen Tragödie*. Münich.

Johansen, H. Friis. 1972. "Sophocles 1939–1959." *Lustrum* 7. 94–288.

Johnstone, Keith. 1981. *Improvisation and the Theatre*. London.

Joplin, P. K. 1984. "The Voice of the Shuttle is Ours." *Stanford Literature Review* 1.1. 25–53.

Jouan, Francois. 1966. *Euripide et les légendes des Chants Cypriens, des origines de la guerre de Troie a l'Iliade*. Paris.

Juffras, Diane M. 1993. "Helen and Other Victims in Euripides' *Helen*." *Hermes* 121. 45–57.

Just, Roger. 1989. *Women in Athenian Law and Life*. London.

Kamerbeek, J. C. 1953. *The Plays of Sophocles. Part I: The* Ajax. Leiden.

Kanellis, A. 1969. *Catalogus Faunae Graeciae. Pars II: Aves*. W. Bauer et al., ed. Thessaloniki.

Kannicht, R., and B. Snell, edd. 1982. *Tragicorum Graecorum Fragmenta*. Vol 2. Göttingen.

Kassel, Rudolf. 1985. "Hypothesis." In W. J. Aerts, J. H. A. Lokin, S. L. Radt, N. van der Wal, eds. *ΣΧΟΛΙΑ: Studia ad criticam interpretationemque textuum graecorum et ad historiam iuris graeco- romani pertinentia viro doctissimo D. Holwerda oblata*. Groningen. 53–59.

Kassel, Rudolf. 1991. *Kleine Schriften*. Edited by Heinz-Günther Nesselrath. Berlin.

Kassel, Rudolf, and Colin Austin. 1983– . *Poetae Comici Graeci*. Berlin.

Katz, B. 1976. "The *Birds* of Aristophanes and Politics." *Athenaeum* 54. 53–81.

Kernan, Alvin B. 1979. *The Playwright as Magician: Shakespeare's Image of the Poet in the English Public Theatre*. New Haven.

Keuls, Eva. 1985. *The Reign of the Phallus*. New York.

Kiso, Akiko. 1984. *The Lost Sophocles*. New York.

Kitto, H. D. 1960. *Greek Tragedy*. London.

Klima, E., Bellugi, U., et al. 1979. *The Signs of Language*. Cambridge, Mass.

Knox, Bernard. 1961. "The *Ajax* of Sophocles." HSCP 65. 1–39.

——. 1979. "Euripidean Comedy." In *Word and Action: Essays on the Ancient Theatre*. Baltimore. 250–74.

Kock, Theodor. 1880–88. *Comicorum Atticorum Fragmenta*. 3 vols. Leipzig.

——. ed. 1927. *Ausgewählte Komödien des Aristophanes*. Vol. 4: *Die Vögel*. 4th ed. Revised by Otto Schroeder. Berlin.

Koenen, Ludwig. 1959. "Tereus in den *Vögeln* des Aristophanes." In Hellfried Dahlmann and Reinhold Merkelbach, eds. *Studien zu Textgeschichte und Textkritik* 83–87. Cologne.

Koenen, Ludwig, and Sara Bonnycastle. Forthcoming. "Euripides' *Kresphontes*." In S. Bonnycastle, T. Gagos, and L. Koenen, *Restoring Greek Drama*. Ann Arbor.

Komornicka, A. M. 1967. "Quelques remarques sur la parodie dans les comédies d' Aristophane." QUCC 3. 51–74.

Konstan, David. 1990. "Aristophanes' *Birds* and the City in the Air." *Arethusa* 23.2. 183–207.

——. 1995. *Greek Comedy and Ideology*. Oxford.

Konstan, David, and Matthew J. Dillon. 1981. "The Ideology of Aristophanes' *Wealth*." AJP 102. 371–94.

Körte, Alfred. 1938. "Pherekrates." In *Paulys Real Encyclopädie der classischen Altertumswissenschaft* 19.2. 1985–91.

Kovacs, David. 1989. "Euripides, *Electra* 518–44: Further Doubts about Genuineness." *BICS* 36. 67–78.

Kowzan, Tadeusz. 1975. *Littérature et spectacle*. Mouton, the Hague.

———. 1983. "Les comédies d' Aristophane, véhicule de la critique dramatique." *Dioniso* 54. 83–100.

Kraggerud, Egil. 1990. "Apollon als Regisseur: zur Problematik der euripideischen *Alkestis*." In Teodorsson Sven-Tage, ed., *Greek and Latin Studies in Memory of Caius Fabricius*. Studia Graeca et Latina Gothoburgensia No. 54; Acta Universitatis Gothoburgensiae. Göttingen. 97–109.

Kraus, Walther. 1985. *Aristophanes' politische Komödien*. Vienna.

Kuiper, J. 1907. "De Pirithoo Fabula Euripidea." *Mnemosyne* n.s. 35. 356–59.

Lacan, Jacques. 1968. *Speech and Language in Psychoanalysis*. Translated with notes and commentary by Anthony Wilden. Baltimore.

Lakoff, George. 1980. *Metaphors We Live By*. Chicago.

Lamberton, Robert, and S. I. Rotroff. 1985. *Birds of the Athenian Agora*. Excavations of the Athenian Agora, Picture Book no. 22. Princeton.

Langerbeck, Hermann. 1963. "Die Vorstellung vom Schlaraffenland in der alten attischen Komödie." *Zeitschrift für Volkskunde* 59. 192–204.

Laroque, François, ed. 1990. *The Show Within: Dramatic and Other Insets. English Renaissance Drama (1550–1642)*. Proceedings of the International Conference held in Montpellier, 22–25 November, 1990.

Lawler, Lilian. 1942. "Four Dancers in the *Birds* of Aristophanes." *TAPA* 73. 58–63.

Lesky, Albin. 1983. *Greek Tragic Poetry*. Translated by M. Dillon. New Haven.

———. 1966. *A History of Greek Literature*. Translated by James Willis and Cornelis de Heer. New York.

Liddell, H. G., and R. Scott. 1940. *A Greek-English Lexicon*. Revised by H. Stuart Jones. Oxford. 9th edition.

Lissarague, François. 1990. "Why Satyrs Are Good to Represent." In Winkler and Zeitlin, *Dionysos* 228–36.

Lloyd, Michael. 1992. *The Agon in Euripides*. Oxford.

Lloyd-Jones, Hugh. 1961. "Some Alleged Interpolations in Aeschylus' *Choephoroi* and Euripides' *Electra*." *CQ* 11. 171–84.

———. 1967. "Heracles at Eleusis: P.Oxy. 2622 and P.S.I. 1391." *Maia* 19. 206–29.

———. 1996. *Sophocles: Fragments*. (Loeb Classical Library. *Sophocles* III.) Edited and Translated by Hugh Lloyd-Jones. Cambridge, Mass.

Lloyd-Jones, Hugh, and N. G. Wilson. 1990. *Sophoclis Fabulae*. Oxford.

Long, Timothy. 1978. "Pherecrates' *Savages*: A Footnote to the Greek Attitude on the Noble Savage." *CW* 71. 381–82.

Lonsdale, Steven. 1993. *Dance and Ritual Play in Greek Religion*. Baltimore.

Luppe, Wolfgang. 1985. "Dikairchos' *hypotheseis tôn Euripidou mythôn* (mit einem Beitrag zur *Troades*-Hypothesis). In *Aristoteles Werk und Wirkung* I. Vol. I, *Aristoteles und seine Schule*, 610–15. Berlin.

MacDowell, Douglas M. 1971. *Aristophanes' Wasps, Edited with Introduction and Commentary, and Appendixes by Douglas MacDowell*. Oxford.

———. 1983. "The Nature of Aristophanes' *Akharnians*." *G&R* 30.143–62.

———. 1995. *Aristophanes and Athens: An Introduction to the Plays*. Oxford.

MacMathuna, Seamus. 1971. "Trickery in Aristophanes." Diss. Cornell.

Maitland, Judith. 1993. "Tripping the Light Fantastic: Treading the Gender Boundaries in Aristophanes' *Ecclesiazusae*." *Drama* 2: *Intertextualität in der griechisch-römischen Komödie* 212–21.

Maquerlot, Jean-Pierre. 1990. "Playing Within the Play: Towards a Semiotics of Metadrama and Metatheatre." In Laroque, *The Show Within* 39–49.

March, Jennifer R. 1989. *The Creative Poet*. BICS Suppl. 49. London.

———. 1989. "Euripides' *Bakchai*: A Reconsideration in the Light of Vase Paintings." *BICS* 36. 33–65.

Marshall, C. W. 1996. "Amphibian Ambiguities Answered." *EMC* 40n.s. 15. 251– 65.

Martin, R. A. 1989. "Metatheater, Gender, and Subjectivity in *Richard II* and *Henry IV*, Part I." *Comparative Drama* 23. 255–64.

Marzullo, B. 1970. "L'interlocuzione negli *Uccelli* di Aristofane." *Philologus* 114. 181–91.

Massenzio, Marcello. 1970. *Cultura e crisi permanente: la xenia dionisiaca*. Rome.

Matthews, Gary. 1993. "Euripides and Mimesis: *Helen, Orestes*, and I*phigeneia at Aulis*." Diss. University of California, Berkeley.

Mayer, M. 1892. "Mythistorica 3: Tereus." *Hermes* 27. 489–99.

McDermott, Emily. 1989. *Euripides' Medea: The Incarnation of Disorder*. Pennsylvania State University Press.

McLeish, Kenneth. 1980. *The Theatre of Aristophanes*. New York.

Meier, Christian. 1993. *The Political Art of Greek Tragedy*. Cambridge.

Meineke, August. 1839–57. *Fragmenta Comicorum Graecorum*. Berlin.

Merkelbach, Reinhold. 1950. "Πειρίθου κατάβασι." *Studi Italiani di Filologia Classica* NS 23. 255–63.

———. 1974. *Kritische Beiträge zu antiken Autoren*. Beiträge zur klassischen Philologie 47. Meinesheim am Glan.

Merkelbach, Reinhold, and M. L. West. 1977. *Fragmenta Hesiodea*. Oxford.

Mette, H.-J. 1967–68. "Euripides (inbesondere für die Jahre 1939–1968). Erster Hauptteil: Die Bruchstücke." *Lustrum* 12–13. 5–403.

———. 1981–82. "Euripides (inbesondere für die Jahre 1968–1981). Erster Hauptteil: Die Bruchstücke." *Lustrum* 23–24. 5–448.

———. 1983. "Perithoos-Theseus-Herakles bei Euripides." *ZPE* 50. 13–19.

Metz, Christian. 1974. *Film Language: A Semiotics of the Cinema*. Oxford.

———. 1974. *Language and Cinema*. The Hague: Mouton.

———. 1991. *L'enonciation impersonelle, ou le site du film*. Paris.

Michelini, A. N. 1987. *Euripides and the Tragic Tradition*. Madison.

———. 1989. "Neophron and Euripides' *Medea* 105–80." *TAPA* 119. 115–35.

Mielziner, Jo. 1965. *Designing for the Theater: A Memoir and a Portfolio*. New York.

Mihailov, Georgi. 1955. "La lègende de Térée." *Annuaire de l'Université de Sophia, Faculté des Lettres* 50.2. 77–199.

Miller, H. 1948. "Euripides' *Telephus* and the *Thesmophoriazusae* of Aristophanes." *CP* 43. 174–83.

Moorton, Richard F. 1989. "Rites of Passage in Aristophanes' *Frogs*." *CJ* 84. 308–24.

———. 1987. "Euripides' *Andromeda* in Aristophanes' *Frogs*." *AJP* 108. 434–36.

Muecke, Frances. 1977. "Playing with the Play: Theatrical Self-Consciousness in Aristophanes." *Antichthon* 11. 52–67.

———. 1982. " 'I Know You—By Your Rags': Costume and Disguise in Fifth- Century Drama." *Antichthon* 16. 17–34.

———. 1984. "Plautus and the Theatre of Disguise." *CSCA* 17. 216–29.

Mylonas, G. E. 1961. *Eleusis and the Eleusinian Mysteries*. Princeton.

Nagy, Gregory. 1990. *Pindar's Homer: The Lyric Possession of an Epic Past*. Baltimore.

———. 1995. *Poetry as Performance: Homer and Beyond*. Cambridge.

Nauck, Augustus. 1926. *Tragicorum Graecorum Fragmenta*. 2nd ed. Leipzig.

Nesselrath, H.-G. 1990. *Die attische Mittlere Komödie: ihre Stellung in der antiken Literatur-kritik und Literaturgeschichte*. Berlin.

———. 1996. "Die Tücken der Sprecherverteilung: Euelpides, Peisetairos und ihre Rollen in der Eingangspartie der aristophanischen Vögel." *Museum Helveticum* 53. 91–99.

Newiger, H.-J. 1957. *Metapher und Allegorie: Studien zu Aristophanes*. Zetemata 16. Munich.

———. 1975b. "Die *Vögel* und ihre Stellung im Gesamtwerk des Aristophanes." In Newiger, *Aristophanes und die alte Komödie* 266–82.

Newiger, H. -J., ed. 1975a. *Aristophanes und die Alte Komödie*. Darmstadt.

Norden, Eduard. 1926. *P. Virgilius Maro, Aeneis Buch VI*. Stuttgart. 3rd edition.

Norwood, Gilbert. 1931. *Greek Comedy*. London.

Obbink, Dirk. 1993. "Dionysus Poured Out: Ancient and Modern Theories of Sacrifice and Cultural Formation." In Carpenter and Faraone, *Masks of Dionysus* 65–86.

Ober, J. 1989. *Mass and Elite in Democratic Athens: Rhetoric, Ideology, and the Power of the People*. Princeton.

Ober, J., and B. Strauss. 1990. "Drama, Political Rhetoric, and the Discourse of Athenian Democracy." In Winkler and Zeitlin, *Dionysos* 237–70.

Oder, E. 1888. "Der Wiedehopf in der griechischen Sage." *RhM* 43. 541–56.

O'Higgins, Dolores. 1990. "Narrators and Narrative in the *Philoctetes* of Sophocles." *Ramus* 120. 37–52.

Olson, S. Douglas. 1989. "Cario and the New World of Aristophanes' *Plutus*." *TAPA* 119. 193–99.

O'Regan, D. E. *Rhetoric, Comedy and the Violence of Language in Aristophanes' Clouds*. Oxford.

———. 1991. "Politics and the Lost Euripidean *Philoctetes*." *Hesperia* 60. 269–83.

Ostwald, Martin. 1986. *From Popular Sovereignty to the Sovereignty of Law*. Berkeley.

Padel, Ruth. 1992. *In and Out of Mind: Greek Images of the Tragic Self*. Princeton.

———. 1995. *Whom the Gods Destroy: Elements of Greek and Tragic Madness*. Princeton.

Padilla, Mark. 1992. "The Heraclean Dionysus: Theatrical and Social Renewal in Aristophanes' Frogs." *Arethusa* 25. 359–84.

Page, D. L. 1950. *Select Literary Papyri*. Cambridge, Mass.

———. 1962. *Poetae Melici Graeci*. Oxford.

Paoletti, M. 1982. "Arula di Medma e tragedie attiche." In A*parchai: Nuove richerche e studi sulla Magna Grecia e la Sicilia in onore di P.E. Arias* I. 371–92. Pisa.

Parsons, P. J., ed. 1974. *The Oxyrhynchus Papyri*. Vol. 42. London.

Pasquali, Giorgio. 1951. "Arte allusiva." In *Stravaganze quarte e supreme*. Venice.

Patrick, James. 1975. "Charlie Parker and Harmonic Sources of Bebop Composition: Thoughts on the Repertory of New Jazz in the 1940's." *The Journal of Jazz Studies* 2.2. 3–23 (June 1975).

Pavis, Patrice. 1976. *Problèmes de sémiologie théâtrale*. Montréal.

Pearson, A. C. 1917. *The Fragments of Sophocles*. Cambridge.

Pecirka, Jan. 1976. "The Crisis of the Athenian Polis in the 4th Century B.C." *Eirene* 14. 5–29.

Pelling, Christopher. 1990. *Characterization and Individuality in Greek Literature*. Oxford.

Pfister, Manfred. 1988. *The Theory and Analysis of Drama*. Cambridge.

Philippart, H. 1930. "Iconographie des Bacchantes d'Euripide." *Rev. belge de philosophie et d'histoire* 9. 4–72.

Pianko, Gabriella. 1963. "Un comico contributo alla storia della musica greca, *Chirone* di Ferecrate." *Eos* 53. 56–62.

Pickard-Cambridge, A. W. 1962. *Dithyramb, Tragedy, and Comedy.* 2nd ed. Revised by T. B. L. Webster. Oxford.

——. 1968. *The Dramatic Festivals of Athens.* 2nd ed. Revised by John Gould and D. M. Lewis. Oxford.

Pollard, J. R. T. 1977. *Birds in Greek Life and Myth.* London.

Pozzi, Dora. 1991. "The Polis in Crisis." In Pozzi and Wickersham, *Myth and the Polis* 126–63.

Pozzi, Dora, and John Wickersham, eds. 1991. *Myth and the Polis.* Ithaca.

Pratt, Louise H. 1993. *Lying and Poetry from Homer to Pindar: Falsehood and Deception in Archaic Greek Poetics.* Ann Arbor.

Preller, Ludwig. 1894–1926. *Griechische Mythologie.* 4th ed. Revised by Carl Robert. Berlin.

Pucci, Pietro. 1961. *Aristofane ed Euripide. Richerche metriche e stilistiche.* Atti dell' Academia Nazionale dei Lincei 358, Memorie, Cl. di Scienze mor., stor. e filol., ser. VIII, vol. 10, fasc. 5. Rome.

——. 1967. "Euripides Heautontimoroumenos." *TAPA* 98. 365–71.

——. 1987. *Odysseus Polutropos: Intertextual Readings in the Odyssey and the Iliad.* Ithaca.

——. 1994. "Gods' Intervention and Epiphany in Sophocles." *AJP* 115.1. 15–46.

Race, W. H. 1982. *The Classical Priamel from Homer to Boethius.* Leiden.

Radt, Stefan. 1977. *Tragicorum Graecorum Fragmenta.* Vol. 4: Sophokles. Göttingen.

——. 1985. *Tragicorum Graecorum Fragmenta.* Vol. 3: Aiskhylos. Göttingen.

Rau, Peter. 1967. *Paratragodia: Untersuchungen einer komischen Form des Aristophanes.* Zetemata 45. Münich.

Reckford, Kenneth J. 1987. *Aristophanes Old-and-New Comedy, Vol. I: Six Essays in Perspective.* Chapel Hill.

Rehm, Rush. 1992. *Greek Tragic Theatre.* Routledge.

Rehrenböck, G. 1985. *Pherekrates-Studien.* Diss. Vienna.

Reinelt, Janelle G., and Joseph R. Roach, eds. 1992. *Critical Theory and Performance.* Ann Arbor.

Restani, Donatella. 1983. "Il *Chirone* di Ferecrate e la nuova musica greca." *Rivista Italiana di Musicologia* 18. 139–92.

Rhodes, P. J. 1986. "Political Activity in Classical Athens." *JHS* 106. 132–44.

Ribbeck, Otto. 1875. *Die römische Tragödie im Zeitalter der Republik.* Leipzig.

Riedweg, Christoph. 1990. "The Atheistic Fragment from Euripides' *Bellerophon*." *ICS* 15. 39–53.

Righter, Anne. 1962. *Shakespeare and the Idea of the Play.* London.

Ringer, Mark. 1998. *Electra and the Empty Urn: Metatheater and Role-Playing in Sophocles.* Chapel Hill.

Rivier, A. 1975. *Essai sur le tragique d'Euripide.* Lausanne.

Robert, Carl. 1920. *Griechische Heldensage.* Berlin. Vol. 2 [in 3 "books"] of Preller, *Griechische Mythologie.*

Roberts, D. 1989. "Different Stories: Sophoclean Narrative(s) in the *Philoctetes*." *TAPA* 119. 161–76.

Roberts, Jennifer T. 1982. *Accountability in Athenian Government.* Madison.

Robertson, H. 1980. "Heracles' 'Catabasis.'" *Hermes* 108. 274–99.

Rogers, Benjamin Bickley. 1907. *The Plutus of Aristophanes.* London.

Rohdich, Hermann. 1968. *Die Euripideische Tragödie: Untersuchungen zur ihrer Tragik.* Heidelberg.

Romer, Frank. 1983. "When Is a Bird Not a Bird?" *TAPA* 113. 136–38.

Ron, Moshe. 1987. "The Restricted Abyss: Nine Problems in the Theory of *Mise en Abyme.*" *Poetics Today* 8.2. 417–38.

Rose, Margaret A. 1979. *Parody / Metafiction*. London.

Rosen, Ralph. 1988. *Old Comedy and the Iambographic Tradition*. Atlanta.

Rosenmeyer, T. G. 1954. "Gorgias, Aeschylus and *Apatê*." *AJP* 76. 225–60.

———. 1963. *The Masks of Tragedy*. Austin.

Rothwell, Kenneth S., Jr. 1995. "Aristophanes' *Wasps* and the Sociopolitics of Aesop's Fables." *CJ* 93.4. 233–54.

Rothwell, Kenneth S., Sr. 1987. "Representing King Lear on Screen: From Metatheatre to Metacinema." *Shakespeare Survey* 39. 75–90.

Roux, R. 1976. "Un maître disparu de l'ancienne comédie. Le poète Cratès, jugé par Aristophane." *Revue de Philologie* 50. 256–65.

Rowland, Beryl. 1978. *Birds with Human Souls: A Guide to Bird Symbolism*. University of Tennessee.

Ruffini, Franco. 1978. *Semiotica del testo: l'esempio teatro*. Rome.

Russo, C. F. 1994. *Aristophanes: An Author for the Stage*. Tran. Kevin Wren. London.

Rusten, Jeffrey. 1982. "Dicaearchus and the Tales from Euripides." *GRBS* 23. 57–67.

———. 1989. *Thucydides: The Peloponnesian War, Book II*. Cambridge.

Saïd, Suzanne. 1987. "Travestis et travestissements dans les comédies d'Aristophane." In Ghiron-Bistagne, *Anthropologie et Théâtre* 217–50.

Sancho-Royo, A. 1983. "Analisis de los motivos de composicion del Ciclope de Filoxeno de Cithera." *Habis* 14. 33–49.

Schlegel, Augustus W. 1846. *A Course of Lectures on Dramatic Art and Literature*. Translated by John Black. Original published 1809. London.

Schlesinger, Alfred C. "Indications of Parody in Aristophanes." *TAPA* 67. 296–314.

Schmid, Wilhelm. 1929–1948. *Geschichte der griechischen Literatur*. Vols. 1–5. Munich.

Schmidt, M. 1970. Review of A. Cambitoglou and A. D. Trendall, *Apulian Red-Figured Painters of the Plain Style* and A. D. Trendall, *Red-Figured Vases of Lucania, Campania, and Sicily*. *Gnomon* 42. 826–30.

Schroeder, O. 1926. "PROKNH." *Hermes* 61. 423–36.

Schwinge, E. 1977. "Aristophanes und die Utopie." *WJA* 3. 43–67.

———. ed. 1968. *Euripides*. Wege der Forschung 89. Darmstadt.

Scodel, Ruth. 1980. *The Trojan Trilogy of Euripides*. Göttingen.

———. 1993. *Theater and Society in the Classical World*. Ann Arbor.

Scolnicov, Hanna. 1987. "Theatre Space, Theatrical Space, and the Theatrical Space Without." *Themes in Drama* 9: *The Theatrical Space* 11–26. Cambridge.

Seaford, Richard A. S. 1981. "Dionysiac Drama and Dionysiac Mysteries." *CQ* 31. 252–75.

———. 1988. *Euripides* Cyclops. *Edited with Introduction and Commentary by R. A. S. Seaford*. Oxford.

———. 1994. *Reciprocity and Ritual: Homer and Tragedy in the Developing City-State*. Oxford.

———. 1996. *Euripides* Bacchae. *Edited with Introduction and Commentary by Richard Seaford*. Warminster.

Seale, D. 1982. *Vision and Stagecraft in Sophocles*. Chicago.

Seidensticker, Bernd. 1978. "Comic Elements in Euripides' *Bacchae*." *AJP* 99. 303–20.

———. 1982. *Palintonos Harmonia. Studien zu komischen Elementen in der griechischen Tragödie*. Hypomnemata 72. Göttingen.

Segal, Charles P. 1961. "The Character and Cults of Dionysus and the Unity of the *Frogs*." *HSCP* 65. 207–42.

———. 1971. "The Two Worlds of Euripides' *Helen*." *TAPA* 102. 553–614.

———. 1981. *Tragedy and Civilization: An Interpretation of Sophocles*. Cambridge.

———. 1997. *Dionysiac Poetics and Euripides' Bacchae*. Princeton. 2nd ed.

———. 1988. Review of S. Goldhill, *Reading Greek Tragedy*. CP 83.3. 234–37.

———. 1990a. "Violence and the Other: Greek, Female, and Barbarian in Euripides' *Hecuba*." TAPA 120. 109–31.

———. 1990b. "Philomela's Web and the Pleasures of the Text: Ovid's Myth of Tereus in the *Metamorphoses*." Lecture version. University of California at Berkeley, March 1990.

———. 1993. *Euripides and the Poetics of Sorrow. Art, Gender, and Commemoration in* Alcestis, Hippolytus, *and* Hecuba. Durham.

———. 1995. Review of Seaford, *Reciprocity and Ritual*. BMCR 6.7. 651–57.

———. 1995. *Sophocles' Tragic World: Divinity, Nature, Society*. Cambridge, Mass.

Segal, Erich. 1973. "The φύσι" of Comedy." HSCP 77. 129–36.

Sidwell, K. 1993. "Authorial Collaboration? Aristophanes' Knights and Eupolis." GRBS 34.4. 365–89.

———. 1994. "Aristophanes *Acharnians* and Eupolis." CM 45. 71–115.

———. 1996. "Poetic Rivalry and the Caricature of Comic Poets." In A. Griffiths, ed., *Stage Directions: Essays in Honour of E. W. Handley*. BICS Supplement 66. 56–80.

Sifakis, G. M. 1971. *Parabasis and Animal Choruses*. Oxford.

Silk, Michael S. 1993. "Aristophanic Paratragedy." In Alan Sommerstein et al., eds. *Tragedy, Comedy, and the Polis* 477–504.

———. (forthcoming) *Aristophanes and the Definition of Comedy*. Oxford.

Simon, Erica. 1968. "Tereus: Zur Bedeutung der Würzburger Schauspieler-Scherbe." In *Festschrift des Kronberg-Gymnasiums* 155–61. Aschaffenburg.

Slater, Niall W. 1985. *Plautus in Performance: The Theatre of the Mind*. Princeton.

———. 1988. "Problems in the Hypothesis to Aristophanes' *Peace*." ZPE 74. 43–57.

———. 1993. "Space, Character, and ΑΠΑΤΗ: Transformation and Transvaluation in the *Acharnians*" In Alan Sommerstein et al., eds., *Tragedy, Comedy, and the Polis* 397–416.

———. 1990. *Reading Petronious*. Baltimore.

Slater, Philip. 1968. *The Glory of Hera*. Boston.

Snell, Bruno, ed. 1971. *Tragicorum Graecorum Fragmenta*. Vol. 1. Göttingen.

Solmsen, Friedrich. 1967. "Electra and Orestes: Three Recognitions in Greek Tragedy." *Mededelingen der Koninklijke Nederlandse Akademie van Wetenschappen, Afd. Letterkunde* 30. 2.

———. 1968. "Zur Gestaltung des Intriguenmotivs in den Tragödien des Sophokles und Euripides." In Schwinge, *Euripides* 326–44.

Sommerstein, A. H. 1980. *The Comedies of Aristophanes, Vol. I:* Acharnians. Warminster.

———. 1981. *The Comedies of Aristophanes, Vol. II:* Knights. Warminster.

———. 1983. *The Comedies of Aristophanes, Vol. III:* Wasps. Warminster.

———. 1984. "Aristophanes and the Demon Poverty." CQ 34. 323–33.

———. 1985. *The Comedies of Aristophanes, Vol. IV:* Peace. Warminster.

———. 1986. "The Decree of Syrakosios." CQ 36. 101–8.

———. 1987. *The Comedies of Aristophanes, Vol. VI:* Birds. Warminster.

———. 1989. *Aeschylus* Eumenides. Cambridge.

———. 1993. "Kleophon and the Re-staging of *Frogs*." In Sommerstein et al. *Tragedy, Comedy, and the Polis*. 461–76.

———. 1994. *The Comedies of Aristophanes, Vol. VIII:* Thesmophoriazusae. Warminster.

———. 1996. *The Comedies of Aristophanes, Vol. IX:* Frogs. Warminster.

Sommerstein, A. H., S. Halliwell, J. Henderson, and B. Zimmermann, eds. 1993. *Tragedy, Comedy, and the Polis*. Papers from the Greek Drama Conference (Nottingham, 18–20 July 1990). Bari.

Spariosu, Mihai I. 1989. *Dionysus Reborn: Play and the Aesthetic Dimension in Modern Philosophical and Scientific Discourse.* Ithaca.

Stam, Robert. 1992. *Reflexivity in Film and Literature: From Don Quixote to Jean-Luc Godard.* New York.

Stanton, Domna, ed. 1992. *Discourses of Sexuality: From Aristotle to AIDS.* Ann Arbor.

States, Bert. 1971. *Irony and Drama: A Poetics.* Ithaca.

———. 1983. "The Actor's Presence: Three Phenomenal Modes." *Theater Journal* 35. 359–75.

———. 1985. *Great Reckonings in Little Rooms: On the Phenomenology of the Theater.* Berkeley.

Steffen, Wiktor. 1965. "Der Hilferuf in den *Netzfischern* des Aischylos und sein Fortleben im griechischen Drama." *Eos* 55. 35–45.

Stewart, Susan. 1979. *Nonsense: Aspects of Intertextuality in Folklore and Literature.* Baltimore.

Stinton, T. C. W. 1990. *Collected Papers on Greek Tragedy.* Oxford.

Stoessl, F. 1945. "Die *Phoinissen* des Phrynichos und die *Perser* des Aischylos." *Mus. Helv.* 2. 148.

Storey, I. C. 1988. "The Date of Kallias' *Pedetai.*" *Hermes* 116. 379–83.

———. 1990. "Dating and Re-dating Eupolis." *Phoenix* 44. 1–30.

———. 1993. "Notus est omnibus Eupolis?" In Sommerstein et al., *Tragedy, Comedy, and the Polis.* 373–96.

Strohm, Hans. 1967. *Euripides: Untersuchungen zur dramatischen Form.* Zetemata 15. Münich.

———. 1968. "Trug und Täuschung in der euripideischen Dramatik." In Schwinge, *Euripides.* 345–72.

Styan, J. L. 1975. *Drama, Stage, Audience.* Cambridge.

Süss, Wilhelm. 1954. "Scheinbare und wirkliche Inkongruenzen in den Dramen des Aristophanes." *RhM* 97. 306–13.

Sutton, Dana F. 1975. "The Staging of Anodos Scenes." *Revista di Studi Classici* 23. 356–64.

———. 1980. *The Greek Satyr Play.* Meisenheim am Glan.

———. 1984a. "Vase Paintings Illustrating Satyr Plays." *The Ancient World* 9. 119–26.

———. 1984b. *The Lost Sophocles.* Lanham, Md.

———. 1987. *Two Lost Plays of Euripides.* American University Studies, Series 17: Classical Languages and Literature, vol. 4. New York.

———. 1988. "Evidence for Lost Dramatic Hypotheses." *GRBS* 29. 87–92.

———. 1994. *The Catharsis of Comedy.* Lanham, Md.

Süvern, Johann W. 1835. *Essay on the* Birds *of Aristophanes.* Translated by W. Hamilton. London.

Suzuki, Minoko. 1989. *Metamorphoses of Helen: Authority, Difference, and the Epic.* Ithaca.

Taaffe, Lauren K. 1987. "Metatheater and Gender in Aristophanes' *Ecclesiazusae.*" Diss. Cornell University.

———. 1993. *Aristophanes and Women.* London.

Taillardat, Jean. 1965. *Les images d'Aristophane.* 2nd ed. Paris.

Taplin, Oliver P. 1971. "Significant Actions in Sophocles' *Philoctetes.*" *GRBS* 12. 25–44.

———. 1978. *Greek Tragedy in Action.* Berkeley.

———. 1983. "Tragedy and Trugedy." *CQ* 33. 331–33.

———. 1986. "Greek Tragedy and Comedy: A *Synkrisis.*" *JHS* 106. 163–74.

———. 1987. "The Mapping of Sophocles' *Philoctetes.*" *BICS* 34. 69–72.

———. 1993. *Comic Angels and Other Approaches to Greek Drama Through Vase-Painting.* Oxford.

Thiercy, P. 1986. *Aristophane: Fiction et Dramaturgie*. Paris.

Thompson, D'Arcy W. 1936.² *A Glossary of Greek Birds*. 2nd ed. Oxford.

Trendall, A. D. 1967. *The Red-Figured Vases of Lucania, Campania, and Sicily*. Oxford.

Trendall, A. D., and T. B. L. Webster. 1971. *Illustrations of Greek Drama*. London.

Ubersfeld, Ann. 1977. *Lire le théâtre*. Paris.

———. 1981. *L'école du spectateur*. Paris.

Ussher, R. G. 1990. *Sophocles: Philoctetes*. Warminster.

Van Looy, Herman. 1991. "Les fragments d'Euripide I: ΑΙΓΕΥΣ—ΙΠΠΟΛΥΤΟΣ ΚΑΛΥΠΤΟΜΕΝΟΣ." *L'Antiquité Classique* 60. 259–311.

Vernant, J.-P. 1980. *Myth and Society in Ancient Greece*. Translated by J. Lloyd. Atlantic Highlands, NJ.

———. 1983. *Myth and Thought among the Greeks*. Translated by J. Lloyd. London.

———. 1990a. "Tensions and Ambiguities in Greek Tragedy." In Vernant and Vidal-Naquet, *Myth and Tragedy*. 6–27.

———. 1990b. "The God of Tragic Fiction." In Vernant and Vidal-Naquet, *Myth and Tragedy*. 181–88.

———. 1990c. "The Masked Dionysos of Euripides' *Bacchae*." In Vernant & Vidal-Naquet, *Myth and Tragedy*. 381–412.

Vernant, J.-P., and P. Vidal-Naquet. 1990. *Myth and Tragedy in Ancient Greece*. Translated by J. Lloyd. Sussex.

Vickers, Brian. 1973. *Toward Greek Tragedy: Drama, Myth, Society*. London.

Vickers, Michael. 1989. "Alcibiades on Stage: Aristophanes' *Birds*." *Historia* 38.3. 267–299.

———. 1997. *Pericles on Stage: Political Comedy in Aristophanes' Early Plays*. Austin.

Walton, Kendall L. 1990. *Mimesis as Make-Believe: On the Foundations of the Representational Arts*. Harvard.

Warmington, E. H. 1936. *The Remains of Old Latin*. Vol. 2: *Livius Andronicus, Naevius, Pacuvius, and Accius*. Harvard.

Waugh, Patricia. 1984. *Metafication: The Theory and Practice of Self-Conscious Fiction*. London.

Webster, T. B. L. 1967a. *The Tragedies of Euripides*. London.

———. 1967b. *Monuments Illustrating Tragedy and Satyr-Play*. BICS Supplement, 20. London.

———. 1969. *An Introduction to Sophocles*. London.

———. 1970. *Studies in Later Greek Comedy*. 2nd ed. Manchester.

Wecklein, N. 1888. "Über fragmentarisch erhaltene Tragödien des Euripides." *Sits. der Akad. d. Wiss.* 99–109.

Welcker, Friedrich G. 1839. *Die griechischen Tragödien mit Rücksicht auf den epischen Cyclus geordnet*. 2 vols. Bonn.

West, Martin L. 1974. *Studies in Greek Elegy and Iambus*. Berlin.

———. 1980. "Tragica IV." *BICS* 27. 17–22.

———. 1983. *The Orphic Poems*. Oxford.

———. 1992. *Ancient Greek Music*. Oxford.

White, John Williams. 1914. *The Scholia on the Aves of Aristophanes*. Boston.

Whitehead, D. 1986. *The Demes of Attica 508/7–ca. 250 B.C.: A Political and Social Study*. Princeton.

Whitlock Blundell, Mary. 1987. "The Moral Character of Odysseus in *Philoctetes*." *GRBS* 28. 307–29.

———. 1988. "The *phusis* of Neoptolemos in Sophocles' *Philoctetes*." *G&R* 35. 137–48.

——. 1989. *Helping Friends and Harming Enemies: A Study in Sophocles and Greek Ethics.* Cambridge.

Whitman, Cedric. 1964. *Aristophanes and the Comic Hero.* Harvard.

Wilamowitz-Moellendorff, U. von. 1875. *Analecta Euripidea.* Berlin.

——. 1903. *Timotheos: Die Perser, aus einem Papyrus herausgegeben.* Leipzig.

——. 1935. *Kleine Schriften.* Paul Mass, ed. Berlin.

Wiles, David. 1990. "Shakespeare and the Medieval Idea of the Play." In Laroque, *The Show Within* 65–74.

Wiles, Timothy. 1980. *The Theater Event: Modern Theories of Performance.* Chicago.

Willems, Alphonse. 1919. *Aristophane. Traduction avec notes et commentaires critiques.* Paris.

Wilshire, Bruce. 1982. *Role Playing and Identity: The Limits of the Theatre as Metaphor.* Bloomington.

Winkler, J. J. 1990. "The Ephebes' Song: *Tragoidia* and *Polis.*" In Winkler and Zeitlin, *Dionysos* 20–62.

Winkler, J. J., and F. I. Zeitlin, eds. 1990. *Nothing to Do With Dionysos? Athenian Drama in Its Social Context.* Princeton.

Winnington-Ingram, R. P. 1948. *Euripides and Dionysos.* Cambridge.

——. 1969. "Euripides: Poietes Sophos." *Arethusa* 2.2. 127–42.

——. 1980. *Sophocles: An Interpretation.* Cambridge.

Wise, Jennifer. 1998. *Dionysus Writes: The Invention of Theatre in Ancient Greece.* Ithaca.

Worthington, Ian. 1989. "Aristophanes' 'Frogs' and Arginusae." *Hermes* 117. 359–63.

Zaganiaris, Nicholas J. 1973. "Le mythe de Térée dans la litterature greque et latine." *Platon* 25. 208–32.

Zannini Quirini, Bruno. 1987. *Nephelokokkygia: la prospettiva mitica degli* Uccelli di Aristofane. Storia delle religioni 5. Rome.

Zeitlin, Froma I. 1980. "The Closet of Masks: Role-Playing and Myth-Making in the *Orestes* of Euripides." *Ramus* 9. 51–57.

——. 1981. "Travesties of Gender and Genre in Aristophanes' *Thesmophoriazusae.*" In Foley, *Reflections of Women in Antiquity* 169–217.

——. 1982a. *Under the Sign of the Shield: Semiotics and Aeschylus' Seven Against Thebes.* Rome.

——. 1982b. "Cultic Models of the Female: Rites of Dionysus and Demeter." *Arethusa* 15. 129–57.

——. 1990. "Thebes: Theater of Self and Society in Athenian Drama." In Winkler and Zeitlin, *Dionysos* 13–17.

——. 1990. "Playing the Other: Theater, Theatricality, and the Feminine in Greek Drama." In Winkler and Zeitlin, *Dionysos* 63–96.

——. 1993. "Staging Dionysus between Thebes and Athens." In Carpenter and Faraone, *Masks of Dionysus* 147–82.

——. 1994. "The Artful Eye: Vision, Ecphrasis, and Spectacle in Euripidean Theatre." In Goldhill and Osborne, *Art and Text* 138–96.

——. 1995. *Playing the Other: Gender and Society in Classical Greek Literature.* Chicago.

Zielinski, Thaddeus. 1885. *Die Gliederung der altattischen Komödie.* Leipzig.

Zimmermann, Bernhard. 1985. *Untersuchungen zur Form und Dramatischen Technik der Aristophanischen Komödien 1: Parodos und Amoibaion.* 2nd ed. [=Beiträge zur Klassischen Philologie 154]. Meisenheim.

——. 1986. *Untersuchungen zur Form und dramatischen Technik der Aristophanischen Komödien II.* Königstein.

——. 1986. "Überlegungen zum sogenannten Pratinasfragment." *Museum Helveticum* 43. 145–54.

——. 1992. *Dithyrambos: Geschichte einer Gattung*. Hypomnemata. Heft 98. Göttingen.

——. 1993. "Comedy's Criticism of Music." *Drama 2: Intertextualität in der griechisch-römischen Komödie*. 39–50.

Zuntz, G. 1955. *The Political Plays of Euripides*. Manchester.

Index